THE *W*RITER'S WAY

Read Chp. 16

THE WRITER'S WAY

Jack Rawlins

California State University at Chico

THIRD EDITION

Houghton Mifflin Company BOSTON TORONTO
Geneva, Illinois Palo Alto Princeton, New Jersey

Senior Sponsoring Editor: Dean Johnson
Associate Project Editor: Magdalena Hernandez
Senior Production/Design Coordinator: Sarah Ambrose
Senior Manufacturing Coordinator: Priscilla Bailey
Marketing Manager: Charles Cavaliere

TEXT CREDITS

"No Room for Children" by Rasa Gustaitus is reprinted by permission of the Pacific News Service and the author. "The People Versus" by Steve Rubenstein, © San Francisco Chronicle, 1982. Reprinted by permission. Excerpt from *The Right Stuff* by Tom Wolfe. Copyright © 1979 by Tom Wolfe. Reprinted by permission of Farrar, Straus & Giroux, Inc. Excerpt (pages 36–37) originally appeared in "Real Women Do Eat Food" by Warren Leight, *Mademoiselle,* August 1989. "Twenty Good Reasons to Cry" by Stanley Bing from *Esquire,* June 1987. Copyright © 1987 Stanley Bing. Used by permission of the author. "Protect Your Inalienable Right to Steer Tanks," Adam Hochschild, Copyright © 1989 by Adam Hochschild. Reprinted by permission.

Cover art by David Hockney
 Jardin de Luxembourg 10th August 1985
 photographic collage 35" × 32$^{1}/_{2}$"
 © D. Hockney 1985

Cover Designer: Harold Burch, Harold Burch Design, New York City

Printed in the U.S.A.

ISBN 0-395-74533-0

456789–QM—99 98 97 96

CONTENTS

Part Two

PLANNING AND DRAFTING 39

Part Three

Part Four

MODES OF WRITING   267

Chapter 14
Personal Writing   268

Chapter 15
Writing to Inform   298

Chapter 16
Writing an Argument, Part I: Thinking It Through   332

Part Five

THE RESEARCH PAPER 397

PREFACE

There have been a lot of writing textbooks published in the past decade. This is the only one that begins early enough in the writing process to make a real difference.

When I first taught people to write, I entered the students' writing process at the finish. I'd show students polished, professional essays, point out their features, and say, "Write something like that." Then I'd look at what they had written to see if their works had the features of a good essay. But this approach didn't work very well. I was too late.

Then the "process-revolution" taught me how to enter the writing process during the composing stage. I'd show students the mythical steps a writer goes through to produce an essay, beginning with brainstorming, and say, "Go through these steps." Then I'd have them write, observing and conferring as their essays evolved. This approach worked better, but something was still missing. The results were often wooden and perfunctory. I was still too late.

By the time I wrote the first edition of *The Writer's Way*, I realized that the big stuff goes on before the brainstorming, before the particular writing project is even imagined. An instructor should be there when the writer is figuring out why she writes, what writing is supposed to do, and what good writing is. Students can reproduce the features of good essays or walk through the steps of the writing process endlessly and gain nothing if they're working with a mistaken definition of writing and its purposes. If a student has the impression that writing is supposed to hide her ignorance, get her good grades, or demonstrate her mastery of technical features or skills (such as outlining or using lively verbs), then writing practice—process-based or otherwise—will simply reinforce her misunderstanding. Until students write for the reasons successful writers write, they won't write well.

So I based this book on what I had learned: 1) good writing begins with real, strong reasons to write; and 2) good reasons to write answer all questions about technique. A successful writer is doing something of importance to himself; that sense of purpose guides all of his writing decisions. He asks himself, not "What's the rule?" or "What do good essays do?", but "What works?". The main goal of *The Writer's Way* is to teach writers to ask themselves, "Does this work?", and to look for answers in their own purposes. This approach pays off, I know, because I've used it in my own classes and I've had a lot of feedback about it from other instructors who report the same level of success.

This way of thinking is based on the linguistic principles known as the "whole-language" or "natural-language" approach. Its best-known spokespeople are Frank Smith and Kenneth and Yetta Goodman, and its premise is that people learn best by emersing themselves in the whole thing to be learned, often surrounding themselves with examples of what it looks like and how it's done. Moreover, they should do it in a context in which the thing to be learned offers immediate, demonstrable personal rewards. These might be aesthetic or emotional rewards ("That feels good.") or utilitarian ones ("I can get things done with this."). By extension, a writer must write from an attitude that says, "I do this *as myself*; I do this for me." This commitment to making writing a part of one's real life, Frank Smith calls, "joining the club of writers." All of us learn to speak in such a context, and with such an attitude. We can learn to write the same way.

What's New in the Third Edition

When we invited users of the Second Edition to tell us how to improve it, most of them said to leave it alone. Fill out some thin spots, rethink the sequencing here and there, but don't make any radical changes in course. I took their advice. I'm hoping that the Third Edition is the same good book as the Second, with a lot of little improvements.

The only new feature in its entirety is Chapter 13, on student publishing. It seemed an oversight that the writing process, as *The Writer's Way* presented it, never included the step for which all the other steps are merely preamble: going public. Chapter 13 shows students lots of likely ways to get their works into print.

Some chapters in the process section have been moved. The chapter on thesis, purpose, audience, and tone has been placed in front of the first draft chapter, where most writers seem to address those issues. Peer editing has been moved back, so that it now follows revising and organizing discussions. The critical-thinking chapter has been taken out of the process sequence and made a part of the book's discussion of argumentation, where most users found themselves working with it.

Two chapters from the Second Edition have been divided in two to make them more swallowable doses: *organization* (now divided into one chapter on mapping, outlining, and paragraphing and another on abstracting) and *argument* (now divided into reasoning and persuading).

All the material on software applications for writers has been updated to keep pace with current advances. The chapter on research methods has a new section on electronic data searches; the peer editing chapter models collaborative editing in computer conferences; the argument chapter models how electronic conferencing is changing the nature of argumentative discussion in our culture; and the new publishing chapter discusses publication via electronic networks and desktop publishing applications.

There are eighteen new student essays, some longer than the Second Edition's typical nine-hundred-word essay for users who want models for writing to greater length.

The *Writers' Workshop* sections have been reworked to make them more classroom-friendly. Each workshop still walks the readers through a hands-on writer's experiment, but now it leads to a new section headed "Your Turn" in which the readers are asked to undertake a task like the one they've just seen done, a task designed to be used as a classroom group activity.

In several places readers said the cooking in the Second Edition was good, but the portions were just too small. I've added larger helpings, in the form of further discussion or additional models, in many places in the book, but mainly in the six areas where readers most often wanted more help: audience, critical thinking, peer editing, argumentation, paragraphing, and revising to greater length.

Acknowledgments

Some of the new materials in the Third Edition profited from the helpful advice of Steve Metzger, Casey Huff, and Carolyn Dusenbury. Ten recent students have added their names to the list of generous writers and classroom friends who let me use their essays for free. Their names are in the Index of Essays at the back of the book. Bonnie Ellis helped polish the bibliographies in Chapter 19.

I also thank the following people for their reviews of the third edition of *The Writer's Way*:

Mary McCaslin Thompson, Anoka Ramsey Community College, MN
Michael A. McMahon, Rochester Institute of Technology, NY
C. R. Embry, Truckee Meadows Community College, NV
Bonnie Ellis, Kellog Community College, MI
John Peterson, University of California, Irvine
Thomas Dean, Cardinal Stritch College, WI
Laura J. Scavuzzo, University of Southern California
Mary F. O'Sullivan, Western Wisconsin Technical College
Barbara Bell, Francis Marion University, SC
Deidre Hughes, Fullerton College, CA
Kevin LaGrandeur, Hofstra University, NY

To the Student

This book is divided into five parts and two appendices. Part One is an introduction to the natural-language attitude toward learning to write. It will acquaint you with the way the book thinks before you undertake specific writing activities, so I encourage you to read it straight through before doing anything else.

Parts Two and Three are a step-by-step walk-through of the writing process: from first thoughts through brainstorming, drafting, rethinking, organizing, stylistic polishing, and cosmetic editing. There are too many pages to read at a sitting, and you'll want to start writing before you've read it all. So read through it chapter-by-chapter as you write, focusing on those chapters that address places where you tend to get stuck.

Part Two covers "prewriting," all the messy, creative things a writer does to find things to write about and generate reams of text around them. Part Three assumes the creative production is largely done and it's time to evaluate, rethink, reshape, and polish. In reality, though—as the book says over and over—the creating is never done. Rewriting is much like "prewriting" all over again.

Part Four gives you advice and practice for three essay modes: personal writing, writing to inform, and argument. These chapters assume a knowledge of Parts Two and Three, so in theory you should read all of Parts Two and Three first. But your course may assign these chapters early, so you'll end up reading them at the same time you read Part Two. In fact, everything in all of the chapters relates to everything else. So you may find yourself reading Chapter 5 and discussing writer's block at the same time you are reading Chapter 14 and trying to write an essay on your Uncle Stanley, all the time wishing you had already read Chapter 11 on eliminating wordiness, but knowing that will have to wait.

Part Four is the most fun, because that's where most of the student essays are. Each chapter has several complete essays that illustrate specific writing lessons, and each ends with a Treasury, a short collection of student essays simply to be read, enjoyed, and inspired by.

Part Five discusses the term paper, that big four-to-six week project some of your college instructors will eventually ask you to write. Even if you're not writing a term paper in your writing class, these two chapters will help you with basic academic writing skills: how to quote; how to avoid plagiarism; how to use the library; how to cite a source and make a bibliography; and so on.

The two appendices are on special topics that have no place in the sequential logic of the writing process: essay-test taking and collaborative writing. If your course is focusing on writing for college courses, Appendix A will be of interest to you. It's also a handy thing to refer to later on in other courses. If your course is asking you to write in a collaborative team, Appendix B will be useful. If you haven't thought about writing in teams before, I hope you will look into Appendix B and let it talk you into it. In the world outside of school, writing is almost always a team effort. School can help people get ready for it.

The *Writers' Workshop* sections at the ends of most of the chapters are different from the main text. These practical sessions are similar to the lab section of a science course: first you watch a hands-on demonstration of one of the concepts presented in the chapter, then in the section headed "Your Turn," you try it yourself. They're designed to get your hands dirty with writers' work.

J.R.

THE WRITER'S WAY

Part One

INTRODUCTION TO WRITING

Chapter 1

LEARNING TO WRITE

In the rest of this book, we'll talk about what to do at the moment you're writing. But here in the beginning I want to talk about the long run: What do you do *in your life* to learn to write well? Writing is a long-term project. In these first two chapters I'll lay out the lifelong approach to writing that makes good writers.

Learn Like a Baby

As far as we know, the way a baby teaches itself to talk is an excellent way to learn language skills. Generally people without speech handicaps learn to speak effortlessly, happily, and voluminously in seven years or so, starting from nothing. And everyone gets it right; have you ever met a grownup who didn't know where the adjectives go or hadn't mastered his interrogatives? Almost everyone I've ever asked says she likes to talk, and as a species we do it well—most of us find listening to each other talk fascinating.

Let's assume that the best writing program you can set up for yourself is as much like the Baby's Way as possible. Here are the baby's guiding principles; after each, in italics, we'll talk about how the principle can be translated into one that applies to you and your writing. In other words, we'll just cross out *baby* and *talk* and substitute *college student* and *write:*

1. It takes a long time—years. *So learning to write will take a while. There is no trick or device or weekend workshop that will hand good writing to you.*
2. The baby practices constantly—not fifteen minutes a day, not an hour a day, but all the time, as an ongoing part of living. *So writing must be a part of your daily life—you can't just write once a week or when an assignment is due.*
3. The baby works hard, but the work doesn't *hurt*, and it doesn't leave the baby exhausted, resentful, or hostile to talking. *So writing*

should be work, but it shouldn't hurt, and it shouldn't leave you exhausted, resentful, or determined never to write again.

4. The baby needs constant exposure to models. He must be surrounded by adult speech, and the more he hears the easier the learning is. There's no alternative to listening: If the baby doesn't hear English, he can't learn to speak English. *So you need constant exposure to examples of good writing. The more you've read, the easier it is to learn to write. There's no alternative to reading: If you haven't read essays, you can't write an essay.*

5. The child wants it desperately. You don't have to make him talk, and bribing him doesn't help much. He wants to learn for two reasons. First, language is powerful: If you can talk, you can shape the world around you. Linguist Frank Smith calls this the "I'd Like Another Jelly Donut" principle of language acquisition. Second, language is a primal joy, like music. Babies babble long before they know sounds can "mean" things, just because it's fun. *So you have to want to write, for real reasons. Wanting a good grade, wanting to impress the teacher, or wanting to be a writer won't work. There are only two reasons that work: Writing makes you powerful, and writing is a basic aesthetic joy, like music. If you aren't writing for one of these reasons, you can't write well until you are.*

6. The whole world expects the child to learn. Not talking is a sign of severe psychological trauma. The child is treated as a *talker* from before he utters his first word, not as a *person learning to someday talk.** So the world must expect you to write and treat writing as an expected, normal human activity. You must call yourself a writer, not a person trying to learn how to write.*

7. The baby isn't graded, criticized, or corrected. He learns without ever being told he's wrong or he's failed. No parent was ever stupid enough to say, "No, Baby, 'Dada' is wrong; say 'Daddy.'" Instead, parents say, "That's right, I'm your daddy" when the baby says "Dada." *So you won't learn by being graded, criticized, or corrected. You can learn without ever being told you're wrong or you've failed. But you need the same kind of feedback the baby needs: feedback that focuses on what you write and not how you write it, and feedback that models what you're trying to do—you write "Dada" and a teacher shows you "Daddy."*

8. It's easy to try *too* hard or care in the wrong way or focus on the wrong things. If we tell the baby to watch his speech carefully, to try hard, or that speaking correctly is terribly important, he won't speak better; he'll become tongue-tied. *So if you try hard to "write well" or tell yourself that writing is terribly important,*

---

*This notion is at the heart of Frank Smith's philosophy of how people learn languages.

you probably won't write better; you'll give yourself writer's block. The more you write in fear or write to avoid error, the worse you'll write.

9. The child teaches himself. Grownups can help by setting up an environment where talking is encouraged, but they can't explain to him how to do it. *So you'll have to teach yourself to write. Teachers can encourage, but they can't explain how to do it.*

10. It's subconscious. The child isn't aware of how he's learning or what he's doing, and after he's learned he can't say what he knows. Teaching the child to be conscious about language making doesn't make him talk better; it makes him talk worse. *So writing is subconscious too. You won't be aware of how you're learning, and after you've learned you won't be able to say what you know. The more you try to make good writing happen by conscious control, the more you'll prevent good writing.*

11. The child practices all aspects of talking at once, holistically. He never breaks language into pieces, or sets up a graded series of tasks to be mastered one before the other. No child ever said, "First I'll master nouns, then move on to verbs; first I'll learn declarative sentences, then work on interrogatives." No parent ever said, "No, Baby, don't ask questions; you haven't mastered imperatives yet!" Nor does the child say, "Whole words are too hard for me; first I'll master some basic consonants and vowels, then try putting them together in simple monosyllables." Instead, the child starts out trying to say the whole messages that matter to him the most. *So you should practice all aspects of writing at once, holistically. Don't break language into pieces and try to learn by exercises or drills. Don't "work up to" writing by steps. If you want to learn to write essays, begin by writing whole essays.*

The Eleven Blinders

If the Baby's Way works so well, and we all know it does because we've been through it once, why don't we use it when we learn to write? Because we've all been taught a set of rules about how to learn that is the opposite of the baby's. Nobody says the rules out loud, but we act by them anyway, and they guarantee you won't write well. I call them the Eleven Blinders, and they sound like this:

1. You can learn everything about writing in a composition class, in four months.
2. You can learn to write just by talking about writing or being lectured to about writing two or three times a week, and writing once a week.
3. Writing is naturally exhausting, humiliating, dissatisfying labor, and most people sensibly avoid writing like the plague.

4. You can learn to write without having read very much. You can write essays without having read essays.

5. You can learn to write without caring much and with no real purpose, the way you learn fractions. You can write without joy. If you have no real reason to write, then grades, bribes, threats of shame, arguments about how "writing is important," or an inspirational teacher will make up for it.

6. No one really expects you to write well, or like writing, or find any use for writing in your life. Writing is something a few anti-social people called "writers" do and sensible people avoid. You'll never really be a writer; you'll always be someone trying to write.

7. You'll learn by being told everything you do wrong—how else will you ever learn to do it right? You'll learn by being told how bad your writing is. You'll be inspired to do better by feeling like you've failed every time you write. The reason you write so badly is because your standards aren't high enough.

8. You learn best by raising the worry and fret level high and "trying harder." You learn by taking attention away from message and content and putting it on mechanics, grammar, and writing rules. Good writing is getting the commas in the right places, having an introduction and conclusion, avoiding misplaced modifiers, and having transition between sentences.

9. You'll learn to write just by having a teacher tell you how.

10. You write well by taking conscious control. You write "good grammar," for instance, by studying grammar rules and following those rules as you write sentences. The less conscious control you exercise, the more you slip into error.

11. You master writing by breaking it up into pieces and steps and practicing them separately. Before you write an essay you do spelling drills, transition and sentence-combining drills, subject-verb agreement exercises, and outlining and thesis-statement-making activities.

And what has been the harvest of *that* approach to language learning? It couldn't be more disappointing. Most of us write in pain and fear and write only when we're forced to. Writing seems pointless and profitless. We feel fake when we write and dissatisfied and full of self-loathing when we've written. We never learn to write easily—writing is always something we grind out. We stare at the typewriter for an hour, then squeeze out a crabbed paragraph and collapse, swearing there's nothing more in us to say—and go off to chatter with friends for the rest of the evening. Until you rid yourself of the Eleven Blinders and replace them with the Baby's Way, you'll write like that, and nothing this book or any teacher or any course can do for you can make much difference.

The Four Basics

The Baby's Way can be reduced to four keys. To learn any language—Russian or formal essay English—you need four things: exposure to models, motivation, practice, and feedback. But in each case you need the right sort—not just any kind of exposure, motivation, practice, or feedback will do. They're also in order of importance: You need exposure more than motivation, motivation more than practice, and practice more than feedback.

Exposure

Exposure, all by itself, will teach you most of what you need to write. Babies learn to talk by listening, not by talking. If I sent you to live in England for a year, you'd come back speaking in British accents and using British vocabulary, without consciously practicing, doing drills, or being corrected. Saturate yourself with eighteenth-century prose for a couple of months and you'll come out thinking in eighteenth-century prose.

We make language the way we see it made. We have no other choice. So we should expose ourselves to models that are written the way we want to write. And being exposed to one thing doesn't teach us to do another, so we must expose ourselves to exactly what we want to write. A lifetime of reading cartoons won't teach us how to write formal essays. If you want to write essays, read essays.

Exposure works faster than you'd imagine. It only takes a Western movie or two to catch on to how Western movies "go." If you read Erma Bombeck essays for twenty minutes every evening for three weeks, afterward you could probably write a pretty good Bombeckian essay.

Ordinary reading will work, but a special kind of reading works better: *reading for the craft*. If someone loved to watch dance and went to a ballet, how much would she learn about dance by watching? A little. But if a practicing dancer went to the ballet, how much would she learn? A lot. The difference is in the way the two people watch. The first watches like an audience. The second watches like an apprentice. Experiencing art doesn't teach you to make art well by itself. Watching movies doesn't make you a director. But once you decide to study directing, every movie you watch is an education.

To write, you must read the way the dancer watches dance and the director watches movies: for the craft, not merely to experience the *effect* of the art, but to see how the effect is wrought. The masses see a movie like *Airplane!* and laugh; the artist sees *Airplane!* and, while laughing, studies how the director makes us laugh. How do essays end? Most people have seen it done hundreds of times but haven't noticed how. To learn, as you go on with your reading life, notice with a small part of your mind how each writer you read solves the problem of ending. After a while, you still won't be able to say how endings go, but you'll know, and when you write you'll do it *like that.*

You need a second kind of exposure as well: Besides exposure to the finished product, you need exposure to the writing process. If you wanted to learn to make automobile engines, you'd need to see more than just finished engines; you'd need to see people making engines, from initial brainstorming and design to final machining and testing. You need to see writers at work, reacting to prompts, doing research, organizing drafts, cutting, line editing. Writing is the only complex skill we're asked to master without a lot of time spent seeing someone do it.

This second kind of exposure is hard to get. When was the last time you watched a skilled writer rewrite a draft? For most of us, the answer is "Never." Where can you go to get such exposure? To a writer's colony. There's probably one meeting in your composition classroom.

Motivation

To write well, you have to want to. How obvious. If someone hates tennis and plays only when he's forced to, we expect he won't play well. Yet in our world we usually accept hating to write and try to work around it: Of course you hate to write—doesn't everyone?—but we'll force you to write with grades or convince you to care by telling you no one will hire you if you can't write. That doesn't work. If you can't find real, personal reasons to write, you won't write well. Period.

Luckily, those reasons aren't hard to find. Every human loves writing, the way we love music, dancing, or talking. All children are dying to write, and scribble long before they can make letters. We even love the supposedly unrewarding parts of writing, like spelling—as you know if you've ever done crossword puzzles or jumbles, or played Hangman, Scrabble, Word Search, Boggle, Perquacky, Spill and Spell, Four Letter Words, or any of the other games that fascinate schoolkids and make game manufacturers rich. We love language as stuff, and love to play with it like clay; we love puns, word games, tongue-twisters, the latest slang phrase, rhymes, and secret codes like Pig Latin. Even the people who "hate English" in school write secret notes to each other in class the minute the teacher's back is turned and rush off to read the latest Garfield book or see a movie or listen to a rap album, all of which are forms of literature and are made out of "English."

Nor do we have to work hard to develop high standards. Children, when they begin writing, have to be taught to *lower* their standards, or they'll fuss over and polish every letter and every punctuation mark and never get beyond the first word or two.

But something gets in the way of all that natural language love, because most people, by the time they're grown up, say they don't like to write. And when they try to motivate themselves, things get worse. They try harder, and hate writing more. People usually write poorly not because they don't care enough, but because they care too much. Most people who "hate to write" care so much that they dare not do it—the chance of failure and pain is too high. I can prove it: You're at a party and find out the person you're talking to is an English teacher. Suddenly you realize that the way you use English "matters." Does that make you speak better, or worse?

We let fear of criticism and failure kill a lot of things we once loved. We all love to dance and sing as children, but when we grow up we learn to raise our standards, critique our dancing and singing sternly, and think about how we sound or look to others. As a result, we decide we "don't like" dancing and singing, and never do it where anyone can watch. But it's not the dancing and singing we don't like; it's the value system we've learned to impose on it.

So what can you do? First, turn off the language cop in your head, the voice that's policing you for errors and failure. Write the way you used to play with clay or paints—to see what comes of it, without fear of reprisal. Remember how badly you drive when a police car is on your tail? No one creates well in fear or when motivated by self-contempt.

Second, use writing to accomplish something you passionately want to do. Some time ago my daughter and I began music lessons. She was nearly tone deaf, so the program started with very simple tunes like "Three Blind Mice." Molly was doing pretty well, pushed along by a bubbly teacher and a rabidly supportive parent. Then one day she came home from a friend's house. She had heard the soundtrack album from the Broadway musical *Annie*. She sang me "Tomorrow," a song of breath-taking difficulty. And she sang it beautifully. Suddenly her musical training took off, helped by the *Annie* album, which I immediately bought. Her standards for her own singing went through the ceiling. The moral: You learn by finding tasks worth the work. For most writers that means, say something you care passionately about to an audience of real people, and get as a reward their thoughtful response to what you said—not how you said it.

Exposure and motivation will almost teach you to write well by themselves. From his college days to his sixties, my father never wrote a word except to fill out insurance forms and write an occasional business letter. But he read voraciously all that time, mostly in anthropology and the sciences. In his sixties he went to Africa, encountered the Bushmen, and suddenly he wanted to write a book about them, his own life spent hunting, and humankind's relationship to the wilderness. And he wrote a very nice book. Whether it won a Pulitzer Prize isn't the point; the point is he could write well without much more than a lifetime of reading and a passionate need to say something.

Practice

Of course, you have to write to learn how to write, and the more you write the better. But it's possible to practice without learning much from it. First, you must practice exactly the skill you want to get: You can practice diagramming sentences all day and all night and learn very little about writing essays. Second, practice is almost useless without exposure and motivation. Babies can "practice" talking all they want, but they never learn to speak French unless they're surrounded by French speakers, and doing something over and over again won't make you remember it if you don't care, as every generation of sentence diagrammers has proved.

Feedback

When you're learning, you try something and see what happens. You hit the tennis ball and watch where it lands. That's feedback. Writing has no built-in feedback system. You write the essay and hand it in, and it's like playing tennis in the dark: You hit the ball, it flies off into the blackness, and you learn nothing. You need to know where the ball went. You need readers who will tell you: Were they convinced? Was the explanation clear? Did the opening paragraph capture their interest? Did they like the writer's voice? Were the jokes funny?

The biggest difference between how babies and adults learn language is this: Babies need one kind of feedback and adults need two. The first, the kind they both need, focuses on the message. The baby says, "I'm hungry," and the parent replies, "What do you want to eat?" You write an argument saying that mandatory drug testing is an invasion of one's right to privacy, and your reader replies, "But who wants to go up in an airplane knowing the pilot may be doped to the gills?" This kind of feedback is the more important of the two, and most school writers rarely get it, so you'll probably have to go find it. Cultivate people who will read your work and react to it the way they'd react if you *said* it in a lively conversation in the living room at home.

The second kind of feedback looks at the *manner*, the *way* in which you said it. Babies can't understand conversations that begin, "Let's look at how you made that sentence and consider alternatives," but adults can.

This kind of feedback is the root of most of the grief we feel about our writing. If you ask someone who "hates to write" where they learned to hate it, they'll usually say, "My Xth-grade teacher ripped every paper I wrote to shreds, covered every page in red ink, and I've been afraid to write ever since." We know the damage it does, yet against all evidence people remain convinced that critical feedback focusing on language mechanics is the single most necessary element in a successful writing program. I teach future public school teachers, and they're always ready to tell me that students can't learn if you don't mark all their mistakes, and many students demand that I mark their writing up, like patients who demand that the dentist's drill hurts so they know they're getting their money's worth.

So let's set the record straight. Feedback is the least important of our four basics. Content-focused feedback is much more useful than language-focused feedback, and the wrong kind of language-focused feedback is worse than none at all.

The most destructive kind of feedback is, of course, the most popular: error marking. Our culture has a love affair with error marking, so let me give you five of the many reasons why you can't learn to write that way. First, error marking hurts most people so much that they can't stand to learn from it. Second, it overloads the writer: The essay comes back a blur of red, and the writer doesn't know where to begin. Third, it speaks to the what and not the how: It labels what's wrong, but doesn't tell you why or how to prevent it. It's as if a tennis coach watched you serve for fifteen minutes and said, "You're serving into the net," and walked on. I *know* that!; tell me how to fix it! Fourth, because error marking works best on minor mechanical features (spelling, noun-pronoun agreement) and worst on big issues (thesis, structure, tone, intention), it implies that minor mechanical features are the most important aspect of writing. Fifth, it equates good writing with error-free writing, yet we all know that we get no pleasure at all as readers from writing that merely avoids errors. Both implications strip writing of its true purposes and rewards.

So what kind of language-focused feedback helps? Chapter 10 is all about that, and writers will tell you later in this chapter (beginning on p. 13), so I'll be brief now. Feedback helps when it is offered as suggestions (instead of orders) given to help accomplish what the writer wants to do, only better (instead of to correct errors or follow rules or do what the teacher wants). Ideally, the writer says to the reader, "I'm trying to do *this*; how could I accomplish that better?" And the reader says, "Maybe if you did a little of *that* it would work better."

Why Explaining Language Doesn't Work

One doomed method of learning to write is so popular I want to single it out for refutation: learning to write by having someone explain to you how. When I was young, it seemed obvious that the way to learn to write was to read great writers explaining how they did it. So I did, and I found out that Hemingway or Faulkner or E. B. White was no more aware of what he was doing than you and I are.

Writing can't be explained, for three reasons, any one of which is enough by itself to doom teaching by explanation to failure.

First, there's too much to know. How many things do you need to know to write an essay? Five billion? At least. If you learn ten things per class session, you and your teacher will be in your graves before you get to semicolons. Of course, most of the five billion you already know. So go learn what remains the same way you learned the others—by listening, talking, reading, and writing.

Second, English is too complex and too subconscious to explain. The simplest things we know about language are beyond our power to express. What's a noun? What does *of* mean? We *know*, but we can't say what it is that we know. Seven-year-olds know more about English grammar than any linguist can put into words. And linguists, who spend their lives learning to explain how English works, don't necessarily write well as a result.

We do lots of subconscious things that we do worse the more we try to be aware of what we're doing as we do them: falling asleep, typing, and reading, for instance. If you're a good typist, you know that ordering yourself to type by conscious command guarantees you'll type at a snail's pace if you can type at all. Instead, you have to let go and not think about it. Language is the same way.

We've all done enough sentence diagramming to know that formal language study doesn't get into our writing very easily. Robert Gorrell, an authority on composition teaching, decided one term that, if he did nothing else, he was going to teach his class how to use *lay* and *lie* correctly (if you don't know the rules, a handbook will tell you, but you don't need to know to appreciate the story). First he explained the difference. Then he gave *lay/lie* exercises at the beginning of every class meeting, all term long. By the end of the term, every student was a master at completing *lay/lie* exercises . . . and their use of *lay* and *lie* in their writing hadn't changed.

Inspired by Gorrell and somewhat disappointed to discover that both my children (then aged three and seven) said *lay* where Standard English demands *lie*, I decided to see if their love for their father could withstand a campaign to convert to *lie*. I explained the "right" way to use the words and corrected my children every time they were "wrong." We all worked like dogs. After about a year and a half, we began to see results, and now they do it "right" most of the time unless they're in a hurry or are interested in what they're saying. They only hated me for correcting them some of the time. But while they were partially learning that one grammatical fact with great labor, they were learning thousands of others, unconsciously, painlessly, and perfectly, by talking and listening.

But the Battle of *Lay* and *Lie* was not without its rewards. One day Max, my youngest, was playing Robot, which she called Robock. She happened to say *lay*, and I said, "No, Max, it's *lie*." She replied in a metallic voice, "Robocks say *lay*."

The third reason writing can't be explained is that language is conventional. Something is conventional if it's made of conventions: rules that have no reason or logic to them, but have simply been agreed upon by a group of people because it's convenient if everyone does it the same way. Table manners, dress codes, and rules of the road are conventional. Do we drive on the right side of the road because it's somehow better than the left? No. It's just less bloody if we all agree to do it that way.

Conventions can't be explained or figured out, because conventions have no reasons. Let's take two examples. "If you're thinking about buying a new car" sounds everyday; "If you are contemplating the purchase of a new automobile" sounds snooty. How would you explain to someone learning English why that is or how you figured it out? How do you explain to someone why "a great many people" is formal, "many people" is colloquial, "a lot of people" is informal, and "a whole bunch of people" is very informal? Conventions aren't explained to you; you live around them and after a while you "just know."

What Good Is a Composition Class?

A composition class can't tell you how to write, but it can help you with each of the Four Basics: exposure, motivation, practice, and feedback.

Exposure

A class can't give you the thousands of hours of reading you need, but it can help by exposing you to a world of great writing you might never encounter otherwise and by helping you practice the art of reading for the craft, so the reading you do for the rest of your life will be writer's training. More important, it can expose you to models of the writing process. A writing class will surround you with other writers' writing, so you can see how they do it.

Motivation

A writing class can help you find real reasons to write by introducing you to the great writers who inspire you and make you say, "Lordy, I wish I could do that!" And it can help by giving you a real audience of classmates who will react enthusiastically and thoughtfully to your work and by surrounding you with writing artisans who are excited by language, reading, and writing and who will quicken your excitement for these things. The club of writers usually, though not always, holds its meetings in classrooms.

Practice

A writing course may be the one time in your life when you can treat writing the way it should be treated, as an ever-present, integral part of your thinking, reading, and conversing. You'll never have it so good again, believe me.

Feedback

Feedback is a writing course's best gift, because it's the one thing you can't give yourself. A writer's most precious possession is a thoughtful colleague willing to read her writing carefully and offer considered advice.

In life, you're lucky to find two; in a writing class, you should be surrounded by them. Think of it—the university spends a fortune just to round up twenty-five people whose job it is for four months to help you write.

What Good Is This Book?

This book will do you no good unless you're busy reading, writing, and talking about writing with your colleagues, and so come to it as a craftsman who is elbow-deep in his craft, fresh from making writers' decisions, and full of questions.

A few years ago I decided to fulfill a lifelong dream and learn to sail. I read several books, all of which said, "Beware the gibe, when the boom swings violently from one side of the boat to the other. If you gibe carelessly, you may destroy your boat and the people in it. Here's how to avoid it. . . ." I read the words, but they meant nothing to me. I went out on the water, got in a position where I had to gibe, and almost destroyed the boat and the people in it. "Good heavens!" I said. "Why didn't someone warn me about this?" Then I went back and reread the pages on gibing, and—wonder of wonders!—I found everything they said pertinent, clear, and unforgettable. So go gibe; then we'll be ready to talk.

How Can I Write Well Right Now?

So much for idealism; what about cold reality? What if you have an essay due this Friday in class, and you haven't got two years to do the reading and writing you should have been doing all along? We can use the principles of exposure, motivation, and feedback to find a way to write well today.

> Since you need exposure, write in a language you already know—your speaking language. Or write in a form you've read a lot of: a comic strip, a sports column, a fairy tale, a sitcom script, a personal narrative, an ad, a movie review.

> Since you need motivation, write something you want to write; say something that matters to you; write to people you want to talk to; write something you'd love to read.

> Since you need feedback, find a classmate—a fellow member of Frank Smith's club of writers—and spend an hour two days before the essay is due kicking a rough draft around. Ask your classmate what he thinks in response to what you said. Ask him how the essay could be made to work better. Pay him back by doing the same for his rough draft.

Sometimes you only have to do the first of these three. Here's a writer who learned to write well overnight by using the language she spoke. Her first draft began like this:

> The use of phonics as we discussed after reading Weller's book is like starting at the end of learning to read in which no meaning or insight is given to the context of the concept of reading.

In conference, I asked her to *say* to me what she meant. She did, in strong, plain English. I said to her, "Look—you talk easily and well. So trust your talk, and talk your papers." Her next essay (on how to teach spelling) began

> Spelling should be taught as a subject separate from reading. Good reading skills do not mean good spelling skills. Spelling is learned by writing.

Beautiful!

Now here's a writer who learned to write well overnight by writing in a form she knew well. Her first essay began like this:

> As a teacher of young children the act of censoring literature is an important task. This prevents bad material from entering the classroom. On the other hand, who has the right to judge what is considered "bad material?" However, our society has a set of basic human values and it is necessary to protect these morals through the act of censorship in regards to text books and other various forms of reading material.

That's in trouble. Her second essay was a narrative, and she wrote like this:

> Finally, the moment had arrived. Summer was over and the first day of school was just three days away. Jennifer was so eager and anxious to go to school. She got up bright and early, put on her favorite jeans, her new tee-shirt, and her new blue tennis shoes. Her mom and dad were still asleep, so she made her own lunch and left a note telling them she went to school early because she did not want to be late for her first day. With her lunch pail in one hand, and her Pee-Chee folder in the other, she set out for her little journey to the bus stop alone.

So sometimes when good writing seems very far off, it's really close at hand and we only have to learn to reach out our arm for it.

WRITERS' WORKSHOP

What Helps, What Doesn't

Many of the chapters in this book end with "Writers' Workshop" sections like this one. If you would like a word on how they work and how you might read them, see the Preface.

My first attempt at a "big" piece of writing was an adventure story I wrote in the sixth grade. I slaved on it for weeks and was hugely proud of how long it was. I gave it to my teacher and waited antsily for his reaction. After several weeks, I asked how it was going, and he took it from the filing cabinet where it had been lying since I gave it to him, wrote "AA" on it, and handed it back to me. He had never looked at it. The grade was just to shut me up. That was in 1957, and I've never written another story. It still hurts to think about it.

Chapter 1 is about the model for "good writing" and the image of ourselves as writers we carry around with us. We construct that model and that image from lessons learned in experiences like mine. Some of the lessons are good, and we should keep them. Sometimes they're poisonous and keep us from writing well, and we have to unlearn them. Every term I ask my students to examine their past for the events that shaped their attitudes toward writing, and then to turn the responses into conclusions: What works, what doesn't? What experiences make for strong, happy writers and what make for frightened, weak ones? Here are some typical responses. After you read them, I'll invite you to add your own experiences to the conversation.

In the eighth grade our teacher assigned an autobiography. We bought a blank photo album, filled it with old family photos, and wrote about each one. It was fantastic. There was no grade, no marks, just a comment: "It sounds like you led a very exciting life!" I still have that album and will always cherish it. The teacher could have ruined it with a grade and red pen marks.

I can honestly say that I loved to write, until I had Mr. Del Rio in my junior year. The whole year was grammar. It wasn't terribly awful until he made us write papers to include certain types of phrases and clauses. They had to be underlined in red, so he could identify them quickly. The papers had no meaning at all.

I never did believe that what I learned in school was writing. Real writing was the stuff that gave you goose bumps when you read it. I wrote at home and kept the products in a box in the closet. I certainly couldn't take it to school to be scrutinized for grammar mistakes.

I remember my high school English teacher telling us that if he finds one grammar error, he will not finish reading your paper. It didn't matter if you had a terrific paper or not. Ever since, I have been dwelling on my sentence structure and where I should put a semicolon, instead of just writing. I wish I could have had a teacher who would have allowed me to write just for the heck of it.

I wrote a poem that delighted me. I thought it would make the teacher laugh. I got an A on it. I didn't continue writing poems. An A is a lousy response to a poem.

I enjoy writing because as far back as I can remember my dad read to me often, at least once each night. When I learned to write (not spelling correctly or with any punctuation to speak of) I would write stories that were take-offs from books my dad had read to me.

In school I would hear the words "write a paper" and I would fill with dread. But I loved to write letters to my friends. Writing itself isn't what I fear, it's knowing it's going to be evaluated and scrutinized.

In college I tried to do exactly what my teachers asked. I stopped trying to please myself, in order to please them. My teachers chose the subjects, most of which I couldn't understand or had no meaning to me, and I knew I must say what they wanted me to say. After I spent hours on a paper, I'd look at it and hate it.

My earliest recollection of writing is the scribbles Mom and Dad would proudly send to Grandma and Aunt Mary. Mom and Dad were great models. They were prolific writers. Mom was always jotting things down: grocery lists, letters, notes to babysitters. Dad wrote forestry articles, lists of things to do

*around the home, 4-H lesson plans, checks. Armed with cray-
ons and then pencils, my siblings and I were encouraged to
draw or write, as long as we left the walls alone. A favorite
writing assignment was writing our birthday menus. I also
loved writing checks when playing house.*

*When I was exposed to Ken Macrorie's concept of "Engfish,"
I realized I had spent at least fifteen years of schooling per-
fecting a language I would never use again once I left school
behind.*

*I've been writing a weekly newsletter for my church. When I
began I was preoccupied with mechanical errors. After a while
I realized the audience wasn't interested in being grammar
critics, but was interested in what the newsletter said.*

*The teacher assigned an argument essay: "I want 250 words,
broken down into fifty words in five paragraphs." I barely
listened; I was busy figuring out how I was going to wow him
with my unshakable argument that Al Haig was the infamous
"Deep Throat" in the Watergate investigations. When he returned the essay, each paragraph had a number beside it: 35,
71. His comment: "I will be unable to grade your paper until
you comply with my rules." I had to rewrite until I had five
paragraphs and each paragraph had exactly fifty words. I finally got an A, but I didn't care any more.*

*My teachers have always wanted the standard five-paragraph
essays. I end up saying everything in the first two paragraphs,
and everything else is a bunch of stuff even I don't understand.*

*Three friends and I decided to put together an underground
newspaper. We were the talk of the school. No one knew who
we were. I would love it when someone sitting in class would
start laughing at some article. One of us overheard some students saying, "Okay, so we know they're in fourth-period PE
and drive mini-trucks. Now all we got to do is find out who
they are so we can kill them."*

*In the eighth grade, we spent the majority of each day copying
grammar facts off the blackboard. The rest of the hour was
spent doing exercises from the grammar book. The final exam
was a 200-word paragraph in which we had to label every
word—noun, pronoun, type of verb, etc.*

I never really liked writing until the fifth grade. Before that all I wrote were book reports. Then one day the teacher told us to write an excuse for not doing our homework. I rambled on about how my pet dragon ate my assignment and how I got a Ferrari for my birthday and got arrested for going 140 miles an hour (pretty good lie for a ten-year-old). My teacher liked it so much she printed it in the school newspaper. I was really excited and wrote other stories just for fun. Next year, I had a teacher who made us diagram any grammar errors we made. I was turned off to writing until high school.

I remember when I first learned to hate writing. In the fourth grade I decided to write a fantasy story about a magic ring that would make me invisible. I was scribbling away when my teacher came by. She marked all the misspelled words and the punctuation mistakes in bright red ink. She lectured me on using good handwriting, not "chicken scratch." I never did finish that story.

For years after that I had trouble writing. I know it sounds ridiculous for such a small incident to have affected me so much, but it did. I would erase my first draft so many times I would wear holes in the paper. I wrote with my arm circled around my paper so no one could see what I was writing, and if someone tried to comment or correct it I would tear it up and throw it away.

In third grade I wrote something about how our pet raccoon couldn't have babies because we didn't have a daddy raccoon—stuff that was very important and puzzling to me. The only feedback was a red circle around the word "racoon." —

Discussion

Obviously, many people are feeling a lot of pain about their writing. And the people in these histories are the system's *successes*, those who thrived and went to college, most of them intending to become teachers! But there's comfort to be taken here, too. All of us writers are having the same experiences, reacting the same way, thriving on the same things, and being curdled by the same things. We're all in this together, and we agree on what helps and what doesn't. For instance, being read to a lot by your parents helps; being forced to push your personal message into cookie-cutter patterns like five-paragraph essay paradigms doesn't. Critical feedback in the form of conversation with a mentor making suggestions about alternatives helps; critical feedback in the form of red-pen line-editing corrections doesn't. All we have to do is do the things that help and avoid the things that don't.

So what should you do to become a healthy writer? First, tell your own story. Get clear on what assumptions about writing you now own and where you got them. Second, using the histories in this section and your own experience, make a list of things that work and things that hurt. Third, reject the poisonous messages you've been fed. Finally, create for yourself a writing environment that nourishes you as a writer. If writing for yourself nourishes you, do it. If writing for grades curdles you, don't.

These aren't easy things to do. But there's little point in talking about how to outline or develop a thesis or revise until you do.

Your Turn

In this chapter you've been listening to a conversation about how people learn to write. It's time to join the conversation. Make your own contribution to the collection of tales in the Writers' Workshop. Write a two-page narrative detailing everything you've done or had done to you that has helped form your writing or your view of yourself as a writer. Which helped? Which hurt? Remember to go back to the beginning—most people's attitudes toward reading and writing are formed long before they get to school. And think about what isn't in your life as well as what is—sometimes lacks are profoundly educational, like never seeing your parents reading for pleasure.

When you're done, as a class pool all your anecdotes and from them make up histories of the generic healthy writer and the generic unhealthy writer. What kinds of things, in general, have healthy writers done and had done to them? What kinds of things have unhealthy writers done and had done to them? What would a person do if she were setting out to create for herself the perfect writer's upbringing and environment?

MORE THINGS TO DO

---

1. Write a one-page essay telling which of The Eleven Blinders (p. 5) is your personal curse that obstructs your writing the most.

2. Write a two-page essay exploring how well your writing career up to now has provided you with The Four Basics (p. 7).

Chapter 2

WHAT MAKES WRITING GOOD

In Chapter 1 we talked about how writing skills are acquired. Now let's talk about what the goal of writing is. When you set out to "write well," what exactly are you trying to accomplish? You can't write well until you know the answer—until you can say, "Good writing does *this*!" You can't play baseball well until you know that the objective is to run around the bases and reach home plate.

You'd think the answer was obvious, but it isn't. Many students are trying to "write well" by trying to accomplish the wrong things. For instance, a lot of people try to write well by studying grammar and working hard to eliminate grammatical errors when they write. But it doesn't work, because good writing isn't simply writing with all the grammatical errors taken out, any more than a great football game is simply one where no one is offsides.

The good news is, what makes writing good is something simple, something you already have. Most people tell themselves that they can't write well yet because they lack something, something that's very hard to get: They don't have a big enough vocabulary yet, or haven't lived a rich enough life yet, or mastered the semicolon yet, or learned Latin yet. Great writers have written without any of these things, and you can too.

Let's look at a piece of the real stuff and see what it's got. Here's a good essay. What does it have that bad essays don't have?

MAKING A BRAVE NEW WORLD WITH NO ROOM FOR CHILDREN

RASA GUSTAITUS

The man came running toward us as we were doing a few last stretches after a morning turn around the Golden Gate Park track. A small figure trailed behind him.

He came alongside and passed—a youngish man in excellent condition, with carefully groomed mustache, blue and red jogging shorts, appropriate shoes and socks. His companion, not nearly as sure-footed and falling farther behind every minute, turned out to be a little girl of maybe three, at most four, in a hooded green winter coat that flopped loosely around her. She too passed us. But a few dozen feet away, as she realized the man was receding hopelessly into the distance, she stopped, stretched her arms toward his back, and wailed: "Daddy!"

He was way out of hearing range now. Sobbing, she stood alone in the sand on the track that surrounds an enormous grassy playing field. More runners passed her, turned to glance, and ran on.

I went over and took her hand. "He'll be back," I said. "See, he's just turning the bend. Soon he'll come around again."

She stopped crying and I led her to the bleachers. Her nose was running, but I had nothing to wipe it with. After a while, the man passed again. "Thanks," he said to me; and, to the child, "I told you it's all right as long as you can see me." Again we watched his back recede.

"I have three daddies," the child said.

"Oh? And how many mommies?"

"Well, there's my mom, and you, and . . ."

"I'm not your mommy," I hastened to correct her, so as to avert yet another abandonment. "I'm just a friend."

We talked a bit more, but it was time for me to leave. So I advised her to sit there and watch, hoping the man was a two-mile and not an eight-mile daddy—whether or not his position in her family was daddy one, two, or three.

The scene stayed in my mind: the vigorous running man and the tiny sniffling girl, with the too-heavy coat slipping off her shoulders, left behind. It struck me that the image summed up what has happened in many American communities, in places where new gourmet bakeries and physical fitness studios open daily and families are increasingly scarce.

Most of the adults seem overscheduled with personal self-improvement efforts. They're out there running, getting body work, practicing martial arts, writing novels, learning to paint after forty, dabbling in psychic studies. They are full of vigor and enthusiasm.

Meanwhile, the children are sent to McDonald's for dinner and parked endlessly in front of TV sets. They run their favorite movies through the videocassette player, and then turn on their radio stations. While the adults seek out wholesomeness to keep their aging systems at optimum levels, the children wind up with junk food for body, mind, and soul. They have multiple parents with whom they cannot keep up.

I tried, recently, to find a children's jazz dance class for my twelve-year-old daughter, only to discover that the two big studios nearby cater to adults.

"The parents are working; they don't have time to take the children around," explained one teacher. "You'll find some children's classes in Marin County or the East Bay."

One after another, the family neighborhoods of U.S. cities have taken this turn, toward a refinement that begs larger questions. The single people who move into houses vacated by dying Irish widows here have good taste. And childhood fantasies are not entirely absent: among the new shops in my neighborhood is one specializing in handmade stuffed animals. But most customers are adults buying for other adults.

In a local flat, a single mother laid off from her job as a school-bus driver speaks of the isolation she feels as she struggles to get by with her two-year-old son. Nearby a feminist-established Women's Building boasts a lot of activities, and most of them have "child care provided"—an obligatory service for feminist events. "But how about something you do *with* children?" asks this mother. . . .

Congress has approved the expenditure of $177.1 billion for the MX missile, just for starters. Economies will be made on school lunches and educational support services. But armed defense may be irrelevant to a society that ignores its children. It is already on a fast-track, self-destructive course. ❖

(Pacific News Service)

What Good Writing Isn't

Let's list the things that a good essay *doesn't* need:

A large vocabulary. We all know almost all of Gustaitus's words. Complex sentences.

A brand new idea. Gustaitus isn't saying anything that hasn't been said before.

An argument that's absolutely and exclusively true. The essay has a nice thesis, but the opposite—that our society is built around catering to children—is just as true.

The last word on its topic. The essay doesn't end discussion of how our society deals with its children; it just adds a little something to it.

Profound thinking. The ideas in the essay aren't subtle or brainy.

Extensive research or expertise. Gustaitus's only "research" she got off the front page of the newspaper—the MX missile budget.

Extraordinary experience. I've had experiences like Gustaitus's encounter on the jogging track several times. I bet you have too.

Since the essay doesn't have these things, they can't be what makes good writing good, and you don't need to have them either.

There are things Gustaitus's essay *does* have that make it *better* but that won't make the essay good by themselves: transition between ideas, overall organization, thesis, examples, conclusion, unambiguous language. If you have them, they'll make your writing better, but they're not the heart of writing, the way reaching home is the heart of baseball, so they won't make your writing good unless you have the "other thing" too.

There are things the essay must have but for which it gets no credit at all: spelling, punctuation, sound usage, and the other mechanical aspects of writing. You'd never say to a friend, "Oh, I read the most wonderful article in the paper yesterday. Such comma placement! And every word spelled just right!" You must do the mechanics when you write, but they won't make your writing "good" at all—only legal—and you still need to have the "other thing."

What Good Writing Is: The Sense of Audience

The "other thing," the key that separates good writing from bad, is a sense of *audience*. Writers who write for the wrong reasons think of writing as a mechanical act with certain "good" surface features, and when they write, they try to make an essay that includes them: correct spelling, an outlinable structure, a thesis statement, a large vocabulary, complete documentation of sources, and so on. That approach produces essays like Dr. Frankenstein's early experiments: However meticulously you sew the bits and pieces together, it's never going to get up off the operating table and walk. Writers like Gustaitus write *to people* in order to *do* something to them. They know we're out there reading them.

You already knew that. And (this is the really wonderful thing) you already know how to do it, too. All children begin their writing careers by writing the messages they think will pack the biggest wallop for their readers: "I love you." "I am Erika." "Come to my party." But somewhere along the line we forget we know it. A friend of mine once asked his students to write dialogues. He suggested to one student that if she had the speakers say less than the whole truth the scene might get more dramatically interesting, because the reader would then have to look behind the words. The writer replied, "But you didn't say we had to make the dialogues interesting." All we have to do is remind ourselves of the secret that writer forgot.

We all can spot writing that knows we're reading it in an instant, and we all warm to it. On a final exam in a course on how to teach writing, I asked students to discuss how to react to students' writing errors. One writer began her exam, "I <u>like</u> errors, for several reasons." Immediately I knew she knew someone was reading her. That sentence announces, "I'm saying something *you* don't expect." The underlined <u>like</u> even tells the reader how to stress the line in her head—it's a guide to our imagined reading out loud.

Once you get the secret of good writing firmly in your mind, you think in a different way about writers' decisions. Instead of saying, "What's the rule?" when a question arises, you say, "What works? What does my reader want? What am I trying to do to him?" For instance, let's say you're writing your way through an essay and you approach the conclusion. You have a decision to make: Should you summarize the essay in the final paragraph? With the old attitude, you recall someone telling you that in an essay you should "tell them what you're going to tell them, tell them, then tell them what you told them." So you summarize. With the new attitude, you ask yourself, "Does my reader want or need a summary? Will a summary conclusion read well?" For most essays the answer to both questions is no. Readers can remember what they've read, don't need to be told it more than once, and don't appreciate it if you do. In other words, summary conclusions usually *don't work.*

Having a Reader in Your Head

All writers have colleagues read their work and tell them how it reads. We'll practice doing that in Chapter 10. But no reader has the time to tell you how every line you write works, and you need to know, so you need an imaginary reader in your head. As you write every line, you imagine a first-time reader reading it and guess how she responds. The more you hear the reader's responses, the better you can decide how to react to and control them, and the better you'll write.

When I talk of hearing the writer's responses in your head, I mean it in the most literal way. If you write, "When you change the oil, be sure to change the oil filter too," you should hear your reader responding, "Why?", or "How?", or "What's an oil filter?" If you're writing a recipe for novice cooks and you write, "Then add a tablespoon of oregano," you should hear your reader responding, "What's oregano? Where can I get some? What's a tablespoon?" If you write, "All U.S. Presidents in this century have been owned by the oil companies," you should hear the reader responding, "How do you know? Can you prove it? That sounds awfully wild to me. The heck you say," and so on. If you write, "Cleaning up our environment is a humongous task," you had better realize that some readers will respond, "This person talks like a kid," or "This guy doesn't speak my language."

It isn't a sure thing: "I say *X*, and my reader responds *Y*." Instead, it's a matter of guesswork and probabilities. Different readers react differently; you can't make everyone happy; and anyway you can only deal with one imagined response. If you write, "Gun control violates the right to bear arms guaranteed by the Constitution," you'll evoke a firestorm of reactions:

Right on!
Just another gun nut.
Not that old cliché!

What does the Constitution say?
Is that what the Constitution really means?
So we can't control guns at all?
Can't we change the Constitution?
No it doesn't—the Bill of Rights says that.

You can't speak to all these voices, at least not all at once. You must choose. That's okay, as long as you respond to *one of them.*

Nor does this mean you have to do what the reader wants. You may want to frustrate him, make him mad, trick him—but you have to know how he's reacting to being frustrated, angered, or tricked, and you must be doing it to him for a reason. And the reader doesn't need to be *pleased* all the time; he just needs to be able to look back, when the reading is over, at what was done to him and see the reason for it—he says, "I see now why the writer refused to tell me what was going on until the end—he had his reasons."

So the good writer doesn't write and then ask herself what she wants to *say* next; she writes, then asks herself what her reader expects to *hear* next. The text becomes more than a series of the writer's statements; it becomes a dialogue, the writer's statements alternating with imagined reader's comments, questions, objections. We'll see that dialogue written out on pp. 33–37, and again on pp. 117–118.

Why doesn't the dialogue "just happen," since the writer's thoughts are following one another logically whether there's a reader or not? Because writing looks different to the writer and to the reader. To the writer, the jokes are always funny, the digressions always worth the time, the argument always persuasive, the description of how to do something always crystal clear. Writers have no need to ask of themselves, "Huh? Can you give me some examples? Can you say that in different words? How did you get to that conclusion?" But readers do. You need to get outside yourself and say, "I know it works for *me*, but will it work for *her*? I know it's clear to *me*, but I already understand it; how might someone who doesn't already know it misunderstand? I know I'm convinced, but I started out convinced; how might someone who strongly disagrees refute me?"

Giving the Readers What They Need

Good writing gives readers everything they need to read you well. Good readers are busy doing lots of jobs; it's your job to assist them.

They're summarizing on lots of different levels, so you must give them paragraphs, sections, and an essay that are summarizable.
They're looking for an answer to the question "Why am I reading this?" so you have to have a purpose.
They're looking for the large organizational principle that makes the pieces of the essay fall into place, so you must have one.

> They're trying to read *through* the sentences, so you must have transition and purposeful sequence.
>
> They're trying to put what they're reading to personal use—"What good is this to me?"—so you must give them something they can use.
>
> They're trying to resolve their doubts, answer their questions, and overcome their objections, so you have to provide them with the means—the data, the reasoning—to do that.
>
> They're looking for touchstones—striking lines and catch phrases on which they can hang blocks of text, remember them, and encapsulate them—so you must give them some.
>
> They're judging the reliability of your information, so you have to tell them where you're getting it, in footnotes or some other citation system.
>
> They're learning to trust you, so you have to be present in the text and acknowledge their presence.

Readers do lots of other jobs too. The clearer you are on what those jobs are, the more assistance you can offer and the better you'll write.

Seeing Writing as Performance

Good writing knows it's a performance. Good writers are hams on the page. They feel the presence of the audience the way a stage actor does; the only difference is the writer's audience must be imagined. Writers who underline, like the test taker on p. 26, are usually good writers, because underlining is a guide to dramatic reading—an underliner expects the reader to read the text aloud to his mental ear. People who read aloud well are usually good writers, and a simple way to write well is to *write something you'd love to read out loud.*

It Really Works: Three Proofs

If good writing isn't so much a matter of skills or features as a matter of having a reader firmly in mind, we should be able to prove it in three ways. First, if we take writers and teach them via skills and features, like five-paragraph organization, their writing shouldn't get remarkably better. And it doesn't, as most of us probably know personally from trying to learn to write that way. Second, if we take writers who are trying to "make essays" and tell them to write to and for real people instead, their writing should get better fast, since most of us know how to do that already. And it does happen that way. Here's a passage from an essay on hypnotism, written by someone with no sense of humans reading him:

> For some types of material, learning while in an actual state of hypnosis is best, while for other types of material, it is better to study in a waking

state with post-hypnotic suggestions providing the improvement. Rote memorization is best done in a hypnotic state, but material of a technical nature which requires integration into one's present knowledge of the subject area should be done in the waking state. The reason that technical material can't be effectively learned while under hypnosis is because the subconscious mind lacks the ability for critical and inductive reasoning. Only the conscious mind has this ability. However, post-hypnotic suggestions can help to improve the learning of technical material.

I asked the writer to rewrite it like he was talking to real people, and he produced this lovely stuff:

If you're trying to learn a foreign language, memorize a definition or a speech, or anything which requires rote memorization, then it is best to do it in an actual hypnotic state. However, technical material is another matter. You can memorize the material easily enough, but all you can do with it is repeat it, just like a parrot. With post-hypnotic suggestions, you can improve your ability to concentrate, retain, and recall the technical material.

Third, we should be able to find good writing that "breaks the rules" because breaking the rules does what the writer wants to do to the reader. Here are two examples. The first is a paragraph from *The Right Stuff* by Tom Wolfe, describing how it feels to watch a fighter plane land on an aircraft carrier.

This was a *skillet!*—a frying pan!—a short-order grill!—not gray but black, smeared with skid marks from one end to the other and glistening with pools of hydraulic fluid and the occasional jet-fuel slick, all of it still hot, sticky, greasy, runny, virulent from God knows what traumas—still ablaze!—consumed in detonations, explosions, flames, combustion, roars, shrieks, whines, blasts, horrible shudders, fracturing impacts, as little men in screaming red and yellow and purple and green shirts with black Mickey Mouse helmets over their ears skittered about on the surface as if for their very lives (you've said it now!), hooking fighter planes onto the catapult shuttles so that they can explode their afterburners and be slung off the deck in a red-mad fury with a *kaboom!* that pounds through the entire deck—a procedure that seems absolutely controlled, orderly, sublime, however, compared to what he is about to watch as aircraft return to the ship for what is known in the engineering stoicisms of the military as "recovery and arrest". . . . As the aircraft came closer and the carrier heaved on into the waves and the plane's speed did not diminish and the deck did not grow steady—indeed, it pitched up and down five or ten feet per greasy heave—one experienced a neural alarm that no lecture could have prepared him for: This is not an *airplane* coming toward me, it is a brick with some poor sonofabitch riding it (*someone much like myself!*), and it is not *gliding,* it is *falling,* a thirty-thousand-pound brick, headed not for a stripe on the deck but for *me*—and with a horrible *smash!* it hits the skillet, and with a blur of momentum as big as a freight train's it hurtles toward the far end of the deck—another blinding storm!—another roar as the pilot pushes the throttle up to full military power and another smear of rubber screams out over the skillet—and this is nominal!—quite okay!—for a wire stretched across the deck has grabbed the hook on the end of the plane as it hit the deck tail down, and the smash was the rest of the fifteen-ton brute slamming onto the deck, as it tripped up, so that it is now straining against the wire at full throttle, in case it hadn't held and the plane had "boltered" off the end of the deck and had to struggle up into the air again.

(pp. 20–22)

Here are some of the conventional essay-making rules Wolfe breaks:

Avoid run-on sentences.
Make paragraphs about four to seven sentences long.
Have a thesis statement.
Avoid redundancy.
Keep adjectives to a minimum.
Avoid exclamation points.
Avoid parentheses.

Now here's a rule-breaking essay by Steven Rubenstein.

THE PEOPLE VERSUS

It was 3:02 P.M. The trial was nearly over. The jurors filed into a small room and the bailiff locked the door behind them. The defendant and his family got up and walked down the stairs and across the street into the bar.

They didn't say anything. The family—the defendant, his parents, and his brother—sat down. The defendant ordered a soda water and everyone else ordered beers. When the drinks arrived, they drank them. It was 3:18 P.M.

There wasn't anything to talk about, really. The only thing to talk about happened three months earlier. The 21-year-old defendant, with his best buddy beside him, drove off the road and into a tree. The buddy was killed and the defendant, as he would do for weeks afterward, cried.

The jury had something to talk about, because they had to decide whether the defendant was guilty of manslaughter. But the defendant and his family didn't have to decide anything. All they had to do was wait.

It was 3:27 P.M. The waitress asked the defendant if he wanted another glass of soda water. He said no.

The father left to go to the store and returned with a bag of licorice. He offered it around the table. The defendant didn't feel like any licorice. What he felt like doing was looking at the clock again. It said 3:56 P.M.

Somebody got up and punched a number on the jukebox. The Everly Brothers sang, "Bye Bye, Love" but it didn't take very long. When they were through, it was 4:01 P.M.

"I wonder," said the brother, "if they picked a foreman yet."

The bartender was polishing a large jar of pickled hard-boiled eggs that sat on the bar. Everybody watched him do it. The father asked if anyone wanted a pickled egg. Nobody wanted one.

A copy of the newspaper was lying on the next table. The father picked it up and turned to the horoscopes and read the one for Sagittarius out loud. His son was a Sagittarius.

"You make a dazzling comeback after an error. All is forgiven."

The defendant tried to smile.

The prosecutor stood on the courthouse lawn and talked to the defense lawyer. He lit a cigarette and said he didn't expect to win and that, if he did win, he wasn't going to feel very good about it. But the law says if you drive your car too fast and it goes off the road and into a tree and your best friend dies, you can be sent to jail for a year. The number of the law is 192(3)(b).

The defense lawyer and the prosecutor watched the cars cruise down State Street. It was about 5:00 P.M., which would have been rush hour if Ukiah had one.

At 8:59 P.M., the foreman of the jury rang the buzzer. The family settled into their seats and the judge put on his robe. The defendant tucked in his blue cowboy shirt but none of the jurors saw him do it because, as they filed into the courtroom, they all looked the other way.

The foreman handed the verdict to the bailiff and the bailiff handed it to the judge.

"We, the jury, find the defendant guilty . . ."

The jurors, as they left the courtroom, told the defense lawyer how sad they were and how they talked for six hours and how, in the end, there was nothing else they could do if the law says you are guilty if you drive your car too fast and it goes off the road and into a tree and your best friend dies. ❖

(*The San Francisco Chronicle*, Nov. 20, 1982)

Here are some of the essay-making rules Rubenstein breaks:

Avoid redundancy.
Avoid run-on sentences.

Add short sentences together to avoid choppiness.
Omit needless qualification ("... which would have been rush hour if Ukiah had one.")
Reveal topic, thesis, and purpose in the opener.

Wolfe and Rubenstein break the rules because breaking the rules "works." Wolfe wants to overload the reader and make her slightly hysterical, to re-create the carrier's atmosphere of chaotic bewilderment. Rubenstein wants to be repetitive and boring, because he seeks the horror of tedious time-filling against a backdrop of unthinkable nightmare.

The rest of this book will offer you scads of rules for good writing. They're good rules, and your writing will usually get better if you follow them. But trying to write well by following the rules is the long, hard road, and I'll keep encouraging you to take the shortcut: Ask, "What works?" And there is no answer to that question until you imagine what you write working *on somebody*.

RITERS' WORKSHOP

Hearing Readers' Reactions

It's hard to hear readers' reactions, because no reader speaks them out loud, except for one in a thousand—the occasional "I don't believe it!" or "All politicians should be hanged!" that bursts out as we're reading the newspaper. Writers have to learn to imagine the other silent 999 reactions.

Let's watch readers try to say all one thousand responses out loud. I let my class read the first few sentences of a student essay one sentence at a time, asked them to say out loud what they were thinking in response after each sentence, and recorded their conversation. Here's the passage, beginning with the title, with some of their reactions in italics.

Writing Outside Oneself: A Lesson Plan

What does "writing outside oneself" mean?
Must be some kind of teacher's manual.
Is there "inside" and "outside" writing?

In order to make beginning writing students feel comfortable about
their writing, we encourage essays that are very egocentric.

> *This isn't for me—I'm not going to be a teacher.*
> *What does "egocentric" mean?*
> *I know what it means, but I'm not sure what an egocentric*
>   *essay is—got any examples?*
> *Isn't "egocentric" a bad thing to be? It has very negative conno-*
>   *tations for me.*
> *He's assuming all teachers teach that way.*

We ask them to write about their own lives, to describe their favorite
place or their grandmother, to write about their favorite holiday, or
to tell a story about something that happened to them.

> *OK, thanks for the examples.*
> *I know what he means by "egocentric" now.*
> *That's "inside writing" I suppose—so "outside writing" must*
>   *be nonpersonal, objective writing?*
> *Is he in favor of doing this or against it?*
> *Why do "we" do this?*

These essays allow the students to loosen up.

> *He's telling us why now.*
> *He thinks it's a good thing.*
> *How does egocentric writing make people "loose"?*
> *I thought the problem with most writing was it was TOO loose.*

They write more freely and with greater confidence when they discover that it's OK to write about themselves.

> *He's giving us more reasons for doing it.*
> *I hate writing about myself.*
> *I've been writing personal essays since kindergarten—I'm sick*
>   *of it.*
> *Why is he telling us this? What does he want?*

When one of their fellow students laughs at their funny story about
getting caught toilet-papering a boyfriend's house, they know that
they can write this way and have an effect on someone.

> *More examples of how personal writing does good things.*
> *I bet he's going to say there's a problem with doing it that way.*
> *He's going to say "but" sooner or later.*

Helping writers understand this, however, can be both a blessing
and a curse.

> *There's the "but."*
> *I knew it—he's going to say there's something wrong with*
>   *doing that.*

He's told us about the blessing; what's the curse?

He's either going to tell us not to do personal writing or he's going to suggest a way to keep the virtues of personal writing and avoid the "curse."

As you can see, readers in a crowd are busy folk, generating a messy blizzard of responses. And in reality it's much worse than what we see here—I've printed three or four reactions to each line, whereas there were usually twenty or thirty in the room. From that blizzard, Bob, the writer, has to choose which responses to address. He can't address them all, and he wouldn't want to. He can't talk to all audiences. If I'm not interested in teaching writing, or if I'm a teacher who thinks personal writing has no place in college, Bob has nothing to say to me except "Goodbye." And he can't please all tastes: For every reader who is scared off by words like *egocentric*, there's a reader who will be repulsed by the mention of toilet paper. And he can't respond to all legitimate demands at once. While some readers are saying "What does that mean?" others are saying, "Like what, for example?" and others are asking, "Why?" Bob can only answer one at a time and put the other questioners on hold. So Bob defines his chosen audience and imagines a likely scenario, a set of responses the bulk of his chosen audience is likely to share, whatever additional personal axes they may be grinding. Here's the text again, with the single audience response Bob chose to imagine.

Writing Outside Oneself: A Lesson Plan

What does "writing outside oneself" mean?

In order to make beginning writing students feel comfortable about their writing, we encourage essays that are very egocentric.

He's talking to teachers of beginning writing classes.
What's an "egocentric" essay?

We ask them to write about their own lives, to describe their favorite place or their grandmother, to write about their favorite holiday, or to tell a story about something that happened to them.

Why do teachers do this?

These essays allow the students to loosen up.

Why is that?

They write more freely and with greater confidence when they discover that it's OK to write about themselves.

Got any examples?

When one of their fellow students laughs at their funny story about getting caught toilet-papering a boyfriend's house, they know that they can write this way and have an effect on someone.

I see that, but why are you writing?

Helping writers understand this, however, can be both a blessing and a curse.

What's the curse?

Of course writers don't write out the two halves of the dialogue like this or even consciously formulate the reader's silent contributions. But it must be going on unconsciously, because when writing works, we'll always find the imaginary exchange if we look for it.

This insight solves one of the great mysteries of writing: *What makes one thing follow another?* Why do we read one sequence of sentences and say "That flows" or "That has transition," and we read another and say "That's choppy"? *The flowing text follows a likely scenario of reader responses and expectations; the choppy text doesn't.* We'll return to this principle in Chapter 6 when we're attacking the mysteries of organization and transition.

Your Turn

Let's go looking for this hidden dialogue in other texts. First we'll try it on someone else's text; then you can try it on your own. Here are the opening lines of an essay. Cover them with a piece of paper and pull the paper down slowly to reveal one line at a time. (If you read the whole text at once, this game doesn't work.) After exposing each line, write down all the reactions, wants, and expectations you're experiencing in response to it. Try to have lots. When you've gone through the text, look it over and write a half-page about how successfully the author predicted and dealt with your responses—do his lines and yours dovetail into a coherent dialogue?

> I keep hearing one line from women, over and over, a line that causes my heart to sink:
>
> "I'll just have . . . a salad."
>
> Oh, no, I think, not again.
>
> Then I look around. At table after table men are downing pasta, gorging on shellfish, lustily wrenching apart Cornish hens.
>
> And there next to them are women, nibbling on radicchio.
>
> Maybe taking "just a bite of yours."
>
> Nice dinner.

Okay—obviously food is complicated and symbolic and our society stresses thinness and youth and many women feel pressure to look like the women in fashion magazines and some women do in fact have a weight problem or diet problems or . . .

Enough. It's time to eat.

Let me put it another way. If men are the reason you're avoiding food . . . eat. Because, as far as men are concerned, women who eat food are much more attractive than women who avoid it.

I swear to you.

(Warren Leight, "Real Women Do Eat Food," Mademoiselle, *August 1989)*

Now do the same thing with your own writing. Sit down with a classmate and the opening passage from one of your recent essays. Read your text out loud line by line, beginning with the title, and have your colleague write down two or three of her reactions, predictions, wants, and expectations. Then jointly write a half-page essay on how successfully the essay predicted and dealt with the reader's responses. When you're finished, switch roles and do the same thing to the other author's essay.

MORE THINGS TO DO

1. To practice writing as performance, write a one-page essay you'd love to read out loud to the class. You might draw from the following prompts:

The worst restaurant you've ever been in
The oddest person you've ever known
The kind of food you hate the most
The thing in your life that most clearly says to the world, "This is me."

2. Examine a piece of your own recent writing for its sense of audience. How many signs that you know a human being is reading you are present on the page? Does the opening of the essay tell the reader who he is and how he can use what you're about to give him? How many of the reader's jobs listed on p. 28–29 are you actively helping him do?

Part Two

PLANNING AND DRAFTING

Chapter 3

FINDING SOMETHING
TO WRITE ABOUT

The next eleven chapters imagine that you'll be going through a series of steps called the writing process: prewriting, drafting, structuring, style polishing, mechanical editing, and so on. The step-by-step approach can be helpful if you find writing overwhelming, because it reminds you that you don't have to do everything at once. For instance, you can, and should, do a lot of playful, unpressured creating before you turn your thoughts to rule-following and obedience tasks like punctuation. But there's a danger to steps: They suggest that the writing process is a lot neater and more regimented than it really is.

We think of the writing process as linear: First you take notes, then you outline, then you write a first draft, then a second, and so on. The steps are real, but writers don't do one, then the other; instead, they do them all, all the time. The mind's a messy thing: It will leap from note-taking to paragraph writing to outlining to rewriting. While you're writing page 7, it will be rewriting page 5 and thinking up great lines for page 10 or another essay. You must let your brain go about its messy business. The writer's rule is, *"Take what comes, whenever it comes."* I never tell myself when I will outline; rather, there usually comes a time when I'm writing and the outline offers itself to me in a moment of clarity. At that moment, I must grab it. And whenever I write, I have a notepad at my elbow—it's there right now—to catch all the mental overflow.

So don't let the fact that Chapter 5 is about note-taking convince you to shut off your note-taking mind forever when you go on to Chapter 6. Use the writing process to help you, not to close doors.

Where Do Good Essays Come From?

"I can't think of anything to write about" is a cry heard in every composition class in the land. Yet we know there's something not right about that, because we all talk all the time with our friends. So we must be defining friendly conversation and writing in different ways, ways that make conversation easy and writing difficult.

For instance, many people think that writing begins with a rare moment of inspiration or a bizarre or unique experience. Not so. Writing essays is like being funny. A comic isn't a person who happens to have funny things happen to him; he's a person who knows how to see the potential for humor in whatever happens. Similarly, an essayist lives a life like yours; he just sees the potential essay in what he experiences. Here's the essayist John Gregory Dunne explaining how it's done:

> My house was burgled twice and the two resulting pieces netted me a lot more than the burglars got. I can recall one columnist who eked three columns out of his house burning down: one on the fire, a second on the unsung dignity of fire fighting, and a third on his insurance adjuster and a long view on the charred artifacts of a lifetime. So avid for material is your average columnist that once, when my daughter caught my wife and me *flagrante delicto*, I seriously wondered if there was a column in it. (As it turned out, only a column mention.)

Once you catch on to the trick, essay topics will jump out of the bushes.

The difference between the panicked student with "nothing to write about" and the confident writer bursting with more things to write than there is time to write them is ultimately one of imagined audience and purpose. The panicker tries to write to instructors, bosses, or other authority figures, and tries to say something uniquely new, totally brilliant, and absolutely right. The happy writer tries to write to peers or novices (people like herself or people who know less than she does) and she only asks herself to say something her peers will sympathize with or the novices can learn from. Once you think this way, you realize that everything you know or have experienced is of use to someone, because people who haven't experienced it can profit from your knowledge and people who have will appreciate knowing they're not alone:

> If you've ever been anywhere, you can tell people who haven't been there what it's like.
> If you've ever done anything, you can show how to do it to people who don't know.
> If you've ever read a book, seen a movie, or eaten in a restaurant, you can review it and tell potential customers whether it's worth the money.
> If you've ever suffered, you can assume others are suffering the same way, and you can assure them what they're going through is normal.
> If anything ever happened to you that was funny, touching, or infuriating, you can share the feeling with others.

In a way you don't even have to "know anything"; you can write about your ignorance, confusion, and doubt. Write about how bewildering it is to be a freshman on campus, how hilariously confusing it was the time you tried to program your VCR guided only by the instructions in Japanese English, how unsure you are that college is the right place for you, or how you're of two minds about getting married.

To convince yourself that most good writing springs from minds and lives like yours, consider these essay theses from my students' recent work:

> I went home for vacation and had to listen to my father tell me one more time how he disapproves of my life.

> I went to "Back to School" night, and no one was there.

> Mornings with my two-year-old are a joyous, comical circus.

> I wonder if this semester I'll finally get organized and actually get something out of school.

> Why are men genetically unable to clean bathrooms?

> The last time I got panhandled I said no. I felt guilty, but I'm not sure I should have.

> My mother never listens.

> I may have finally found a car mechanic I can afford and trust.

> It's the second week of the term and I'm already burned out.

And, for my final bit of evidence, there's a splendid essay on the following page about the most trivial of subjects.

THE EGG AND I REVISITED

KRIS TACHMIER

Kids can be finicky eaters. My own three-year-old son will put up determined resistance if he sees one Brussels sprout on his plate. One hour after dinner that singular Brussels sprout will still be on his plate, undisturbed. Similarly, my seventeen-month-old daughter cringes at the sight of a carrot and immediately clamps her jaws shut, making passage into her mouth by a fork laden with the vegetable impossible. But I really have no right to single out my children when their own mother is the classic persnicketist: I cannot and will not eat eggs.

Ever since I can remember, I have hated eggs. I'm not really certain why—maybe it's their texture, or maybe it's the notion that they're really hen ova, or maybe it's the idea that eggs can assume so many disguises. A Brussels sprout will always remain a Brussels sprout; a carrot remains a carrot; but an egg will scramble, fry, poach, coddle, benedict, and devil in the twinkling of an eye. I simply cannot trust eggs.

For a while, my childhood breakfasts included some sort of egg concoction, but the minute my mother stepped out of the kitchen I would sneak over to the sink, tilt my plate upside down, and watch the shimmering yellow creation slip down into the darkened cavity of the drain. This bit of cunning was a great success until one fateful morning. I must have left a few damning fragments of eggy evidence. I was interrogated by my mother: how long, how often, how come? The next morning a glorious bowl of Cheerios was awaiting me. The egg and I were finally separated.

In the years following, my mother learned to keep eggs out of my path, but all her efforts were not enough. During lunch at high school I would invariably sit next to someone who would pull a hardboiled egg out of his sack (together with one of those miniature salt shakers) and sit there happily sprinkling and munching on it. Too bad he never stopped long enough to notice me turning green on his left . . . I might have spoiled his appetite. And there was always some inconsiderate friend who ordered egg salad sandwiches at restaurants. The mixture would always be thick and runny, and globs of it were forever dripping out of all sides of the sandwich.

With marriage, I realized that my attitude toward eggs was a little ridiculous. I decided to give the egg a second chance. I can remember the event clearly: the morning sun was shining, the smell of fresh-perked coffee filled the kitchen, and there, flattened out in submission on my plate, was one fried egg, barely distinguishable for all the salt and pepper I had poured over it. I resolutely picked up my fork, stabbed a section of the egg, thrust it into my mouth, gulped it down, felt it rumbling its way toward my stomach, and blanched as I realized it was rocketing out of my mouth. So much for a second crack at the egg.

Today I still keep my mouth empty of eggs, but my refrigerator is full of them. For the last year or so I've been raising chickens. Every day I march out to the coop and gather a half-dozen freshly laid eggs. As soon as I have several dozen I call up friends to check if they want any eggs free of cost. I think the operation a stroke of genius: I have cleverly combined charity with penitence. ❖

Assuming you hate at least one kind of food, I'll rest my case. Now let's look at some practical ways to encourage those potential essays to make themselves known to us.

Five Principles for Getting Good Ideas

We need some labels. We'll call the spark from which an essay grows a *seed*. And we'll call the thing that causes that spark (the newspaper article you read, the conversation you overhear in the grocery store, the ad you see on TV) a *prompt*. Brains that find seeds easily follow five principles:

Don't begin with a topic.
Think all the time.
To get something out, put something in.
Go from little, concrete things to big, abstract ones.
Connect.

We'll talk about each in turn.

Don't begin with a topic. Essays rarely begin with subject matter alone. Why would a person say out of the blue, "I think I'll write about linoleum, or the national debt"? Nor are essay seeds always "good ideas"— they often aren't *ideas* at all, in the sense of whole assertions. Seeds come in many forms:

Questions: "Is there any real difference between the Republicans and the Democrats anymore?" "Why is Ralph so mad at me?"

Problems: "I'm always behind in my work." "Violent crimes against women are on the increase."

Intentions: "I want to tell people about what's really going on in this class." "I want to let people know about alternatives to the phone company."

Theses: "There are cheaper alternatives to the phone company." "Old people are the victims of silent injustice in our culture."

Feelings: "I was furious when the instructor suddenly announced there would be a term paper no one knew about due in three weeks." "I was surprised to see my father crying."

Think all the time. If you have a sense of humor, you know that the surest way to prevent yourself from being funny is to have someone (even yourself) demand that you be funny *now*. Comedians since time began have bemoaned the fact that people introduce them to friends by saying, "This is Milton. He's a riot. Be funny, Milton." Thinking's the same way. Being put on the spot is the surest way of preventing the creative juices from flowing.

So don't expect to discover a seed by sitting down for a scheduled half-hour of profundity. Minds that think well think all the time. One prolific student wrote that she goes through the world "looking for *writable* things" and her friends think she's weird because she scribbles notes to herself at parties.

Thinking all the time sounds like work, but it isn't. Your mind works all the time whether you want it to or not, the same way your body moves all the time. Any yogi will tell you that it takes years of practice to learn to turn the mind *off*, even for a minute or two. And it's physiologically impossible for your brain to get tired, which is why you can study or write all day, go to bed, and find your mind still racing while your body cries out for rest. So I'm really not asking your brain to do anything new; I'm just asking you to *listen* to it.

To get something out, put something in. One popular, poisonous metaphor for thinking is the lightbulb clicking on over our head—the notion that ideas spring from within us, caused by nothing. To become good thinkers, we have to replace that metaphor with another: Think of thoughts as billiard balls on a pool table, idle until other balls—external stimuli—slam into them and set them in motion. Seeds are *reactions*—we have them in response to other things. A thinker thinks as life passes through him, and does what I call "talking back to the world." Many of us have learned to separate input and output modes: We are either putting information into our brains or asking our brains to put out thoughts, but we don't do them at the same time. I call such people data sponges. But when things are going in is the best time to try to get things out. Let the incoming bounce off you and strike sparks. People do this naturally until they've been taught to be passive; try reading a book to a three-year-old, and listen to her mentally react to everything she hears or sees, or take her to a movie and watch her struggle not to talk back to the screen.

Are you a data sponge or a reactor? Answer the following questions:

Do you find yourself silently talking back to the newspaper when you read it?

Do you write in the margins of books you read?

Are at least 25 percent of the notes you take during course reading or lecture your own thoughts, questions, doubts, and reactions?

As you meet up with life's outrages, do you find yourself complaining to imaginary audiences in your head?

After a movie, do you feel like you're going to burst until you find someone to talk about it with?

When you listen to a speaker or a teacher, do you find yourself itching to get to the question-and-answer period?

If you said yes to these questions, you're not a sponge. If you said no, you're going to have to practice your reacting skills.

Any external stimulus can be a prompt, but, just as seeing water makes us realize we're thirsty, the best writer's prompt is another piece of writing. So if you're looking for something to write, *go read something.* Go read the newspaper or *Newsweek* and note your reactions. My student Megan McKay saw a magazine ad for hair color that rubbed her the wrong way, and she wrote this:

BRUNETTES ARE BEST

Would someone please enlighten me as to how hair color affects your ability to have fun? I have never made the connection, yet I'm continually told that "blondes have more fun." Oh, really? How so? I'm not a blonde and have never felt my life to be lacking in excitement. I've had my fair share of dates, boyfriends, and rowdy nights. Imagine, and me only a poor brunette.

Can we examine these "blondes" now? I use the term loosely because many so-called "blondes" are natural brunettes. This makes them, then, *brunettes* having fun, doesn't it? Many men say that blondes are more striking. Now excuse my ignorance, but it seems to me that a blonde in the midst of a horde of California blondes is "just another blonde." I have been told I stood out in a crowd of women because of my lovely brown hair.

Women with darker hair are surrounded by an air of mystery. Words like "smoldering" are frequently applied to us. Fie upon these lighter women. Brunettes have the true allure. So go check out Clairol's brunette section, Blondie! ❖

I used to ask my students four times a term to write an essay, and they would scrounge within themselves for seeds. Then I learned to phrase it differently. I said, "Once each week, while we're doing other things, react to something you've read, write down the reaction, and give it to me." Now they write fifteen times a term, and they never, ever complain about not having anything to say.

You can use your reading to prompt you in two different ways. The first is to let it make you think, as Megan did. The second is to let it inspire the craftsman in you. You read the piece and say, "Wow! I like that. I'd never have thought to do it. Maybe I could do something sort of like it." That's called *modeling*. Modeling reminds us that prompts aren't always *content*; we can also be inspired by *technique* (the tone, the structure, the narrative device). When you use a model, you can stick close to the original if you want to, but you don't have to; often what you're inspired to produce becomes something quite your own. Here's an inspiring model, a description by the poet e. e. cummings of his father:

> My father . . . was a New Hampshire man, 6 foot 2, a crack shot & a famous flyfisherman & a firstrate sailor (his sloop was named The Actress) & a woodsman who could find his way through forests primeval without a compass & a canoeist who'd still-paddle you up to a deer without ruffling the surface of a pond & an ornithologist & taxidermist & (when he gave up hunting) an expert photographer (the best I've ever

seen) & an actor who portrayed Julius Caesar in Sanders Theatre & a painter (both in oils & watercolors) & a better carpenter than any professional & an architect who designed his own houses before building them & (when he liked) a plumber who just for the fun of it installed all his own waterworks & (while at Harvard) a teacher with small use for professors . . . & my father had the first telephone in Cambridge & (long before any Model T Ford) he piloted an Orient Buckboard with Friction Drive produced by the Waltham watch company & . . . my father's voice was so magnificent that he was called on to impersonate God speaking from Beacon Hill (he was heard all over the common) & my father gave me Plato's metaphor of the cave with my mother's milk.

Here are two essays students were inspired by cummings's model to write:

Dave's porch has everything you ever wanted in a porch and more & it is located right next to the freshman dorms & you sit there in the sunshine & you can meet tons of people and most of those people are girls & they like to drink beer & we are always drinking beer on the porch & that way we can meet girls & we like the porch because it has a big chair on it and it's comfortable and the porch is made of redwood and Dave and Phil built it (with Dave's dad's wood) & it's sturdy & it's small but it's fine & you get to see all the people drive by & I can't think of where I'd rather be than on Dave's porch.

(Jeff Ochs)

My ex-boyfriend was a baby-faced, wavy-haired blonde with blue eyes that could be warm as a smile while his thoughts would be as cold as ice scraping against raw metal and he could charm anyone like an alligator and you couldn't get away because he would find you and follow you silently and he would watch and find out every move you made and he would just wait and wait until you made a wrong move and then he would pounce with words like claws and he was a better liar than anyone I ever knew and he would look at you with those alligator eyes and you would freeze like a deer caught in headlights because he knew you were scared and he wanted you to be scared because he let you know that he would hurt you if you ever crossed him because he collected guns and throwing stars that he would throw, embedding them deep into wood, and he would always carry two knives on his belt, one visible and one hidden, and you knew they were there and he knew that you knew and that's what he wanted and he would manipulate anyone like a chess piece (not that he ever learned to play chess, it was a sissy game) and he would do whatever he could to whoever he could to get what he wanted with that alligator smile that was like someone walking over your grave and he wants to be a politician.

(Kathleen Siemont)

Modeling gets you started, but it is just as good at getting you unstuck when you're in a rut. We'll watch it do that on pp. 377–382.

Go from little, concrete things to big, abstract ones. This principle is a logical consequence of the one before. Since ideas come best in reaction to life's incoming billiard balls, the best thinking follows a predictable course: from little, concrete bits of experience to large, abstract implications. You see an ad on TV, start thinking about it, and it leads you to speculations on American consumerism, media manipulation, and the marketing of women's bodies. Or you see a parent disciplining a child in a grocery store aisle just for being alive, and it makes you think, "Why are people without training or talent allowed to do this all-important job called child raising?" or "Parents need time off too."

Here's the path my mind traveled from a little particular to a big issue. I was sitting doing nothing one day when my eyes fell on a box of Girl Scout cookies. The box had on it a picture of a girl and the slogan "I'm not like anyone else." I reacted. I thought, "Gosh, that sounds lonely." And I valued the reaction enough to notice it and think about it. It led me to a big issue: How does American love of individuality affect Americans' ability to be members of a culture? And I formulated a thesis: Americans love their individuality so much they'll cut themselves off from everything and everyone to get it. Being "unlike everyone else" is a curse because it means you're cut off from other human beings by your differentness. I was raised a proud individualist, and I've only recently realized that the reward for being unique is loneliness.

Many of the essays in this book model this progress from a minor personal experience to a big issue. In "Why I Never Cared About the Civil War" (p. 383), Shawni Allred studied a muddy pool of water in the fifth grade and used the experience to discuss what's wrong with traditional classroom teaching styles. In "Given the Chance" (p. 374), Melissa Schatz met Stacey, and her experience with her led her to question the entire state drug rehabilitation program. And it has to be this way, because that's just how brains work. We don't walk down the street and spontaneously think, "California's drug rehabilitation program is a sham," but after trying to get Stacey into the program and meeting a stone wall, we do.

Usually the first sentence of the essay tells you whether the writer knows the secret of starting small or not. Essays on friendship that begin "Friendship is one of the most important things in life" indicate that the writer doesn't know it and are doomed. Essays that begin "Mary was my best friend in high school" indicate that the writer does know it and will thrive.

Connect. Those who think well make connections between things. An essay begins when two previously unrelated bits in the brain meet and discover a connection. Usually it's a new stimulus hitching up with an old bit stored long ago in the memory: The incoming billiard ball hits an old one that's just lying there, and they fly off together.

Here's what connecting feels like inside. One day I was sitting in an English Department faculty meeting, and we were discussing an administrative change. A colleague said, "We couldn't do that until we were sure our people would be protected." I thought momentarily, "I wonder how he knows who 'his people' are." Months later, I was vacationing in a small mountain town and picked up the local newspaper. On the front page was an article about the firing of a group of nonunion construction workers. The boss had asked the union for workers, but there were none available, so he trained out-of-work mill workers. Later the union rep showed up, announced that union workers were now available, and insisted that the others be fired. Something clicked, and I had an essay. My colleague's attitude and the union rep's were the same: "I'll watch out for my people, and everyone else can watch out for himself." I wanted to talk about why people think that way and how they learn to rise above it.

How did I make that connection? Perhaps I had opened up a file in my mind labeled "People who think in terms of those who belong and those who don't" and dumped anything related in there as it came in. Or perhaps I had spent the last few months unconsciously checking everything that came into my brain against the faculty-meeting remark for a possible link. That all sounds like work, but we all know that when something "clicks" in memory, we haven't "worked" at all—in fact, the way to bring to the surface the connection that's on the tip of the tongue is to forget about it and let the unconscious do its work unwatched.

The more UNlike two things are and the less obvious the connection, the more fresh and stimulating is the connection when you make it. Find the connection between mountain climbers and skydivers and people will nod; find a connection between inflation rates and incidence of breast cancer and the world will open its eyes. This is the Head Principle. Mr. Head was an aviation engineer who got interested in downhill skiing. Apparently no one had ever connected aircraft technology and skiing before; Mr. Head took a few runs down the hill and realized that he could make a better ski if he simply made it with the principles and materials used in making airplane wings. He invented the Head ski, the first metal ski, and made millions of dollars. He then did the same thing to tennis, inventing the Prince racket. Apparently aircraft engineers didn't play tennis either.

The Head Principle says you can't predict what will connect with what. So you can't tell yourself what information to seek. You can only *amass experience and information voraciously* and stir it all up together. If I had been formally researching stupid faculty remarks, I'd never have thought to read up on Northern California construction workers. If you're writing about Charles Dickens and you read only about Charles Dickens, you're just making sure you won't make any connections except those other Dickens critics have already made. Instead, go read *Psychology*

Today, read President Nixon's memoirs, see a movie, watch a documentary on insect societies, or visit a mortuary. As you talk back to all of it, keep asking yourself, "What is this like? What does this remind me of? When have I thought things like this before?"

It's easy to block seeds from coming by practicing the exact opposite of these five principles. Just set aside a time for thinking, cut yourself off from the outside world by locking yourself in a stimulus-free study room, and look within yourself for a uniquely original idea. If you're doing any of that, your seed-finding regimen needs overhauling.

Writing from Rage

If the due date is near and you still can't find something to write about, there's an almost sure-fire out: *Write from rage.* I once had a composition student who wrote one dead essay after another, each full of flat clichés and careless mechanics. I tried every trick in the book to get her to write something that mattered to her. Nothing worked. She got a D in the course. Two weeks after the end of the term I got a letter from her—a beautiful letter, full of fine, lethal irony. She cursed me up one side and down the other. The letter was beautifully punctuated and typed, too. She finally had found something important to say. I only wished she had found something to make her mad sooner.

Not all anger makes good essays, but most of us have more than enough that does. The other day a student came to me to discuss an argument she was beginning to plan. "What are you going to write on?" I said. She said something so abstract my nose started to bleed. I said, "Has anything made you mad recently?" She said, "Sure." "What?" "Well, I just got done with a production in the Music Department, and they schedule the rehearsals in such a way that now I'm weeks behind in all my classes. They, in effect, force students who want to be in the productions to shaft all their other courses." "A perfect essay thesis!" I cried. "Write on that."

You may feel that anger is inappropriate to essays or that it warps your thinking. Perhaps. But even if you don't *end up* furious in the last draft, anger can get you started.

There are two places in this book that continue this conversation about finding things to write about: Chapter 15 talks about finding informative seeds (p. 299), and Chapter 16 talks about finding argumentative ones (p. 333).

Finding Essays in Your Life

Whatever you tell people, some remain convinced they "have nothing to write about." I asked my class for a volunteer who "had
nothing to say," someone whose life had been "nothing special."
(It *was* special, as you'll see, but she didn't think so, and that's the
point.) The volunteer (Sally) and I talked for twenty minutes. Then
Sally and I looked at what she had said, looking for essay seeds.
Here's our conversation, with the seeds in parentheses.

JR: Tell me about yourself. What do you do?

S: I'm a student. I work in a restaurant, and I enjoy sports.

JR: What kind of sports do you do?

S: I used to compete in track, but now it's for my own enjoy-
      ment. (*Compare being athletic in formal competition
      with being athletic just for fun, arguing that athletics
      outside of organized competition is healthier, more fun,
      less stressful.*) I run, play basketball, cross-country skiing,
      downhill. I play a little bit of volleyball, swimming, soft-
      ball. I've only just started cross-country skiing. I really like
      it because of the solitude; there's more physical exercise.
      Downhill I like because of the speed and getting accuracy
      down. (*Write to downhillers, arguing that cross-country
      skiing is less crowded, cheaper, better for your body, and
      better for your spirit.*)

JR: What did you do in track?

S: Shot put and half mile. I had a lot of strength from
      weightlifting.

JR: Did you ever take any flak for doing something that was
      as "unfeminine" as putting the shot?

S: Sure. We were considered jocks. There was a lot of stereo-
      typing. . . . (*Write to large, strong girls, sharing your experi-
      ence pursuing a "manly" sport and encouraging them not
      to be intimidated; or defend the thesis: Even after the*

women's movement, female athletes still face prejudice.) I was used as a guinea pig for a program. Since I was a good athlete, they wanted to see how strong they could really make me. But I ended up getting injured. They didn't provide the equipment I needed—belts and stuff like that. I strained my back. From trying to squat too much. (*Write to beginning women weight trainers, offering training tips and cautioning them about the dangers.*)

JR: Tell me about your past. What was your childhood like?

S: We grew up fairly poor. My mom divorced when I was seven, so it was just the girls in the house: my two sisters, Mom, and me.

JR: What was it like when your parents divorced?

S: I was happy about it. I was scared to death of my father. He hit us a lot. The way I look on it now, that was the only way he had to communicate. That's the way he was raised. I was scared to death of him and anyone who was ever going to raise a hand to me. It caused many problems with our relationship. To the point where I didn't know him—though he doesn't live very far from my hometown. (*Write to children of divorce, sharing your feelings and the insights you've gained from the experience; or write to children physically abused by their parents, sharing your experiences and your feelings; or defend the thesis: Sometimes divorce is good for the children of the marriage.*)

JR: How did your father's treatment of you affect you?

S: It made it hard to be affectionate with people—I'm beginning to outgrow that. Also I felt like I was a bad person, but that's also because he would tell me bad things about myself. I wanted to be a lawyer all my life, but he always told me, "Nope, you'll never be good at that, you'll never be good at that." And he told me that so many times, I tell myself that. He wanted a boy. (*Write about what it's like growing up with parents who tell you you're bound to fail; or write about what it's like being a girl in a family where a parent wanted a boy.*)

JR: Did you always live in the same place when you were growing up?

S: No, in high school we moved and I had to change schools. My mom thought I was a little too radical and the neighborhood was a bad influence on me.

JR: Do you agree?

S: No. There was definitely a better grade of education in
      the new place, but the new high school was in a richer
      neighborhood and was really into cocaine. The girls were
      all daddy's little girls, they got everything they wanted,
      they didn't have to work for anything, the guys all thought
      they were cowboys, which I thought was funny, since they
      probably never had been near a horse. (*Write a satire laugh-
      ing at the foolishness of parents who move to upper-
      middle-class neighborhoods in the mistaken belief that
      they're escaping the problems of poverty or the city; or
      defend the thesis: "Better neighborhoods" aren't always
      better.*)

JR: Were you doing drugs?

S: I drank a lot, but never when I was playing any sport,
      because it would screw me up. (*Defend the thesis: We
      should fight drug abuse by helping kids find something
      they love so much they won't risk losing it.*)

JR: How did you ever survive long enough to make it to
      college?

S: I had the influence of my mother, which was very posi-
      tive, very striving. She works in a field where very few
      women do, general contracting: multimillion-dollar build-
      ings. She doesn't have a college degree, so she doesn't
      have a title, but she travels all over the country, part
      engineer work, part administration; she heads a marketing
      team. . . . She's a super-intelligent lady, and the kind of
      person who, when something isn't supposed to be possi-
      ble, can get it done. (*Write about your mother and your
      relationship with her, showing the ways she helped you
      survive your youth.*)

JR: It sounds like your mom was a very good influence.

S: Almost too much so. I'm in awe. And I have a stepfather
      who's a doctor and very successful, who's also very intelli-
      gent. (*Write about the pluses and minuses of having a
      stepparent; or write about the pluses and minuses of
      having parents who are superheroes.*)

JR: What are your plans?

S: I intend to go overseas and teach. That's what I'd like.
      Teach English for a while. (*Write to English majors, de-
      fending the thesis: You should consider teaching English
      overseas for a year or two.*)

That's sixteen essays in twenty minutes from what Sally was convinced was a "nothing" life—and we never even talked about basketball, swimming, or softball! Of course, Sally's life turned out to be anything but ordinary, but the funny thing is that the same thing happens with every life, including yours, when you start looking at it this way.

Your Turn

With a classmate, do Sally-type interviews of each other. Have her interview you for fifteen minutes; then you interview her. Together, find as many essay seeds in each interview as you can. Try to find personal essays, informative essays, and arguments; try to find questions to answer, theses to defend, topics to cover, essay goals to achieve, and specific audiences to write to.

MORE THINGS TO DO

1. Write an essay describing your personal essay-writing process. Step by step, describe the acts you go through, from first thoughts to final proofreading. Be as detailed as possible. Do you use a pencil, a pen, a typewriter, or a word processor for the first draft? What size paper do you take notes on? Do you rewrite as you go, or do you write through a draft, then rewrite?

2. For two days, record (in a notebook or journal) all the concrete stimuli that prompt a reaction in you: fragments of conversation overheard in the grocery store, startling ads on TV, unusual moments in class. Take three and recast them as essay seeds, the way we did with the grocery store anecdote on p. 49.

3. Find two prompts in a recent issue of the newspaper or your favorite magazine. Write essay seeds in reaction to the prompts.

4. Practice writing from rage. Make a list of things that have made you mad recently. Take one, decide what you want to do about it, and make an essay seed from it.

5. Recall a restaurant, store, or movie you've been to that you really loathed. Write a paragraph reviewing it.

6. Write a one-page essay like the egg essay on pp. 43–44: an essay about something utterly trivial, like the contents of your purse or your secret fondness for going to the laundromat.

Chapter 4

THESIS, PURPOSE, AUDIENCE, AND TONE

At some time during the essay's growth you must discover answers to four big questions: What's my thesis? What's my purpose? Who is my audience? What tone shall I use? Ask the questions now . . . but don't get wed to your answers.

I'm running a risk by putting this chapter here, before the first draft, because you might sensibly conclude that a writer first commits herself to thesis, purpose, audience, and tone, then begins to draft. Not exactly. The chapter is here because you should start thinking about these things now, but if you conclude that you are supposed to *settle* them now, I've done you more harm than good. Most writers have a sense of thesis, purpose, audience, and tone when they begin writing—in fact, drafting without that sense can be almost impossible—but they never close the book on them, and if a better thesis or purpose comes along, they welcome it. Staying committed to your first tentative thesis is like marrying the first person you go out with: It would be a miracle if you ended up with the best person, or thesis, for you. Instead, free-write a draft or two and see what turns up first.

So you need a delicate balance of purposefulness and flexibility. You need a destination when you get in the car—"I'm going to San Antonio"—or you just sit in the driveway. But you also need to be free to spin the wheel and dump your plans the moment the journey reveals a better road.

How soon you arrive at firm answers to the four questions above depends a lot on what kind of writing you're doing. With informative writing, you may know the answers now, before you begin drafting. Technical or scientific writing often is sure of audience, purpose, and tone, and has a thesislike hypothesis, long before the writing begins, when the experiment or project is first being designed. Argumentative writing or writing that searches for self-knowledge may not discover the final version of the answers until a very late draft.

You must especially keep the book open on thesis, because it can mutate right up to the last draft. Writing out an argument often shows you that you believe something quite different than you thought you did—that's why writing has been at the heart of higher education for a thousand years or more—and if you write down your thesis when you start and promise to stick to it through thick and thin you're just promising to remain ignorant of everything the writing will teach you. "How can I know what I think until I see what I've written?" writing teacher James Britten says.

One day someone mentioned in class that the opening pages of *The Catcher in the Rye* and *Huckleberry Finn* were strikingly similar. I was intrigued and decided to write an analysis of the two writers' styles. That sense of purpose (without thesis, at that point) led to another, and I found myself comparing the way Huck and Holden Caulfield use language. That led me to compare their characters generally, and that led me to talk about Holden's concept of phoniness, which led me to the hypocrisy of American phony-hating, and (to my great surprise) to Holden's fear of death and Americans' inability to confront death. There I stayed. And in the progress I went from siding with Holden to disliking him to hating him to loving him. At each stage in the writing, I knew to the best of my present knowledge what my purpose and thesis were, and at each new stage I let the old knowledge go and embraced a new purpose and thesis. When I started, Americans' relationship with death was the farthest thing from my mind.

Topic

Topic is the thing you're writing about, the subject matter: abortion, inflation, recent advances in running shoes, the box-and-one defense in basketball, cholesterol, your father, your first date, prunes. Of course you need one, but, just as topics don't make good prompts, if you've got a topic you've got almost nothing. You still have all the hard decisions—about thesis, purpose, and audience—to make. I say this only because many writers make sure they have a definite topic and conclude the essay's sound. Far from it.

Thesis

Your thesis is the statement at the heart of the essay—the topic sentence, the core, the point, the *one* thing you have to say. If you boiled the essay down to a one-sentence summary, that sentence would be your thesis. Here are theses for some of the essays in this book:

> "Given the Chance" (p. 374): The State of California's commitment to drug rehabilitation programs is so minimal that it makes it impossible for social service people to help those who need it.

"Why?" (p. 376): Getting sickeningly drunk to celebrate your twenty-first birthday makes no sense, but we keep doing it.

"Why I Never Cared for the Civil War" (p. 383): Traditional ways of teaching school are boring and don't work, but there are powerful, exciting alternatives.

"Sixteen Reasons You Can't Start Your Essay" (p. 380): There are always plenty of "good" reasons not to write, if you don't want to write.

To find out if you have a thesis, ask yourself, "What, in short, am I actually *saying*?" and see if you get a one-sentence answer.

Of the four needful things, thesis is the last you need. Every once in a while a thesis will pop into your head right at the beginning, but more typically you start with a question, a problem, something that needs looking into, and work your way toward a thesis through several drafts. You say, "I wonder why economists can't seem to predict the future accurately" or "Why does Dickens always have an intrusive narrator in his novels?" and start writing to see where the writing takes you, knowing you need to have found a thesis when it's all over.

Many writers shy away from having a thesis because that's where the risk is. That's where you must claim to have something worth saying. Many students say they can't write because they *don't believe anything*, but by that they always mean they want to keep their opinions to themselves, where they won't have to examine or defend them. It's much safer to be a neutral information compiler. It's safer to gather data about nuclear armaments than to take a stand: Should we disarm and, if so, how? It's safer to summarize reviews of a movie than to judge it yourself. Thesis is put-up-or-shut-up time. Stick your neck out. Of course, you may get it cut off, but that's why writing is more exciting than addition and subtraction.

It's also easy to write a series of bold assertions without a thesis—a hundred insights about a movie that never come together to say any one thing, never lead to a single vision of the film. That kind of writing leaves the reader saying, "What do I *do* with all these great bits and pieces?" This is a major problem in school, where you're often handed a topic and required to find something to say about it. Accept the fact that no amount of gathering data on the topic or making solo assertions about the topic will by itself fulfill your obligation to find a thesis.

Does all writing need a thesis? Almost. There are a few kinds of writing that are in effect thesis-less: an automobile service manual, a description of cell mitosis, a review of control methods for soybean cyst nematodes. But even informative writing is better off with a little thesis because that's where the "Read me!" push comes from; that's what tells us *why* we're being given the information and how we're supposed to use it. A manual on servicing your car gains horsepower from the thesis,

"Working on your own car is easy, is rewarding, and can save you lots of money." Here are the little theses for some of the informative essays in this book:

"Leaving Nothing on the Table" (p. 317): Armed with a little information, you can make sure no car salesman ever pushes you around again.

"The Last Stop for America's Buses" (p. 325): If you understand how Mexico's bus system works, your vacation will be less expensive, more exciting, and a lot more educational.

"The Basics of Handgunning" (p. 327): With a little training and some wise guidance, you can overcome your prejudices about guns and maybe even add an exciting hobby to your life.

Don't ask too much of your thesis. Don't tell yourself you can't write until you have a message that's a universal, absolute, and original truth. Kris Tachmier proved that "Eggs make me sick" can be a great thesis (pp. 43–44). Your thesis need only be something that matters to you and is of use or interest to your audience. Reread Chapter 3 if you need to be reminded of the power of simple theses.

You don't always have to be able to state your thesis to yourself. Some people like their thesis written out, on a 3 × 5 card perhaps, even taped to the wall above the typewriter, because it keeps them on course. By all means, if it helps you, write it down, and if you tend to write without a thesis, force yourself to spell it out. But some of the best writing has a thesis that can be felt but only partially put into words. If you can't write your thesis down, but your heart assures you that you're doing something real and important, leave the thesis unstated.

Similarly, you don't have to state the thesis explicitly in the essay. Some theses get spelled out; others are only *felt*. In George Orwell's "Shooting an Elephant," he tells how he, as a minor British official in India, was forced by the pressure of an expectant mob to shoot an elephant that had gotten loose from its owner. He tells you exactly what the lesson of the story is:

And it was at this moment, as I stood there with the rifle in my hands, that I first grasped the hollowness, the futility of the white man's dominion in the East. Here was I, the white man with his gun, standing in front of the unarmed native crowd—seemingly the leading actor of the piece; but in reality I was only an absurd puppet pushed to and fro by the will of those yellow faces behind. I perceived in this moment that when the white man turns tyrant it is his own freedom that he destroys.

Other essays have theses that are implied, lightly touched on, or constantly evolving: essays like "Dear Governor Deukmejian" (p. 378), "Where Did Louise Go?" (p. 388), and "Why?" (p. 376).

Some audiences and purposes demand an explicit statement of thesis, and others don't. Scientific and technical writing demands an explicit thesis; fiction almost never states its point, and at the higher levels of essay writing, where the line between nonfiction and fiction is very thin, stating the thesis is more the exception than the rule. The essay called "Dad" (p. 271) states no thesis, and wouldn't be better off if it tried to.

Where does the thesis statement go in the essay? For people who like canned essays, there is a canned answer: at the end of the first paragraph or introduction. For uncanned writers, you can't answer that question until you think through purpose and audience.

Purpose

Thesis isn't enough. You need something more; you need answers to questions like

> Why am I writing this?
> What do I hope to accomplish?
> What's the task this essay sets out to perform?
> What use is the essay to the reader?

The surer and stronger your purpose, the easier it is to write. If you're writing not just to sell a thesis but to save the world by making readers face the horrors of impending nuclear holocaust, or if you're writing not just to package information but to help soybean farmers fight nematode infestations and save their crops, you write better. Suddenly, the writing matters.

Most of the purposes we think of first are unhelpful ones:

> To complete the assignment
> To get a good grade
> To write a good essay
> To learn about topic X
> To practice researching, thinking, and writing
> To convince your audience of your thesis
> To increase their knowledge
> To touch them emotionally

The problem with all these purposes is they don't tell you what to do. A writer is constantly faced with decisions: How should I say this? Should I put this piece of information in or not? Should I do X, then Y, or the other way around? What tone should I use? Writing "to get a good grade" or "to write well" or "to increase the audience's knowledge" gives you no answers to such questions. Even writing to learn about a subject isn't a good purpose, because it won't help you answer two major writer's questions: "What do I keep and what do I throw away?" and "How do I sequence my data?" *The better a purpose is, the more it answers such writer's questions.*

The more precisely we define the purpose, the clearer such answers get. If our purpose is "I want to write a great essay," our purpose will answer no questions at all. "I want to write a great character sketch" is only a touch better. "I want to capture the essence of my friend Sally" is better. When we get to something as specific as "I want to capture Sally's ambivalence: She talks like a feminist and acts like a sex object; then I want to use her as an example to argue that her dilemma is typical of the women's movement, which has always found it easier to talk liberated than act liberated," we've got a purpose that will really help us make choices.

Like theses, purposes can't always be written down. What are you really trying to *accomplish* by writing your life story? I really can't say . . . but when I read Russell Baker's *Growing Up,* I know something important is going on. So if you find your purpose is unsayable but your gut tells you you're doing something important, trust the gut. If, on the other hand, you know you're given to writing without a purpose, make yourself spell it out.

Are thesis and purpose the same thing? No, but often they're so alike the distinction between them seems picky: If your thesis is "Television advertising trains Americans in lust and dissatisfaction," your purpose may be to convince your reader that television advertising trains Americans in lust and dissatisfaction. Big deal. But you should make the distinction anyway, because writing merely to convince your audience of your thesis isn't the strongest kind of motivation you can muster. For instance, most literary criticism is thesis-strong but purpose-weak; you read it and say, "Okay, I'm convinced that Shakespeare was strongly influenced by Elizabethan treatises on animal husbandry, but so what?" Ask "What use is this thesis and to whom?" and you'll avoid the "So what?" response. You'll write the TV advertising essay better if your purpose is to arouse Americans to righteous indignation and move them to do something about the corrupting filth pouring into their living rooms every night. Then no one will ask, "So what?"

Audience

Write to a specific audience. A purpose is always an intent to do something *to someone,* and you must be as clear about who you're doing it to as about what you're doing.

It's hard to remember we need an audience because when we write it seems so apparent that there's no one there to read. We write alone, and so tend to write to a blank wall. But if we do that, we sound like those people who find themselves on television and talk to the camera as if it's only a hunk of metal and glass. You must write directly to an imagined person listening, and the more clearly you know who she is, the more surely you know how to talk to her.

Have an audience more specific than "anyone interested in what you have to say," because that audience doesn't tell you how to write. The narrower your audience, the easier it is to write. Let's assume that the trustees of your college have just decided to raise student tuition . . . again. You decide to write an essay decrying this. Your purpose is clear: to stop the fee hike. Now, who should you write to? There are many groups who have a say in the matter: students, parents, college administrators, state legislators (since they control the state university's purse strings), teachers, and citizens (since they elect the legislators). Within these groups are smaller groups: Within the student body there's a group of students who think it's okay for rising costs to be borne in part by the students; there's a group that's violently opposed; there's a group that doesn't care; there's a group that hasn't heard about the issue; and there's a group that's on the fence.

Each audience has to be talked to in a different way. The students who are violently opposed to fee hikes need to be preached to like brothers; those who think the hike's a good idea need to be persuaded they're wrong; administrators need to be shown alternative ways to pay the university's bills; citizens need to be convinced that it's ultimately to the benefit of the society that bright kids can afford to go to college.

Purpose and audience tell you how to write. How true this is becomes clear when you read something meant for someone you're not:

When you read a technical manual that's way over your head
When missionaries come to your door to convert you and *preach* to you as if you already had the faith, and you don't
When the media publish private in-house memos from branches of the federal government or big corporations
When you overhear friends discussing you

Those texts aren't wrong; they're just wrong *for you*. All the writer's decisions were right—for someone else.

Purpose and audience tell you what to say, how to say it, how to structure, where to begin—in short, everything. Writers constantly encounter questions that begin, "Should I . . . ?" Should I include a thesis statement? Should I begin a sentence with *and*? Should I use slang? Should I summarize in my conclusion? Mechanical writers want absolute answers: A good writer always includes a thesis statement in every paragraph, never begins a sentence with *and*, avoids slang, and restates the thesis in the final paragraph. But there are no absolute answers to "Should I" questions; instead, all such questions are answered by referring to purpose and audience. Ask yourself, "What am I trying to do?" and "Will doing what I'm considering doing aid that purpose or hinder it?" If you can't get clear answers to your "Should I" questions, it can only mean that your sense of purpose and audience is weak.

Since there is no more important insight about writing than this, let's watch that principle at work solving some common "Should I" questions.

Example #1: *Should you use slang, like "chill out," "word up," or "clueless"?*

It depends on whom you're writing to and why. Slang is trendy. Last year every young person I knew was saying "I'm clueless." Now no one says "I'm clueless." So if you want what you write to last long, avoid slang because it will soon be out of date. Slang also marks you as a member of a certain group. If you're talking to members of that group, using slang may help you get accepted. If you're talking to others, using slang may advertise the fact that you're not one of them. You may or may not want to do that. In the sixties many black activists methodically used black slang when talking to white audiences, in effect saying, "I don't have to speak your dialect to be worth listening to."

Example #2: *How should you structure the essay?*

It depends on whom you're writing to and why. How-to essays usually go through a process step by step, because the reader is trying to go through the process herself with the essay as a guide. Technical reports usually begin with summary, conclusion, or recommendations, because they're read by bosses who don't have time to read the whole thing and want *the answer* where they can see it in a glance. Newspaper articles always put their most important information first and their least important information last, because newspaper readers skim the openings of articles, pick the ones worth reading, read until their interest flags, and quit. Arguments often start by declaring that there's something that needs fixing in the world but hold off telling the reader what the thesis is. The idea is to win the reader's attention but give the writer time to talk him into agreeing with her. In each of these cases, organization is dictated by what you're trying to do to the reader and what he's reading you for.

Example #3: *How much information should you give, and what style should you write in?*

It depends on whom you're writing to and why. A few years ago, I was given the job of rewriting our university's course catalog. At that time, course descriptions read like this:

> Structure of the English Language: Basic study of English morphology and syntax, making use of the practical contributions of traditional, structural, generative-transformational grammars and other approaches to analysis of English structure.

I said to myself, "This is useless—no student can understand it, so how can it help him choose his courses?" I rewrote the descriptions in this way:

> Structure of the English Language: How words are made, and how words are added together to make sentences.

I thought this was a great improvement. But my new descriptions were all thrown out and the old ones kept. The argument for doing so went like this: I was wrong about who read the catalog and why. Catalogs aren't read by students; they're read by faculty advisors and admissions officers at other schools. They need to know exactly what topics a course covers, so they can decide when to give transfer credit, for instance, and they aren't troubled by weighty terms like *morphology*. My revision of the catalog made it useful to a new audience and useless to its old one.

Example #4: Should you state the essay's topic in the introduction?

It depends on whom you're writing to and why. I once read an essay called "The Greatest Game Fish in the World." It was a three-page narrative, describing in mouth-watering detail the excitement of angling for and catching a wonderful game fish the author neglected to identify by name. At the end of the narrative was one short paragraph: "Do you want to know what it is? It's carp." End of essay. Magnificent. You see, the writer knew that his readers (subscribers to a fish and game magazine) despised carp as garbage, so he hooked them with the story, stunned them with the punch line, and ended.

Rules of writing won't tell you to write essays that keep the topic secret until the last sentence. Such strokes of genius are dictated by a sense of audience and purpose so finely tuned that the writer can hear the audience out there reading every line and can play them like fish.

Your sense of audience tells you what to say and what to do, and since you need to know *exactly* what to say and do, you need to know *exactly* whom you're talking to. The typical essay audience is defined much more narrowly than the reader realizes (until something goes wrong and the reader finds herself excluded). There's more to it than "how much does the reader know?," although that's often primary. The writer has to answer questions like, How old is my reader? How frightened is he of what we're about to do? How resentful? What are his values? What can he afford? How physically able is he? How sophisticated? How educated? Does he have a sense of humor, an eagerness to learn, a sense of history, a sense of pride?

To prove that writers do this, look at any of the essays in Chapter 15 and ask, "How much do I know about the imagined reader?" If the writer has done his homework, you can write a complete personality profile and personal history. In "Leaving Nothing on the Table" (p. 317), Hyman's audience at first appears to be "people interesting in buying a car," but we know more. They're interested in saving money, they're intimidated by the aura of the high-pressure, manipulative car salesman, they've never bought a car before (how do we know that?), they know next to nothing about how cars are priced and sold, they haven't gone car shopping yet (they haven't seen a car sticker, for instance), and they've decided on what make and model of car they want, so they don't need advice on making those decisions. They aren't interested in a used car, they don't want to buy just any car they can get the best deal on, and they're willing to go to a bookstore and do a little research. John Mercer's audience in "Last Stop for America's Busses" (p. 325) are people who haven't been to Mexico but would like to go, who know nothing about Mexican public transportation, who are shy about going because they're worried about being out of their depth, but who like adventure and aren't looking for luxury and security. They're probably young or middle-aged, and they travel to encounter the culture. They know very little about the Mexican national character. They have a sense of humor about the little disasters of traveling. And so on.

Writers construct these personality profiles in their heads because if they don't, they don't know how to write. Imagine Hyman's dilemma if he decides to write to "everybody who is thinking about buying a car." Some members of his audience will need a lot of help choosing a make and model; some will only have $1500 to spend; some will know how to bargain but will need a lot of help setting up financing; some will need room for six kids; some won't care about expense; some won't speak or read English; some will hate bargaining, and some will thrive on it. What should he do? He can't meet everybody's needs. He has to choose. The more narrowly he defines his listeners, the easier it becomes to write.

Writers who try to write, not "to" some *one*, but just "about" some *thing* usually end up writing something that's useful to no one. Here's the opening from an essay which, tellingly, has no title:

> Dance forms are characterized by the use of particular movements. The various forms of dance require differing degrees of body mathematics usage, strength, endurance, practiced ability, innate ability, and mental concentration.
>
> Butoh dance movement requires all of the above. The precision of body placement, the strength needed for sustained positions, the endurance necessary to sustain positions, the repetitive exercises to build strength and endurance, the natural ability to execute movement, and the high level of concentration are the components of the body and mind for the Butoh dancer. The development of these enable the dancer to tap inner and outer spheres of energy movement. The physical body is the initiator, receptor, and giver of these energy realms.

Our first question may be, What does this mean? But the question that must be answered first is, Who is this for, and how is he supposed to use it? Once the essay declares an audience and purpose, meaning becomes a handleable problem:

Your First Butoh Concert

If you're a longtime lover of dance, you probably think you've seen it all. But the first time you attend a concert of Butoh, the new, exciting blend of Eastern philosophy and Western modern-dance technique, your immediate response may be, "But they're not *dancing* at all!" Well, they really are, but they aren't doing anything you're used to calling dance. Butoh looks odd, because it thinks a different way about movement than other schools of dance do, but once I walk you through it you may find it's something you want to see again and again—and perhaps try yourself.

Our dependence on knowing our audience is easiest to see in informative writing, where we know we have to keep our reader's level of expertise in mind at all times, but it's equally true of arguments, because in an argument you're trying to get the reader to give up his position and move over and join you, and he isn't going to budge until you understand who he is and what makes him tick so you can talk to him in his own language. Here's the first paragraph of an essay that didn't do that homework, arguing for the death penalty and titled "Make Them Pay":

There are many people in this world that are against the death penalty. They think it is wrong, inhumane, cruel, and unusual, etc. They feel that no one has the right to take someone else's life. But what about the life that was taken by the criminal in question? What gave them the right to take an innocent life? I feel that the death penalty is sufficient punishment for violent crimes such as murder and rape. Crimes like these are repulsive and should be considered crimes against humanity. Those who commit them should pay with their lives, not only as punishment for their sick mistakes, but also as a lesson to others that such offenses will not be tolerated in this society.

Since I oppose the death penalty, this argument is addressed to me, but it does such a bad job of predicting my responses that I just find myself digging in and becoming more and more resistant to the writer's cause. It keeps assuming, for instance, that if she can convince me that the crimes are heinous I will grant her thesis; but we all know the crimes are heinous, and I don't oppose the death penalty because I think rape is no big deal—my opposition is on entirely other grounds. She has no idea who she's talking to; once she knows her listener, she'll realize that none of that paragraph is getting her job done.

You may think the refutation to my argument is on any newsstand—how can writers need specific audiences when the *Times* and *Newsweek*s of the land are full of essays apparently for everyone? There are several explanations. First, the readership for a magazine like *Newsweek* is far narrower than you'd imagine, which is why it doesn't have a circulation of 250 million; second, magazines with broad audiences suffer from it, which is why *Newsweek* is always trying to be a little bit of *People,* a little bit of *Sports Illustrated,* a little bit of *The New York Review of Books,* and a little bit of *Entertainment Weekly,* and not really giving any reader enough of what he wants; third, for every magazine that struggles to keep a broad readership, there are a hundred that go the easier route and talk just to Mac owners, or dirt bike aficionados, or scuba divers; and fourth and most important, the essayists in *Time* and *Newsweek* who try to write to mixed audiences are the best writers in the country, and even they end up infuriating and alienating half their readers much of the time. You can write to everyone . . . if you're good enough and want to work that hard.

What about writing to and for yourself—writing for self-expression or to find out what you really think? No purpose in writing is more honorable or more valuable to you. Write for yourself, by all means . . . but don't give it to someone else to read. If you're writing for yourself, then as soon as you've written, the writing has achieved its purpose, so file it somewhere. The instant you ask someone else to read it, you imply that it's useful to him also; it's then no longer self-expression, but rather communication. Another way of saying this is, there are no answers to "Should I" questions in self-expressive writing except "Do whatever feels right"—and that answer won't help you tell what's working and what isn't or how to make a draft better.

If you want to do more thinking about how audience drives your writing, there are many places in the book that continue the conversation. Chapter 2 begins it, especially in the Writers' Workshop section. Chapter 15 continues it, especially in the sections on "Using Paragraph One as an Attitude Checker" and "Avoiding COIK Writing." Chapters 16 and 17 both discuss audience throughout, as a core part of the arguer's task. Chapter 18, on term papers, raises the issue in the section called "Setting Yourself a Good Task." Check them out.

Tone

Tone is the emotional mood of the writing and is described by the adjectives we use to describe people's moods or personalities: angry, gentle, frustrated, formal, snide, comical, silly, melancholy, conciliatory, contrite, professorial, stuffy, casual, arrogant, hip, hyperactive, ebullient, and so on. Style is famously defined as "the *way* of saying it," the thing you have left when you remove the content. Style is what makes the same lyric and same melody sound different when sung by Frank Sinatra and

Mick Jagger. Tone and style are nearly the same thing, and I'll treat them as one, calling it tone.

The first rule of tone is, *have one;* sound like a person with a distinct, living personality. If you write like a machine, you'll bore yourself and your reader. There are kinds of writing where quirkiness and colorfulness are distractions—medical research, for instance—but that's no reason to sound dead. I'm not going to tell you how to have a tone because you already know. You already know how to sound angry or ironic or sad or indignant; you do it every time you talk.

Some people never choose tone because they think tone is chosen for them, determined by topic, thesis, audience, or our own personality. That's not so.

Tone isn't determined by topic or thesis. Sometimes we think that linguistics must be talked about in academic jargon, basketball in sports slang, sex in clinical, moralistic, or pornographic terms, and nuclear holocaust in a somber tone. But any topic and any statement can be presented in any tone. You can do standup comedy about being burned alive (as Richard Pryor has done) or write scholarly disquisitions about why a pie in the face is funny.

Tone isn't determined by the author's personality. Some people think you write the way you are: If you're a warm, funny person you write in a warm, funny style, and if you're a cold, clinical person you write in a cold, clinical style. But that's only true if you can't control your writing. A writer should be able to be charming on the page whatever kind of heartless louse he is in life.

Tone isn't always determined by audience, though it's natural to think so. We usually talk to children in childlike language and to sex therapists in clinical terms. But we don't have to. Remember the black activist (p. 64). If we're trying to make the point that sex therapists get so distanced from their subject they come to think of sex as plumbing and mechanics, a clinical tone might be just the wrong thing to use.

Tone is determined by purpose. What are you trying to *do?* What tone will further that cause? If you're trying to inflame the rabble, dispassionate objectivity is the last tone you want; if you're trying to advance scientific knowledge, inflammatory passion is probably a handicap. There is no "good" tone in the abstract; there is only tone that achieves its ends. So if someone is telling you, "That's good writing" and "That's bad writing" irrespective of purposes, you're being misled.

The more tones you have at your command, the better; writing everything in the same tone is as impractical as hitting every golf shot with the same club. Writing in one tone all the time is also boring, like eating mush at every meal or never wearing any color but blue, and any time we bore ourselves we write badly. Learn to delight in changing tones like you delight in changing clothing styles. Imagine writing a letter to

your bank telling them they've once again fouled up your checking account. Try several different tones:

Sarcastic: I have to hand it to you guys—I never thought you'd find
a new way to foul things up, but you have.

Sympathetic: We all make mistakes—I know, I make them myself
all day long. I appreciate the load of paperwork you guys are under.
I know how it can happen, but you seem to have gotten my account
confused with someone else's.

Ironic: I know it's incredible, but you seem to have made a mistake.
Alert the media.

Furious: You incompetent idiots. I'll make you pay for this. You
know less about banking than I do about termitophiles.

Indignant: I have never in my twenty-five years as a businessman
witnessed anything like the level of administrative incompetence
that is the daily norm in your bank . . .

Suppliant: I don't want to make a nuisance of myself, but might I
ask that you re-examine your records for my account? There seems
to be a mistake somewhere, and I know it's probably mine, but . . . ❖

Don't think of tone as merely cosmetic. Some people, if they think
about tone at all, think of it as a surface thing, like the paint job on a
car: What really matters is what's under the hood, the content. Yet tone
matters as much as, and sometimes more than, content. We judge our
presidents more by their style than their content. Who cares what they're
actually saying? What matters is, do they feel like nice guys, and do we
feel liked by them? A writer may disapprove of that fact, but he lives
with it, and he consequently crafts his tone as carefully as his content or
structure. To prove this, let's take an opening paragraph and discuss how
the author's tonal choices reflect his subtler purposes:

For the moment—but only for the moment—it will be safe to assume
that we all know what is meant by the word "word." I may even consider
that my typing fingers know it, defining a word (in a whimsical conceit)
as what comes between two spaces. The Greeks saw the word as the
minimal unit of speech; to them, too, the atom was the minimal unit
of matter. Our own age has learnt to split the atom and also the word.
If atoms are divisible into protons, electrons, and neutrons, what are
words divisible into?

(Anthony Burgess, "Words," in Language Made Plain*)*

Burgess comes off as a playful, easygoing fellow with a quiet sense of humor and a sense of language play—sentence two is a joke, and the phrase "the word 'word' " is meant to tickle. He's personal—he uses *I* and recognizes the reader via the *we's*. He's informal—he uses dashes, for instance. He concretizes—he talks about his fingers. He summarizes his own words in the "if atoms are divisible" phrase. So he's working hard to be personable and easy to read. Yet he's learned, and he's willing to use his learning: "whimsical conceit" is a sophisticated phrase, and "conceit" is used in its classical sense, meaning not "vanity" but "bit of cleverness."

Burgess's simile—words are like atoms—is meant to contribute to the atmosphere as well. He's trying to say, "Linguistics is as exciting as atomic physics." That may not work for you, but in 1964, when the paragraph was written, atomic physics was the most exciting intellectual game in the world. Every red-blooded American bookworm wanted to be an atomic scientist when he grew up. Atomic physics has now become a dirty business, but imagine Burgess saying, "Linguistics is as exciting as working with Steven Spielberg on a sequel to *Jurassic Park*," and you'll feel what he wanted you to feel.

How do all these tonal choices support Burgess's purpose? He's writing a book on language for laymen. He knows that linguistics is traditionally dry, frightening, and irrelevant to nonacademics, so he works hard to keep things lightweight. He tries to make it easy reading, yet he wants the reader to think, so the jokes and the occasional hard word make you work. Finally, the simile says "This is exciting stuff!" in an attempt to whip up some reader interest.

None of this is determined by Burgess's subject matter, audience, or personality; *Language Made Plain* doesn't sound like other introductions to language, nor does Burgess always sound like that.

To appreciate how large a part tone plays in writing, become sensitive to it in everything you read. Every piece of writing, like every person, has an affect, an emotional feel—an unstated message like "I'm just like you" or "We're all unemotional scientists here" or "This is strictly business." Notice it, then read for the craft to see how the author got it.

Revising for Thesis, Audience, and Purpose

Here's a first draft that's full of interesting stuff but that hasn't yet
tried to answer the four big questions.

NO TITLE WORTHY

ALBERT PIERCE

I think I got the date right. There isn't much else worth remembering.
Oh, my thesis! A little advice for all you folks out there who still
fall into the category defined by that all too oft-quoted song which
I believe says something about those who have not yet accumulated
enough scar tissue and believe that they still fit the category label
"young at heart" (an interesting little concept when one stops to
ponder its complexities): Boys and girls, marriage is for the birds. I
could easily use stronger language, but, believe it or not, I'm turning
this in as a representation of my consummate skill at argumentative articulation.

   And you wonder what revelatory message I could possibly relate
that would have any significance to your life? Frankly, I'm not sure
that I give a damn if you read this or not.

   Perhaps I should explain that it is quickly approaching two in
the morning and that I didn't get any sleep last night either. I am
perusing the bottom of a bottle of Jack Daniel's (I should have bought
two) and my grammar, as well as my sense of good taste, are at a
state so low as to not have been experienced before in my lifetime.
No doubt, having read this far, you concur.

   As to the matter at hand, my wife left me twenty-nine days
ago, upon the date of my 37th birthday. So why, I hear you cry, are
you still so damn depressed? Because marriages spanning twelve
years just don't end that easily. First you have to go through two
years of hell while you're still living together but don't know you're
going through hell. Then your lady informs you that it's over. Naturally you don't believe it, and in your vain attempt to sway the
opinion of your soon-to-be-estranged mate, discover all kinds of

things which she never told you about. Excuse me a minute while I pour myself another drink.

At any rate, during the week that it takes you to find an apartment, she discovers that she has made a terrible mistake. And so begins the reconciliation. Now you are totally enamored of each other. You talk incessantly. You have sex in the kitchen. This lasts about two weeks.

After this period begins the stage in which she doubts that the two of you can really make it after all. Wednesday after the Sunday upon which she professed undying love, she tells you she "needs some space" and she hopes you will "always be her friend." This is followed by the Thursday when she won't talk to you except to say that she doesn't want to talk to you. You buy a bottle.

Excuse me, I need more ice.

This last event is quite predictable. It happens within three days prior to the due date of at least three large school projects. No problem!

And now for the first time in your life you discover real pain. I just wrote another poem and put it under her windshield wiper. I will probably never know if she reads it. I will never see her laugh, cry, complain. Twelve years. It wasn't worth it. Don't get married. It's three A.M. I'm going to bed now.

The horsepower is great, but Albert knows he hasn't a clue about who he's talking to or what he hopes to do to the reader. So far it's just personal therapy.

Albert and I discussed possible audiences and purposes until he decided to write to his brother John, who was just getting married, and by implication all other newlyweds on their honeymoon. His purpose would be to prepare them for the inevitable agony of divorce. This decision gave him structural principles to combat the rambling of the first draft: The essay would be a letter, and it would be a sort of list enumerating strategies to minimize the agony. The decision would also give him some much-needed distance and perspective on himself. His tone would be much the same as the first draft, mocking irony toward marriage, but less self-indulgent, self-pitying, and hostile to the reader. Here's how the next draft came out:

BEST-LAID PLANS

Dear John:

I loved your wedding. The flowers were lovely, and the bride looked radiant.

I'm writing to offer you the benefit of my experience as you start out on this new phase of your life. Marriage is a big step. It requires planning and foresight. You should be receiving this about two weeks after the ceremony, so the first flush of love is past and it's time to start planning for your divorce.

You may think I'm being a little hasty, but consider. More than half the people who get married these days get divorced. That means the odds are against you. Wouldn't it be wise to take some precautions? Having some practical experience in this area of the human experience, I will be your mentor.

First off, accept the coming divorce as an inevitability. Begin thinking of your spouse as "your future ex-wife." The agony of divorce is largely in the surprise.

Second, accept the fact that the person you're living with isn't the person you'll have to deal with during the divorce. Your loving spouse will overnight become a ruthless enemy bent on domination. You will be amazed at the similarities between dealing with an ex-wife and a gigantic corporation planning a hostile takeover of your company.

In fact, accept the fact that your spouse isn't the person you think she is *right now.* During the divorce proceedings, she will cheerfully tell you that everything you thought you knew about her was a lie: she never liked you, she always thought your jokes were lame, she really hated sex with you and just did it out of a sense of duty, etc., etc.

Now that you have the right attitude, what practical steps can you take? Prepare for the divorce in a businesslike manner. Do exactly what you would do in a business relationship with a shifty partner. Trust no one. Make sure you have at least seven bank accounts, so when her lawyers find three or four of them you'll be left with something. Make sure everything you own of value is heavily mortgaged. Have no significant liquid assets, except whiskey, which will be tax deductible after the divorce as a medical expense. Don't count on your premarital agreement saving you—all legal contracts can be broken. Most important of all, fight for your own interests. Let the other guy look out for the other guy; she will, I assure you.

Lay plans to handle the sense of worthlessness. Start seeing a therapist *now,* to get a head start. And don't make the novice spouse's mistake of severing all ties with members of the opposite sex. I'm not advising having affairs, but when the break comes you'll need women friends to pat you on the head, say you've still got what it takes, and listen as you say loathsome things about your ex.

Know the traditional behavior of the divorcing spouse and expect it. For instance, there is the False Reconciliation. She discovers that she has made a terrible mistake. Now you are totally enamoured of each other. You talk incessantly. You have sex in the kitchen.

This lasts about a week. Wednesday after the Monday when she professed undying love, she tells you she "needs some space" and she hopes you will "always be her friend." This is followed by the Friday when she won't talk to you except to say that she doesn't want to talk to you. You go into shock. This will always happen three days prior to the due date of at least three large school projects. Plan ahead!

If you take this advice, divorce, like thermonuclear war, can become an unpleasant but survivable disaster. And incidentally, since these realities have nothing to do with the personalities involved, I'm sending a copy of this letter to your wife, with suitable pronoun changes, to be fair. After all, after the divorce I'm hoping to stay friends with both of you.

Your Turn

Here's a first draft of an essay that hasn't yet committed itself to a thesis, audience, or purpose—it's just "everything I'm feeling on this issue." Write down three potential audiences, three theses, and three purposes for the essay; then pick one of those audiences, one thesis, and one purpose and write an opening paragraph for a revision draft of the essay directed to that audience, thesis, and purpose.

UNTOUCHABLES

DUNCAN THOMSON

Women! Can't live with them, can't get near them, drink another beer. Sweet dreams. Is it in the eyes of the beholder? I think not. You see them every day on campus, do they acknowledge you? Maybe, maybe not. They say that love comes from the heart, for a guy, I think it comes from his zipper most of the time. For a gorgeous girl, I think it comes from her attitude. Maybe you truly just have to know someone until you can truly judge them.

She was my *Cosmo* woman, my runway girl, I still think about her and miss what we once had. I feel so stupid for letting her get away to pursue her modeling career. It's over now but for the longest time I couldn't even think about another woman. Life really didn't seem worth living. Will I ever meet her again? I'm looking and she's out there, I just don't know who she is. Is this her?

It's Friday night and you're ready to hit the town. If you're under twenty-one it's a piece of cake, but if you're over twenty-one that means a night at the bars. Why we go, man, I'll never know. You're getting ready. You pick what you think will make you the most attractive person on the face of this earth. Now I feel like a million bucks. There is so much confidence in this bathroom as I stare into the mirror. You see, Mike's is to many of us guys the ultimate place to meet women. From 9 PM till 1, the place is completely packed with both sexes.

This is it, the time to find my Christy Brinkley, Elle McPherson. Anything is possible. This is the place where confidence becomes reality: dance, rate the pairs in the room, buy her a drink, throw some one-liners, anything to strike up a conversation. "Those are the most beautiful eyes I've ever seen." It may be corny but it does lead to an interesting conversation.

I'm all fired up as I wait in line to get in. We're going out to get drunk and meet women. Is this paradise or am I just stupid? The fellas and I head for the bar. "Two pitchers and three shots please." No, why oh why did I order shots? Oh well, here we go again.

There she is, oh god, just look at her. Blond hair, blue eyes, but that's not where my eyes are wandering. What curves! The complete package. I can feel my body start to shake. "Hey, bartender, one more shot please." I feel sick, I start talking to myself: Relax, Jerkface, you haven't even talked to her yet. I still have this really nervous feeling inside but on the outside I still have that confident 90210 look.

I'm really starting to feel good from the alcohol. That other girl who didn't look so hot earlier is all of a sudden looking good. So many women! Blondes, brunettes, tall, short, skinny, voluptuous, and of course the total packages. Most other women call them sluts but I think they got it so they flaunt it. Why are they so hard to meet? I'm a nice, attractive person with a lot going for me. I stumble over to talk to one. "Do you want to dance?" I say. "Maybe next song," she replies. I turn to say hello to a friend and the snooty little bitch is gone. She was just another untouchable.

Some of these girls are so incredible, most men don't even have a chance with them. You have got to have either money, some kind of title, or something that makes you desirable. Everything you try is wrong. I know I'm probably not going to meet this woman in a bar but it's a good place to start.

Let me tell you, when you get to date one of these women just once, your whole world is great. Each day is bright, the sun is shining. Everyone looks at you with this girl, the other guys are thinking, "What? That little dork with such a hot woman?" The world is your oyster. Your dreams become reality. I know, no woman has enough power to do that. Wrong! An untouchable woman is the best thing in the world.

Then that day will come, she's gone. No heart, no soul, worthless. It crushes you for at least six months. Eventually you get over it. Is that why I'm still in this bar?

I'm heading home, with nothing but a piece of pizza in my hand. I get home and grab that little black book and dial for a girl until I pass out. Women! Can't live with them, can't get near them, drink another beer.

God life is great.

MORE THINGS TO DO

---

1. Pick three topics you know something about. For each one, make up a thesis concerning it, an audience that would be interested in hearing the thesis, a purpose for you writing it and them reading it, and a tone that would suit the purpose. For instance, if you've worked at McDonald's, your list might look like this:

Topic: Working at McDonald's
Thesis: "Work somewhere else; the hours are long, the pay is
  low, and the prospects are nowhere."
Audience: Teenagers looking for their first job
Purpose: To discourage them from working at McDonald's,
  thus saving them a bellyful of grief
Tone: Casual, mockingly funny, in teen language, a bit sarcastic
  toward McDonald's

2. Pick any essay in this book and answer the following questions about it:

What's the topic?
Does it have a thesis? If so, what is it?
Is the thesis stated or implied?
What's the assumed audience?
What's the purpose?
What's the tone?
How does the tone suit the purpose?

3. For each of the following opening paragraphs, decide what the work's thesis, purpose, audience, and tone are. How does the tone suit the purpose?

A. The Brookfield Unified School District maintains an educational program which provides special learning opportunities for pupils who, after consideration of all pertinent data, evidence exceptional intellectual capacity. Recently your child was identified as having demonstrated a significant number of characteristics of intellectual giftedness. Therefore, he/she was nominated to participate in the identification process for possible inclusion in the program.

B. I GIVE UP. I have finally decided that Miss/Ms. Right isn't going to walk through the door. Never would I have thought that I would end up resorting to a public appeal such as this. I've been to bars, churches, the YWCA, the YMCA (was that a mistake), NOW, and every possible spot this wonderful mystery woman might be, all to no avail. This is my last resort. If you desire to help a frustrated and very nice guy, read on.

C. After hunting through a parking space, wading through a crowded registration line, and forking out $375, I expect to be entertained. That's why I decided to sign up for a film class. Besides, I needed three General Ed. units, and English 37, seriously titled "American Film as Literature," seemed to fit the bill (no pun intended).

At the first class meeting, I watched twenty graduating seniors from Signa Phi Nothing attempting to add and wondered why. Was the course an easy A, as the Greek connection implied? Or was there more to it?

4. Write a half-page evaluation of one of your classes and its instructor. Write versions for each of the following audiences:

A. A friend who's coming to campus next term
B. The instructor
C. The department chair

Afterward, write a paragraph on how the different audiences led you to write in different ways.

5. Recall one time recently when some restaurant, store, school course, etc., mistreated you in some way. Write brief letters about the experience to three different audiences in three different tones. Write the first as a personal newsletter to a friend, treating the experience with comical outrage. Write the second to someone in the organization—the dean, the manager, the boss—complaining about the treatment with righteous indignation. Write the third to the letters to the editor section of a newspaper, in a tone of calm, reluctant reasonableness: "I don't want to do this, but I must, for the public's welfare."

Chapter 5

FROM FIRST
THOUGHTS TO DRAFTS

In this chapter we'll take that set of good intentions we fleshed out in Chapter 4 and turn it into a bunch of pages of loose, unforced text (called a draft) that's crying out for rethinking, reshaping, and resaying (called revision). Some writers like to expand by writing whole drafts, and if you're one of them, you can roll a piece of paper into the typewriter or call up a blank file, type "Page 1" or a tentative title, and begin. But most people find that thought intimidating and prefer to work up to drafting. In fact, you need never encounter the first draft at all. This chapter shows you ways to back into drafts without ever facing the Terror of Page One. In other words, you can "prewrite," and then go directly to revision if you want to.

Many people, without saying so, have decided that the kicking-around stage shouldn't have to happen, and that if it does something's wrong. Once I asked my students to write an essay stating where they stand on censorship in the public schools. A student came into my office on the verge of tears and furious with herself; she said, "I can't write this paper; I've tried, but I just can't." I said, "How come?" She said, "Because I keep going round and round. First I thought, 'Well, I'd censor books that had explicit sex,' but then I thought, 'Maybe it's good for children to know that sex exists, and maybe it's wrong to make sex a big mysterious deal.' And at one time I figured I'd say that I'd censor stuff I personally found distasteful, but then I thought, 'What if everyone censored everything they didn't like?' So that didn't seem to work. I tried to make a list of works I thought should be censored, but when I tried to make arguments for why they should be censored, I couldn't explain what was wrong about them except I just didn't like them. What is censorship, anyway? I've decided I don't even know what the word means. Like is it censorship when an advertiser on TV tells a network it won't buy advertising time if the network runs a special on abortion? I just don't know what I'm doing, so I can't write the paper. What's wrong with me? I could always write before."

To all that I responded, "But everything you've said *is* the paper! All that lovely, messy, fragmented mind-changing and wandering and reexamining and tripping over things is what's *supposed* to happen. Hooray! Your brain is on the move."

The following pages will help you adopt this strange new attitude. First I'll give you five principles to guide your thinking; then we'll talk about how to translate them into concrete practices. After that, we'll talk about what to do if, after making all the right moves, you're still bothered by writer's block.

Five Principles

Give yourself a lot of time.
To get something out, keep putting something in.
Don't "work" at thinking, and don't think by rules.
Don't be too sure of where you're going.
Practice the behaviors that foster thought.

We'll talk about each one.

Give yourself a lot of time. How obvious. Yet no rule of writing is broken more often. We wait until the last minute before a paper is due, conning ourselves into believing that we write better under pressure. But we don't.

Thought processes never end, so you'll never have "enough time." So use all the time you have. Turn a part of your mind to the task of nibbling at the project from the moment the assignment is made, and return to it off and on throughout the day, every day, until it's handed in.

To get stuff out, keep putting stuff in. Don't cut off the input just because you're now on output mode. The billiard balls of the mind soon come to rest unless they collide with something new. Keep them careening around by sending in a constant stream of new, varied stimuli.

Don't "work" at thinking, and don't think by rules. Thinking is like making language: It's too complex, too subtle, too unconscious to do by the numbers. You must *let* it happen. If you ask people to describe how they think, the good thinkers say they don't know, and it's not wise to try to find out. A watched mind rarely boils.

Every writing day teaches me that truth. I write from nine to five, thinking hard. At the end of the day, I pack up and point my weary brain toward home. During the fifteen-minute walk, I let my mind go . . . and the best ideas of the day begin popping into my head. I hit the front door running and reach for the notebook to catch them before they slip away.

Don't be too sure of where you're going. Geniuses have something in common: a talent for working without rigidly defined goals. They're willing to let the investigation work itself out and discover where they'll end up when they've gotten there. Less creative minds want to know exactly where they're going before they start. The genius wisely says, "How can I know I'm going to invent the laser or discover the theory of relativity when no one knows such a thing exists yet?" If we only do the tasks we can define ahead of time, we limit ourselves to discovering only what we already know.

Sometimes school teaches you the reverse, by telling you that you need discipline and structure and by requiring you to use outlines, thesis statements, and other tools that force those skills. Those tools are nice, but if in mastering them you close doors, your writing will get more and more mechanically competent, but your best stuff will remain on the other side of those doors.

Practice the behaviors that foster thought. Good writers don't know how they think, but they do know what behaviors and conditions make thoughts come best. Once I asked a group of students to describe their writing process. One student thought for a while and began, "I always take a shower before beginning the last draft." I knew he was a writer, because he knew what worked for him, and he did it, however ridiculous it seemed.

A writer does whatever *works*. If music helps the thoughts flow, listen to music; if it doesn't, don't. But beware: I'm not saying do whatever feels good. Some writers drink because it helps them write, but most writers drink because they'd rather drink than write.

Seven Techniques for Making Words Come

I can't tell you what behaviors will make *your* brain work best—I would never have guessed that someone would write better if he took a shower before the last draft—but I can recommend some of the most popular ones. We all think better when we're busy with our eyes, ears, mouth, or hands, so not surprisingly these seven techniques are just stylized forms of reading, talking, and scribbling.

Reactive reading. This is what you do when you read if you're not a data sponge (p. 46), and we practiced it in Chapter 2 (pp. 33 ff.), so we know how to do it. I'll just add two cautions. First, *write your reactions down.* Don't assume you'll remember. No one wants to interrupt her reading to jot down notes, but you must. You can do it in the margins if the margins are big, the book is yours, and you know you'll have time to reread and collect your reactions. But it's better, though more disruptive to reading, to react on a large notepad by your side as you read.

Second, to guard against slipping into data sponge mode, make sure that at least half of what you write down is *your own:* the thoughts, questions, doubts, and feelings that come in response to the text. If you're not sure about the distinction between transcribing and reacting, draw a vertical line down the middle of the note page and transcribe on the left side of the page and react on the right. If comments on the right side are few and far between, you'll notice.

Brainstorming. Any talking you do with colleagues is good. Brainstorming is just an extra messy kind of talk. Brainstorming differs from the conversations we hold with friends every day in four ways: (a) Brainstorming is done as fast as possible; (b) brainstorming is unstructured—you try to spit out single words and phrases as well as sentences or whole thoughts, and you take whatever comes, however fragmented, however ill-phrased, however apparently irrelevant; (c) you have no standards; and (d) you record everything people say.

The trick is to stop screening and judging. To brainstorm well, you must have absolute confidence that no one (including your internal critic) will say, "What a dumb idea" or laugh at you or back you into a corner. All contributions must be welcome; unproductive contributions will be tossed later, but they will have helped by contributing to an atmosphere of uncritical fecundity of thought.

The rest of the tools are forms of scribbling. Writing is a great way to think, but most people, when they try to write, try to write *essays*, and essays are structured, rigid, scary, difficult, demanding things. So we get intimidated, try hard, and shut down. To stop that, you have to write something that doesn't look like an essay—an *unessay*, in short. What constitutes an unessay is a personal thing. Some people feel that anything written on a note tablet or in pencil isn't an essay, so they can write on note tablets or with pencils without fear. You must find your own way. We'll talk about five popular kinds of unessays: notes, maps, journals, letters, and discovery drafts.

Note-taking. For most of us, notes "don't count." So we write them quickly, without premeditation, without forcing, and we usually write them well.

Note-taking goes best when you're busy doing something else. Don't set aside a time for note-taking; instead, take notes while you read, talk, listen, brainstorm, write the first draft, and so on.

Mapping. Mapping is my students' favorite prewriting tool. You can map to *find* a seed too, but it's usually used now, when you've found one. Write the seed in the center of a piece of paper and circle it. You don't need a thesis or a great idea—you can start with a word, a suggestive phrase, a visual image, a picture. Now begin brainstorming or free associating connections between the seed and other thoughts. Let the other bits be whatever they are—words, sensations, questions. Write each bit down as it comes on the paper somewhere, circle it, and draw a line from it to the bit on the page it seems somehow connected to. Work out from the seed in all directions, letting bits cluster as they will. Try to connect

everything in the map to something else in the map, so you're making a spider web, or highway system, or whatever you want to think of it as. Above is the map of the essay about the sinister boyfriend on p. 48:

If a bit doesn't seem related to any other bit, don't worry about it; just write it anywhere and circle it. Don't demand that you know what the bits or connections mean. If you're uptight, push away from *thinking* and push toward *feeling*. If you momentarily run dry, keep doodling or retrace the spider web, so your hand keeps moving and invites your brain to contribute.

If, as you're mapping, you catch glimpses of essay structure, record them somewhere. If you notice, for instance, that many of your bits concerning industrial pollution are about the history of the problem, many are about public opinion on the issue, and many are about the federal government's role in the problem and its solution, you can try to cluster the bits around three main arteries in the map, respectively labeled "history," "John Q. Public," and "Feds." But you needn't do any of that now. You're *generating*; you can sort, label, sequence, and analyze later.

When you map, watch for two danger signs, both symptoms of too much self-control. The first symptom is choo-choo trains—strings of bubbles in series:

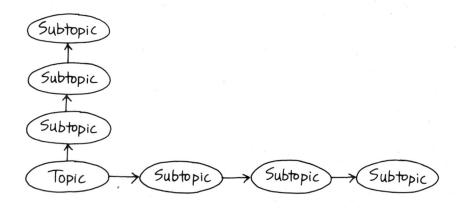

(For some reason, choo-choos almost always appear vertically.) The second is monochromatic bits: bits that are all nouns, all verbs, or all any one thing. They'll almost always be *nouns*. If you see these danger signs, counter them: Map in 360 degrees, with lots of branches and forks; draw connecting lines between one bit and several others; make bits that are adjectives, images, smells, letters, pictures, whatever. Linear, nouny thoughts are just a drop in the bucket of what's in your head.

Don't think you're now committed to writing an essay that follows the map. You don't owe a map, or any other prewriting tool, anything. If you have to prove this to yourself, take a part of the map that you like, move it to the center of a new piece of paper, and map around it.

Journals. A journal is a notebook or binder where you dump everything you think, feel, or observe. It's written to and for you, and you write in it every day or nearly every day—not just when a good idea strikes. It's the only one of the prewriting tools that you use on schedule, so it gives you a lot of writing practice. But there's more to it than that: It teaches you to monitor your mind and heart constantly, as a part of life, and to value what's pouring out of them. We're always moving, breathing, thinking, and feeling; if we're writers, we observe and record what we think and feel. Most good writers keep journals, at least for a year or so until the monitoring habit is firmly established.

People who don't keep journals can't figure out what people who do keep journals find to put in them, so here are some entries from the journal of my student Susan Wooldridge, who's kept her journal going for more than twenty years and hasn't run out of things to put in it yet:

Happy morning.
Tiniest sprouts in our herb garden. Sunlight on our plants.

Aristophanes—
"Who's there?"
"An ill-starred man."
"Then keep it to yourself."

Perhaps the heaviness will leave soon. Perhaps I can will it away, perhaps it will just lift. All right, why is it here. Heavy dreams. Kent interested in someone else, though not truly, I knew that in the dream. Heavy weather. Anger at myself for having a job so basically useless to the world and to me. Every day. Morning energy lost on it.

André Malraux said of Goya:
    "He discovered his genius the day he dared to give up pleasing others."

I urge Smokey into the large field, recently plowed, we trot, canter, turn, figure 8, etc. I watch our shadow galloping across the field and try to convince myself that this, truly, is my childhood dream come true. Me galloping through a green field with my own beautiful horse. Sometimes it feels right. Sometimes I feel guilt. Self-indulgence! Bad Sue. You should be out in the ghettoes carrying bundles of food to the starving and poor.

Doing office work. Typing like an automaton. Breathing stale smoke smells guardedly through my nose, occasionally flailing a broken fly swatter at a spiraling bumpy fly that refuses to land except on fragile typewriter parts.

Cows in the fog, dumb and heavy. Vague clumps of cows, a hog and sows in pale rows in a bog of weeds and grass and cows vacant as glass in the fog.

Words. Reasons, worries, flight.
Birds. Nested birds.

Think, when I have worked on a poem for a certain time, if it isn't getting better, if it doesn't intrigue me, it's not going to be any good.

Opened the dictionary to "fipple flute" while looking up "apposite," and found a lovely reproduction of fingerprints on this post-Halloween morning.

We went, with the rent, for another chat with Clarence and Grace. Good folk in their way. Clarence like a big cumbersome child, devilish. Grace somewhat shy, somewhat sly. Real country folk. She had pet pigs once. Cows. Clarence delivered milk during the depression. Real Illinois farmers. Clarence has been to 4 funerals this week, friends.

There will be snow tonight. And perhaps tomorrow I shall speed, skate, spin on thick ice.

Our tree is lying frozen outside. I just got the strange idea that at some level, the tree had consciousness, awareness of dying, even an ability, at an unheard level, to call to us, to appeal. But I am making this up.

And oh, this curse of words, endless rumination, introspection and self-exposure. Here it is: I am a writer I am a writer I write I write I am a person who writes I am a woman I am a woman who likes to write, who chooses to write. I am a writer. No more fudging on this one, Susan, this drive will not be submerged, this is a need, a want. So follow it. Do it. Hell. Hello. Hell, Hello.

There are two things worth noting here. First, in conventional terms *nothing has happened* in Susan's life. She sees cows. She looks a word up in the dictionary. Nothing more. As always, it's the watchful eye and heart of the writer that makes things worth saying, not the experiences themselves. Second, these entries aren't mini-essays or proto-essays. They're written for the journal-keeper—an audience of one. Writing to others is different.

The last two tools ask more of you than the first two, because they both ask you to write sequential sentences.

Letter writing. Most of us write well when we write letters, because we're writing as ourselves to a real audience we feel we can talk to. Write about the events of the day if that's all you feel up to; if you want to ask more of yourself, write, "I've been mulling over this thing for this essay I'm writing for a class. It's about . . . ," and block out the essay for your reader.

Discovery drafts. A discovery draft is a first draft that's purely exploratory; you just keep saying things and see where they lead you. You ask nothing, but hope that by the time you're done, you've written yourself to a sense of what you're going to do.

In a discovery draft, you're doing what Ken Macrorie, the writing teacher, calls *free writing*—brainstorming in running sentences. In its most extreme form, you write for a predetermined period of time, and keep writing sentences no matter what happens. If you have nothing to say, write, "I have nothing to say" over and over until you find something else to say. Write song lyrics, gibberish, "The quick brown fox jumps over the lazy dog," or whatever, but keep writing sentences. It seems odd that writing nonsense would lead anywhere, but the physical act of writing turns your mind on. It's just another way we're trying to break out of the old bad habit of trying to think *first, then* write.

Behind all of these devices are some shared ideas about how to get stuff out of your head onto paper:

Be physical. Your hands make your brain go. Don't try to think in your head; concretize it, on paper.

Be messy.

Don't judge. Take what comes—all of it. You can pick and choose later.

Go for volume. More is better.

Throw nothing away. Don't erase, cross out, or crumple-and-heave.

Work fast—the faster the better.

Ask questions; don't demand answers.

Explore nonlinear, nonprose, nonverbal ways to say things. Brainstorm words. Write poems. Draw pictures.

Break things up. Write fragments. Use little file cards for notes. Take your favorite sentence from the discovery draft and map around it.

Be wasteful. Map, brainstorm, or free write three, five, or ten times as much stuff as the essay can use.

Anything that does these things is good; anything that doesn't is bad. And that's true after the prewriting stage is supposedly over. That glorious noncritical openness that says to our minds and hearts, "I welcome anything you want to send me, in any form, at any time" we want right up to the copyediting stage.

Two Last Prewriting Don'ts

Don't outline. I don't encourage you to outline in the beginning, because it's usually asking too much of yourself. To outline you need to not only generate material, but also cluster it, sequence it, and usually organize it around a thesis. That's more than most of us can do in the beginning, and it's inviting the critical rigidity we've been working all chapter to get rid of. Map instead.

Don't wait till you're done prewriting to begin writing. Some people begin prewriting by writing a draft. Some people prewrite in their heads for days and weeks before touching paper. Some people scribble piles of maps and heaps of notes. But no good writer waits until she's "ready," knows what she's going to do, has all the answers, because that moment never comes, so she'll never write. Jump in.

Defeating Writer's Block

However well you practice the art of backing into the first draft, there comes a time when your brain says you're no longer just playing prewriting games and are now writing An Essay. At that moment, writer's block becomes a danger. Everything we've practiced in this chapter so far helps reduce it, but if it remains a problem for you, it's time to approach the problem in another way. Let's talk about where writer's block comes from and ways to make it go away by attacking it at the source.

Writer's block is another name for stage fright. You have a mild case of it if, when you write, you get dry in the mouth and feel yourself tightening up. You have a serious case if you stare at blank paper unable to squeeze out a line. Every writer feels some fear, just as every actor feels some stage fright, because writing is a big deal, like starring in the school play. If you're one of the lucky ones, the fear adrenalizes you, pumps you up for the performance. If you're not, the fear makes you stiff, tentative, awkward, a dull shadow of your usual lively, fascinating self. We can't let that happen.

People get writer's block because they define writing and their relationship to it in terms opposite to the ones we practiced in Chapter 1. They don't feel like writers. So they try to be someone they're not when they write, and write to fake it. They write to people they aren't comfortable talking to. They equate their writing with their self-worth: "If I write a bad essay, I'm a bad person." So they ask too much of themselves, try too hard, and write to avoid failure. We have to replace those attitudes with healthy alternatives.

Call Yourself a Writer

Most people don't feel like writers when they write; they feel like ordinary people posing as writers. As long as you feel that way, you'll write to avoid detection. You can't play good tennis if you're telling yourself over and over, "I'm really not a tennis player, I'm really not a tennis player." You're not someone practicing to someday be a writer; you're a *writer*, right now, the same way you've been a talker since you began talking.

As Frank Smith says, you're a member of the Club of Writers as soon as you choose to join, just as you're a "real" tennis player the moment you believe you are one. It isn't a matter of skill level: Talkers join the Club of Talkers even *before* they can talk, and I know people who have published a few books and still doubt they are "real writers" yet.

Chapters 1 through 4 have already suggested lots of ways you can help convince yourself you deserve to belong. Write something that matters to you, so you have a purpose you honor. Read some good writing just before you write, to make you feel a part of the writer/reader community of intellectual exchange. Use your reading as a model, and write in imitation (p. 48). You can go even further and pretend you're an author you revere: If you like Hemingway, try to write as he would have written, and tell yourself this isn't you writing, but Hemingway acting through you. (You know why this works if you've ever pretended you were Michael Jordan and seen how much your basketball game improves, or stuck a can of chewing tobacco in the hip pocket of your softball pants even though you don't chew. You're tapping into the powers of the eagle or the wolf, acknowledging your membership in the Club by using its secret handshake.)

Write as Yourself

The less you have to disavow yourself when you write, the less writer's block will touch you. I just encouraged you to become Hemingway, so this seems to be a contradiction, but it really isn't. Writer's block comes from fear of being judged and found wanting. If you become someone else, you're safer: "This isn't me writing; it's Hemingway." It's like being at a costume party. But you can also go the other way and accept yourself as you are; then you don't need the disguise.

To help you be yourself, *don't write; talk.* Since most of us are used to being ourselves when we talk, if we talk on the page we'll feel that it's the real us writing. We're also better at talking because we've done so much more of it, so we'll be more successful writing talk.

Obviously, a first draft you've *spoken* isn't ready to hand in, but I have two responses to that. First, good writing is probably much closer to speech than you think. Almost every beginning writer is far too willing to abandon the virtues of talk. Second and more important, just because a talked draft needs work doesn't mean you shouldn't use talk to get you started. Anything that gets words out of yourself and onto the paper is good at this point. Use talk to get the words out, then revise out the vices of talk later.

There are many ways you can use your skill at talking to help you write. If you're badly blocked, you may want to go to the extreme and dictate your text into a tape recorder and then type a transcript. Once I was asked to edit the narrative for a film on conservation. The author of the text said it didn't sound like a person talking, and he asked me to fix it. Instead of rewriting the text, I turned on my tape recorder, read the first paragraph of the text to see what it said, and tried to *talk* the content—without looking at the written text—into the recorder. I worked my way through the text in this way, and the product was the same text, now in the language of a human speaker, not a stiff and artificial writer.

You can use talk without reaching for the tape recorder. When you're writing and you get stuck—you know what you want to say but can't find words that aren't awkward and ponderous—stop writing, back away from the paper, clear your head, and try to *say* it simply—out loud, if it helps.

If you have trouble talking to the air, find someone who will listen. When I'm stuck, I jump up from my desk, run into a neighbor's office, say, "Listen to this for a minute," and try to spill what I'm trying to say, without thinking too much about it, into his astonished ear. With luck, I like what I hear and can run back and type it onto the page.

Remind yourself to use your talking language by using *contractions:* *can't, won't, it's, I'm, there's,* and so on. Every time you write *cannot* or *it is,* you remind yourself that you're not allowed to be you when you write; every time you write *can't* or *it's,* you'll remind yourself that's not so.

Create Your Own Best Audience

People get tense when they try to talk to people they're afraid of. You'll make it easier on yourself if you write to someone you can talk freely to.

Most people either write to the wall or write to either of the two toughest audiences in the world: the instructor and the whole world. The instructor is hard to write to because she knows more than you, and she's judging (grading) you as well as reading you. (I know that in reality you *are* writing to the instructor and writing for a grade, but there are some realities it's wise to forget, and this is one of them.) Writing to the whole world is hard because there is little you can say that the whole world wants to hear. If you're writing on agricultural economics in America and you try to write something that small farmers, farm laborers, labor union organizers, agribusiness tycoons, and presidential economic advisors will all profit by, you're asking too much of yourself. These groups know different things, have different needs and values, and speak different languages.

The audience that's easiest to write to is small and homogeneous; it's made up of people with the same interests, values, level of sophistication, and education. It knows less than you on the subject. It wants what you have to offer. It doesn't threaten you; it's not made up of people who are richer than you, higher class than you, academically more advanced than you, or whatever makes you feel at a disadvantage. It's pulling for you: friends, family, pen pals, classmates. You may not be able to write to such an audience in the last draft, and you'll want to learn to write to other audiences eventually, but it's a good place to start.

Take Your Ego Out of the Loop

We get stage fright because we feel our ego is on the line: If we fail, we've proved we're bad, stupid, inept people. The essay *is us,* and we crash if it crashes. To escape that fate, we have to unlearn the ego identification. You *are not* the essay. If it crashes, you can still be a worthy person who occasionally writes essays that don't work.

The first step in this unlearning is to realize that we choose to equate our egos with things, and can as easily choose not to. I can go out and play soccer badly and not grieve, because I am not my soccer game, but if I write badly I must hate myself, because I am my writing. But there is nothing inherent in soccer or writing that makes me assign those values to them—I choose it. I have the power to move writing over to the "It's not a big deal" category any time I want.

Second, realize that the result of assigning such import to an action is destructive. I may tell myself that I'm helping me write well by caring so much, but in fact the only result is that I can play soccer without fear (and therefore boldly, joyfully, and well), but I dare not write—there's too much to lose.

Third, understand how audiences read. *You* think the essay is you, but *they* don't. I learned this lesson when I observed a master class for classical guitar. A student played with extreme stage fright—trembling fingers and the like. The master said, "You fear because you think the audience listens to *you.* They do not. They listen to Bach, or Villa-Lobos. You are merely a messenger. You are nothing. They don't hear you. Remember this, and you'll disappear. Then there is no reason to be afraid."

When I began playing violin in the local symphony orchestra, I discovered the truth of his words. At first, I imagined the audience listening to every note I made, and I was paralyzed by the greatness of my responsibility. Then after the concert I would talk to my friends and ask them how it went. "That Beethoven is a great piece," they would say, or, "I loved hearing the Mozart again." And they never, ever said, "You played really well" or "You missed a note in the slow movement." In fact, people who knew I was in the symphony would compliment me on how well the orchestra played in concerts *I wasn't in!* I realized I was free to play for fun and enjoy myself, trusting the audience to ignore me and hear *the music.* In the same way, your reader reads *the essay,* not *you,* and notices *what it says,* not *how well you write.* Again, the reality may be that your instructor *is* reading for how well you write, and, again, that's something best ignored.

One way to practice circumventing the ego is *imaging.* Also called visualization, it's a therapeutic technique being used to combat everything from cancer to writer's block. You imagine the problem going away or being solved, in graphic, concrete mental images. Cancer victims are encouraged to imagine friendly little creatures in their bodies attacking and devouring the cancer cells. People with chronic stress are taught to lie down and imagine the tension running down from their shoulders, through their arms, and out their fingers onto the mattress. Imagine yourself writing effortlessly. Imagine words flowing effortlessly and powerfully from your brain, down your arms, and onto the paper. The ego disappears simply because there's no role for it in the model. For imaging to work, the images must be of your own making, since only you know what symbology carries magic for you, and you must believe it will work.

Purposely Do What Frightens You

The last step in taking the ego out of the loop is to prove to yourself the essay really isn't you by screwing it up and noticing you didn't die. Make a list of what you're afraid of doing wrong when you write. What constitutes failure? Breaking grammatical rules? Misspelling words? Looking stupid? Sounding infantile? Being wordy and clumsy? Once you have the list, go do, abundantly and gleefully, all the things on it. Break every grammatical rule you can think of. Purposely misspell a few words—mutilate the English spelling system (doesn't it deserve it, after all it's done to you?). Say some dumb things. Write in baby talk. Take half a page to say one sentence worth of thought.

Put the dread moment of failure behind you. If you write a lousy paragraph, write, "Boy, was that a lousy paragraph, and I don't care" right after it. If you feel the weight of the teacher's expectations looming over you, write a caricature of him, or a parody of professorial style. If you feel constrained to be dignified when you write, tell dirty jokes and relate comic misadventures from your wild youth. If typing makes you uptight, because you're waiting for the inevitable typo that will despoil the clean page, make several typos now so the damage is done.

The more precisely you define your personal writing demons, the more precisely you can plot their overthrow. Once upon a time a blocked writer discovered he was telling himself as he began, "I'll die if this turns out to be mediocre." So his writing guru ordered him to *strive to write a mediocre essay*—ordered him to write "This is a mediocre essay" at the top of page one, in fact—and he found that, not only could he write without the old constriction, but when he strived for mediocrity he surpassed his expectations.

Lower Your Standards

We're talking about the damage done by *feeling obligated.* A football player who chokes because he's anticipating getting clobbered is said to "hear footsteps." Most people write hearing footsteps: the footsteps of their own critical selves, coming to clobber them for not measuring up.

Most writers are burdened with obligations: obligations to the English language, to the spelling system, to the rules of grammar, to the noble art of composition, to their parents, who are paying for their college education, to instructors, to the demands of the five-paragraph format. All those obligations instill fear and make it harder to write. To silence them, *lower your standards,* fool around, and indulge yourself at every turn. Ask as little of yourself as possible.

It works. Here's how Lewis Thomas, a modern master of the essay, discovered the benefits of not trying hard when he turned from writing medical research and tried his hand at essay writing for the first time:

> The chance to . . . try the essay form raised my spirits, but at the same time worried me. I tried outlining some ideas for essays, making lists of items I'd like to cover in each piece, organizing my thoughts in orderly sequences, and wrote several dreadful essays which I could not bring myself to reread, and decided to give up being orderly. I changed the method to no method at all, picked out some suitable times late at night, usually on the weekend two days after I'd already passed the deadline, and wrote without outline or planning in advance, as fast as

I could. This worked better, or at least was more fun, and I was able to get started.

(*Lewis Thomas*, The Youngest Science)

Three years after that beginning, those essays won the National Book Award.

If your guilt reflex tries to tell you that excellence lies in sweating the details, assure it there will be ample time for that during the polishing stages. Write the last draft to suit others, and write everything else to suit yourself. After all, when in the writing process do you owe other people (audiences, bosses, teachers, grammarians) anything? Not till the moment you hand the essay in. Writing's one great advantage is that none of it "counts" until you say it does. Don't throw this advantage away by insisting you write well from the first page of the first draft. Who cares how good the first draft of *Moby Dick* was?

Once you know your internal voice of self-criticism is active, you can set up a writing regimen that denies it an opportunity to speak. Just forbid yourself to reread what you write until you are at the end of it. Another solution is to use the voice's input to your advantage. Make a rule that you never cross out anything. When the voice says that something you wrote isn't good enough, leave it and write onward, saying it all over again better or discussing what you didn't like about it. That way the voice of criticism becomes a force for *more* writing, not less.

Sheer speed helps, because it prevents you from thinking about what you're doing too much. Good early-stage writers write fast. Your normal composing pace should be as fast as your fingers will move.

Sidestep the Thing That Blocks You

Identify the thing that stops you from writing, and figure out a way to go around it. If blinking gives you writer's block, just don't blink. It sounds simple, but it isn't. A friend of mine was once telling me about a brilliant friend of hers who had writer's block—literally hadn't written anything in years. "Why?" I asked. "Because," my friend said, "every time she wrote a paragraph she read it, found it disappointing, and quit." "That's easy to fix," I said; "Just don't read what you've written." "Obviously," said my friend, "but you only say that because you don't have writer's block." Moral: Blocked writers feel compelled to do the thing that prevents writing.

It's easy to say you don't do that, but most of us do, at least a little. Do you ever refuse to begin the essay until you sweat out a title? Do you ever refuse to write the body of an essay until you've ground out an opening paragraph that refuses to come? Do you ever write and rewrite a sticky passage, refusing to go on until it's just right? Do you ever interrupt the steady flow of words to check a spelling in the dictionary? All these behaviors may be excuses to stop writing. I've known would-be writers who made writing impossible by insisting that they type letter-perfect pages, beginning page one over and over again at the first mis-hit key.

There are an infinite number of ways to stop yourself, but three are so common we'll name them.

Fear of page one. A colleague of mine, Dwight Culler, said he used to roll the paper into the typewriter and stare at page one in blank terror. Then he got an idea: He rolled the paper into the typewriter, typed "page 10" at the top . . . and found he could write with relative ease. Today he's a renowned literary critic, and he's still beginning on page ten.

Fear of the page limit. This is where you are assigned a ten-page paper and are terrified you'll never find enough to say to fill ten pages. Attack this in two ways. First, fill pages quickly: Write by hand (handwriting gets fewer words on a page than typing does) or double-space, use large margins, and ramble—be as wordy and redundant as you please. Pile up text until you're well past the page limit. Now the problem is no longer how to stretch to fill the assigned space, but how to *cut down* to fit into it. It may all be an illusion, but you'll feel better nonetheless. Second, don't let yourself know how many pages you've written. Write on 3 × 5 cards, in pocket notebooks, or on legal pads. Best of all is a word processor, because you write what amounts to one endless page.

Fear of the essay. This is perhaps the most common source of writer's block. This chapter is full of ways to write unessays (pp. 84–89). For many writers, just writing in pencil is enough to remind them that the draft isn't really an essay yet. And writing on cards instead of full-size pages works in the same way.

My favorite way of writing an unessay is abstracting (Chapter 7). Instead of trying to write a first draft, I tell myself I'll just write a rough paragraph summary of what I expect to say. I write the abstract very quickly and messily, like sketching a rough outline of a scene before your eye forgets the general layout. If all goes well, with the pressure off I can simply keep on writing, letting the abstract grow into several pages before I realize what I'm doing.

Quit When You're Hot, Persist When You're Not

Writer's block is worst when you're starting up, so we need a trick for that special moment. Every time you stop writing, whether it's for five minutes or five months, you run the risk of finding out you're blocked when you come back. Get around the problem by quitting when you're hot. Take a break on a winning note, not a losing one. Stop writing when things are going well, when you feel strong and know where you're going next. When you're at a loss, don't let yourself quit; stick with it until the block dissolves, words come, and you've triumphed momentarily.

The principle behind this is basic behavior modification. If you quit when you're stuck, you're in fact rewarding your failure: You're learning that if you get stuck you get the reward of getting to eat, to stretch, to escape. If you stick it out, wait until the words come, and then quit, you reward success. At first it seems contrary to logic: Why stop when the words are flowing? The answer is only apparent when you try it: If you quit when you feel good about the writing, you feel good all during the break and come back to the typewriter feeling strong. If you quit when you're stuck, your break is filled with dread and worry, and the return to the typewriter feels like the climb to the scaffold.

When I encourage writers to do this, someone always says, "But I'd be afraid I'd forget what I was going to do next." My point is that you must lick that fear, or it will cripple you. Every writer thinks silently, "What if I try to write tomorrow (or in five minutes) and discover I've lost it?" If you don't learn how to make stopping and restarting easy and painless, you'll never dare stop writing.

The longer the break, the more important it is to quit knowing what you'll do next. When I break for five minutes, I want to know what sentence I'm going to write when I come back; when I break for the day, I typically finish with a sketchy paragraph summary of where the discussion is going in the next few passages—a map of tomorrow's journey.

But what about the first time you start writing? As chapters 3 through 5 show, there is no such moment. Your work is always in process. And if there is a moment when the essay "starts," you can use the quit-when-you're-hot principle if you can think of just two things to say. Pick the two easiest things you plan to say in the essay, write one, and quit, comfortable in the knowledge that next time you can begin with the other one.

Throwing Money at the Problem

You can't learn to write by throwing money at the problem . . . except in this case. Perhaps the most fruitful thing you can do to rid yourself of writer's block is to spend $500 or $1500 on a word processor. Word processors reduce writer's block in lots of ways. They're *fast*, and speed dissipates fear all by itself and helps you write like you talk by letting your fingers almost keep up with the speaking voice in your head. They're *quiet* and *physically effortless*, so the technology disappears and you seem almost to think directly onto the page. They're *fun*, so they turn writing into play. The page you're working on is endless, so you lose sight of how much you've written and get over your Fear of the Page Limit. And the text you produce is infinitely malleable, so revision and correction become almost a game, and the fear of Having to Do It Right the First Time goes away. If you can't afford to buy one, try to borrow time on a friend's machine or find the university's word processing center where machines are available to students.

One last word. You can always devise strategies to overcome writer's block, if (a) you can define precisely what frightens you and (b) you really want the block to go away. It's worth the time to ask youself if you really do. The reward for having writer's block is enormous: It means you don't have to write. It's always easier and safer to be paralyzed than to write. Writing's a risky thing—when we write, we put our intellect, our taste, our personality, and our values on display. I've suggested ways to minimize the risk, but if in the final analysis you'd rather be paralyzed and safe, no tip, no book, no teacher can make you do what you don't want to do.

THINGS TO DO

---

1. Write a one-page essay critiquing your personal prewriting regimen for how well it follows the five principles on p. 82.

2. Carry a small notebook with you for three days. Frequently turn your thoughts to your essay seed and record your musings in the notebook.

3. Make a map from your seed.

4. Write a ten-minute timed free write on the seed.

5. Pick the sentence from the free write in exercise 4 you liked the best, write it at the top of a new page, and free write for ten minutes on it.

6. Write a real letter to a real friend of yours, in which you tell him the usual letter news and then say something like, "I've been thinking about this essay I'm writing for my comp class. It's about. . . ." Then tell your reader the essay, keeping him interested.

7. Read an author you really like for ten minutes. Then, while the sound is still in your ears, write a quick half page *that author* would write on a seed of your choosing.

8. Write a one- to two-page essay in which you (a) gauge how much you're hobbled by writer's block, (b) say exactly what form your fears take—what are you afraid will go wrong or happen to you? At what point do you get stuck?—and (c) plot strategies for either doing what you're afraid of or sidestepping it.

Part Three

REVISING AND EDITING

Chapter 6

ORGANIZATION, PART 1: MAPPING AND OUTLINING

The Spirit of Revising

Now that you've written the piece, it's time to rewrite it. No step in the writing process is so badly done by so many writers as rewriting. Shake a tree and a dozen good first-draft writers will fall out, but you're lucky if you get one good rewriter.

Most of us give ourselves rewriter's block by buying into one or more of several bad arguments. Many writers convince themselves they're just first-draft writers by nature. "I hate rewriting," they say, as if that was an argument against it; "My rewrites are always worse than my first drafts." Other writers define rewriting in the least helpful terms and equate it with mechanics: Rewriting is proofreading, checking grammar and spelling, and replacing words with better words. Others define rewriting in negative terms: Rewriting is looking for errors and blemishes and eliminating them.

As long as you hold any of these beliefs, rewriting will be an unproductive pain. Instead, adopt a new mindset:

Rewriting is rethinking, experimentation, adventure, boldly going where no first draft has gone before.

Rewriting is positive, not negative: You're enriching and expanding, not correcting. It adds, not deletes.

Rewriting, like writing, fries the biggest fish first: You give first priority to the big deals—What am I saying here? Who's reading this, and what does she want from me? What goes with what?—and last priority to cosmetics like spelling and grammar rules.

However good your first drafts are, if your rewrites aren't significantly different, and better, it proves that you don't know how to rewrite, not that rewriting doesn't work. Was Fred Astaire such a good dancer that he didn't profit from rehearsal? Heavens no.

The next six chapters will help you catch that new spirit. But before we talk about strategies, there's something you can buy that will make it all much easier: a word processor. Word processors destroy the whole idea of separate drafts. In the old days, you'd write the first draft, then ask, "What needs work?" On a word processor you're constantly composing and adding and deleting and polishing and tinkering and rethinking and resaying, in one seamless process of writing/rewriting, from the first free-writing steps. And word processors remove the labor penalty from changing your mind or trying something different. Without a word processor, every time you rewrite something you have to retype everything that follows. In other words, when you get a good revision idea, you pay for it through the nose. With a word processor, you can finish the paper, decide to change the title, punch it in in a few seconds, and the revision's complete. You can write five different opening paragraphs, keep them all till the last minute, then pick the one you like, and make the others disappear by hitting a key. And finally, rewriting on a word processor *feels good*, like playing a video game, except better because it's free. You can explore, fool around, see what happens. Rewriting by crossing out and substituting by hand on a typed draft feels like chopping up your children.

Of course, you can rewrite well without a word processor; people have done it for centuries. But it's harder—so much so that more and more universities are making computer ownership an admission requirement. If you can't afford one and can't borrow your roommate's, there are alternatives. You can rent time on a machine at a word processing center. Most colleges have computer labs and word processing rooms scattered across campus, available to students in one way or another.

Organizing

Organizing isn't something you do at any particular step in the writing process or do only once; it's something you play with from the moment you begin thinking about the project to the moment you begin the final editing. You must always be on the lookout for a glimpse of the grand design, a good way to begin, or a good way to end.

You take what comes. If a sense of structure comes in the prewriting or the first draft, of course you'll take it. If you want to risk a carefree outline before the first draft, go right ahead. But remember two things. First, most people can't organize something until they've said it, and organizing is just about the hardest part of writing, so asking yourself to organize before the first draft is a great way to give yourself writer's block. Second, even if you've gotten lucky and caught a glimpse of structure early, *restructure* after the first draft anyway. Break the essay into pieces and try putting them back together in other ways. There is almost no way your first tentative try at putting the pieces together would turn out to be the best one.

Before we talk about specific organizing tools, let's talk about acquiring organizing skills in the long run.

Learn to organize by reading for the craft. Organization is hard in part because we never get much practice in it. A lifetime of talking leaves us unprepared to organize, because talk is linear—we say something, then add something to that, and something to that, and end up with what I called choo-choo-train writing when I see it in print. We practice organizing when we write, of course, but few of us write enough to get the practice we need. Yet you can practice organizing every day, just by reading and noticing the design of what you read, the way a child practices talking by listening. To write, you impose structure on material; to read, you perceive the structure another writer has imposed on his. Not surprisingly, colleges teach students to read exactly the same way (with outlining, etc.) they teach them to structure their writing. And remember, with structure as with every other aspect of writing, you have to read the kind of thing you're trying to write. Textbooks can teach you how to structure textbooks, but they can't teach you how to structure personal essays or business letters.

By the way, word processors, which help your writing in so many ways, make large-scale organizing harder, because you can only see twenty lines or so of the text at any one time. You can't map on a monitor screen at all, and outlines soon become too big to see on the screen in a single glance, which defeats their whole purpose. Do your *composing* on a word processor, but figure you'll have to do your whole-essay organizing by hand, on a piece of paper, with a pencil or pen.

Organizing tools are simply *road maps:* simplified pictures of the whole, with most of the details thrown away so you can get an overview. You're driving down a highway in Pennsylvania heading for Maine and all you can see is the next hundred yards of highway; you look at the map and say, "Ah! I just head east until I hit the Atlantic and then follow the seaboard to the left."

Use your road maps wisely. *After you make the road map, look at it critically.* A lot of writers outline and pay no attention at all, as if the ritual act of outlining appeased the wrathful god of organization. This is as pointless as shooting a basketball without watching to see if it goes through the hoop or not. You must *judge* what the outline reveals to you.

On the other hand, *don't let a road map push you around.* It can't tell you how good the essay is. Some rotten essays outline beautifully; some great essays defy outlining (see p. 373 for an example). Never let a mechanical device talk you out of your writer's judgment. If you have a great opening passage that won't fit in your outline, keep the opening.

Organizing is a messy business that has no tidy step-by-step timetable, but if we try to isolate precisely what we're doing when we shape an essay it comes down to four basic acts:

Finding the grand design: seeing the shape of the essay as a whole
Clustering: putting all the bits that belong together in piles
Sequencing: putting one cluster after another
Connecting: leading the reader from one cluster to the next

For each of the last three, there is a tool:

> For clustering: mapping
> For sequencing: outlining
> For connecting: abstracting

We're going to talk about organization tools *minus* abstracting in this chapter, because abstracting is a big subject all by itself. We'll meet it in Chapter 7.

I've called the four things *acts* instead of *steps* because there is no rigid order in which they're done. The grand design may come to you in a flash in the prewriting; you may have to work your way toward it, through clustering, sequencing, and connecting. Sometimes you can dash off an abstract before you begin the first draft; often abstracting is the very last organizational task you perform. In all this, there is only one true "First do *X*, then *Y*": You probably can't sequence until you've clustered. Beyond that, it's a free-for-all; take what comes.

The Grand Design

An essay isn't five thousand words, or eight hundred sentences, or twenty-five paragraphs; it's *one thing* in which all those words, sentences, and paragraphs play a part. To have that unity, you must see the essay the way a knowledgeable fan sees a baseball game: not as a series of unrelated times at bat, throws, pitches, and base-stealing attempts, but as a purposeful sequence of events where one event causes another and the pieces can only be understood in terms of the large pattern—in short, as a game.

That vision of how the whole thing hangs together I call the grand design. Here are grand designs for four of the essays in this book:
"Why I Never Cared for the Civil War" (pp. 383–384):

> Begin with the problem: I "did well" in school but was bored and learned little. Then explain the source of the problem: School was boring and irrelevant. Then provide alternatives: There are ways to make classrooms exciting and useful. Then conclude with a gleam of hope: I remember about paramecia because of the trip to the pond.

"Consider Nuclear Energy" (pp. 386–387):

> Declare thesis: We need nuclear power. Acknowledge the reader's horrified response. Refute all the reader's arguments against nuclear power. End with an appeal to reason: Please just don't be close-minded.

"Why?" (pp. 376–377):

> Narrate the experience of turning twenty-one and getting dangerously, idiotically drunk. To make the point that I was acting on reflex, after

each idiotic act repeat the refrain: "Why? Because it was my twenty-first birthday." End with the cycle being repeated with my roommate: Nobody learns.

"Europe and the Starving Student" (pp. 322–325):

> Begin by encouraging the nervous student that a trip to Europe is really doable on his budget. Tell the reader you need six things, in this order: motivation, a travel budget, a cheap airline ticket, a knowledge of the Youth Hostel system, familiarity with the European railway system, and a passport. Explain how you get each of the six. End by admitting that this Spartan kind of traveling isn't for everyone.

The brain needs this kind of overview, both when we write and when we read. And we all read and write by glimpsing the overall plan; the only question is, how large a chunk of text can you do it to? We can all do it to sentences: "I'm going to the store now" is *one* thing, not six, for all English speakers. Some of us can do it to paragraphs. Good readers can do it to essays. Great readers can do it to books. You do a version of it when you reduce an essay to a thesis statement or retell the plot of a movie in a minute to a friend.

We feel how necessary a grand design is when we're reading and can't see one. When most of us read an organic chemistry textbook, we understand the material so poorly at first that we read each sentence individually and try to record its information in our brains one bit at a time, and as a result, after we've read a few sentences we understand nothing and remember nothing.

It's probably enough if your grand design lists the essay's large tasks in sequence: "I'll start by doing A, then I'll do B, and I'll end by doing C." But ideally it includes reasons why as well: You say, "I'm starting here for a reason, then doing this next for a reason, and finally I'm ending there for a reason." Here's a grand design for "Making a Brave New World with No Room for Children" (pp. 23–25) *without* reasons:

> First, I'll tell the story about the jogger and his child. Then I'll give some more examples of the problem. Then I'll generalize, and argue that it's a problem at the root of the new society. Finally I'll conclude with an "if this goes on . . ." prediction of doom.

And here's the same grand design *with* reasons:

> First, I'll grab my reader's interest and sympathy with the story about the jogger and his child. Then I'll convince him that the problem is widespread by giving him some more examples. Then I'll generalize, and argue that it's a problem at the root of the new society, to convince him that the problem isn't superficial. Finally I'll conclude with an "if this goes on . . ." prediction of doom—to frighten him and get him moving toward change.

Even if you don't spell out your reasons, they must be in the back of your mind, or you have no rationale for putting one thing in front of another.

Ideally you make up your own design the way you make up your thesis. But in fact there are some basic ways to put things together, so the same grand design appears over and over again in different essays, the same way the same paragraph structure is used in a million different paragraphs, and you're almost fated to reinvent the wheel. "Making a Brave New World" repeats a popular grand design for discussing social ills: Begin with a human-interest example of the problem; show that the problem is widespread; explain what caused it; then speculate about dire future consequences if we don't take steps. Here are some other time-tested grand designs:

> For a restaurant review: Follow the customer through the stages of the meal. First discuss the ambiance, then the service, then the menu, then the salad, the soup, the main course, the dessert, and the bill.

> For an investigative essay: Pose a fascinating question. Gather data toward an answer. Answer the question, and discuss the implications of your answer.

> For an argumentative essay: Declare a thesis. Marshal arguments, supportive evidence, and examples to prove it. Finally, discuss the implications of the thesis.

Sometimes the grand design is dictated for you by a prescribed format. In lab reports, for instance, you summarize the experiment and its findings in the introduction, describe what was done in the experiment in the methods section, reproduce the data gathered in the results section, and discuss your findings in a discussion.

If you've got a grand design, you've licked organization. But most people have to work their way toward theirs, through mapping, outlining, and abstracting.

Clustering

Most people start putting bits together in piles as soon as they start prewriting, though it's possible not to and to produce writing that is literally just a series of bits. Here's an abstract (a quick summary) of an essay that's still in bits, about a best friend:

> Randolph will always be my best friend. He's vivacious. He's always stubborn. He can always pick me up when I'm feeling low. He always loved soccer and played well; he started a team when he moved away. He draws great caricatures. At age eighteen he got interested in ballet and is still studying seriously. He fell in love with a girl whose parents

sent her to Chicago to get away from him; he went after her, and now they're traveling through Central America together. He's a thrill-seeker who never doubts himself.

But for most of us the mind rebels and we categorize as a matter of course. If you're writing on anorexia, your thoughts fall into categories like "What causes it?" "What kinds of treatment are there for it?" "Why did no one ever hear of it until recently?" "How can you spot an anorexic?" "What should you do if someone you know is one?" If you're writing about your best friend, you naturally find your thoughts falling into categories like her physical appearance, her personality, her relationship with men, her relationship with her parents, and so on. Soon you begin to see categories within categories: Within the category for personality is your best friend's sense of humor, her spontaneous, uncontrollable rages, and her inexplicable love of trash, like soap operas and TV dinners. If you think of each thought or idea as a slip of paper, you can think of the categories as manila folders in a filing cabinet, cubbyholes in an old-fashioned desk, or wastepaper baskets spread out on the floor, and you toss all related slips into a single folder or cubbyhole or basket and label it. For a very short paper, you may do this in your head; for a longer paper, you'll probably do it in a notebook; for big projects like term papers, the wastebaskets may be real—you'll physically snip your notes into pieces and file the pieces in real folders or boxes or tubs.

You can represent the categories and subcategories graphically in a number of ways. Outlines use indentation and a heading system of letters and numbers:

I. Intro to Cross-Country Skiing

    A. What you need to get started

        1. Necessary gear

            a. poles

                a-1. Poles should be long enough to reach from the floor to your armpit when you're standing.

You can see an outline as a branching-tree diagram:

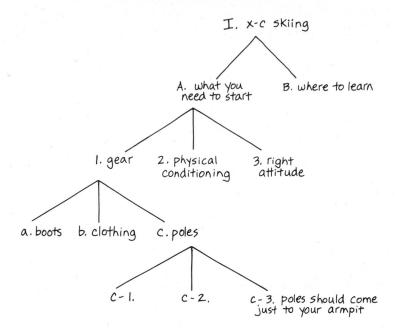

Or you can make a pie chart, where the categories are slices and the subcategories are slices of slices:

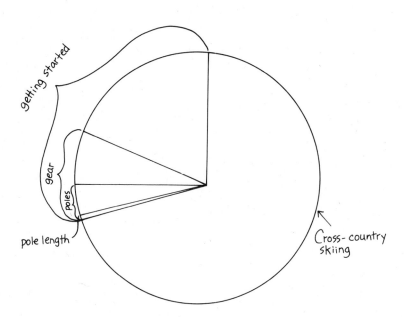

The hardest part about clustering is that bits keep wanting to be in several categories at once. If you're writing a character sketch of your roommate and you want to talk about the time she talked to her mother on the phone, got furious, and took it out on you and her boyfriend, which wastebasket does that bit get tossed into?

Her relationship with her parents
The way she treats her boyfriend
What she's like as a roommate
How she deals with anger

There's no easy answer, but everything has to end up in only one place, and that's precisely the mess you're trying to untangle by clustering. When you encounter such a problem, put a copy of the bit in every basket where it might work. Later you'll see where it worked out best and delete all the others.

The connections between things can take a while to reveal themselves. Here's an abstract of an apparently structureless student first draft that went through a few revisions before the links made themselves known:

Tony can fill a room with excitement. He's very handsome. He used to have a mustache, but he shaved it off. He tells marvelous lies. He wants to be a professional actor. His eyes mist over when he talks about emotional things. He can talk well on almost any subject. Women melt before him. Tony has worked very hard at karate. He's as graceful as a panther. When he fights, his eyes burn with a passionate wildness. On stage, he acts with unpolished, startling energy. He sweats when he acts. Last week he told me that he wasn't happy. He said he was burned out. An old back injury had suddenly recurred. He said he feared he was going insane. Today I saw him walking down the street, wearing the latest fashions and beautifully tanned. He smiled a hard plastic smile. He talked excitedly about a potential job and hurried off without a backward glance. He's twenty years old. He lives at home with both his parents. He has no job and doesn't want to go to college. He stays out and parties heavily until two or three o'clock in the morning. His mother always waits up for him.

That sounds almost random. If we take each of the five paragraphs in the original essay and summarize it in a topic sentence, the essay doesn't look any better:

Tony is energetic and attractive.
He's an eager conversationalist.
He's an expert at karate.
Last week, he said he was miserable and acted rushed and insecure.
He's twenty and has no prospects.

Yet there is one master wastebasket, with three subbaskets in it, and sub-subbaskets in each of the three. Tony has power (social, sexual, physical), but can't find anything to do with it. Karate gave him a bit of an outlet, and acting a bit, but acting is only professional faking, and Tony does too much of that already. With all his gifts, he's burned out and directionless—he's wasting his time in pointless partying, and can't get it together enough to leave his parents. The wastebasket arrangement looks like this:

Thesis: Tony is wasting his great talents.

I. Tony has power and talent to burn.

  A. Sexual: Women swoon over him.

  B. Social: He can walk into a room and every eye will turn to him.

  C. Physical: He's a panther at karate.

  D. Psychic: He's a dominating force on the stage.

II. But he can't seem to do anything with his power.

  A. He's burned out.

  B. He wears slick duds but looks dead inside.

  C. His body's failing him.

III. He's twenty years old, but still living like a child.

  A. He just goes partying every night.

  B. His mother still waits up for him.

If we rewrite the abstract using *that* structure, it looks great:

Tony is so attractive he can walk into any party and fascinate everyone there in five minutes. He has so much natural energy that he's an expert at karate and a stirring actor. Yet he tells me he's burned out and miserable, and he seems empty, in a hurry but with nowhere to go. He's twenty years old, but without a future; he spends his time going from one meaningless party to another, with his mom always waiting up for him.

When you've finished clustering, go through your bits and see what never found a wastebasket to belong to. Deciding what to do with each ill-fitting or homeless bit is when you debug the structure:

If you can't decide whether to throw something away or keep it, check to see if you're still sure of your purpose.

If the bit's important but seems to have nowhere to go, maybe you need to make a new basket.

If you can't decide in which of two baskets it should go, maybe the two baskets are really parts of a bigger basket.

Don't try to keep everything. If you've prewritten well, you should have much more stuff than you end up using, because when you wander you make lots of false starts and head down lots of blind alleys. If you aren't throwing a lot of stuff away, I worry that you're either critiquing and editing yourself as you compose or you're thinking in terms of topic instead of purpose—that is, you're writing an "everything there is to say about anorexia" essay.

Mapping

The best clustering tool in the world is *mapping,* which is described in Chapter 5 (pp. 84–86). Take every piece of the essay—every argument, insight, fact, quote, whatever—and attach it to the map, either by making it a bubble of its own, a subbubble, or a sub-subbubble. Theoretically, you can map every sentence until you have sub-sub-sub-subbubbles, but in reality you almost never need to go that far before you see the grand design, any more than you need a road map marking every tree and footpath along the highway.

Mapping has three advantages over outlining and abstracting, which we'll talk about next. First, you can map in all 360 degrees of the circle, and you can connect anything on the page to anything else on the page via a line, so you can categorize much more flexibly than with an outline or abstract, where you can only make *lists.* Second, a map has no starting and ending points and no sequence—there's no order to the spokes on a wheel—so mapping forces you to rethink sequence. Third, a map has a center, so it's good practice in unifying and locating a thesis. There's no center to a list.

The trick with mapping, as with all structuring tools, is to *learn* from doing it. Let's debug the map on the facing page for the essay "Legalize Hemp" (pp. 183–184). That map tells me six things about the essay. First, the strength of the essay is clearly at Bubble A, where Todd has seven reasons to support his thesis. But Bubble B, which logically should be a thesis statement for all of A, hangs alone in the map. I'd subordinate the seven arguments under the three categories in B: politics, economics, and environment. When Todd does that, he'll see that he's got lots of good economic arguments, some good environmental ones, and *no* political ones, so he'll have to find some or drop politics from B.

Second, the map dramatizes how often the first draft repeats itself. The last paragraph of the draft, for instance, begins and ends with points that are already in the map (C and D), and Todd should think about deleting the repetitions unless they're purposeful.

Third, Bubble E hangs alone and unexplained, a clear sign that the single sentence about false propaganda in the draft's last paragraph needs lots of explanation and development.

Fourth, Bubble F seems to be an oddball. It's from a different point of view than the rest of the essay, and it contradicts the arguments in G

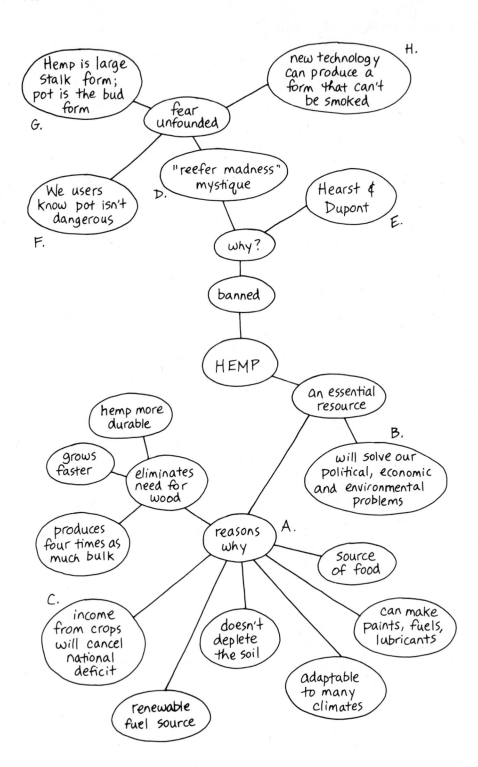

and H, because if pot is harmless we don't need to argue that hemp can't be smoked. I'd consider dropping it.

Fifth, Bubble G isn't clear, and that's important because the reader really has to understand that point if the argument is to work. I'd expand the sentence in the essay to a full discussion.

Sixth, E and H are out of place. In the map, they're with F, G, and H, which are all in paragraph 2, but in the essay they're as far away as they can get, in the last paragraph. I'd bring them together, then decide where in the grand design they all belong.

Sequencing

Once you get things in bunches, you must put one bunch in front of another. The trick, as always, is to think about how your reader reads. The hemp essay consists of two big parts: (1) proving that hemp is a useful resource and (2) refuting the charges that it's a dangerous drug that should be illegal. Which should Todd do first? The first draft does part 2, then part 1. I think it works better in the other order, because the reader needs to be convinced that hemp is of value before the rebuttal makes sense. How can you rebut a response the reader hasn't even had yet?

Outlining

The most popular tool for sequencing is *outlining*, which we see everywhere: Instructors often outline their lectures on the blackboard, books are outlined in their tables of contents, textbooks often end each chapter with an outline summary, church services and conventions often hand out programs that outline events in chronological order, and so on. To outline, you list the contents of the map's main bubbles in a vertical column, each item headed with a capital Roman numeral; you list the subbubbles indented under them, headed with capital letters; you list sub-subbubbles indented again, headed with Arabic numerals; and so on. There are sample outlines on pages 107, 110, and 373.

Outlining may be popular, but it's fraught with peril. Mapping sets you free, but outlining locks you up, and I've known a thousand writers blocked by outlining. If outlining makes your writing go dead, don't do it; if you do it, here are two rules to help you remain alive.

First, *don't let the outline buffalo you.* Writers cower before outlines. For instance, people will tell you that all the entries in the outline must be grammatically parallel: all noun phrases or all verb participles. Or they'll tell you that if you have an A section you must have at least a B section. Phooey. Don't follow rules for rules' sake. Do what helps you. If having an A section without a B section lets you see the grand design, do it.

Second, *outline statements, not topics.* For the same reason that finding a topic doesn't help start an essay (p. 45) and having a firm topic doesn't mean the first draft has accomplished anything (p. 58), outlining topics doesn't get you very far, because it doesn't tell you if you've *said* anything yet. I can outline topics without learning anything about the essay behind them. Here's a nice-looking outline on a topic I know nothing about and have nothing to say on:

I.   Disarmament: the present crisis

II. Historical causes

    A.   The birth of the bomb

    B.   The cold war

    C.   Past attempts at solutions

III. Popular current disarmament proposals

    A.   American proposals

    B.   Russian proposals

    C.   Why they don't work

IV. My solution

A topic outline is really just a generic grand design, like those on p. 106, waiting for an essay; it will help you a little, but not nearly as much as an outline with the essay's content included. To have that, outline *statements:* whole sentences, with predicates.

Connecting

Once you've clustered and sequenced, you are *not* done. Something remains, something invisible and therefore hard to produce, but in some kinds of writing it's the most important structural feature of all. It's called *transition* (or momentum). It's *between* the items in your sequence, and outlining won't help you get it—in fact, outlining often makes transition problems worse instead of improving them.

Some kinds of writing aren't really made of pieces, but are instead made of steps along a path, and in such writing the crucial organizational question is not what comes after what but rather how you get from one to the other. In such writing, the thought process is everything, and any organizational tool that doesn't focus on it won't help you see if the writing is working or not. An outline encourages you to not think about the matter by cutting the writing up into parts, labeling each one, and thereby suggesting that the parts stand next to each other but never connect. If you outline thought-process writing, good writing can look bad and bad writing can look good. "Where Did Louise Go?" (p. 388) is a great essay that looks like a mess when outlined, as its outline on p. 373 shows.

What exactly is transition? Let's begin by feeling it. In transitionless writing, the separate pieces of information (clauses, in grammatical terms) stand next to each other without connecting, like shy strangers at a party. When you read it, you feel like you're coming to a complete stop at each period, and each clause has to regain the lost forward momentum:

> I think requiring deposits on soda bottles is unfair. I clean up my own litter. How much is a clean roadside worth to Americans? Glass is not something we're likely to run out of soon. Why should people be forced to do something they don't want to do?

Transitional writing connects the pieces together, so we read *through* them all as a unit; the stop signs are gone and our momentum never flags. Just adding *and*s won't suffice:

> I think requiring deposits on soda bottles is unfair, and I clean up my own litter, and how much is a clean roadside worth to Americans?, and glass is not something we're likely to run out of soon, and why should people be forced to do something they don't want to do?

Transition requires seeing how the pieces relate to each other. It requires what grammarians call *imbedding:* putting pieces inside other pieces.

By the time you graduate from college, you're expected to read and write in a spectacularly *imbedded* style. Here's a sentence from a student essay about Buddy Bolden, the legendary blues man, in three degrees of imbeddedness. Here it is in logical order but in bits and pieces:

> There are some things historians agree on. Bolden played cornet. No one could play like him. His fellow bandmembers said so. Even Jelly Roll Morton said so. Morton was egocentric. Bolden worked as a barber. He had his own business. By noon, he was working on his second bottle of whiskey. You had to go to him before noon if you wanted a decent hair cut. He gradually went insane. He was committed to a state mental hospital. That was in Louisiana. He was committed in 1907. He died there twenty-four years later.

Now rewritten by me in moderately transitional, imbedded form:

> There are some things historians agree on. Bolden played cornet like no one before or after him could do, for one thing. His fellow bandmembers said so. Even Jelly Roll Morton said so, and he was egocentric. Bolden worked as a barber, and had his own business. By noon, he was working on his second bottle of whiskey, so you had to go to him before noon if you wanted a decent hair cut. He gradually went insane and

was committed to the East Louisiana State Hospital. He was committed in 1907 and died there twenty-four years later.

And finally in the author Beth's original version—a single virtuosic sentence:

> Historians agree that Bolden played the cornet as no one before or after him was able to do (accounts of everyone from fellow bandmembers to the egocentric Jelly Roll Morton confirm this), that he was self-employed as a barber (one to whom—if a decent haircut was important—you went before noon, by which time he was usually working on his second bottle of whiskey), and that he gradually went insane and was committed in 1907 to East Louisiana State Hospital, where he died twenty-four years later.

Sometimes with transitionless writing the ideas have no reason for being in the order they're in. But more typically, the writer has excellent reasons for her sequencing; she's just forgotten to let the reader see what they are. Formless writing is like trying to go in several different directions at once; unconnected writing is like driving down a highway and stopping every mile for no reason. All you have to do to fix the transition problem is spell out the missing links:

> The teacher puts the most important notes of the day on the overhead. This system is helpful when it comes to the test because we know what he considers the most important points. It is much easier to study this way. Trying to memorize one entire chapter is difficult.
>
> Rewrite: *When he lectures, he puts the day's most important points on the overhead projector; this is helpful when it comes time to study for tests, because you don't have to memorize the entire chapter.*

> Dr. Leland's humor is the best thing about the class. He literally keeps you rolling on the floor with laughter. His great sense of humor keeps you attentive also, because you don't want to miss out on a good joke.
>
> Rewrite: *The best thing about the class is Dr. Leland's sense of humor, which keeps you rolling on the floor while it holds your attention—you don't want to miss the next joke.*

If you're wondering how transition-rich your writing is, use two tests: First, how do you compose? Do you write a sentence, then stop and think of another sentence to write? If so, your writing will probably read stop-and-go too. Do you write *through* your sentences, with a sense of one carrying you to the next one? If so, your writing will probably read with momentum too. Second, read your writing out loud. If you can read it well, without having to get up a new head of steam after the periods, you're probably transition-rich. But you must give a lively reading: A monotone will obscure everything under the wet blanket.

So transition has something to do with reading pace, and it has something to do with the connection between ideas. But there's a third, better way to conceive of transition: in terms of the unspoken dialogue between reader and writer we practiced voicing in the "Writers' Workshop" section of Chapter 2 (p. 33 ff.). The better you articulate the reader's imagined half of the dialogue and respond to it, the better your transitions will be. Here's writing teacher Sheridan Baker talking about how to put a "funnel-shaped" paragraph together. He's just given an example of a funnel-shaped paragraph and is now going to discuss it:

> Now, that paragraph turned out a little different from what I anticipated. I overshot my original thesis, discovering, as I wrote, a thesis one step farther—an underlying cause—about coming to friendly terms with oneself. But it illustrates the funnel, from the broad and general to the one particular point that will be your essay's main idea, your thesis.
>
> *(Sheridan Baker,* The Practical Stylist)

We can prove the existence of transition here by making visible the reader's expected responses:

Now, that paragraph turned out a little different from what I anticipated.
In what way was it different?

I overshot my original thesis.
Why did you do that?

[Because] I discovered, as I wrote, a thesis one step farther.
What kind of thesis?

An underlying cause.
What was it about?

About coming to terms with oneself.
So your previous claim was wrong?

[No,] the paragraph still illustrates the funnel.
In what ways?

It still goes from the broad and general to the one particular point that will be your essay's main idea.
What's that idea called?

Your thesis.

If we take the transition-poor passage we looked at on p. 115, we can't imagine any likely reader response that the text responds to:

I think requiring deposits on soda bottles is unfair.
Why?

I clean up my own litter.
So what?

How much is a clean roadside worth to Americans?
I don't know—what's the answer? Why does it matter?

Glass is not something we're likely to run out of soon.
So what?

Why should people be forced to do something they don't want to do?
Because people don't want to do things that are good for society as a whole—isn't that why we have laws?

Reader response comes in an infinite variety of forms, but 90 percent of it is variations on four basic questions. If you can learn to ask them yourself and then answer them, you will go a long way toward solving all transition problems. Here are the questions and what you must do to answer them:

Like what, for instance? (Give examples.)
So what? (Say why it matters.)
Why? (Give supportive arguments and reasons.)
What does that mean? (Explain.)

If you want to force yourself to have more transition, use *connectors*, the words and punctuation marks that signal strong, specific relationships between clauses:

and	so
but	still
yet	first, second, etc.
because	thus
since	even though
therefore	for instance
nevertheless	furthermore
however	moreover
instead	finally
rather than	although
also	too
for example	in fact
in other words	consequently
while	on the other hand

But, for instance, means "I'm going to qualify what I just said or disagree with it in some way." *So* means "I'm going to draw a conclusion from what I just said." *Instead* means "I'm going to offer an alternative." The more specific punctuation marks—the semicolon and the colon— send the same kind of message. The semicolon means "The next clause is the second half of the idea started in the previous clause." The colon means "Now I'm going to enumerate or list examples of what I just said."

Some connectors are quite precise about the logical relationship between the two things they connect, and some aren't. *Nevertheless* and *for example* are precise, for example; *and* isn't. Push yourself toward the precise ones.

If you want to exaggerate your transition for practice, stuff your writing with connectors. But don't do it forever. Reading excessive connectors gets boring quickly, like having someone give you directions as you drive along a route you know perfectly well. Here's Sheridan Baker's paragraph (p. 117) with all transitions telegraphed by me:

> Now that example isn't a simple example of what I've described, because it turned out a little different from what I anticipated. The difference is that I overshot my thesis, which I did because I discovered, as I wrote, a thesis one step further—in other words, an underlying cause—which is about coming to friendly terms with oneself. But the basic idea is still valid, because the paragraph still illustrates the funnel, in that it goes from the broad and general to the one particular point that will be your essay's main idea—in other words, your thesis.

As your structure becomes stronger you'll find you need that kind of signposting less and less.

Paragraphing

We now have the tools to tackle an oft-asked question: how do you know when one paragraph is over and it's time to indent five spaces and begin a new one? For most writers paragraphing just happens—let it. Don't think about it at all unless (a) you regularly write entire pages with no paragraph breaks, (b) your paragraphs are typically three sentences or less, or (c) your instructor tells you it's a problem for you.

If it is a problem, attack it with the tools in this chapter. Poor paragraphing is not a disease, it's a symptom; the disease is poor structure. If you treat the disease, the symptom will disappear. Well-organized, transition-rich essays paragraph themselves.

If you ask people what a paragraph break means, most of them will say it means one topic is finished and another is about to begin. In practice, that doesn't help much. It can work for the rare piece of writing that is truly a series of subjects, but most writing isn't. Remember what we learned way back in Chapter 4: Topic is almost nothing in writing, thesis and purpose are everything. Remember what mapping showed us: Everything is connected to everything else. Remember what we learned about transition: One thing doesn't just follow another; one thing leads to another. In Chapter 9 we'll meet the same idea in different language: Every topic is a subtopic of a larger topic. For all these reasons, trying to make paragraph breaks when one topic ends and another starts will only drive you mad.

Mapping, outlining, and transition help us to healthier ways of thinking of paragraphs. A map shows us that our essay is a kind of branching tree—a trunk that divides into main limbs, which themselves divide into branches, which themselves divide into twigs. Think of a paragraph as representing one section of the tree. But how large a section?—a main limb, or a branch, or only a twig? The answer is, however much you can keep straight in your head at once or your reader can take in without a break is a good size. As long as you've clustered well, any section of the map will make a unified paragraph, however large it is, because the pieces in any section of the map belong together—that's what a map is all about. Once you glimpse this, you can just put the paragraph breaks when you or your reader need a rest.

We can also think of paragraphing in terms of outlining. The outline breaks the essay up into tasks or statements, and breaks them up into subtasks or substatements. Any section or subsection of the outline can logically be a paragraph, so you can begin by trying to make a paragraph break between every subsection, or every sub-subsection, and simply move left in the outline to a larger section if the paragraph seems abrupt or move right to a smaller subsection if it's unwieldy.

But the best way to think about paragraphing is in terms of transition. We write from one thing to another, so the paragraph break can never signify an ending—only *a breather,* a momentary pause in the midst of the reader's forward progress. Writing is full of breathers: tiny breathers between phrases (commas); slightly bigger breathers between sentences (periods); big breathers between paragraphs; and very long breathers between sections or chapters. You can always make the sentence or the paragraph longer or shorter, just as you can decide to cut the day's drive short and find a motel at two in the afternoon or drive on through the night. It's just a matter of how much work you want to take on in one push. But you can't paragraph at all until the writing flows from one thing to another seamlessly, any more than you can decide to drive on through the night if you're driving in three directions at once.

You put paragraph breaks in two places, then: when the reader needs a little breather before continuing and when you want to shock the reader by pulling him up short. The reader doesn't want to brake to a full stop every half mile, which is what he'll have to do if you write a lot of very short paragraphs. He doesn't want to drive across the country without stopping, which is what he'll have to do if you write in one continuous paragraph. He wants to drive in comfortable blocks of time with rests between, and for most adult readers that turns out to be about a quarter to a half a page—four to nine sentences. The more experienced the reader, the longer he can drive without a rest stop.

But you don't have to do what the reader wants or expects. Short paragraphs startle the reader into full attention with an unexpected stop, like hitting the brakes a second or two after starting up from a stop sign. In George Orwell's essay "Marrakech," the first complete paragraph is

> As the corpse went past the flies left the restaurant table in a cloud and rushed after it, but they came back a few minutes later.

Long paragraphs intentionally exhaust the reader, like forcing him to drive thirty-six hours without sleep, leaving him strung out and overstimulated (Tom Wolfe's paragraphs on pp. 30–31, for example).

Since paragraphing is the art of controlling your reader's reading tempo, the best way to learn it is to read your own writing out loud well and see where the big dramatic pauses fall.

You shouldn't have to build paragraphs by rules and regulations, but if you're stuck, you can always fall back on what I call McParagraph, the Big Mac of the writing world. Like the Big Mac, it ain't special but it gets the job done, and if you use it a lot your writing will be serviceable, although it probably won't excite you. In the McParagraph you state a thesis up front, then spend the rest of the paragraph doing one of the following tasks:

> Back the thesis up with reasoning or evidence.
> Illustrate the thesis with examples.
> Explain the thesis in more detail.
> Explore the consequences: If the thesis is true, so what? Then what?

If these four tasks look familiar, it's because you just saw them on p. 118 when we were talking about meeting readers' needs. Good writing is really just one thing, and mapping or paragraphing or keeping the reader in our thoughts or writing thesis statements always takes us to that same good place.

What's Next?

We've done a lot in this chapter. We've clustered, we've sequenced, and we've checked for transition from sentence to sentence. But there's one thing left to do, and it's big enough to deserve its own chapter.

THINGS TO DO

1. Practice reading for the craft by finding an essay you admire in a magazine (not a newspaper) and describing its organizing principles:

    a. Describe its grand design.

    b. State the purpose, task, or thesis of each paragraph.

    c. Describe the logical structure of any two paragraphs. Is either one a McParagraph? If so, which of the four paradigms on p. 121 does it use?

    d. Choose a paragraph and write out the imaginary reader's half of the dialogue, in the manner of pp. 117–18.

    e. Choose a three-paragraph passage and circle all connectors (see p. 118). If you see stretches of text that have none or few, write in the connectors the writer left implicit.

2. Pick an essay from Chapter 15 or 17 and do the five tasks in Exercise #1 with it.

3. Write a first draft of an essay and do the following tasks with it:

    a. Map the draft, letting the structure change as the mapping suggests it should.

    b. Critique the map, as we did with the hemp essay map. Make a list of questions that need answering and problems that need addressing about the map.

    c. Redraft the essay, using the map as a guide to paragraphing. Try to make each section of the map its own paragraph.

    d. Critique the paragraphing: Do some paragraphs seem abruptly short for no reason? Are some paragraphs tiringly long? Do some paragraphs seem to lack transition? How can you solve these problems by reparagraphing or resequencing?

    e. Pick a two-paragraph passage and circle all connectors (p. 118). Everywhere connectors are rare, add them—resequence the sentences if necessary.

    f. Choose a paragraph and write out the imaginary reader's half of the dialogue, in the manner of pp. 117–118.

4. Write a first draft of an essay and do the following tasks with it:

a. Outline the draft, letting the structure change as the outlining suggests it should and making sure to outline statements, not topics (p. 114).
b. Redraft the essay, using the outline as a guide to paragraphing. Try to make each section of the outline its own paragraph.
c. Critique the paragraphing: Do some paragraphs seem abruptly short for no reason? Are some paragraphs tiringly long? Do some paragraphs seem to lack transition? How can you solve these problems by reparagraphing or resequencing?
d. Pick a two-paragraph passage and circle all connectors (p. 118). Everywhere connectors are rare, add them—resequence the sentences if necessary.
e. Choose a paragraph and write out the imaginary reader's half of the dialogue, in the manner of pp. 117–18.

Chapter 7

ORGANIZATION, PART II: ABSTRACTING

The invisible thing called *transition*, which in Chapter 6 I said exists between sentences that seem to follow each other purposefully, exists between paragraphs too. But it's harder to see there, and harder to make sure your writing has it there, for the same reason that it's harder to remember where you were headed after you stop for a week than it is after you stop for five minutes. But we still need it, so to make sure you have it, you need to make an *abstract:* a one- or two-paragraph summary of the essay. If you can write a transition-rich paragraph, you can write a transition-rich essay, just by *shrinking the essay to paragraph size.*

An abstract (also called a précis or a summary) is like soup left on the stove—you begin with a gallon of soup, set it to simmer, come back in four hours, and you've got all the substance, now reduced to an inch of sludge on the bottom of the pot. Here are abstracts for three of the essays in this book:

"Leaving Nothing on the Table" (p. 317):

> A used car salesman wants you to pay as much as possible; you're trying to pay as little as you can. There are three strategies. 1) The "Take my wallet, please" approach, where you pay the sticker price, is easy, but the most expensive. 2) The "Take a few dollars off and I'll buy it approach," where you argue the salesman down a few hundred dollars, is better. But the best is Option #3, the "Take this offer or shove it" approach, where you get the "invoice cost" from *Edmund's Car Prices,* add the cost of each option, plus service charges, and add a reasonable profit—perhaps 5%. Tell the salesman that total is your final offer on the car. He'll probably take it.

"Top Chicken" (p. 285):

> It's recess and we all rush to the monkey bars. I check out my next opponent—she's a pushover. Now it's my turn. I attack. She counterattacks, but I escape her grasp and start to take her down. The crowd is screaming. Her grip loosens and she falls to the turf and hobbles off,

humiliated. I strut back to the end of the line, pick at a callus, and check out my next opponent.

"Consider Nuclear Energy" (p. 386):

Electricity can't meet California's energy needs. We have to consider nuclear power. Yes, I know you hate the idea, but population will continue to grow, and all technological alternatives either are inadequate or pose serious environmental threats of their own, so we really have no other choice.

   I know—you're saying nuclear power isn't accident-proof. But we live with acceptable risk every day; the safety factors on nuclear power plants are extreme, in accordance with the damage an accident might cause; and the projected deaths from a disaster are fewer than we slaughter on our nation's highways each year. What about waste disposal, you ask? The solution isn't cheap or easy, but it works. I know the issues are frightening and complex, but it's too important a decision to just make with a knee-jerk response—think about it!

You can approach abstract writing from two different directions. You can try to glimpse the whole essay at once in your head and write it in a single mental breath, without looking at notes or drafts. Or you can construct the abstract sentence by sentence from the draft itself. To do that, read the first paragraph or two of the draft—the section of the draft that seems to do the first big opening job or make the first big statement—and summarize it in a sentence; then summarize the next chunk of text, and so on through the essay. Unless the draft is longer than five pages, try for roughly one sentence in the abstract for each full-size paragraph in the draft.

   Both kinds of abstracts have things to teach you. The in-one-breath abstract is good at diagnosing *content:* It answers the question "What, exactly, have I *got* here?" The constructed abstract is good at diagnosing *structure:* It tells you how the pieces of the essay go together.

   Abstracting is the most wonderful structuring tool there is. Mapping is good at setting you free, outlining is liable to tie you up and make you rigid, but abstracting can point out every strength and weakness of your present essay design and make it easy to see better alternatives. Usually an essay that abstracts well is a good essay, and you can't say that about mapping or outlining. Abstracting demands more from you than either outlining or mapping does, so it may come later in the writing process, but it also tells you much more than they do.

   Abstracting an essay is like hooking your car up to one of those wonderful machines they have in high-tech repair shops that checks your car fifty different ways in minutes. It will answer every large-scale revision question you can ask of a draft:

Did you find something to say?
Do you like the voice that's speaking?

Did you accomplish your task?
Is there a sense of beginning and ending?
Do you have reasons to support your claims?

And so on. The beauty of the abstract is that, since you're looking at a paragraph instead of several pages, the answers are easy to see. But the question the abstract answers best is, "Does it flow?" The abstract's special genius is for diagnosing large-scale transition, the smoothness with which big pieces of text follow each other. Mapping can't touch this and outlining often makes transition problems worse.

There are only a few ways to go wrong with abstracting. One is to write what tech writers call a *descriptive* abstract, where instead of doing the essay in miniature you *describe* what the essay is or does. It usually begins like this:

I'm going to . . .
This essay is a description of . . .
How to . . .
In this essay I said . . .
An introduction to . . .

Descriptive abstracts are useful to readers, but they have no place in revision, because they aren't diagnostic: They tell you what you hope you did or are intending to do, not what you've actually *got*. It's easy to write a great descriptive abstract for an essay you haven't written and will never write: "This essay solves the problem of world overpopulation, suggests a workable cure for cancer, and proves to everyone's satisfaction that Elvis is really alive."

To avoid writing descriptive abstracts, make sure of three things: (1) The abstract duplicates the draft's structure; (2) the abstract and the draft speak from the same point of view—if the draft doesn't say "The essay argues that . . . ," neither should the abstract; and (3) the abstract contains the core content of the draft—the thesis, the point, the answer to the question, the main reasons why.

Another way to go wrong is to try to write the abstract by *extracting* sentences from the draft as is. With a certain kind of writer—one who writes summarizing topic sentences in her paragraphs—you can get away with this, but few writers do that all the time, and probably those who do shouldn't. With most writing, you'll have to *compose* the abstract's sentences yourself.

A last way to go wrong is to write the abstract as several very short paragraphs. Write the abstract as a single paragraph—at the outside perhaps two—so you can see how one sentence runs into the next. If you have trouble making the paragraph hang together, *that's the abstract doing its job:* making you face the fact that you need to resequence the draft.

How long should an abstract be? You can abstract to any length (see pp. 125–26 for proof), and each length will teach you something different.

If you want to know how strong the thesis is, abstract down to a sentence. If you want to see the basic design at its broadest, abstract down to four or five sentences. The longer the abstract becomes, the better you see how the little pieces fit and the less able you are to see the core.

Still, there are norms. With a three- to seven-page essay, you seem to learn the most from an abstract the size of the ones on pp. 125–26: six to ten sentences, a quarter to a half a typed page, one substantial paragraph. Don't assume that as the draft gets longer the abstract follows suit. A map of Cleveland isn't necessarily bigger or smaller than a map of Africa.

Some kinds of writing don't abstract well: narratives, step-by-step processes, lists and enumerations, or anything that's a collection of bits and pieces rather than a flow. Abstracting also can have trouble handling *openers,* so if your abstract makes your opener look bad, don't assume it's telling the truth.

Learning from Abstracts

I said before that abstracting is the most wonderful structuring tool there is. But it's a hard tool to master, so many people do a little abstracting, find it relatively unprofitable, and set it aside. Let's watch abstracting pay off in three different ways.

Critiquing the Constructed Abstract

If you write a constructed abstract (p. 126), following the structure of the draft rigidly, you then look at the abstract hard to see how well it reads, judging it as a piece of writing unto itself. You must *follow the sequencing of the draft slavishly.* If you revise as you abstract, you'll hide the draft's weaknesses and the abstract can't tip you off to them. It's like lying to the doctor about your symptoms.

Let's practice on three abstracts written by students from their drafts:

> ***Abstract A*** Mark Twain is the best writer in American literature, because he could do things Cooper and Whitman couldn't do. Cooper's works were inconsistent and unrealistic. Whitman was also very influential, and liberated American literature from taboos about sex and free verse. Twain tackled taboos more successfully. In summation, American literature was shaped by Twain, Cooper, and Whitman. Twain was unique in his tact, the vividness of his descriptions, and his frank honesty. He died penniless and mad, cursing the human race. Hemingway said that all modern American literature comes from *Huckleberry Finn.* ❖

Diagnosis: The abstract has a lot to say, and it seems excited by it. The voice seems direct and forceful—not boring. The abstract starts right off with a meaty first sentence that wastes no time and gives itself a worthy task to perform. So far, so good.

What needs work is sequencing. It's hard to get logically from one sentence to the next, and there's little sense of overall direction—the abstract doesn't seem to go *from* a starting place *to* an ending place. The general sense that "there's a problem somewhere" is enough to tip us off to the need for a rewrite, but we can get specific about where the problem manifests itself:

1. Sentence 3 seems to contradict sentence 1.
2. The *also* of sentence 3 implies this is the *second* of something, but we can't see the first.
3. *In summation* comes in the middle of things, and it doesn't summarize, since it tells us something new.
4. We can't see how "He died penniless and mad" is logically connected to anything.
5. The last sentence doesn't seem to end anything.

We can fix all these problems by resequencing:

Rewrite A Hemingway said all of modern American literature sprang from *Huckleberry Finn.* Why would he say that? What's so special about Twain among the other great early American writers? Two things: he did what greats like Cooper and Whitman did, only better—like break social and artistic taboos; and he had things they didn't have, like tact, descriptive accuracy, and, most of all, a willingness to look at the dark side of human nature. That willingness was so uncompromising that it drove him mad and left him penniless. ❖

Now that the abstract works, we must do the thing without which the abstracting process is pointless: *Rewrite the draft* to match.

Abstract B A favorite way to spend Friday night for many people is to watch hardball. My nephew plays and is talented and confident. I wonder if my five-year-old son will have the chance to build his confidence. Some kids make it through without getting hit by the ball. Many parents oppose the use of the standard hardball because it's dangerous. Cost and tradition are the biggest reasons for not changing over to the ragball. The Little League Association needs to adopt the use of the ragball in this beginning league; it works just as well. Why should a potentially dangerous ball be used when technology has produced a good and safe alternative? ❖

Diagnosis: This abstract reads badly, but it's really just a short step from excellent. Its virtues are that it has a strong case to make, it makes a moving personal connection with the argument, and it expresses it in clear, unforced language. But it consistently refuses to tell us *why* we're being told these things. We're two thirds of the way through the piece before we get a clue as to what the issue is, and then it comes indirectly by way of a prepositional phrase ("for not changing over to the ragball"). All we have to do is *telegraph the transitions*. Beyond that, we need make only one sequencing change: Put the refutation of the opposition's argument ("cost and tradition are the biggest reasons . . .") *after* the declaration of thesis. You can't address the rebuttal before you've stated your case:

> ***Rewrite B*** A favorite way for my family to spend Friday night is to watch hardball. My nephew plays with confidence, but sometimes I wonder if my five-year-old son will have the chance to build his confidence. Not all beginners get hit by the ball, but many do, and those who do often are injured and quit in fear. But there's a way to avoid that: switch from the conventional hardball to the ragball. It works just as well as the hardball without the danger. Why should a potentially dangerous ball be used when technology has produced a good and safe alternative? The only arguments against it are cost and tradition, but certainly the added expense is worth it and tradition isn't worth the cost in frightened children and injuries. ❖

Since an abstract's greatest gift is its ability to diagnose transition, you want to exaggerate transition by using lots of connecting words (p. 118). If you don't, the abstract is so short it can make perfectly sequential prose seem disjointed and stiff. Once you've loaded the abstract with connectors, go back and make sure all the connections they represent are unmistakable in the essay itself.

> ***Abstract C*** The search for a golden tan is an annual quest for students. Tan skin is risking skin cancer, premature aging, and wrinkles. A tan is a status symbol, but it doesn't necessarily make you a better person. I'm pale and have heard all the pale jokes, but I still don't think a tan is important. The stereotypes applied to pale people are just as bad as those applied to tan people. A tan may be nice now, but it can create wrinkles that will last a lifetime. I may never be tan, but I'll have smooth skin when I'm old. ❖

Diagnosis: If this abstract sounds okay to you, you aren't asking enough of your abstracts, because this is transition gridlock. Every sentence seems to read in a vacuum, unconnected to the sentences before and after, and we cannot for the life of us read with a sense of forward movement. A clue in the language is the lack of connectors: Not one sentence begins with a *but* or a *so.* So we have to start stringing thoughts together and expressing the ties between them:

> ***Rewrite C*** The search for a golden tan is an annual quest for students, but tanners don't realize what danger they're in: tanning is risking skin cancer, premature aging, and wrinkles. A tan may make you look great now, but it can create wrinkles that will last a lifetime. Of course, a tan is a status symbol, so not having one means you have to put up with a certain amount of guff. I know—I'm pale and have heard all the pale jokes and the stereotypes. But you can learn to live with it. And there are payoffs later: I may never be tan, but I'll have smooth skin when I'm old. ❖

The original has four transitional signposts: the four *but*s. The rewrite has ten: *but, but, of course, so, I know, but, and, but,* and two colons.

Learning from the In-One-Breath Abstract

There is much to be learned by forcing your abstract to follow the draft slavishly, but there is also much to be learned by abstracting out of your head and learning from the places where the abstract and the draft differ. Write the abstract in one breath, then compare the abstract to the draft, and when you find differences choose which you like better. *If the abstract altered the essay in some way, it probably had a good reason.* Here's an in-one-breath abstract of "Legalize Hemp" (pp. 183–184):

Hemp is a wonderful crop that can solve a lot of the world's problems. It grows faster than wood, produces more bulk, and is more durable, so it will help save trees. It's a renewal fuel source, it can replace fossil fuel lubricants, and it's a healthy source of essential food elements. It's also an easy crop to grow, and it's easier on the soil than most crops. So why aren't we growing it now? Because the lumber industry and the paper industry conducted a "reefer madness" scare campaign against hemp back in the fifties. Those fears aren't true, because we have the technology to grow a strain of hemp that can't be smoked. ❖

That abstract has found a more powerful sequence and has jettisoned a lot of troublesome repetitions and asides that were in the first draft. All Todd has to do is rewrite the essay using the abstract as a template.

Learning as You Abstract

The first two techniques let you learn after the abstract is written, but the easiest time to learn is when you're writing it—when you're looking at the draft and deciding precisely how to summarize each paragraph and get from one sentence to the next:

If you look at a paragraph and it's hard to summarize it, ask yourself if the paragraph is clear about what it's saying.

If it takes two or three sentences of the abstract to summarize one paragraph, ask if the paragraph shouldn't be two or three paragraphs.

If you find yourself passing over chunks of text without representing them in the abstract at all, ask if they're doing worthy work in the essay and are in the right place.

If you can't make one sentence link to the previous one in the abstract, ask if the essay has a logical connection from idea to idea there and if it makes the connection apparent.

If you find that the new sentence in the abstract sounds like something you've already said, ask if the essay repeats itself.

In short, every time the act of abstracting *makes you stop and think,* ask what's causing the holdup and if it's a problem in the draft. Let's abstract the following draft paragraph by paragraph, noting how it's going along the way.

BE BEAUTIFUL OR BE NOTHING

DONNA JOLLIFF

Due to the nature of the advertising media today, most people are unhappy with their physical appearance. Daily, when we watch TV, go to movies, read magazines or billboards, we are struck with the destructive reality that our bodies aren't good enough. Either we're too skinny or too fat. And if we are one of the lucky few to possess a terrific body, then the face to go along with it is somehow imperfect. Only about 1% of the population can meet the standards imposed by the supermodels of our time.

> *(Summary: Advertising is making all of us hate the way we look.* That paragraph summarizes pretty easily and seems to be a strong assertion. So far, so good.)

Tanning beds, body wraps, liposuction, wrinkle-preventing cremes, NutraSweet, and the list could go on endlessly. These are only a sampling of the products which have come about as a result of advertising. Every company, it seems, has something to offer us to help us improve our bodies, to make us feel better about ourselves. The truth is we, as a nation, are much worse off now as a result of all of those things which came about to make us better. Cancer has increased, and new diseases have been manifested as a result of the terrible things we've given and done to our bodies. People on the whole are much heavier now than they were years ago, before today's high standards came about.

> *(Summary: Every company offers products to improve our bodies. The truth is we're sicker and fatter now as a result.* There are two slight signs of trouble here. First, it took two sentences to summarize the paragraph, which is always something to be investigated, and sentence 3 follows sentence 2 logically but the text doesn't spell the transition out. We could add a connector, and make the two sentences one: *"But ironically we're sicker and fatter now. . . ."* Second, it's not clear why ads telling people their bodies need work should make people fatter, so the logic of that should be explained.)

Bulimia and anorexia nervosa are two diseases commonly suffered by young women who feel they are overweight. Oftentimes, the victims never had anything to worry about in the first place, weight-wise. Last summer I spent a lot of time with my sister, and I was given the opportunity to get to know her friends really well. Iris was one of her long-term friends who I had never known personally. It had never dawned on me that she was extremely skinny, to the point of being bony. She admitted to us over dinner that she was resorting to extreme measures, meaning throwing up most of the food she took in. Since this was the first I had heard of the problem, I probed a bit. She told us of her bingeing and purging, "but you have to consume food which will easily come back up, stay away from breads." I was shocked. Here sat next to me a vigilant worshipper of the much desired and sought-after perfect body.

(Summary: Bulimia and anorexia nervosa are two diseases commonly suffered by young women and sometimes men. Last summer I got to know my sister's friends. Iris admitted she was bulimic. Whoa. We've got transition problems. There's no visible connection between sentence 1 and our abstract's previous sentence; there's no visible tie between sentence 1 and sentence 2; and it takes three sentences to summarize the paragraph. We need to add explicit transitions where they exist, resequence where they don't, and reparagraph to mark the major changes of topic.)

Even though Iris had received professional help from different psychologists, her obsession just wouldn't go away. Fat has become one of the ultimate taboos of our society. The advertisers have made sure of that. Last summer, I went to a modeling interview. I was told I had potential. In the next breath, the woman asked me, "How much weight do you think you need to lose?" Succumbing to the insult, I feebly offered, "Fifteen pounds?"

(Summary: Iris's problem wouldn't go away. Advertising has made fat one of our ultimate taboos. At an interview I was asked how much weight I needed to lose and guessed fifteen pounds. Problems of transition and paragraph unity continue here. Sentence 1 seems to belong to the previous topic, sentence 2 doesn't seem to connect with the sentences before or after it, and sentence 3 leaves us hanging. I'd put sentence 1 into a paragraph devoted to Iris's story, put sentence 3 into the next paragraph, and write a better thesis statement than sentence 2 to head it.)

"To start" was the woman's reply. At the time, I weighed 140 pounds and in height I was just inches from the 5'7" mark. The question is, have we gone too far? Through the infliction of unsightly norms, have we set irreversible trends? Perhaps a reduction in advertising, period, is what we need to see next. Then, as people become unaccustomed to seeing perfect people every day, the incorporation of imperfect, real people can take place. Then people might be able to relax a little and be more at ease with their unique, human bodies.

(Summary: "To start," the woman said. I wasn't fat then. Have we gone too far? Maybe we should reduce advertising until we become accustomed to imperfect people again. We seethe same kinds of problems again: too much apparently unrelated material in a paragraph, paragraph breaks in the midst of things or major topic changes without paragraph breaks, and transitions not spelled out.)

A rewritten abstract that addresses these problems might go like this:

Last summer, when I met some of my sister's friends, I was horrified to discover that her friend Iris, an apparently normal girl, was bulimic. Then I began to notice how many diseases and neuroses about our bodies all us supposedly normal people actually have—bulimia and anorexia nervosa, for example. What causes this? I think it's advertising and the media: Every movie, every company is telling us our bodies aren't good enough by presenting us with impossible standards to compare ourselves to. For example, once when I weighed 140 pounds, a woman at a modeling interview told me I'd have to lose fifteen pounds—"to start!" Something has to be done—perhaps limiting the amount of advertising we see—until people are once again at ease with their human bodies. ❖

So careful attention to your abstract can teach you a lot, but I don't want you to think you have to work so hard. If you simply scribble an abstract off the cuff and note that it says something and says it in plain English, or you just summarize the essay to a friend in conversation, it will be the most profitable five minutes in your whole writing process.

THINGS TO DO

1. From the following abstracts, write a half-page revision plan discussing changes you would make in the drafts they were made from.

    a. Because information learned in conjunction with music is retained accurately and for a long time, music can be considered an effective learning tool. Rating a child's musical abilities can cause egotism, self-doubt, or total rejection of music. While providing educational benefits, music also promotes creativity and reveals the beauty surrounding knowledge—an essential in the learning process. Music when incorporated into the school curriculum must not be performance-oriented or stressful in any way.

b. Most articles on surviving in the backcountry tell how to live off the land, but I think they ignore prevention. Real survival is knowing how to avoid the dangerous situation in the first place. One survival article showed how a guy snowed in on a deer hunt couldn't start a fire, couldn't retrace his steps, etc. With a little forethought, none of this would have happened. An important factor in survival is keeping your head. Once I went goose hunting without my pack, got lost, panicked, and spent a cold night out. I learned my lesson. To survive, you don't need to know how to live off the land—just take the right equipment and keep your head.

2. Rewrite the abstracts in activity 1 to improve the essay as much as you can.

3. Pick an essay in this book and abstract it three different ways:

a. Write a constructed abstract (p. 126).
b. Write an in-one-breath abstract (p. 131).
c. Write a descriptive abstract (p. 127).

4. Find an essay you admire in a magazine (not a newspaper) and abstract it in the three ways listed in activity 3.

5. Write a first draft of an essay and do the following tasks with it:

a. Write a constructed abstract of the draft.
b. Write an in-one-breath abstract of the draft.
c. Using both abstracts, write a half-page critique of the draft, listing problem spots in the abstracts and mapping out revision strategies to solve them.
d. Write a new abstract incorporating the solutions in c.

6. With the abstract produced in activity 2, 3, 4, or 5, do the following tasks:

   a. Circle all connectors (p. 118).
   b. Add connectors between sentences that lack them.
   c. If there are places where connectors don't seem to work, resequence the sentences of the abstract to eliminate the problem.

Chapter 8

BEGINNING, ENDING, AND TITLING

Beginnings, endings, and titles are worth special attention. Not only are they key moments of contact with your reader, they're superb touchstones, telling you all kinds of things you want to know about the essay. Essays that can begin well, end well, and be titled well are usually good through and through. Too many writers treat these three tasks as formulaic rituals, conventions to be followed by rote and without reference to the reader: For the introduction, they write a flaccid inverted-funnel paragraph; for the conclusion, a needless summary; and for the title, a flat declaration of the topic. Who cares if these things all come off as dead as last week's news? We do. So let's explore some alternatives to the empty conventions.

Beginnings

When you call a stranger on the phone, you often know everything you want to say except the first sentence. Once a thing's under way, momentum helps carry it along—but how do you begin?

The basic rule of introductions is, *if you can't find a good opener, have none.* No introduction at all is better than an empty, formulaic one. Perhaps because in social situations introductions are formulaic, meaningless things—"And now, a man who needs no introduction . . ."—we think of essay introductions the same way—like this opener to an essay telling how linguist Frank Smith feels about teaching reading via drills and exercises:

> After reading Frank Smith's book *Reading Without Nonsense* you could tell that the author has very definite views on how to teach people to read. He lets the reader know exactly how he feels about different techniques of teaching children to read. One example he cited was how he felt about children doing reading drills and exercises.

Here's how an essay (on a slightly different question) that refuses to waste a word gets on with it from the very first sentence:

Frank Smith feels that reading via food labels, street signs, and board games is a good way to learn to read, because to learn to read, children need to relate the words to something that makes sense.

Read through your latest draft until you find a sentence that really starts something, that wades into your substance, and throw away everything above it. Become comfortable with the idea that it takes a while to write your way into the essay's real business, and look at the first paragraph or page of the first draft with the *assumption* that it was a warm-up and should be trashed. Remember also that a good introduction is one of the two hardest parts of the essay to write (the other being the conclusion), so you will probably discover it quite late in the writing of the first draft, since you're supposed to compose by writing the easiest part first and the hardest last.

The Three Tasks of an Introduction

Introductions are worth keeping if they do three tasks:

Declare the topic: Let the reader know what the essay he's going to read is about.

Say, "Read me, read me!"

Define the purpose: Imply that the writing has a task to perform and that the task matters.

An introduction can skip some of these three if it has something better to do—remember the carp article (p. 65), where the author purposely refused to say what the topic was until the last word of the essay.

Declaring the topic. This is easy and doesn't amount to much—in fact, it's hard to write an introduction that doesn't do this. So do it fast. *A whole sentence is too much*, because it invariably sounds like, "In this essay I'm going to talk about . . ." Reveal topic as you're doing more important things:

If you're an average, somewhat chubby individual wanting to get some healthy, not overly strenuous exercise, you should consider bicycling.

When you start working as a pizza delivery person, you're going to get a new view of life.

Most of us, if we're honest with ourselves, will admit we've thought about committing suicide.

Each of these first sentences reveals the topic in passing, while it does the more important jobs of beginning to define purpose and win an audience.

Saying "Read me, read me!" A beginning says, "Read me, read me!" by winning our interest and making us want to read it—it's a sales pitch.

I don't have to tell you how to do it because you know how: Just write openers like the ones that make you want to read on. Audiences and tastes differ, but most people agree on what writing that wants to be read looks like and can spot it in the first sentence. Here are some openers that make you want to read more:

> In late July 1982, Presidential Press Secretary James Brady sued the gun company that made the pistol used by John Hinckley.
> Einstein did it. Shakespeare did it. Howard Hughes did it.
> Grandpa drank too much beer the day he jumped into the pool wearing his boxer shorts.
> Most Americans do not get to experience the excitement and discomfort of train travel very often.
> If you'd like to murder somebody but receive a penance of one year's probation and a small fine, try this: get yourself blind, staggering out-of-control drunk some night and just run over some guy as he walks across his own lawn to pick up his newspaper.
> Many gun control advocates believe in the common-sense argument that fewer guns should result in fewer killings. But it may not be that simple.

These openers make you want to stop reading:

> Handguns are a major concern to many people in the United States.

> Driving under the influence of alcohol is a serious problem in the United States today.

> Bilingual ballots have been in the spotlight for many years.

Everybody can write "Read me" openers. Those who don't just think they're not supposed to; as soon as they get permission to do it, they do it.

Not all sales pitches are fireworks and cutesiness; you can sell with dignity and with class too. My favorite first sentence is the famous beginning of George Orwell's "Shooting an Elephant":

> In Moulmein, in Lower Burma, I was hated by large numbers of people—the only time in my life that I have been important enough for this to happen to me.

You can't say "Read me" more quietly or more powerfully than that.

Defining purpose. The reader needs to know more than that the essay is about something and that it's in a voice he wants to listen to; he needs to know the essay has a job to do and that the job is worth doing—that it *matters.* What the essay is going to give him has to seem worth having. Chapters 1 and 4 talked about writing to some real purpose, so we know how; all the opener has to do is *let the reader see that you are doing it.*

Two case studies. How well do the following beginnings do the three tasks of an opener? Here's the first paragraph of C. S. Lewis's *A Preface to Paradise Lost:*

> The first qualification for judging a piece of workmanship from a corkscrew to a cathedral is to know *what* it is—what it was intended to do and how it is meant to be used. After that has been discovered, the temperance reformer may decide that the corkscrew was made for a bad purpose, and the communist may think the same about the cathedral. But such questions come later. The first thing is to understand the object before you: as long as you think the corkscrew was meant for opening tins or the cathedral for entertaining tourists, you can say nothing to the purpose about them. The first thing the reader needs to know about *Paradise Lost* is what Milton meant it to be.

We know Lewis's subject: How did Milton mean for *Paradise Lost* to be used? We know his task: to tell us how Milton intended his poem to be used so that we may judge it truly. We know that this should *matter* to us: Until we have what Lewis offers us, he implies, we are doomed to misconstrue Milton's poem.

Has Lewis written in a voice designed to make us want to hear it talk on? That depends on who we are. You can't write to everyone, and Lewis doesn't try. He's writing to college literature students primarily, so he speaks in a voice which is learned—to win our respect—but also personal (in terms of *you*) and mildly witty (corkscrews and cathedrals) and in strong, plain language ("know *what* it is"). I think he does well.

Let's look at another writer doing the same three tasks in a different style to a different audience. The writer is Robert Schadewald, writing in *The TWA Ambassador,* TWA's in-flight magazine. The essay is called "How Do It Know?"

> What is the most remarkable device in the world? The electron microscope? Perhaps it's the brain scanner? Or the side-looking radar?
>
> No, it's something that has no electronic circuits, not even any moving parts. According to a joke that made the rounds a few years back, the most remarkable device, in the opinion of one gentleman, is the Thermos bottle, for it keeps hot things hot and cold things cold. Asked what's so remarkable about that, the man replied in awe, "How do it know?"
>
> How indeed.
>
> It used to be that an educated person could keep up with things, could understand how things work. . . . Today's space-age technology leaves the layman out in the cold; the technical specialist is hard-pressed to keep up with developments in his very own narrow field.
>
> Before technology runs away with us all, we've prepared this "uncomplicated" guide for you, explaining how things work. We've chosen six modern-day wonders most of us encounter every day. . . . We con-

sulted experts in each of the various fields, and asked them that simple question, "How do it know?"

Schadewald's topic is clear: how six common modern devices work. His task is clear: to explain to the reader how the machines around him work. We have no reason to read except mild curiosity—we don't *need* to know how a telephone works—so Schadewald invents a need. Technology is running away from us, he says; we're "left out in the cold." Fight back, Schadewald says; I'll restore to you your lost sense of control over machines.

Does Schadewald's introduction say, "Read me, read me"? That depends on who you are and what you want. Schadewald is obviously trying to sell the essay as light entertainment, just the sort of thing the typical traveler wants to kill thirty minutes of flight time without having to work hard. The essay tells jokes, it's chatty and clever and easygoing, it breaks grammatical rules on purpose and for fun. The style is saying, "If you're looking for something technical or profound, this isn't for you."

Different kinds of writing value the three tasks differently. Scientific and technical writing values "Read me" hardly at all, on the theory that purpose (the information the writing offers and its usefulness to the professional reader) is so overwhelming that sales pitches are unnecessary: No doctor ever had to be won over to read about new surgical techniques. As a result, few people read scientific and technical writing for fun. Academic writing values purpose highly in the sense of "What are you trying to accomplish?" but doesn't think about importance and usefulness enough, so when you write in school you have to keep asking yourself, "Why am I doing this and what good is it to the reader?" Entertainment journalism values "Read me" so much it may stoop to misrepresenting the facts to do it: I recently saw a tabloid article claiming in its headline that a new baby in England's royal family had the palace gardener as a father. The article went on to confess that the gardener was just doing some royal baby-sitting. Which of the three tasks you value the most is up to you, but ignore none of them, and keep in mind that the two tasks people most often slight are earning the audience's attention and being useful.

Four Time-Tested Openers

Ideally, your opener comes to you in a flash of inspiration as you're toiling through the first draft. But if it doesn't, it turns out that most good beginnings are variations on a few basic strategies, and you can use one. Here are four.

The thesis statement. You declare up front (usually at the end of the first paragraph) the heart of what you have to say. Beginning writers like this because they can grasp its purpose easily, and teachers and other people in a hurry often like it because they can see right up front what the writer is saying. But people who write to popular audiences almost never do it, because it's usually unexciting unless the thesis is startling and provocative, like the newspaper article a while back that began, "Americans apparently like reading the newspaper more than sex." Technical writing usually demands thesis openers; use them. Don't try to be clever or entertaining then; it won't be appreciated. "Consider Nuclear Energy" (p. 386) uses a thesis opener.

The question. A question opener baldly declares the paper's task, so if your writing is weak on purpose, use this opener to keep purpose before you. You *end* your opening paragraph or passage with a question; the buildup to the question explains why that question needs to be asked and answered, and the rest of the essay works out the answer. This turns the structure of the thesis statement around: Instead of spilling the beans up front and then explaining how and why you know, this form poses a puzzle and seeks a solution. Schadewald's opener (p. 142) is a question opener, and Lewis's (p. 142) is a task that could easily be rephrased as a question: What did Milton intend *Paradise Lost* to be?

The hook. Also known as the grabber or the angle, the hook is the eye-catcher that sucks a reader into the essay like a vacuum cleaner: "The next time you are in Florida, you would do well to remember that it is illegal to have sex with a porcupine in that state" (Charles McCabe). "Polly" (p. 293) and "Dear Governor Deukmejian" (p. 378) open with hooks.

There are countless ways to hook a reader. You can start with a paradox, an idea that seems self-contradictory and therefore demands explanation—like "Americans are getting more liberal and more conservative all the time." You can tease the reader with a promise of excitement to come: "No one noticed that the world changed on August 7, 1984." You can drop the reader into the middle of things so she reads on to find out how she got there—what Latin poets called beginning *in medias res:* "The President looked unamused as he wiped the pie filling off his face." You can hook a reader with human interest, her innate willingness to care for people: "Stella Wilson listens to her baby cry and wonders where the money to feed him will come from."

Newspaper sports sections love hooks:

> A World Series involving the New York Yankees would not be official without a controversy. The 75th Series was stamped as the real thing yesterday at Yankee Stadium.

> Westside High's Cougars did what they had to and nothing more to hand Central a 24–15 defeat Saturday night.

Hooks are healthy things because they remind stiff writers that writing can be playful and dramatic and sly. But a word of caution: Since they work by cleverness and surprise, they can easily be abused. Don't promise what you can't deliver. You gain nothing by hooking a reader only to leave him hating you later. Classroom speeches are prone to this ploy: The speaker shouts, "Murder! Fire! The Martians have landed! Now that I've gotten your attention, I'm going to talk about brands of tennis shoes."

The narrative. Narrative openers work because they say "Read me" and because they get you to concretize and humanize right off the bat: "In the middle of the worst depression in our nation's history, one woman decided to leave her comfortable home and head west looking for a better life." "Given the Chance" (p. 374) and "The Last Stop for America's Busses" (p. 325) have narrative openers.

One subtype of the narrative opener always works as a last resort: the "how I came to write this essay" opener. Explain what started you thinking on the subject: "I was reading the newspaper the other day and noticed an article about the federal government taking over the Coca-Cola Company. I couldn't help thinking. . . ." This has the inherent excitement of a mind at work. It does "Read me" well, but it runs the risk of breaking our first rule about introductions—get on with it—so don't let it run on. There are examples of this kind of introduction on p. 374.

Conclusions

Conclusions are even harder than beginnings. Anyone who's ever found himself stuck in a phone conversation that has outlived its usefulness but won't die knows that. Ending is so hard that we tend to end with meaningless formulas: "Last but not least, I'd just like to thank . . ."; "And so, without further ado . . ."; "Thank you very much for your attention to this matter."

What a Conclusion Isn't

The problem is, it's very hard to figure out what a conclusion is trying to do, and you can't write until you know what you're trying to accomplish by writing. It's easier to say what a conclusion *isn't*.

It isn't a summary of the essay or repetition of the thesis. This is a shock to lots of people, but the fact is that, unless the piece is very long and utterly utilitarian (like an essay on troubleshooting your car's electrical system), a summary conclusion is a waste of time and a deadly bore. Graders like summary and repetition because they make grading easy, and students like them because they solve the problem of what to do at the end, but no one else does.

It isn't a last word. If you write a paper on the national economy, you're *not* going to end all discussion of the national economy. Yet the conclusion must say, "Here we can stop for now"—like a campsite on a walking tour, a home for the night.

It isn't necessary. It's quite okay simply to say the last thing you have to say and stop. Much to many people's surprise, essays without cymbal-crashing conclusions can read well—and a lot better than essays with a last paragraph of filler or needless repetition for conclusion's sake. There's no real conclusion to the essay called "Dad" (pp. 271–272) and it's a mistake to try to fabricate one for it.

What a Conclusion Is

A conclusion is *the place your grand design has been taking you all along*. If you ask a question, you're committed to giving the reader an answer. If you're writing a lab report, you're committed to discussing the significance of what you learned. If you begin with human interest, you're committed to returning to those people so the reader isn't left wondering what happened to them. If you begin by saying, "There's a problem," you're committed to answering the question "What should we do about it?" If you don't have a fairly inevitable ending, you probably lack a strong grand design. Fix the ending by redefining your whole structure, via abstracting.

Since an ending is determined by large structure, it's almost impossible to describe the features of a good conclusion without seeing the essay that set it up. And you can't write out the essay minus its conclusion and then stare at the computer trying to think one up; you have to plan ahead. Here are two essays that did. A student reviewed a local taco stand. His thesis was that it was okay, but nothing compared to the Mexican food he was used to back home in L.A. Here's an abstract of his essay, with his concluding sentence intact:

> When I was young, I learned to love the great Mexican food in L.A., but now that I'm here in the sticks I keep seeking a restaurant that comes up to that high standard. In that search I tried Alfredo's. It was pretty good, but hardly spectacular, and the search continues. Now, if you want real Mexican food, I know a little place not far from Hollywood and Vine. . . .

Here's an abstract of a review of a local counterculture restaurant, titled "Lily's Restaurant . . . And More":

> Lily's has a wide range of sandwiches, all tasty and reasonably priced— and more. Lily's has a clientele ranging from student hippie to lumber- jack—and more. It has soups, vegetarian meals, and friendly, casual service—and more. It's also got cockroaches, so, no thanks, I'm not going back.

But conclusions, like paragraphs or introductions, tend to fall into types. If you haven't found a conclusion yet, you can do one of the following standards, but remember: You should design the whole essay structure around it, the way you plan a whole vacation around the idea that you're driving to Yellowstone.

Some conclusions come to a decision or an answer. "Given the Chance" (p. 374) and "Exactly How We Want It" (p. 372) do this. If you begin by addressing a problem, you naturally end by deciding what's to be done about it. If you begin by asking a question, you end by answering it. This is another benefit to writing a strongly task-oriented opening: It makes your end-point obvious.

Some conclusions come full circle and return to the essay's opening. Hook introductions often end this way, and it's one of the advantages of the hook introduction that it almost hands you this concluding device. A student began a paper on a quiche restaurant by referring to the author of the bestseller *Real Men Don't Eat Quiche*, saying "Bruce Feirstein has obviously not been to Quiche Heaven," and he returned to that in his concluding line: "I don't care what Bruce Feirstein thinks; he doesn't know what he's been missing." If you begin with a human-interest narrative hook about someone, return to that person: "Perhaps, if these changes are enacted, no one will suffer the way Alice suffered again." The essay on the Mexican restaurant does this, beginning with the author's beloved L.A. haunts and returning to them. But notice that coming full circle is *not* summarizing or repeating, though it may look a little like it.

Some conclusions consider the long run. After you've arrived at your thesis and the case is complete, you explore the implications of your discovery. You get outside the argument and reflect on what it all means, see where it leads, or how you feel about what you've found. If you've argued that women are getting more into physical fitness, talk about the long-term implications for women's self-image, standards of female attractiveness in our culture, and sexism. This can work with personal writing, too. Once a student wrote a narrative dramatizing the strong bonds among her peer group when she was fourteen and on the swimming team. She had no way to end, so I suggested a long-run conclusion: Look at the essay from the perspective of today, tell the reader where the members of the group are now and what happened to the energy, innocence, and camaraderie. She added a couple of paragraphs chronicling the teen pregnancies, alcohol-related deaths, and bad marriages that had plagued the team members, and the whole essay got richer and more poignant. "A Moral Victory?" (p. 385) has a brief long-run conclusion.

If you like to dump your thesis into your first paragraph, get to know the long-run conclusion well, because *it's one of the few ways to conclude such an essay without resummarizing.*

Some conclusions are punch lines: startling surprises. If no better conclusion has come to you, you can usually end with your best insight, your snappiest line, your most sparkling thought. An essay whose thesis was that the author's best friend was the nicest, kindest, most wonderful person on earth ended like this:

> If I ever have a daughter, I'll wish for her to be just like Suzy; but if she isn't that lucky, I hope she has a best friend like the best friend I have.

The writer could have used that line anywhere in the essay, but she was wise enough to save it until the end. An essay describing a poor old quirky man who lived alone among hulks of dead refrigerators ended this way:

> He has shirts of every description and a full closet of the very short-legged, wide slacks that you always see at the Salvation Army and wonder who they could possibly fit. They fit Andy.

"Eradicat" (p. 307) and "How to Audition for a Play" (p. 315) both have punch-line endings.

Read for the Craft

Because concluding is hard to witness out of the context of the whole essay, study it by reading for the craft. Every essay or newsmagazine article you've ever read has faced, and probably solved, the dilemma of ending; watch how they do it. But don't study newspaper articles. They start with a bang, so newspapers are good places to learn about "Read me" openers, but they're structured to allow a reader to quit at any moment. So they don't conclude—they just fade away.

Titling

Most people don't take their titles seriously enough. You usually know a bad essay is bad or a good essay is good by the time you've read the title. Ask a lot of your title, and when you can't find a title that fulfills your high expectations, take that as a sign that there's something wrong with the essay. A good title should do the same three jobs a good introduction does: Declare the topic, say "Read me!," and suggest a worthwhile task to accomplish. If your title doesn't do these things, suspect that the essay doesn't either.

Think of titles in terms of degrees of excellence. The lowest degree is no title at all, but that's so obviously an announcement to your reader that you're not writing to be read that I'm going to pretend it would never enter your mind. One step up are titles that just declare topic: "Prayer in School," "Seat Belts," "Friendship," and the like. Among topic titles, the broader the topic the worse the title, just like with essays. The worst is a title like "*Hamlet.*" Better is "Imagery in *Hamlet.*" Better still is

"Images of Disease in *Hamlet.*" I suppose "Images of Gastro-Intestinal Ailments in *Hamlet*" would be best of all.

A mutant form of the topic title is the description, which tells you not the essay's *name* but what *kind* of essay it is:

A Review of the Smokehouse Restaurant
Character Sketch of Tom Russo

The best topic sentence in the world is dull. More important, since no topic, however narrow, ever made an essay, topic titles aren't good diagnostics. You can't rest until you reach the next level, where the title both indicates the topic *and* implies the thesis or task:

The Joys of Racquetball
Mark Twain: America's Finest
Fad Diets Vs. Reality
What's the Matter with Cats?
A Vote for Plastic Surgery

Titles rarely state the thesis baldly, because it's usually wordy and dull. Often the thesis is merely suggested. "A Gamble for Better Education" argues that the state should institute a lottery to help fund public education, for instance. And in art or entertainment writing, sometimes titles have a thesis connection that isn't clear until the essay is under way, like "China Syndrome," a phrase referring to nuclear power plant disasters, for an essay on the poisonous food at a local Chinese restaurant.

If your titles shy away from reflecting your thesis, you can force yourself to by using any of three title formats:

The question: "School Music: Fundamental or Thrill?"; "What Is Pornography?"
The why title: "Why I Hate Advertising"
The declarative sentence: "Breast Feeding Is Best"

If your title identifies a specific topic and promises a thesis or task, the essay probably has them too and is therefore sound. But the best titles do more, as the best essays do more: They say, "Read me, read me!" The title is the moment when you announce that you're writing to real people and you want to be read:

Messin' 'Round with Moses
Tube Addiction
Yes, Virginia, Leisure Is a Good Thing
Anatomy of the Myopic Introvert
Give me *Massive* Doses!
Killing Bambi

One time-honored way of saying "Read me" is by playing with language: an essay on jogging faddism called "In the Long Run," for instance.

Different kinds of writing value the three tasks of the title differently. Science and technical writing values absolutely precise declaration of topic and values "Read me" very little. Another kind of writing values "Read me" so highly it often forgets to declare the topic at all: An essay called "Say Something" is about mealymouthed sports commentators, and "Given the Chance" (p. 374) is about state drug rehabilitation programs. That's clearly inappropriate in technical writing and dangerous anytime, since you're counting on the reader finding your voice so fascinating he'll read on without knowing what you're talking about.

The Colon Title

Finding a title that reveals the specific topic, implies the task, and says "Read me" in a short phrase is hard. Most titles choose to do one or two at the expense of the other(s). One way around that is to stick two phrases together with a colon. Write a phrase that hooks and implies the thesis or task, put in a colon, and then write a phrase that declares the topic. If the thesis for our *Hamlet* essay is that corruption always has its source in sexual desire, our title could be "Venereal Disease: Images of Sickness in *Hamlet*." Sometimes the two halves of the colon title are reversed, and the topic comes first: "Television: The Glamour Medium."

Colon titles are a little bit long and a little bit stuffy, but they get the three jobs done, so as a diagnostic they're unequaled: A good colon title tells you a lot of good things about your essay. But remember that rules never tell a writer what to do; if you've written an essay about your father and it feels right to call it simply "Dad," do it.

THINGS TO DO

1. Describe how successfully the following openers do the three tasks of an opener discussed on p. 140:

> a. The horror of those seconds will forever haunt Cindy Ferguson. She was driving her three sons—the identical twins Tommy and Tony and her baby, Lee—to a party, when suddenly her Vega was smashed from behind. A tremendous explosion hurled her, Tony, and Lee onto the street. Cindy raced back to the car and pulled Tommy's burning body from the wreck, throwing herself on him to smother the flames. . . . As Cindy lay there on top of her son, the other

driver approached her. But when she pleaded for help, he staggered away. ("The War Against Drunk Drivers," *Newsweek*)

b. Early in Campaign '82, supporters of the statewide initiative requiring deposits for soft drinks, beer, and mineral water sold in bottles and cans had every reason to expect success. In late August, Mervyn Field's California Polls showed Proposition 11 favored by a 2–1 margin. In early October, the measure was still ahead 20 points. . . . But the early signs of support came before opponents of the measure—the bottle and can industry, brewers and soft drink makers, most labor unions and supermarket chains—unleashed the full force of their war chest. (Alan Cline, "The Life and Death of Prop. 11," *Chico News and Review*)

2. Pick three essays in this book and write a one-page essay discussing the concluding strategies they use. Do they use one of the four strategies discussed on pp. 147–48? If not, what are they doing?

3. Here is a list of titles from essays on censorship. For each title, answer the question "Which of a title's three tasks does it do?" (p. 140).

a. Why Is Censorship Needed?
b. Who's to Judge?
c. From a Child's Point of View
d. You Want to Read *What?*
e. Censorship: The Deterioration of the First Amendment
f. Censorship

4. Take the titles in activity 3 that don't do all three tasks and rewrite them so they do; make up thesis or content if you need to. Example: "Eating" → "Tomorrow We Diet: My Life as an Overeater."

5. Pick an essay in this book and write four titles for it, one in each of the following formats:

a. The question
b. The *why* statement
c. The declarative sentence
d. The colon title

Chapter 9

MAKING THE DRAFT
LONGER OR SHORTER

It's time to practice the writer's art of writing to the assigned length.

Beginning writers usually think an essay should be as long as it takes to do the task at hand—you write till you've said it all. That almost never works, because in life there's almost always a length limit: The boss says, "Fill three pages and no more." Students often think length limits are invented by teachers, but the professional world is more pitiless about length than teachers are. Once I wrote a 2000-word essay for a national newsmagazine. The editor said, "I like it, but we have a 1050-word maximum." I said okay, and sent her a cut version that was 1100 words. She said, "I like it—but you have to cut fifty words." I said okay, and did. Two days later, she called and said, "We're seven words too long; which seven words would you like to cut?"

In the beginning of your career, the problem is usually that the draft is too short. But after you've been writing for a few years, the problem reverses itself, and the draft is almost always too long. So we'll talk about making drafts longer and shorter, and if you don't need both skills now, you might later.

Two beginning principles: First, don't think about length until late in the writing process—after drafting, after rethinking. Until that time, just write. If the assigned length is long and you shoot for it, it will just give you writer's block and make you pad; if it's short and you try to stay within it, you'll probably never write the ten pages of discovery draft it takes to find out where the final three-page essay really begins.

Second, always try to have too much text. Having too much makes you relax, because you're past the terror of the Required Page Limit, and it makes the final product better, for the same reason that big high schools have better football teams than small ones—a bigger pool to pick from. Brainstorm mountains, write out reams, then keep however much the boss will give you room for.

Making It Shorter

You make a text shorter in one of two ways: Say it all, only faster, or say less.

To say it faster, we need only notice that Chapter 4 reduced essays to single sentences (thesis statements) and Chapter 7 reduced them to paragraphs (abstracts), so any coherent text can be reduced to any size. Just to prove it, here are successively shrunk versions of "A Moral Victory?" (in its full 500-word form on p. 375):

The half-size version:

> In 1984, some white male police officers sued San Francisco, claiming they were the victims of reverse discrimination because they had been passed over for promotion in favor of less qualified minority officers. The U.S. Supreme Court has refused to hear their case. This may seem to be a victory for minorities, but isn't it really a loss for us all?
>
> I'm married to a white male, and I've seen a lot through his eyes. He's an engineering professor who has worked in industry for thirteen years. Unfortunately, reverse discrimination is for him a fact of life. Employers are forced by federal quotas to give preference to Hispanics, blacks, and women.
>
> My sister is also an engineering professor in the same system, but basically what she wants she gets, because the quota system makes her a sought-after commodity. It took my sister a long time to appreciate the injustice of this.
>
> Right now her department is interviewing for a new instructor. The department doesn't actually have an open position, but the university has funding for a certain number of faculty who meet "specific criteria." The candidate is black, so of course she's irresistible!
>
> We feel an awful sense of collective guilt in this country for what we've done to women and minorities, and we should. But can we really right past wrongs by creating new ones? I don't propose that we forget our past, but I think it's time to forgive ourselves and move on. ❖

The quarter-size version:

> The U.S. Supreme Court has refused to hear a reverse discrimination case concerning San Francisco policemen. Is this a victory

for minorities or a loss for us all? My husband is an engineering professor. Unfortunately, reverse discrimination is for him a fact of life. Employers are forced by federal quotas to give preference to Hispanics, blacks, and women.

My sister is also an engineering professor, but basically what she wants she gets, because the quota system makes her a sought-after commodity. Right now her department has a job that's open only to people who meet "specific criteria"—being black, for instance.

Americans feel guilty for past racism and sexism, and we should. But it's time to forgive ourselves, and move on. ❖

The eighth-size version:

Reverse discrimination isn't a victory for minorities, it's a loss for us all. For my husband, reverse discrimination is a fact of life. But my sister gets anything she wants, since she's female, and her department has a job that's open only to minorities. We should feel guilty about our past, but it's time to forgive ourselves and move on. ❖

The sixteenth-size version:

Reverse discrimination is a loss for us all. My husband suffers from reverse discrimination daily, but my sister gets anything she wants, since she's female. Guilt is good, but let's forgive ourselves and move on. ❖

On the head of a pin:

Reverse discrimination is a loss for us all; let's forgive ourselves and move on. ❖

Saying it all faster is a great intellectual exercise—nothing will make you know your own essay better—but the results are usually displeasing, like watching a videotape on fast forward. You'll probably get a better essay with the second approach, saying less. You think, "I'd like to talk about the San Francisco case and my husband's experiences with reverse discrimination and my sister's change of heart and the hiring her department is doing, but I just don't have the time, so instead I'll focus on my sister's change of heart and leave everything else for another day." Think of the draft as a pie, and the final version will be only a slice.

The secret lies in shaking the notion that you're cutting error or waste. What you cut here isn't bad, and you don't throw it away; you save it for another essay.

You need a sense of the essay's *tasks;* you need to be able to say, "The essay is basically doing these three (or six or however many) jobs." "A Moral Victory?" does five large things: states its thesis, backs it up with three examples (the husband's experience, the sister's change of heart, and the department's hiring policy), and uses the San Francisco court case as a prompt (not in that order). "Why I Never Cared for the Civil War" (p. 383) describes Shawni's feelings about grades, confesses she didn't learn much from school, describes a typical counterproductive classroom, argues that tests are hindrances, defines ideal goals for education, offers three examples of alternative instruction (discussion instead of lecture, experiential learning, and broader-based grading), and closes with the example of real education working in her fifth-grade classroom (the pond water experiment). If you articulated a grand design when you were restructuring (p. 104), that will list your major tasks for you. Once you have the list, you just pick one or two items.

You could just select a few of the draft's tasks at random, but usually you see priorities: Job 2 is most important; job 3 merely supports and expands that; job 7 is just a way of introducing the issues; and so on. So you do the high-priority items. For Angela, most important is the thesis, next important is the supporting evidence, and least important is the prompt. For Shawni, priorities aren't as obvious, but she might decide to save the issue of grading until another essay, or focus entirely on testing and alternatives to conventional recall tests, or just write a narrative about the joys of the pond water experiment.

Representing the draft graphically helps this kind of shortening. Write an outline or draw a map; then just cross out a few major sections of the graphic, or pick a section or two of the graphic to be your new essay:

PRUNING

PICKING A SECTION

1st draft   2nd draft

Making a text shorter is pretty easy, but it's good preparation for the harder problem you face when the teacher says "Give me five pages" and you've run dry after two paragraphs. Again, there are two approaches, saying it in more detail and saying more, and again the second is usually a better solution than the first.

Making It Longer by Filling In

Saying it in more detail does *not* mean saying exactly the same thing in twice as many words. It means filling in blanks and providing background detail, explaining yourself more fully, adding illustrative examples, citing statistics. Think of it as responding to a reader's persistent "Tell me more about that." This rewriting doesn't break new ground; it just clarifies, expands, elucidates what's there. An essay is like a drawn portrait. The two-paragraph version is like a happy face—nothing but a circle for the head, a curved line for the mouth, two circles for eyes. Now we're going to go in and start adding details—lips, ears, pupils. Then we can add details to the details—chapped skin on the lips, ear hair, bloodshot eyes.

We can keep adding detail upon detail in effect forever, like sharpening the resolution on a TV screen by increasing the number of pixels.

As always in *The Writer's Way*, you find details to add by asking questions and answering them. And there is a limitless supply of good questions to ask about any text. Here are six productive questions Angela could have asked herself about just her third paragraph in "A Moral Victory?":

> What are the exact proportions of white male to nonwhite, nonmale engineers in her husband's field?
> What are the quotas? What percentages is his company required to have?
> How has affirmative action hiring affected him or his work? How precisely has he suffered?
> How qualified are the affirmative action hirees he's worked with?
> What long-term effects does he think reverse discrimination will have on his discipline?
> What does he say about all this? (Quote him.)

This kind of expanding (like most writing tasks) is pretty obvious in narratives or descriptions. We know that you can tell a story in a sentence ("I got arrested for speeding last night") or you can take two pages just describing the experience of being fingerprinted and the sensations it caused in you, and two more pages describing the features of the cell where you spent the night. Writing classes often try to make this point by asking students to describe a room, then demonstrating that the describing is never done—there is always another level of detail you haven't gotten to.

To make this point, I asked my students to write narratives of recent experiences, just as they might tell them to a friend; then I asked them to take a small portion of the narrative and rewrite it under a microscope, as full of detail as possible. Here's the story Mark Wilpolt told:

> Yesterday the rain stopped and the sun came out. I had been doing homework all day, so I jumped on my bike to experience the drying streets. Along the way I decided to turn the bike ride into a trip to the gym. I arrived at the gym and worked out on the Nordic Track for fifteen minutes. On the way home, I took the scenic route along the creek, enjoying the fall colors, the clear sky, and the foothills, with their new patches of snow, in the background. Who says exercise isn't fun? ❖

And here is Mark's fully realized description of getting from the gym front door to the workout machine:

The entrance to the Sports Club is its own little world. As I walked through the lobby, the day care was on the right. A dozen kids running around the plastic playground as perfect smiling employees in their twenties look on—a Norman Rockwell scene for the 90's. The beauty salon is next: women with big hairdos and long, fluorescent fingernails giving their customers that extra little something they can't get from the workout floor. Then the big-screen TV, surrounded by comfy sofas, and the snack bar, tempting you to just skip the exercise and vedge.

I hand my card to the girl at the front counter. Whoever is on duty, it's always the same: a bubbly smile and a musical "Hello, how are you today?, have a nice workout" as she zips my card through the computer, like she's been waiting all day for me to show up and make her shift. They must major in Smiling, the people who get hired for that position. Tough job.

Next I must negotiate my way past the aerobics room. Why they make that whole wall one giant window of glass I'll never know. Is it so women can see the class going on inside and feel guilty because THEY don't look like that, or so men can watch the proceedings and get their heart rate up in anticipation of their workout? Whichever the case, there's a bench right there in the hall inviting everyone to sit and stare. As I pass, I want to sit and ogle the women of all shapes and sizes who are jumping and twisting and sweating in their Spandex. Of course they'd probably revoke my membership.

In the Big Room, a dozen machines, none of which I know the name of, for shoulders, thighs, chest, back, quads, biceps, even a machine to exercise your NECK for heaven's sake. A ten-thousand-dollar machine to exercise your NECK? Also there's a fleet of Stairmasters, a bank of treadmills, a rank of stationary bicycles, a squadron of rowing machines—and the Nordic Track. None of them going anywhere, but some of them being driven pretty hard. The humorless faces of the exercisers say, "This is serious business."

All the machines call to me, "Me, do me first, No, work on your arms first," but it's hard to hear them because a dozen TV sets suspended in rows where the wall meets the ceiling are blaring, "Watch ME instead!" No way to avoid it—you work out and you watch TV. "Wheel of Fortune" is on. I'm trapped. I get on the Nordic Track and stare. The clue is "Person," five words. The champ has the wheel.

> "I'd like an S, please."
> "Yes, two of them!" DING, DING. "Spin again!"
> "I'd like an R, please."
> "Yes, there are FIVE R's!" DING, DING, DING, DING, DING.
> The champ buys a couple of vowels. ❖

Similarly, any fact-based writing is infinitely expandable (see Chapter 15 for more practice in this art). There is always more to say if we imagine a reader who is more ignorant than the one before. Imagine telling a reader how to change a flat tire, in various degrees of detail:

Short version: Remove the hubcap.

Longer version: Remove the hubcap with the tire iron.

Still longer: Find the tire iron. It's a long iron bar. Stick one end under the lip of the hubcap and pry until the hubcap comes off.

Even longer: Find the tire iron. It's a long iron bar and is probably alongside your jack, either in the trunk or under the hood. Stick one end under the lip of the hubcap anywhere along the circumference and pry until the hubcap comes off.

Longest so far: Check to see if you have hubcaps—Frisbees of shiny metal covering your lug nuts. If you have one, you have to remove it. Find the tire iron. It's a long iron bar and is probably alongside your jack, either in the trunk or under the hood. If you want to stay clean, be careful—it, like the jack, is likely to be pretty yucky if it's been used before. Grasping the iron in your left hand (if you're right-handed), stick the end that is flattened and slightly canted under the lip of the hubcap anywhere along the circumference and push hard on the other end with the flat of your right hand. The hubcap should pop off. If it doesn't work, push harder. Don't worry—you can't hurt the iron or the hubcap. Keep prying until the hubcap comes off, whatever it takes. If it's stuck, try different spots around the lip. Above all, DON'T wrap your right hand around the bar when you're prying— if you do, when the hubcap comes loose, your fingers will be crushed between the iron and the tire or fender.

The infinite expandability of information is why biographies written about the same life can be 100 words long, in the encyclopedia, or five volumes. The life hasn't gotten longer, any more than the portrait gets physically larger when we add eyelashes and mole hairs—we're just looking more closely.

The tricky part is realizing that *arguments or thought processes can be expanded just like information can*. Shawni could easily expand "Why I Never Cared for the Civil War" to book length by researching the degree to which American schools use the lecture-and-test approach to teaching, citing successful classroom alternatives to it, and detailing how they work and why they succeed. Chapter 16 is all about how to do that, so consult it now if you want to see the process in operation.

Making It Longer by Going Further

An even better way to lengthen is to look at the draft and say to yourself, "Okay so far—where do we go next?" You're breaking new ground, and the draft is just a launching pad for the new, larger task. If the first way of lengthening was like adding facial details to a portrait, this way of lengthening is like continuing a road trip: we've already driven from New York to Ohio, and now it's time to get back in the car and do the next stretch of road. Just as there is always another layer of detail to add, there is always somewhere to go next.

This skill is very powerful, because it works best with arguments, where the problem of adding length is the greatest for most of us. It's also something we encounter in this book time and again. It's what we'll do throughout Chapter 16, where we use a sentence or two of draft as a springboard to a few paragraphs of provocative, open-ended discussion about the issues raised there. It's what we'll do in Chapter 10, where we practice the art of reacting to a draft by suggesting connections and extensions that might be included in a revision. It's what we did in Chapter 5, where we brainstorm and free write and loop, except that the prompt for the brainstorming is now a complete draft. It's what we do in Chapter 17, where the networking conference on p. 360 shows how no argument is ever the Last Word because the conversation always goes on and on. It's what we do in Part V, where we sculpt the term paper project to fit the assigned space (p. 402). Over and over again, writing comes down to this fundamental mental game: Write something, then look at it as a starting place, a spark to kindle bigger visions.

Going further comes down to asking two questions: "What's the bigger issue my issue is a little version of?" and "What's the next task that has to be done?" Here are some larger issues to raise and questions to ask next for some of the essays in this text.

"Why I Never Cared for the Civil War":
Some bigger issues:

> Alternatives to the back-to-basics movement
> Why students don't learn
> Current trends in educational reform

Some questions to ask next:

> So why aren't the schools rushing to adopt your suggestions? How can we make them do it?

How does this approach translate to other, more fact-based disciplines like math?

How can we teach entrenched teachers the new approach?

"A Moral Victory?":
Some larger issues:

What changes are occurring in our culture's attitudes toward affirmative action?

Have we made progress? Is the problem of inequity solved? Have we abandoned the cause or changed our minds?

What have been the consequences of the affirmative action program?

Some questions to ask next:

What is the counterargument in favor of quotas?

If we decide we don't like quotas, what do we do now? Do we scrap affirmative action entirely, or is there something short of quotas that works?

All issues connect with all other issues eventually, the way all roads run into each other, so you can continue the journey started by the draft until it takes you anywhere and everywhere. If you start writing about doing away with lecture-based classes and keep going, you'll eventually run into school funding, back to basics, why Johnny can't read, the effect of TV on learning, the effect of tenure on schools, teaching values and ethics, the goal of education and the role of the schools in a free society, student repression and disenfranchisement in American schools, and the antagonism in our society between equality and capitalism. And, just as all back roads eventually run into superhighways, there is no such thing as an issue so trivial that it doesn't lead to big issues, if you have the time: An essay on where to take children on a rainy day leads, in time, to child-raising philosophies, the role of children in our culture, how much we undervalue children, how we deny them fundamental rights, child neglect, child abuse, institutionalized ageism, the movement to empower the young, government funding of family services, teen suicide, American contemporary spiritual poverty, and the role of the church in our society.

Remind yourself that you're trying to make the draft *longer*, not *better*. You're not doing this rewrite because the draft is flawed; you're doing it because the draft did its job well and it's time to move on to *the next* task. Now that you've shown that grading is destructive to learning, it's time to suggest superior alternatives to grading; then it's time to talk about why schools are inherently resistant to the alternatives; then it's time to explore ways to change the schools so they're less resistant; and so on.

WRITERS' WORKSHOP

Making Arguments Longer

When you write arguments is when you're most likely to quickly run dry—you state your thesis, give your reasons, and there's nothing more to say. So let's practice breaking out of that trap. As always, the easiest way to see revision possibilities is to ask other people to read the draft. Ask readers to tell you what tasks remain to be done. Ask them to verbalize their "Tell me more" reactions. Ask them where the argument leads and what bigger issues it connects with.

Here's the process in action. Below are two student arguments that ran out of steam after a paragraph or two. The authors distributed copies to their classmates and asked them to list essay-extending questions about the draft, questions that would open doors, turn the authors on to grand new possibilities, and take the draft further down the road. After the essays I've listed some of the readers' questions, separated into the three types of door-opening questions in this chapter: How can you fill out the portrait more?; What are the big issues this issue is a small version of?; and What is the next task?

SEX AND TV
ANNETTE BYRD

Do you hate turning on the TV and all you see are people touching each other sexually and some taking off their clothes? Well, I'm tired of it. There is much more to human relationships than sex. Yes, some people would agree that sex has a lot to do with a relationship, but sex on TV is what I'm most annoyed with. Sex is enticing and sex does make products sell, but the question is, should sex be thrown around like it's yesterday's lunch? I feel that something has to be done. It would be great if the media would monitor the shows that we see, but in reality they want to broadcast what will sell, and sex sells.

Questions for Annette

1. Filling out:

What are some examples of how sex is portrayed on TV?
How does TV use sex to sell things?
What exactly are the messages we're being sent about sex by
  TV?
What is the price we pay in our lives for this cheapening of
  sex?

2. The larger issues:

How our culture treats sex
Healthy and unhealthy sexuality
How TV influences our values and beliefs
Our culture's portrayal of women
How advertising degrades and corrupts us

3. The next task:

How can we stop the marketing of sex?
Who is ultimately responsible?
How did this get started?
What other ways are there that TV cheapens our lives?

TYRANT!

TRICIA IRELAND

Christopher Columbus should not be regarded as a national hero.
He was a terrible man who worked only for selfishness and greed.
He was not the first on his expedition to spot land; a man named
Roderigo was. But according to his own journal, Columbus took
credit because the first to spot land was to receive a yearly pension
for life.

When Columbus landed in the Bahamas, he took the natives
by force and made them his slaves. Hundreds he sent back to Spain;
others were held captive in their own country. He made them bring
him a monthly quota of gold, and when they did they received a
copper coin necklace. If they were found without a necklace, their
hands were cut off and they were left to bleed to death.

I don't know why we teach our children to admire and respect
Columbus. There exists a terrible amount of ignorance regarding
the truth around him. It's time to teach the truth. Columbus Day
shouldn't be celebrated, and Columbus himself shouldn't be seen
as anything but the cruel tyrant he was.

Questions for Tricia

1. Filling out:

What else did Columbus do, good and bad?—tote up his virtues and vices.

What's the argument for the other side—that he was a great man—sound like?

What's the rest of his story? How did he get the idea to go exploring? How did he die? And so on.

How did the Columbus myth get started?

2. The larger issues:

What's a hero?

How do we pick our heroes? How should we do it?

Tradition vs. the ugly truth in history

The European bias in our view of history

3. The next task:

What about our other heroes, like Babe Ruth and George Washington—are they fables too? Should we also expose them?

Why does this matter, since it's ancient history?—show how this attitude still shows up in our relations with Latin American countries.

How can we change the way we teach our children history so they don't get such Eurocentric, biased views?

Who *should* be our cultural heroes, instead?

Your Turn

Here are two more short student essays. Make lists of essay-expanding questions for each essay like the ones above. Try to ask each of the three kinds of questions. If you want models, consider these questions from other places in *The Writer's Way*:

What exactly do you mean?

How do you know?

Like what, for example?

What assumptions are you basing this on?

What's the logical extension?

Where do you draw the line?

What's the philosophical antithesis?

What are the alternatives to your proposal?

What are the other consequences?

(all from Chapter 16)

So what?
Why?
        (from Chapter 6)

If you want even more inspiration, look at the other places in the book where we react to writing, hoping our reaction will prod the authors to say more: Chapter 2 (the Writers' Workshop especially), Chapter 10 (all), Chapter 15 (the sparkplug essay), and Chapter 17 (the networking conference). Remember not to argue with the essay or critique it—you're suggesting what more there is to do, not praising or blaming what's there.

OPEN THE DOOR
PAULA BONKOFSKY

College-level students shouldn't be punished, or worse, locked out of classes if they arrive late. Certainly if it becomes habit the teacher should speak with the student and affect his or her grade accordingly. But on occasion, students who are never regularly late are late because of circumstances that were out of their control. These students should be allowed to come in and participate with their class. Yes, it really is their class because they paid for it.

SEX, LIES, AND POLITICAL BASHING
KERI BOYLES

Lately, it seems as if you can't turn on the TV without seeing some political campaign commercial blasting the opposition. Instead of telling us what they stand for and what they plan to do in office if they get elected, they spend the majority of their time smearing their opponent. These commercials are exactly the reason why a lot of people are presently disgusted with politicians. Not only are they insulting to the voter, but they skirt the issues as well, focusing on their opponent's flaws instead of informing the voter on what their actual policies are and how they plan to "clean up" the messes that politicians (unlike themselves, of course!) have gotten this country into.

It's time to say enough is enough. These distasteful commercials shouldn't be allowed. Candidates should only be able to state what their beliefs and policies are, without smearing their opponent. Voters would then be able to make logical, rational decisions without being bombarded with all the other pointless garbage they are all subjected to when watching their favorite TV shows. Personally, I don't care if Clinton inhaled or not!

MORE THINGS TO DO

1. Choose an essay from Chapter 15 ("Writing to Inform") and cut it to half its length in two ways:

   a. Say it all, but twice as fast, as we did on p. 154.
   b. Cut the essay's scope in half, using the techniques on p. 154.

2. Do the two tasks of #1 above to an essay from Chapter 17 ("Writing an Argument, Part II").

3. Do Mark's assignment on p. 158: Write a brief personal narrative about an experience you've recently had, then take a single episode or scene from that story and retell it in as much detail as you can. The narrative should be a paragraph or two, the detailed scene at least two pages.

4. Do the informative writing exercise on p. 160: Briefly tell the reader how to do a task like changing a tire; then decide that the reader needs to be much more thoroughly informed, and retell part of the essay in more detail; then decide the reader needs still more information, and retell it in even greater detail. Repeat this as many times as you can.

5. Practice making an argumentative draft longer by having readers ask questions like those in the Writers' Workshop section. (1) Bring copies of an essay draft to class; (2) ask classmates to write a list of questions that will generate more text; then (3) write a revision, at least twice as long as the first draft, addressing some of those questions.

Chapter 10

PEER FEEDBACK

Up to now you've been your own tutor. But outsiders can do some things better than you, and it's time to call them in.

Having colleagues read what you've written and make comments is at the heart of all revising. You say all you have to say; then you give it to fellow writers, and they suggest all sorts of new things to think about, ask questions you didn't think to answer, and point out passages you thought were crystal clear but that they find confusing. Suddenly doors open, you've got lots more to do, and the essay can become something better than you could make it by yourself. Every writer needs this restimulation, and every piece I've ever published has been substantially improved as a result of it. If you have writer's block, it's especially helpful because when you're paralyzed, other people can see all sorts of exciting directions to go in.

Let's begin by debunking some myths about peer feedback. First, peer feedback's first task *isn't* to tell the writer "what's wrong" with the draft; instead, it's to help the writer think farther by suggesting alternatives and connections. I've had class sessions where we've discussed a student's draft for an hour and no one ever pointed out a weakness or made a correction; instead, we spent our time exploring *where the essay could go next* (that's what the chapter on making drafts longer and shorter is all about).

Second, you don't seek peer editing only for the flawed drafts. Every draft profits from peer editing, and the better the draft, the more peer editing the writer will seek, since the project is worth the extra effort.

Third, you don't seek peer feedback only when you're "done." If you wait until you've got the essay just the way you want it, you'll fight off advice as a parent fights off criticism of his children. Ask for peer editing at every stage in the writing process. Before you write at all, bounce your first thoughts off colleagues in casual conversation to see what they think. After you've written a rough first draft, ask someone to give it a quick read to tell you if you're on to something. After a cosmetic polishing, ask for proofreading and copy editing. And every day, talk your thoughts to anyone who will listen, and ask them what they think.

Yet there is a moment in the writing process when you traditionally solicit thoughtful, in-depth reader reaction: after a couple of drafts, when you're pretty sure of what you're doing. The piece isn't *finished*, but it's gone about as far as you can take it by yourself, and it's clearly worded and cleanly typed so the reader won't have to wade hip-deep in debris to read you—which is why the peer feedback chapter is here.

The Art of Taking and Giving Feedback

Most of us, even the pros, take and give feedback poorly. If you're like most writers, *no single thing will help your writing more than learning to use feedback well.* So we're going to talk about the roles of the two parties involved, the writer and the reader.

In the end, peer editing is collaboration and communication. Both parties try to say clearly what they're thinking and feeling; both parties listen hard and work to understand. The writer talks about what he's trying to do, what he's done, why he did it; the reader talks about what the reading was like, where she thinks her responses are coming from, what might be done about it. They work together to figure out what's going on in the draft and where it might go from here. Nobody is trying to win. Nobody tells anyone else what to do. Nobody is "right." Above all, the reader is doing the writer a favor.

The Writer's Role

Most writers respond to criticism in one of two calamitous ways: the defensive response and the submissive response. In the defensive response, the writer fights off everything the reader says and tries to argue the reader out of her reaction. In the submissive response, the writer assumes that anything the reader says is "right" and slavishly agrees to follow any and all suggestions.

The defensive writer thinks of feedback as a contest: The reader is trying to talk her out of doing what she wants to do, and she resists. The less the essay changes as a result of the feedback, the more victorious the writer feels.

To find out if you're prone to the defensive response, ask yourself: If a writing instructor conferred with you on your writing and said only "It's fine" and sent you home, would you feel relieved or cheated? If you said "Relieved," you're guilty of the defensive response—you're bent on escaping punishment and failure. But escape isn't what you're after in feedback; you're after assistance.

To make the defensive response go away, do any or all of the following things:

1. Write to do something to your reader, and focus the conversation on whether you did it. If you're writing to please yourself and a reader says she doesn't like paragraph three, you're likely to tell her silently to put a sock in it. If you're writing to move readers to tears or talk them into breast feeding, when a reader says she finds paragraph three cocky or unconvincing, you'll want to change it. It's like serving a tennis ball into the net: It's not an issue of ego, it's an issue of getting the serve to *work*.

2. Ask for feedback early and often, before the project becomes "finished" in your mind and suggestions feel like rejections.

3. Begin the conversation by asking questions of your reader. Good writers never just hand over the manuscript and say, "Please make it better" or "What do you think?" They attach a sheet of questions, specific things they want to know about how the piece is going:

> Do you understand the title?
> Am I saying anything new?
> When did you realize it was a satire?
> Will parents take offense?
> Was the purpose of paragraph five clear?
> The ending seems lame to me—any ideas about ways to improve it?
> Can you think of other examples I could use here?

Question-asking guarantees that you're peer editing for the right reasons, because it reminds both of you that the reader is *helping you out and doing you a favor.* If you have nothing to ask—if you can only muster vague questions like "Did you like it?," "What's wrong with it?," or "Is it okay?"—the conversation is in trouble.

4. Steer peer-editing conversations away from errors and corrections, and toward additions and extensions: What else would you like to know? Where could I go from here? What are my opponents likely to say in response, and how can I answer them? Our feelings don't get hurt when we're told, "Do it some more."

5. Don't ask your reader to tell you what to do; just ask her to verbalize her responses. You're the writer, so only you can decide what to do; but only readers can tell you *how something reads.* They share their reactions: "I was put off by this"; "I wanted to hear more here"; "This confused me." Then you decide what to do with the information. If they want to give you concrete revision suggestions ("I'd delay giving the thesis until later"), welcome them, but only you can decide whether or not to follow the advice.

6. Don't argue, explain, or justify what you've written—those are all forms of telling the reader to stifle her feedback. Instead, *listen,* ask questions until you understand what she means and what in the text caused her response, ask for revision suggestions if you wish, then *go off and decide what to do.*

7. Wait twenty-four hours before reacting to feedback. However saintly we are, a part of us wants readers to say, "It's utterly magnificent— don't change a word." So it hurts when they don't. In time the pain eases, and we're open to learning.

The submissive response looks "nicer" than the defensive response, but in the end it's just as deadly, because it too means the writer misunderstands why he's writing and why the reader is reading. You'll know you're submissive when your colleagues make suggestions during a class critiquing session and you keep saying okay to whatever anyone tells you, even when two people tell you contradictory things.

You might think the submissive response would be rare, but it isn't. More than half my students want me to just "tell them what's wrong" so they can go fix it. This springs from an attitude we've been fighting off since Chapter 1: We believe there is a thing called "good writing" or "correct writing"; our objective is to do it, and someone who knows what's "good" or "right" will simply tell us how. School drills this notion into us. Teachers mark our drafts and assign revisions that incorporate the marked changes, for instance. You should know by now why that doesn't work. Writing isn't following rules; writing is accomplishing your purposes and having your intended effect on your reader. No one else can tell you if you've done that—not even a teacher. A reader can tell you how she feels and what she'd like, but only you can decide whether that's what you choose to give. I can imagine a reader saying, "These paragraphs are really choppy," and the writer replying to himself, "Good—choppiness is just the feeling I wanted," or a reader saying, "I loved this character," and the writer replying, "Then I'd better rewrite—I wanted him to be a sexist jerk."

To cure yourself of the submissive response, do three things. First, memorize the following truism: *In any critiquing session someone will pick out the best thing in your essay and tell you to get rid of it.* That's because really good bits are unexpected, and some readers dislike anything that disturbs their tranquil slumber. Second, wait a while before deciding to follow someone's advice, and ask yourself, "Do *I want* to do this?" Third, have your work read by readers in groups (your comp class, for instance), and let the different readers talk to each other. They'll disagree with each other, of course. Everyone will want you to "fix" the essay in a different way, and while they're fighting with each other you'll either go mad trying to make them all happy or you'll realize that readers can't tell you what to do.

The Reader's Role

The reader's first job is to help the writer see alternatives and possibilities: What *else* could the essay do? Where might it go next? You do that by doing exactly what you would do in a friendly intellectual conversation if the writer spoke the draft to you instead of writing it: *Share your thoughts on the matter.* Tell the writer what you think about what he said. Ask questions about things you don't understand. If you disagree, explain why. If you agree, add to and extend the conversation. Make connections with related issues. *This conversation is more important than any suggestions you can make about the text itself,* and if you begin with text-based comments—what's good or bad about the document in front of you—you'll probably never come back and have it.

If you're wondering how this job differs from the brainstorming we practiced at the beginning of the writing process in Chapters 3 through 5, it doesn't. Brainstorming often starts with a thesis, an issue, a problem, a question; this brainstorming begins with a *draft*—that's the only difference.

The reader's second job is to let the writer know how the text reads. You can't speak for everyone, since different readers respond differently. Nor is it your job to tell the writer what or how to write. But you can say, "This paragraph confused me" or "I wanted to know more here." Writing is like playing tennis blindfolded: The writer hits the ball, and you tell him where it lands. That's why readers can advise even if they can't write as well as the author or don't know as much: They're in the audience, where the author can never go. They can see where the ball lands, and the author can't.

This kind of feedback can't be "wrong." If you say, "Paragraph one read choppily to me" or "I felt the essay didn't flow logically," the writer can't say, "No, paragraph one didn't read that way to you" or "No, you didn't feel that." Affective feedback—feedback on how the text affects you—is a natural preventive for the defensive response.

Since one reader can only say how something reads *to her*, a writer needs more readers than one. He's not trying to write by majority vote, but he is trying to filter out the personalities for a sense of how the text is working on his audience generally.

If you've done the reader's first and second jobs, there are other services you can perform.

First, you can help the writer identify the source of your reactions. You help a little if you say, "I don't trust this paragraph," but you help a lot if you add, "I think it's because of all the academic jargon." You help a little if you say, "It feels choppy," but you help a lot if you add, "I think it's because you're leaving out transitional phrases."

Second, you can suggest possible revision strategies. You help a little if you say, "The essay seems unstructured," but you help a lot if you add, "Here's one way you could organize it." You help a little if you say, "It feels choppy," but you help a lot if you add, "I think if you add *because* here the reader will see the connection."

We have to be cautious about this. It's not your job to tell the writer how to write, and anything that smacks of telling him what to do invites the defensive response or the submissive response. But if you both keep in mind that your suggestions are mere possibilities, and that the final decision always rests with the writer, specific "here's what you might do" suggestions are pearls of great price. It helps if you *don't ask the writer to accept or reject the suggestion on the spot.* Let him decide that later when he's alone, when he has only himself to answer to.

Third, you can help the writer sort out priorities by frying the biggest fish first. Time is short. Don't waste time picking at punctuation or polishing style if there are matters of purpose, tone, large-scale organization, and logic to discuss. If you point out an awkward sentence, you help a hundredth of the essay; if you find a better way to organize the essay, you help everything. You should both keep asking, what's most important? What are the three things that would help the essay the most? What's the area of greatest need?

It's usually not mechanics. Cautious readers will take refuge in line editing because it's easy, impersonal, and safe. But you only want to talk about mechanics if they're a major problem or all the more important matters have been addressed.

Finally, you can make connections and generalize. In peer editing the writer gets a few hundred pieces of reaction and advice and has to extract from the blizzard a *few* things that most need attention. So both writer and reader must *generalize:* Make broad statements that apply to the essay as a whole. You help the essay a little if you rewrite a sentence for style; you help it a lot if you say, "Generally I'd like to see more active verbs." You help the essay a little if you point out a transition problem here and a paragraph with two subjects there; you help it a lot if you say, "I'd like a stronger sense of structure—I'll bet abstracting would help."

Note patterns. This is especially true if you're line editing. If you repair thirty flawed commas in thirty separate sentences, the writer thinks he has thirty things to learn; if you see that all thirty are the same comma in the same construction in thirty different sentences, you can say, "I'd like commas after long introductory phrases and clauses," and the writer only has one thing to learn.

Peer Editing in Groups

Peer editing can get chaotic when you get twenty-five people in one room all giving feedback at the same time, so you need strict rules strictly enforced to maintain order.

First, stick to an issue once it's raised. If someone raises a question about structure, discuss structure until all comments on structure have been heard. To ensure that this happens, each speaker must obey group editing's Golden Rule: *Make what you say connect with what the previous speaker said.*

Even good, group-minded readers violate this rule with the best intentions. They come to class well prepared, with four comments to make about the draft, and *make them all at once,* in a tidy list: "I've got four things I want to say: first. . . ." When the lecture is finished, someone chooses one of the four points to address at random, and *the other three are forgotten.* Make a single point, let the group work with it until everyone's had his say about it, then make another.

Second, strive for consensus. This doesn't mean you should force everyone in the room to agree—in fact, you want to go the other way and nourish dissent—but the writer needs to know where the whole group stands on the issues raised. If someone suggests cutting the paragraph about the cuttlefish and most of the people in the room agree, the writer had better have superb reasons for overruling them. If the room is passionately divided on the issue, he knows that he has a big decision to make and that it matters. If no one but the speaker seems to care, he can do what he wishes. *But if no one reacts to the suggestion, he can't decide what to do.*

During one of my peer-editing sessions, one student pointed to a paragraph in the draft and said, "I'd cut that—it doesn't seem to fit." Someone else cried, "No—I thought that was the best part of the essay!" People immediately lined up behind both speakers, and the will of the group became clear. Everyone saw the same thing: The paragraph stood out from the rest of the essay as a thing unto itself, and it was interesting, provocative. Half the class wanted to remove it so the essay could go on about its business; the other half wanted to abandon the draft and write a new essay that pursued the richer possibilities in the outsider paragraph. Both solutions are good ones, and the class did a fine job of clarifying the writer's choices for her. But the writer only understood her choices and how important the decision was because *everybody voted.*

All you have to do is, *when you agree, say "I agree"; when you disagree, say, "I disagree."* It sounds easy, but we're reluctant. "I agree" seems simple-minded; "I disagree" seems threatening and unfriendly. You have to keep reminding yourself how important it is. Make a special effort to voice your *disagreement,* since everyone assumes that silence implies consent.

Third, translate comments into concrete revision advice: "You should do X to the draft." Classroom conversation typically starts with sentence fragments, tentative gestures toward statements, or timid questions: "Yeah, but what about the Russians?" "I was wondering about this passage. . . ." "I thought the Amish hated rock and roll." "I had trouble with that sentence." Let the conversation start there, but pursue the issues until they lead to specific *things the writer should do in the rewrite:*

You might discuss the Russians here.

You should explain how this passage connects with the argument as a whole.

You should explain here that the Amish really hate rock and roll.

We'd like to see the sentence rewritten without the *which.*

Readers don't tell writers what to do, so these suggestions aren't orders the writer must obey. If you're worried they might be taken that way, phrase the advice as *wants:* "We want a discussion of the Russians here"; "I'd like to hear more about why the Amish hate rock and roll."

Finally, connect, generalize, and prioritize. Everyone should be on the lookout for ways to tie comments together ("I think what Will is saying ties in with what Eunice said a few minutes ago"). Everyone should keep an eye on the big picture ("A lot of what we're saying seems to come down to structure"; "In different ways, we keep asking to be more fully informed"). Everyone is responsible for identifying the important stuff ("I think that's a really important point"; "I think that's something the essay really needs"). Everyone is responsible for steering the conversation away from the trivial and the particular and toward the big issues ("I'd like to get back to the question of purpose and audience—that seems crucial to me").

The Writer's Role in Group Discussion

A group needs a leader and, since the writer has the most at stake and knows what he wants, he might as well be it.

This role is fraught with peril. If you can't take part without arguing with your readers, defending yourself, or justifying the draft, *say absolutely nothing except a final "Thanks for the help."* But if you have the necessary self-control, you can do yourself a lot of good.

Your main job is to keep reminding the group of the rules, which you do by prompting:

Do others agree with Nell? Could I see a show of hands?

As long as we're talking about structure, what other structural comments do you have?

Wait a minute; before you go on I'd like to know what else you'd like to tell me about style.

So what do you think I should do about it?

Maybe I could do *X.* Would that solve the problem?

Are there other places where that sort of thing happens?

Andy, I hear you disagreeing with what Sheila was saying earlier; am I right?

How big a problem is that?

So what does the essay need the most?

You can also explain what your intentions were. The readers say, "This is how it reads," you say, "This is what I was trying to do," and they say, "Here's how you might change it to get the effect you're after." But be careful. The instant you're perceived as *telling the readers they've read you wrong*, you have to stop, because you'll shut them up. Remember to begin the conversation with questions you want them to answer, so you stay focused on the idea that *they're helping you*.

Line Editing in Groups

In any group editing conversation, there will be dead spots. You will feel an urge to fill those silences with mechanical trivia: "Does the comma come inside the quotation marks or outside?" "I thought *A.M.* was capitalized." In addition, given any twenty readers, there will be at least one grammarian whose purpose in life is to pick nits about punctuation or usage. Since line editing will eat up all the time you have, and since an hour of line editing usually only helps an essay a little, you must suppress these voices by enforcing our old rules with special zeal:

> Only discuss grammar and mechanics when all bigger fish have been fried or when grammar or mechanics problems *are* the big fish.

> Discuss grammar and mechanics only in general terms. Talk only about problems that are habitual. Don't correct spelling errors; tell the writer if spelling is a problem.

> Assign priorities to all mechanical advice. Every essay needs line editing; what the writer needs to know is, how imperative is the need in this case? Are you saying, "Since we've taken care of everything that really matters, we'll tinker with spelling," or are you saying, "My God, we've got to do something about the spelling before we do anything else!"?

Peer Editing in Cyberspace

In the old days, group editing conversations were done with talk, in real time in the classroom. Now it's often done on-line. If your class has access to computers and networking, you can all edit the manuscript simultaneously, comment on each other's comments, and all keep copies of the draft and the comments.

There are some disadvantages: You miss the spark of face-to-face interaction, though with practice you'll learn to feel the faces and personalities behind the screen text. It seems slow at first, because most people type slower than they talk. But there are two advantages that dwarf these problems: You get a permanent record of everyone's thoughts (nine tenths of any spoken conversation is forgotten), and readers can log on at their leisure, over a matter of days, instead of having to produce on the spot in the midst of the shouting match.

Here's what it looks like—a student draft, followed by the same draft after my writing class reacted to it for fifty minutes on the network in the school's writing lab. First, the draft:

MR. AND MRS. NEUTRAL

HENNIE EILERS

The last of the roses had arrived, the dresses were all hemmed, the organ lady was sober and the wedding was soon to begin. Ima was ecstatic. Her knight in shining armor, Gregory Phatti, was about to sweep her off her feet and they would ride off together into marital bliss.

Ima fantasized about the bonding kiss, her beautiful ring and the reception to follow. She mouthed the words that the minister would say and then her vows. For the first time, she said her new last name with her first; "Ima Phatti". She did not get the warm tingly feeling that she expected, instead she realized that for the rest of her life she would here jenny Craig jokes and be reminded of her saddle bags every time she wrote a check. She imagined herself at a party saying "Hi, Ima Phatti . . . but I'm not" while she guiltily held a plate covered with pigs in a blanket. Sweat beaded on her upper lip, she knew that life was truly over if she went through with the ceremony. At that moment, her father took her arm and ushered her down the isle.

Poor Ima went through the humiliating process of accepting her new last name and was rushed off to the reception where she longed to swallow whole pieces of her wedding cake and lick the frosting off each finger, snorting and drooling at her guests. Surely they would approve of her living up to her name.

The name tradition has a long line of women's oppression linked to it. In almost every culture, women and girls were sold by their families or bought by their husbands, and this was called "marriage". Many times, love was not a prerequisite and the wives were often treated as slaves and property by their spouses. When the woman took the man's last name, it was simply a way to show others that she was "his". In today's society where women are struggling for their own power and identity, they no longer should submissively give up their name.

It is unfair that women are expected take on their husband's last name at marriage. It is equivelent to handing him your identity and giving up your family pride. For half of your life you carried your family history along with you every time someone said or read your name.

If your maiden name was "O'Sullivan" and you have fair skin, red hair and blue eyes, it seems completely inappropriate to suddenly be called "Wong." There is a certain amount of information that you can derive from a person's last name. Their heritage for instance and where their family originally came from. Sometimes new acquaintances will know a family member of yours and this can open all new doors into a conversation or even meeting someone that you did not know was related.

During school your name was verbally plastered everywhere. You were always called by your first and last name as to keep all the Jennifer's and John's apart. This made you unique. Your parents sat you down and told you where your name came from and why it was special. They shared with you the lengthy pains that they went through to make sure it sounded good. You took great pride in developing a cool signature that was all yours and would be used for the rest of your life. There is one major flaw to this happy, shinny identity ritual; if you were a little girl no one told you that someday you would no longer be "Sally Smith" but instead "Sally Muelerberger".

In the case of the rich and famous these people would not dream of giving up their last names because their future depends on their identity. I'm sure that Julia Roberts loves her husband and his name dearly but she didn't 'love it' enough to take on the "Lovett". Lisa Marie Prestly would be giving up the legend if she gave up the "Prestly" then again, who would want Michael's name this year? Even though the average woman might not have a famous background or be in limelight of the press, she is still worthy of being recognized as people have always known her.

Two people can still give each other the gift of love and bonding without the woman sacrificing something. Why not join both the couple's names. They could flip a coin as to who's name comes first. Though there is no law saying that the female must take the male's name, ask your fiancee or husband if he would consider taking your name. The answer is probably "No", and when asked "why?", their reply will probably include an ego bit about their manly identity. So what about our womanly identity, we were born with it, so why can't we keep it like our brothers will?

The children of a two name marriage could also have the bonded name. Sure, sometimes the names can be lengthy but what a great way to show the products of such a bonded love. When these children in turn get married, they will each pick the last of the two names and bond it with their spouses.

As for "Ima Phatti" who probably never had an eating disorder prior to her marriage, lets hope that she is kind when naming her children, and informs her daughter of the alternatives to accepting prince charming's ugly name. To "Truly Jones" of Chico, couldn't you have found a better companion than "Steve Boring?" I truly hope your personality does not suffer terribly. ❖

Here's the group-edited version, with readers' comments in boldface:

MR. AND MRS. NEUTRAL

HENNIE EILERS

I don't really get this title (Eric). The last of the roses had arrived, the dresses were all hemmed, the organ lady was sober **Does this matter? (Terry) Is it a joke? (Dan)** and the wedding was soon to begin. Ima was ecstatic. Her knight in shining armor Gregory Phatti, was about to sweep her off her feet and they would ride off together into marital bliss.

Ima fantasized about the bonding kiss, her beautiful ring and the reception to follow. She mouthed the words that the minister would say and then her vows. For the first time, she said her new last name with her first; "Ima Phatti". **I can't believe she never thought about it before—can you make this more believable? (Joan). I think it's clever—don't change it (Tod).** She did not get the warm tingly feeling that she expected, instead she realized that for the rest of her life she would here jenny Craig jokes and be reminded of her saddle bags every time she wrote a check. She imagined herself at a party saying "Hi, Ima Phatti . . . but I'm not" while she guiltily held a plate covered with pigs in a blanket. Sweat beaded on her upper lip, she knew that life was truly over if she went through with the ceremony. **Why was her life over because of a name change? And what about people who change their names from Ima Phatti to Ima Jones? (Stacy). Right—this whole "ugly name" argument is a joke, and it detracts from your important issues—I'd drop it (Eric).** At that moment, her father took her arm and ushered her down the isle. **It's "aisle" (Mark).**
I like this whole intro.—doesn't put the reader on the defensive (Keri).

Poor Ima went through the humiliating process of accepting her new last name and was rushed off to the reception where she longed to swallow whole pieces of her wedding cake and lick the frosting off each finger, snorting and drooling at her guests. Surely they would approve of her living up to her name.

The name tradition has a long line of women's oppression linked to it. In almost every culture, women and girls were sold by their families or bought by their husbands, and this was called "marriage". Many times, love was not a prerequisite and the wives were often treated as slaves and property by their spouses. **Explain how the whole property thing worked—the men owned the land and the name went with the land so the man's name had to survive, and so on. Until recently, widows had to fight to convince banks that they owned the marriage's bank accounts! (Joan). I'd like to know more about the legal history—like, was the wife ever obligated by law to take her husband's name? (Aaron).** When the woman took the man's last name, it was simply a way to show others that she was "his". In today's society where women are struggling for their own power and identity, they no longer should submissively give up their name. **I'd say this sentence later—it seems sort of plopped here (Eric). I agree—we jumped from the narrative to the thesis (Aaron). Why not talk about some other traditions that oppress women right here? (Keri) Talk about matriarchal societies in history—make the point that our way isn't the only way (Mark).**

It is unfair that women are expected take on their husband's last name at marriage. It is equivelent to handing him your identity and giving up your family pride. **Whatever happened to becoming one with your mate?—have we become so individualistic that a marriage can't be a union? (Stacy). Seems like loyalty, commitment have become vices (Jill). I think you Americans have it easy. In Japan, females belong to their husband's family—they're cut off from their own family (Tod). So what you're saying is that we're lucky to be treated halfway decently? And African Americans should be grateful they aren't slaves anymore? Come on (Keri).** For half of your life you carried your family history along with you every time someone said or read your name. **There are two issues here—family history and personal empowerment—and they conflict. Decide which you want to support. Are women trying to keep their ties to their (patriarchal) past, or break out into an autonomous future? Can't have it both ways (Eric). Good comment, Eric (Joan).**

If your maiden name was "O'Sullivian" and you have fair skin, red hair and blue eyes, it seems completely inappropriate to suddenly be called "Wong." **Inappropriate in what way? (Paula). This is racist stereotyping (Jill).** There is a certain amount of information that you can derive from a person's last name. Their heritage for instance and where their family originally came from. Sometimes new acquaintances will know a family member of yours and this can open all new doors into a conversation or even meeting someone that you did not know was related.

During school your name was verbally plastered everywhere. You were always called by your first and last name as to keep all the Jennifer's and John's apart. This made you unique. **There are other ways to be unique—this seems away from the issue of giving up your individuality when you marry (Dan).** Your parents sat you down and told you where your name came from and why it was special. They shared with you the lengthy pains that they went through to make sure it sounded good. You took great pride in developing a cool signature that was all yours and would be used for the rest of your life. There is one major flaw to this happy, shinny identity ritual; if you were a little girl no one told you that someday you would no longer be "Sally Smith" but instead "Sally Muelerberger". **Talk about the awkwardness of changing your name back and forth when you divorce (Jill).**

In the case of the rich and famous these people would not dream of giving up their last names because their future depends on their identity. I'm sure that Julia Roberts loves her husband and his name dearly but she didn't 'love it' enough to take on the "Lovett". Lisa Marie Prestly would be giving up the legend if she gave up the "Prestly" then again, who would want Michael's name this year? **But Lisa Marie got the name by marrying Elvis—doesn't that argue against you? And it's spelled "Presley" (Eric).** Even though the average woman might not have a famous background or be in limelight of the press, she is still worthy of being recognized as people have always known her.

Two people can still give each other the gift of love and bonding without the woman sacrificing something. Why not join both the couple's names. They could flip a coin as to who's name comes first. Though there is no law saying that the female must take the male's name, ask your fiancee or husband if he would consider taking your name. The answer is probably "No", and when asked "why?", their reply will probably include an ego bit about their manly identity. **Why not dramatize this scene and use it as an opener! (Joan). Great idea (Mark).** So what about our womanly identity, we were born with it, so why can't we keep it like our brothers will?

The children of a two name marriage could also have the bonded name. Sure, sometimes the names can be lengthy but what a great way to show the products of such a bonded love. When these children in turn get married, they will each pick the last of the two names and bond it with their spouses.

As for "Ima Phatti" who probably never had an eating disorder prior to her marriage, lets hope that she is kind when naming her children, and informs her daughter of the alternatives to accepting prince charming's ugly name. To "Truly Jones" of Chico, couldn't you have found a better companion than "Steve Boring?" I truly hope your personality does not suffer terribly. **Add some real examples**

(Jill J.) Actually, Truly Boring is a real case (Mark).
Isn't it still a personal decision?—let people do what they want
to (Aaron).
Not really—women feel pressured (Hennie).
I'd like a stronger sense of what harm taking the man's name does—
why is it a big deal? (Jill J.) ❖

Peer-Editing a Peer-Editing Session

Chapter 1 taught us that you don't get better at something just by
doing it—you have to do it, then think about it and learn from it.
That's true of writing, and it's true of peer editing. So after you peer
edit, you have to examine your performance: What went well? What
went badly? Which of the principles of Chapter 10 did you follow, and
which did you forget? How are you going to do it better next time?

Let's practice critiquing a critiquing session. Here's an unedited
first draft. Following it I've written out the peer-editing conversation
my class had about it, with comments about what's going well and
what isn't along the way.

LEGALIZE HEMP: AN ESSENTIAL RESOURCE
FOR THE FUTURE

TODD BURKS

Hemp, falsley known to many as marijuana, is an essential
resource for the future of the planet. In todays age of environmental
awareness is seems silly that we are not taking advantage of such a
valuable commodity. Not only would the legalization of hemp save
our forests, but it would stimulate the presently ailing economy.

Although both marijuana and hemp are derived from cannibis
sativa, you can't get " stoaned " from hemp. You see, hemp is the
large stock form while marijuana is the small " budding " form.
Unfortunately, negative stigmas have been placed on hemp since
marijuana became a popular street drug back in the late thirties.

"The flower was said to be the most violent inducing drug in the history of mankind." Those of us who have experimented with the marijuana form Know this to be false.

The legalization of hemp (marijuana) for personnal use does not concern me. However, the legalization of hemp as a valuable resource would alleviate many political, economic, and environmental ills that plague the world.

To begin, hemp legalization would virtually eliminate the need for wood in paper products. Four times the amount of hemp can be grown on an acre of land than wood. The hemp takes only four months until harvesting, compared to nearly ten years for trees. Furthrmore, hemp paper is more durable than wood paper, lasting four times as long, and it's cheaper to produce.

The adaptibility of hemp to many soils and climates would allow for extensive growth worldwide. Unlike many rotation crops that degrade the soil, hemp roots actually permeate the soil, allowing for more productivity.

Hemp seeds could also develop into daily diets around the world. "The hemp seed is the second most complete vegetable protein, second only to soybeans. However, hemp seeds are more easily synthesized by humans due to the high content of enzymes, endistins, and essential amino acids. "The seeds can also be used to make margarine and a tofu-like substance.

Almost one-third of the hemp seed is oil. Hemp oil can be used in paints and varnishes, eliminating the need for petrochemical oils. The biodegradeable hemp seed can also be used for diesel fuel and lubricant, causing less environmental pollution.

Finally, the rapid growth rate of hemp makes it the number-one renewable biomass resource in the world. "Biomass is fuel, whether it be petroleum, coal, or hemp. " Therefore, hemp can be used in place of fossil fuels. Rather than carbon monoxide hemp gives off carbon dioxide which is naturally synthesized by our atmosphere.

It is obvious that hemp has gotten a bad rap due to the popularity of marijuana as a street drug. Not to mention the false propaganda headed by Hearst and DuPont early in the twentieth cent. However, with todays technology in genetic engineering, we can produce a plant that is purely stalk and is not possible to smoke. Finally, with government regulation and taxation we could virtually wipe out the trillion-dollar deficit hanging over our heads. ❖

Here's the conversation the class had about the essay. Each new number indicates a new speaker. In the right margin I've noted some of the rules we talked about in this chapter that are being followed or broken. *Don't* indicates the rule is being *broken*.

1:

1. Don't forget to begin with the writer's questions.

2: It seemed like you jumped right into your argument, and you could hold off on that a little more—like in your introduction, explain what hemp is, what you're going to use it for, then start saying, "But this is the reason why it's not being used . . ."

2. Fry the biggest fish first.

3: There was one sentence I'd take out: "Those of us who have experimented with the marijuana form know this to be false." That could weaken your case, because we could say, "Oh, it's a pot smoker, he just wants it legal so he can smoke it."

3. Don't raise a new issue before the old issue is settled.

4: He says legalization for personal use doesn't concern him, but I think it does concern him, because I don't see how you can start reforesting the fields of hemp for commercial use without some people doing it for personal use too.

4. Connect with the previous comment.

5: He needs to make more of how he just wants to legalize the genetically engineered plants.

5. Don't raise a new issue before the old issue is settled.

6: A couple of things I thought when I read it: If we have all this hemp, what do we do with the dope? Do we legalize that as well?

7: And this fossil fuel thing: I've heard there's about fifty or so alternatives to replace fossil fuel; the only problem is it's really expensive to do so.

7. Don't raise issues in bunches.

8: Maybe you could argue, "The fossil fuels are limited, this is replaceable . . ."

9: That gets around the cost issue.

10: It ends up you can still grow it in Mexico for a tenth the cost. There's no way we can compete with Third World countries where it grows wild along the road.

11: As far as throwing out the "those of us" sentence, I don't know. Because obviously in the back of the reader's mind they're saying, "Wait a minute—some people have experimented with it, and I'm sure they have something to say about it." But I think that could be a potentially strong argument.

11. Connect with previous comments (in this case, with 3). If you disagree, say so.

12: Everyone seems to agree that the essay should either drop that aside about personal use or develop it more. Let's get a show of hands: How many think it should be dropped? And how many want to develop it? (Rawlins) (The vote is to drop it.)

12. Push to consensus.

13: Todd, didn't you tell me that it's just the stalk that makes the paper and stuff, so there's no reason to even worry about it being misused as pot?

14: You can certainly breed out the THC content—they've been intensifying it for twenty years, so I'm sure you can reduce it by the same genetic engineering.

15: I'm sure if I'm a farmer I'm going to grow hemp when I can grow pot for twenty times the money.

16: I'm confused about whether hemp and marijuana are the same thing, because in the first sentence you say "hemp, falsely known as marijuana," and in the third paragraph you say "hemp (marijuana)."

16. Tell the writer how the text reads to you.

17: Well, they're both *cannibas sativa*, but one is the long stalk form and the other is the flower form. (Author)

17. Don't explain or defend what you've written.

18: So they're from the same family but two separate plants?

19: Same plant, different breeding. (Author)

20: That issue seems to be an important one. Does the group agree that that issue needs to be clarified? (Rawlins) (Signs of agreement throughout the room)

20. Connect, generalize, prioritize.

21: I don't understand that bit about Hearst's false propaganda.

21. Tell the writer how the text reads to you.

22: Don't you remember the "killer weed" business in the fifties?

23: What's that got to do with Hearst and DuPont?

24: At the time hemp was the second biggest crop after cotton, and they were going to use it as an alternative to paper products. Hearst and DuPont rallied against it, because DuPont has the patent on sulfuric acid, which breaks down wood into pulp, and Hearst had huge tracts of forest land, so they didn't want hemp to hurt the wood paper market. That's when they started all this reefer madness thing. (Author)

25: That all sounds like great stuff—I'd put it right into the essay. (Rawlins)

25. Turn comments into concrete revision suggestions.

26: I'd just prefer "cent." to be turned into "century."

26. Don't line edit unless it's a big fish.

27: Me, too.

27. Say, "I agree."

28: How do you spell "stoned"? "S-t-o-n-e-d"?

29: Is spelling a problem in the essay? (Rawlins)

29. Prioritize.

30: Yes. (Several voices)

31: Like what? (Rawlins)

32: "Falsley." "Personnal." "Furthrmore." (Several voices)

33: Also there are two "finally's." When I hear the word "finally" I think, you know, "finally," so when I hear it again I go "Whoa . . ." I just deleted the last "finally."

34: You could say "sorta finally" and "really finally."

35: Before we turn to grammar and mechanics, are there any larger issues anyone wanted to talk about? (Rawlins)

35. Fry the biggest fish first.

36: In the last paragraph when you say "bad rap" I could tell it was your voice. The essay seemed so technical, when I got to "bad rap" I thought, "Gee, it's not so technical anymore."

37: Are you saying you *like* "bad rap" and want more of it, or that you *don't* and suggest Todd take it out? (Rawlins)

37. Turn comments into concrete revision suggestions.

38: It just seems like a contradiction—it sticks out.

39: So you'd like the tone to be more consistent. (Rawlins)

40: One question that I have: There are three large quotes in the paper and you don't say where they come from or who said them or anything. They're just kind of there, so . . .

41: On the first page you talk about "political, economic, and environmental" benefits of hemp. You talk mostly about environmental, and you mention economics at the end, but I really didn't see much about political.

41. Don't raise a new issue till the old one is settled. The vital issue at 40 is never returned to.

42: Is that the thesis of the essay there? Because I thought the end of Paragraph 1 was the thesis.

43: You know, you talk about "negative stigmas" twice, in Paragraph 2 and the last paragraph. I wonder if you need to do that.

43. Don't forget to generalize. 43, 42, and 41 all address the same large issue. This goes unacknowledged until 61.

44: Should this be two sentences?: "Not to mention the false propaganda headed by Hearst and DuPont . . ." Maybe it should be a comma.

44. Don't line edit unless it's a big fish.

45: Is punctuation a problem in the essay? (Rawlins)

45. Prioritize.

46: No. (Several voices)

47: You say it can be used for diesel fuel and lubricant ... I'm sorry, I just don't get that. I don't work on cars.

47. Make I statements instead of telling the writer what to do.

48: I need to know more about hemp roots penetrating the soil. It's not that I don't agree—I'm just not going to buy it until I know what it all means.

49: I hear several of these comments addressing the same issue: You'd like *more information*— what exactly the roots do to the soil, how exactly hemp and marijuana are different, how hemp can be used for diesel fuel. (Rawlins)

49. Generalize and connect.

50: I've been playing with this sentence in Paragraph 2: "You see, hemp is the large stock form, while marijuana is the small 'budding' form." I tried, "While hemp is the large stock form of *cannibas sativa*, marijuana is the small budding form."

50. Don't line edit unless it's a big fish.

51: You could just cross out "you see," couldn't you?

52: The only sentence I had trouble with was "The flower was said to be the most violent inducing drug in the history of mankind." I'm not sure what a "violent inducing drug" is.

53: That's a quote from a book. (Author)

53. Don't defend or explain.

54: I still don't understand it.

54. Your reader's response can't be wrong.

55: I think it should be "*violence*-inducing drug."

56: Okay, it's time to generalize and prioritize. What are your biggest and most important suggestions to Todd? (Rawlins)

56. Generalize and prioritize.

57: Explain yourself more—like the roots and the soil.

58: Make it clearer what the difference between pot and hemp is, and how you can grow one without running the risk of growing the other.

59: Tell us more about Hearst and DuPont—that was interesting.

60: Proofread for spelling.

61: You know, many of your comments relate to structure. For instance, the way the essay talks about stigmas twice, and the two "finally's," and the two thesis sentences, and the way it promises to discuss politics in Paragraph 3 but never does. If we were going to restructure, I thought the very first comment of the day gave us a good design: First list the virtues of hemp, then explain why we're prohibited from using it, relate the history, and *then* argue that the ban should be lifted. That suckers the reader into agreeing before he knows what he's in for. (Rawlins)

Your Turn

Have a classmate distribute copies of his essay draft to the class. Peer edit the draft as a group, in the manner of Chapter 10, in conversation or via computer network if you have one. Then reflect on the conversation or examine the transcript, and individually write a one-page essay evaluating and critiquing the group's performance. Which of the chapter's rules did the group follow? Which did they break? How well did the group leader do her job? And so forth. Form two resolutions for next time: what two things are you going to strive to do differently the next time you peer edit?

MORE THINGS TO DO

Write a page doing to the electronic peer-editing session on p. 180 what we did in the Writers' Workshop section: How well did the session go? What went well? Which comments violate the spirit of Chapter 10? And so on.

Chapter 11

REWRITING

FOR STYLE

At last, we're going to talk about sentence polishing. I've put it off until now, very late in the evolution of the essay, to make a point: Most writers start polishing sentences way too early, and many of them think of it as the heart of rewriting. It isn't. Polished sentences alone never made a piece of writing good. If you're equating rewriting with crossing out weak words and replacing them with strong ones or cutting superfluous adjectives, you're skipping the really important stuff. Think of sentence polishing as installing elegant cornices and finials on a house that is already well founded and weatherproof. No cornice can make up for a leaky roof or a shifting foundation.

"Uncl" and "Awk"

Teachers' two most common criticisms of student writing are that it's vague (traditionally signaled by a teacher writing "uncl," short for "unclear," in the margin) and that it's awkward ("awk" in the margin). Both reactions should be taken seriously if you get them, but I don't think either problem can be attacked only on the sentence-tinkering level. They're big deals, best attacked in big, holistic terms. So we'll talk briefly about ways to attack them before we get into sentence polishing.

Vagueness

Saying that writing is vague means "I can't understand this" or "I'm not sure what this means." That's a matter of communication, not aesthetics, so don't think in terms of prettying up the language. Instead, use our old friends:

> *Write something you care about,* so you're writing to be heard and not to hide.

> *Know your audience,* so you know what language they understand.

Think like a reader. When you read over your own work, don't ask if it makes sense to you; try to imagine how another reader could possibly misunderstand, and write to prevent all reasonable misunderstandings.

Write redundant first drafts. Say all hard things three or four different ways; then pick the way that said it best or combine the virtues of several.

Use talk. Most of us can say things more simply and cleanly than we can write them.

Get lots of feedback from colleagues. This is your number-one weapon against vagueness. Ask readers to flag places where they're confused. Even better, ask them what they think you meant (they may think they understand and be wrong). Then *talk with them* until you've found a way to say it so that what they hear is what you mean. Chapter 10 practices this art.

Don't strive too hard for clarity. It will give you a splendid case of writer's block. Ignore problems of vagueness unless readers tell you you have them, and then only think about them after the loose creative writing stages are behind you. Even then, too much devotion to clarity will make you write like a corporate lawyer, covering your fanny and splitting hairs.

Awkwardness

Saying that writing is awkward means "It just doesn't sound right." That's the hardest of all reader responses to use, because how can you go out and make it sound right when you don't know what "right" is? Right is mostly a matter of what you're used to. Shakespeare sounds awkward when you're not used to him, but he sounds great to me now that I've read him for twenty years. Academic prose or textbook language strikes all novices as awkward, and we professors cheerfully tell students that's their fault and expect them to adjust their ears. Street slang or pop-culture slang sounds awkward to isolated academics who have never heard it before. Since they're in a position of power they can condemn it, until the media use it so much it becomes familiar and ultimately okay—just the way the word *okay* did, in fact.

Imagine a reader saying to you, "This seems awkward to me." When you reread the passage, you say one of three things to yourself: "It seems awkward to me too," "It seems fine to me," or "I don't know if it's awkward or not." In each case you must do something different.

If you say, "It seems awkward to me too," you fix the problem by resaying it, preferably out loud and to real people, until it sounds good. Don't try to locate the problem or repair it mechanically, and don't worry about why one version reads poorly and another works; just trust your ear and take multiple runs at it until one succeeds.

If you say, "It sounds fine to me," things get complicated. In that case your reader may be saying, "It's not in my dialect"—with the implied instruction to forsake your dialect and adopt his. This is obviously a big political issue that transcends questions of writing technique. Do you have the right to your own language or not? Is the reader under any obligation to learn to read your language, or can she demand that you use hers? It's not my business to tell you how to answer these questions. If you decide to write in your own dialect, I can respect your decision and acknowledge your right to do so, but I have nothing to teach you. If you decide you want to write in standard essay English, we've already talked about how in Chapters 1 and 2: You need to have read enough standard essay English to be able to reproduce it, and you need an ear tuned to dialect so you know which dialect you're using. Next, you must know who your reader is and keep him in mind, so you can choose language he's comfortable with.

The key here is knowledge, which leads to choices, which lead to control. The more dialects you know, the more audiences you can reach and the more choices you'll have about what you want to do to them. Because Geneva Smitherman knows both academic prose style and American Black English, she can write with special authority about the politics of dialect and language use in America:

> I saw without qualification that we cannot talk about the black Idiom apart from Black Culture and the Black Experience. Nor can we specify educational goals for blacks apart from considerations about the structure of (white) American Society.
>
> And we black folks is not gon take all that weight, for no one has empirically demonstrated that linguistic/stylistic features of BE impede educational progress in communication skills, or any other area of cognitive learning. Take reading. It's don been charged, but not actually verified, that BE interferes with mastery of reading skills.

We get rightfully defensive when a teacher says "Ugh" or "That's wrong" just because he doesn't know our language. If you get this response, you'll have to be wise enough to paraphrase that hurtful message into "That's not what my ear is used to." Then you'll know you have the power to choose whether to accommodate his ear or stay put and write powerfully enough to convince him he should learn to hear you in *your* language.

The solution in the third case is obvious, but slow. If you say, "I don't know if it's awkward or not," it means you don't have the template of essay English to judge your writing against, so you can't tell if it conforms. You have to develop an ear for it, and you do that the way you learn any language: by immersion. Go read a ton of standard essay English (or whatever kind of writing you're trying to learn). It will take time, but it's painless and there's no substitute.

Wordiness

People call writing wordy when it takes too long to say its say. Excellence of any sort—excellent dancing, excellent quarterbacking, excellent wood-working—has no waste. You fix wordy writing by doing the same job using fewer words.

Attacking Wordiness at the Source

To make a stylistic vice go away, you have to (a) realize where it comes from and (b) want it to go. Wordiness comes from two distinct sources, and each demands a different solution.

The first source is a need for volume. No one in casual conversation ever said, "So, Elisa, what ya been doing, and make sure you talk for at least ten minutes," but school does it all the time, by setting minimum page limits. If the assignment rewards bulk but you haven't much to say, you'll pad.

Don't try to solve this problem by lecturing yourself on the evils of waste. Hungry people steal food; students with two pages of text and a five-page length requirement add filler. In the seventh grade when I did a report on Russia that was graded on length, I called the country "the Union of Soviet Socialist Republics" on every occasion, and wrote the name out instead of using the initials because it made the report longer.

Instead, attack the problem at the source: *Go find more to say.* Redefine the essay's task using the skills in Chapter 9, especially the Writers' Workshop section. Do it until you have more to say than you can squeeze into the allowable space; then wordiness will be a curse instead of your salvation.

The second source of wordiness is the creative process itself. Creating is a messy, wasteful business. You fool around. You try anything and everything. If your first scribblings aren't wordy, you have a much bigger problem called writer's block.

The only problem is, when we write something, we fall in love with it and want to keep it—every word. To fall out of love again, you have to think about your writing in a new way. See the writing as readers see it, and cut anything that doesn't pay them for the trouble of reading it. Think of it like preparing for a backpacking trip: You don't take along everything that might prove useful; you leave behind everything but what you know you'll need. Newspaper editors know this: They look at every word asking not "Does this say anything?" but "Am I willing to *pay for this?"*

Whipping Wordiness Holistically

We'll talk in a moment about mechanical ways to look for flab, but I don't encourage you to begin that way. Instead, stir up a great loathing for flab in your heart and then try to resay leanly whatever you've written that feels like it takes too long.

Begin by getting the sound of flabby writing in your ear:

"The Greatest American Hero" is a TV series which is extremely popular. One could speculate that the reason for this popularity is the theme of the show. This speculation leads us to ask: Well, what is the theme of "The Greatest American Hero"?

Rewrite: *The TV series "The Greatest American Hero" is extremely popular, probably because of its theme. What is that theme?*

It seems reasonable to assume that a writer chooses his setting purposefully. That is to say, the setting is an important element in most stories and is not an implement of random nature. Certainly this must be the case when dealing with a writer of Hemingway's caliber. In his story "Hills Like White Elephants," Hemingway chooses to involve his characters in a conflict which takes place at a train station.

Rewrite: *Writers choose their settings purposefully; certainly Hemingway does. His "Hills Like White Elephants" takes place in a train station.*

It's hard for me to write about Holden Caulfield, because he reminds me so much of myself. The thing about him that reminds me most of myself is the way he deals with girls. The first instance we see in the book of Holden's attitude toward girls is where Holden discovers that . . .

Rewrite: *It's hard for me to write about Holden Caulfield because he reminds me so much of myself—especially in the way he deals with girls. For instance, when Holden discovers that . . .*

Notice that cutting flab is rarely done simply by lining out needless words; a certain amount of rewording and restructuring is almost always necessary.

If you're still not offended by wordiness, write a parody. Take one of your own simple sentences and load it with lard. Here's one of mine in varying degrees of lardification:

Learn to love pith.

You must learn to love pith in your writing.

If you want to be a good writer, you must accept the fact that you will have to learn to love pith.

> In my experience, I have come to realize that anyone who wants to be
> a good writer must sooner or later accept the fact that he will have to
> learn to love pithiness of expression.

This technique works on any stylistic bad habit: Overdose on it until it
disgusts you and you learn to laugh at it.

But if in your heart you still really like wordiness and its benefits,
use this last-ditch argument against it: Pith eliminates errors of grammar
and idiom. Words are like oranges: The more of them you try to juggle
at once, the more likely they'll fall down around your ears. Write less
and you stay in control. In the Hemingway flab passage we looked at, the
writer says that setting isn't "an implement of random nature." That
language is out of control, but the problem disappears in the lean version.
Over and over I see this happen: *The bad writing is in the flab itself;*
trim, and the problems go away.

This idea is especially useful for non-native English speakers. Here
are two non-native writers whose grammar and idiom problems (which
I've put in italics) disappear with a rigorous trimming of fat:

> Sometimes exercising to maintain fitness and good health can get a
> little expensive. However, that is not the case *in* jogging. Jogging is a
> very inexpensive type of recreational activity. Unlike some, jogging
> doesn't require a large investment *on* gear and equipment. The most
> that has to be invested is probably *in* a pair of comfortable jogging shoes.
>
> Rewrite: *Sometimes exercising can get a little expensive, but not
> jogging. It doesn't require elaborate gear—just a pair of comfortable
> running shoes.*

> Oftentimes in writing reports, we encounter a need to quote phrases
> found in other people's writing. When we do this, credits need to be
> given to those quotes by footnoting them. Therefore, this paper will
> *discuss about* the general format for footnotes.
>
> Rewrite: *Often in writing reports we need to quote from someone
> else's writing. When we do this, we must give credit to the author in
> a footnote. Here is a standard format for footnotes.*

Incidentally, a word processor takes fat trimming and changes it
from labor and rejection into a video game. Devouring those words becomes such a game you'll have to stop yourself from gobbling everything
in sight—another good reason to make a major effort to get your hands
on one of those machines.

Concrete Anti-wordiness Strategies

When the holistic approach has taken you as far as it can, you can go flab
hunting armed with specific techniques and things to look for. I have
three favorite mechanical anti-wordiness strategies.

First, *minimize the glue.* Language consists of words that matter and "glue" words that hold them together. Pithy writing has as little glue as possible. Consider this: "There is a wide selection of à la carte items to choose from. Some of the selections are: appetizers . . ." What are the words that matter here? *À la carte, choose* (or *selection,* but not both), and *appetizers.* If we string these three words together with as little glue as possible, we get "Choose from à la carte items like appetizers. . . ." You can work the other way: Look for glue words and cut them wherever possible. After a discussion of ways to teach in public school classrooms, a student wrote, "All of these aspects are important to aid in the learning of the student." What words are glue? *of, these, aspects, are, to, in, the, of, the,* and *learning* or *student* (since they say the same thing). If we rewrite using as few of these as possible, we get "These all aid learning."

Make a list of the glue you like to use, and put at the head of it everybody's Favorite Five: *of, is/are, there is/there are, which,* and *that.* Try never to use these five again, and you'll have gone a long way toward ridding yourself of wordiness. But there are lots of others—*as, as far as . . . is concerned, effect, sort of, kind(s) of, in terms of, regarding, concerning, aspect, experience, situation, proceed to, occur, create, cause, in the form of, on a . . . basis, the reason for this is that, is where, is when, in order to, due to, as a result of.* You'll have to discover which are your personal favorites.

Great gobs of glue tend to accumulate at the beginnings of sentences, as we struggle to get up a head of steam: *It's important to realize that, Remember that, One should note that, The main point here is that.* Most of these introductory gobs end with *that,* so always question any such construction.

Second, *ask, "What's new?"* This is a variation on the glue rule that works on the sentence that *follows* a solid sentence. You ask, "What's new in the second sentence?" and cut everything else:

> They say he heads their list of "most wanted" players. This stems from the fact that he has a .376 career batting average.

What's new in the second sentence? Only the batting average, so add it to the first sentence as simply as possible:

> They say he heads their list of "most wanted" players, thanks to his .376 career batting average.

What's new in the second sentence here?

> In this paper I will discuss the two predominant attitudes concerning interpersonal communication that face Americans today. These two views can be classified as self-oriented and other-oriented.

Only the two adjectives, so add them to the first sentence, trimming the flab from the first sentence as you do:

Americans choose between two attitudes toward interpersonal communication, self-oriented and other-oriented.

Many "what's new?" problems call attention to themselves because the second sentence contains a straight repeat of a phrase from the first, in what I call an overlap:

There are ways to deal with censorship in the schools. One way of dealing with the problem of censorship in the schools is to . . .
Rewrite: *There are ways to deal with censorship in the schools. One way is to . . .*

There are two tests and a final. The tests along with the final are all based on the lecture material.
Rewrite: *There are two tests and a final, all based on the lecture material.*

Eliminate overlaps with colons, pronouns, or dashes:

Incoming freshmen are faced with some tough decisions. Some of these decisions that face them are what classes to enroll in . . .
Rewrite: *Incoming freshmen are faced with some tough decisions: what classes to enroll in . . .*

A good class is General Biology. The class consists of two one-hour lectures a week . . .
Rewrite: *A good class is General Biology. It's two one-hour lectures a week . . .*

One thing I especially don't care for is eating off trays. I think of eating off trays as being a bit tacky.
Rewrite: *One thing I especially don't care for is eating off trays— too tacky.*

Many students are taught to avoid pronouns and dashes because in careless hands they can lead to loose sentence structure, but a writer needs them to avoid wordiness. Not using them because they're tricky is like refusing to eat because it makes your teeth dirty.

Third, *eliminate redundancy.* Redundancy is the writer's word for the special kind of wordiness where you say something more than once. Like wordiness generally, redundancy in a first draft is a good thing—it's just a kind of practicing, trying it a few different ways as you write. But when it comes time for the public performance, the artist only gets to do the act once.

One kind of redundancy we do on purpose, because we mistake it for good writing or because we're told to. "I'll just restate my thesis," you tell yourself, "to underline the point," or "That's so good it bears repeating." And writers are often explicitly told to practice redundancy in school: "Say what you're going to say, say it, then say what you said." This intentional redundancy usually takes three forms:

1. You state your thesis at the beginning of the essay and restate it in the conclusion.
2. Your last paragraph summarizes the essay.
3. You restate the thesis with each new supportive argument: "The first way in which the beliefs of Smith and Anderson are alike is . . ."; "The second way in which the beliefs of Smith and Anderson are alike is . . ."; "The last way in which the beliefs of Smith and Anderson are alike is . . ."

If you think like a reader you'll realize intentional redundancy doesn't work. Real readers hate redundancy; if they want to read something two or three times, they can just reread. *Say it once, well.*

There's another kind of redundancy that's harder to stop, because we don't know we're doing it. When the writer said there was "a wide selection of à la carte items to choose from," she was communicating the idea of choosing twice, since a selection is something to be chosen from—but she didn't know it. Similarly, the newscaster I heard say, "A crowd of over five hundred women marched today to protest against the ERA" was being redundant, since protests are by definition *against* things—but he didn't know it. Here are other hidden redundancies:

As a *result*, this *causes* car crashes.

Smith and Frankel have many *common similarities.*

Litter is a horrible, *ugly blemish* on the land.

The *natural primitive instinct* for survival . . .

Look for covert redundancy especially in two places:

1. Adjectives: *grave crisis, true facts, real truth, added plus, future plans, past experience, basic necessity, general consensus, valuable asset.*
2. Compounds: words or phrases in pairs connected by *and.*

The point of reading is to *comprehend and understand* content.

Censorship is a very *pertinent and important* subject to all Americans.

Scrutinize every compound you write; try to pick the better of the two and throw the other away.

Two Traps to Avoid When Fighting Wordiness

First, don't think on a word-by-word level only, and don't cut only the words that "don't say anything." Here's an opening paragraph from a student's informative essay on a local state historical monument:

In an attempt to help incoming freshmen in their search for entertainment, the so-called editor has asked for another paper. The assignment is to report on a place to go. Sounds simple, but I wanted to write about a place that no one has been to. Not so simple. Then I got an idea. A place that everyone has heard of, but no one has been to: Bidwell Mansion. Of course, to write an "informative" essay, I would have to visit the mansion.

I like that paragraph cut to its central idea:

There's a place in town everyone has heard of but no one has been to: Bidwell Mansion.

Most of the words I cut said something, and a lot of them couldn't be categorized as glue, but I like the big cut anyway. Fighting flab word by word will never let you make such sweeping gestures.

Have I lost meaning? You bet. We lie if we tell ourselves that we edit only meaningless air. Every word added or deleted changes meaning, so if you only cut the words that don't mean anything, you'll cut almost nothing.

When do you stop cutting? *Everything* makes some contribution; *nothing* is essential except perhaps the thesis statement. How much pruning is enough? You'll have to decide. Perhaps you think I cut too much in the Bidwell Mansion paragraph; I don't. There is no right here, only judgment.

Second, don't lose the life. It's easy to get so zealous in your cutting that you ax all signs of personality and vitality. Efficiency in writing is like efficiency in the workplace: It's a good thing, but it's not everything. When efficiency makes us robotic, life isn't worth living.

Pretentiousness

Pretentiousness goes by many names: BS, pompousness, bureaucratic English, bureaucratese, political English, textbook English, Engfish, academic prose, Pentagonese. I call it pretentious prose, or PP for short. You may not know the names, but you know the thing: A campus administrator sends me a memo saying, "A majority of the inquiries coming to my office have been concerned with implementation criteria," and I know she means, "Most of the questions people ask me are about how we're going to do this." You know how to write it too. You're writing the rules of the social club, and you want to say, "If you break any of these rules, we'll kick you out forever." But that doesn't sound important enough, so you write, "Violation of any of these statutes will result in immediate and permanent expulsion."

Pretentiousness is more than just a composition-class issue; it's a disease sickening our entire culture. In many workplaces the rewards for PP are enormous, and you must have the integrity of a saint to resist. It may not be a problem for you yet; people beginning college are usually worried their writing doesn't look pretentious *enough*. But the thirty-year-old readers of *The Writer's Way* unanimously cite the PP section as the most valuable in the book.

Here's what the culprit sounds like (and, in parentheses, what it's really trying to say):

> Along with advanced reading capabilities, the familiarizing of books and words to children should also stimulate their intelligence at all levels. (Reading also stimulates a child's intelligence.)

> He investigated various studies to conclude if improving articulation of production of speech sounds can aid in developing spelling skills. (He read some studies to see if improving articulation helps spelling.)

> A forced stop at all four inlets to this intersection would enable persons to gain a greater ability to assess the traffic situation at present. (If we put stop signs at all four corners of the intersection, people could see the traffic better.)

> Censorship has both its pros and cons which when discussed won't resolve the question of its necessity. If, however, the subject is dealt with from the viewpoint of its utility, the mechanism can be put into perspective. In the case of a schoolroom setting, censorship's intent is to protect the student. (In school, censorship tries to protect the student.)

Wordiness and PP look alike at first, but they have different motives. When we're wordy, we're just writing like we talk—it just takes a little time to boil it down. But we write PP because we're trying to put one over on the reader. It's a moral issue, and so the hardest part of licking the problem is wanting to. Let's begin by acknowledging the payoffs for PP.

Why Do We Do It?

You might think there are more than enough good reasons to avoid pretentiousness: It's ugly, unnatural, dishonest; it prevents communication; it makes it impossible to think or understand yourself; it breeds vagueness and destroys your grammar; readers hate it; every book on writing ever written has said, "Don't do it." But the reasons to *use* it are also strong.

First, *all our authority figures use PP.* We hear it from teachers, bureaucrats, administrators, lawyers, doctors, politicians, scientists, advertisers, and almost everyone with clout. It's one of the few writing problems that is worse in adults than in children and worse in professionals than in students.

Second, *many of us are trained in school to use PP.* When I ask students mired in PP to write in their natural language, they often wail, "But my other teachers keep complaining that my writing sounds too simple, and I've worked for years to make it sound like that!"

Third, *pretentiousness sells.* It gets grades, earns prestige, and opens wallets. When versions of student papers in plain English and PP are submitted to university instructors for grading, the pretentious versions often get higher grades. When plain English and pretentious versions of the same scholarly articles are submitted to academic journals, often the pretentious versions are more readily accepted for publication. Grant proposals set forth in plain English often don't get funded.

Since PP can pay off, but we know we're scum if we write it, we feed ourselves lines to make it okay. We tell ourselves:

"Plain writing is boring; complex writing is fun."

"Great writing is supposed to enrich and ornament its matter." This is what I call the Gettysburg Address Fallacy: the notion that "eighty-seven" is mundane and "four score and seven" is art.

"My substance or my subject is so sophisticated, scientific, or scholarly that I need PP."

"I'll only use PP for certain audiences."

Behind each of these is a complex, stimulating argument about writing and language, but instead of working through each one, I'll fell them all with a single blow by saying, "Okay, there's a grain of truth in each of them, but ninety-nine times out of a hundred the writers I see using PP aren't making their writing better; they're disguising vacuity, preventing communication, and cowing the reader."

Pretentiousness is like liquor to an alcoholic. An alcoholic on the wagon doesn't drink, even in social situations where drinking is appropriate, because he can't stop. If you can use PP when it works for you and leave it alone when it doesn't, good for you. But very few can.

Kicking the Habit

Let's assume you've decided to rid your writing of pretentiousness. How do you do it?

In a way, pretentiousness is the easiest of the great writing vices to lose; it goes away as soon as you choose to stop. Here's a serious case:

Thompson contributed some positive ideologies on the subject of classroom subtleties. It is stated that our educational system is falling prey to worries about destroying a child's psychic and ethnic upbringing. As such, a refusal to teach standard English becomes prevalent in our schools.

I said to the writer, "I can't understand this. But when we talk I understand you fine. Write it like you'd talk it, and try to make what you're saying as simple and like you as possible." Her next essay began like this:

We have discussed different techniques teachers use when teaching children how to read and write. The following are techniques I would use to teach children how to spell in terms of the principles of this course. I would use word association and recognition. In my classroom the children would make bulletin boards, posters, labels, and signs with words they are familiar with and experience in their everyday lives. An example might be a picture of a stop sign with the word "Stop" on it, or words they see on labels in the grocery store.

That's good stuff. And she could write it the moment she chose to.

But in practice it's not always that simple, so here are some props to shore up your resolve.

Go back to this book's roots. Write for real reasons. Find something to say you're passionate about. Think like your reader. Write something you'd love to read. Honor yourself.

Develop an ear for PP. You need an alarm that sounds at the first whiff of fakery. My alarm went off before I got past the introductory phrase of these two opening sentences:

In learning institutions . . .

At the beginning of educational experience . . .

Real people say "in school" and "when you first start school."

Memorize a few touchstones. Touchstones are key words whose presence alerts you to PP; whenever you see them, you know you're being snowed. My favorites are *utilize* (instead of *use*) and *prior to* (instead of *before*).

Cultivate a love of simple beauty. Fall in love with writers who catch rich, subtle truths in plain, strong words: Russell Baker, the authors of the King James Bible, Ernest Hemingway, Robert Frost, Langston Hughes, James Herriot, Alice Walker, Leslie Marmon Silko, J. R. R. Tolkien, Larry McMurtry. And keep strong, simple words by you as touchstones when you write:

Let him who is without sin cast the first stone.

Don't push the river.

A man shoots his own dog.

Give yourself the right to hate and mock PP, even if you find it in the mouths of four-star generals, respected educators, or Presidents. If we let PP cow us, of course we'll want to exercise the same mastery over our readers. Anger is good; laughter is better.

Use parody to liberate yourself. If you still harbor a secret belief that PP is pretty nifty, overdose on it until you're glutted and have to laugh. Rewrite a simple sentence into the worst PP you can manage. Old saws like "The grass is always greener on the other side of the fence" or "Out of sight, out of mind" work well. Try this one:

> Studies of a significant number of choice situations in the main conclude that, when faced with an alternative between an object (either material or abstract) of lesser value and a high degree of certainty of attainment and an object of greater value and a low degree of certainty of attainment, the certainty of the former object renders the object a greater value than the potentially obtainable object. In fact, it has been shown that in cases where the value of the potentially obtainable object exceeded the value of the certainly obtainable object by a factor of two, the uncertainty of attainment still rendered the less valuable object the more profitable choice.

Do you recognize "A bird in the hand is worth two in the bush"?

Trust your talk. We're less willing to be fake when we talk than when we write, so if you suspect you're getting pretentious, talk to yourself or a listener and write down what you say.

Reread your first notes. When we brainstorm, we usually don't bother to posture and inflate, so the language is lean and bold. After you've puffed the language up in the rewrite, look back to your first language and use it if it's better.

Say "Come off it!" to yourself. There are other ways to phrase it: "Write like you talk"; "Quit BS-ing!"; "Get real"; "Who are you trying to con?"; "Just *say* it!" But you need some verbal jolt to use when you lose your grip.

Don't try to be a saint. Pretentiousness is a kind of lying, and ethical people lie sometimes. At such times, you do it and try not to let it become a habit. Once I applied for a research grant. I wrote the application in plain English, to find out what I was saying. Then, shelving my integrity for the moment, I rewrote it in PP. I needed the money, and I got it.

Fighting Pretentiousness Mechanically

If those ten props don't do the trick, you're in luck: PP is *the only* stylistic vice where the mechanical approaches work well. You can rid yourself of PP simply by restraining yourself from using four kinds of words or constructions:

Latinity

Nominalization

The word *of*

The verb *to be*

Latinate words. English is a Germanic language that has borrowed a lot of words from other languages, mainly French and Latin. The Germanic words are at the ancient root of the language—words like *good, foot, dirt, water, mother,* and *eat.* The French words were brought into English largely by contact with French high culture, so the French vocabulary in English tends to feel arty or genteel: *banquet, dine, fashion, genteel, cuisine, honor, virtue, chef.* But our Latin vocabulary was brought into English by scholars, academicians, and scientists, so it feels scholarly, scientific, and clinical: *condition, instinctual, relativity, procedure, effective, factor, element, consideration, criterion, process.* Everybody who knows English grasps this, so when we want to impress a reader with our status as scholar, scientist, or expert, we reach for our Latinate vocabulary. We unconsciously (or consciously) translate our meaning into Latinate synonyms. The police officer testifying in a courtroom wants to say, "I saw the guy who probably did it leave the place with two other white guys—I don't know who they were," but he wants to add weight, so he paraphrases: "The alleged perpetrator was observed to exit the premises in the company of two unidentified male Caucasian individuals . . ."

All PP is very Latinate, and if you avoid Latinate words you can't write PP. How much is a lot? We're not pushing for a zero percent Latinate percentile—that sounds like Hollywood redmen: "White man make us fire stick, make big bang . . ." When typical journalism prose writes a hundred words, about twenty of them will be Latinate. Writers who strive to remain earthy and plain (Hemingway, Robert Frost) have a Latinate percentile as low as 10 percent. PP is typically above 30 percent. If your percentile isn't above 25 percent, PP will be almost impossible for you to write.

Latinate words are easy to flag, because they're marked by distinctive prefixes or suffixes. Assume a word is Latinate if it begins or ends with any of the following:

Prefixes: a- (amoral), ab-, ac-, ad-, ante-, anti-, co-, com-, con-, de-, di-, dis-, e- (eject), em-, en-, ex-, il-, im-, in-, ir-, ob-, op-, per-, pre-, pro-, re-, sub-, super-.

Suffixes: -age, -al, -ance, -ant, -ar, -ate, -ence, -ent, -ible, -ic, -id, -ile, -ion, -ite, -ity, -ive, -or, -ous, -tion, and nouns with -a (data), -is (crisis), -ude (decrepitude), -um (datum), and -y (contingency).

Any word that can take any of these prefixes or suffixes is also Latinate. So *real* is Latinate because you can add *-ity, use* is Latinate because you can add *-al* (*usual*), and *close* is Latinate because you can add *dis-*.

Don't worry about any particular word; you just want a ballpark figure, a sense of how high or low your style is as a rule. You can do as big a block of text as you want, but a 100-word section will tell you what you want to know. Pick a passage that feels typical, count off a hundred words, count how many of them have, or can have, the prefixes and suffixes in the list, and that number is your Latinate percentile.

There are two nice things about the Latinate percentile. First, it turns PP hunting into a game. Second, it gives you the means to document your feeling that you're surrounded by con artists. I can't count the number of students who have said, "You know, I always knew old Mr. *X* was snowing me, but I could never say how I knew. Now I know: It's his 40 percent Latinate vocabulary."

Nominalizations. Nominalizing means making nouns and noun phrases out of verbs and adjectives: *consideration* (a noun made from the verb *consider*) and *stupidity* (a noun made from the adjective *stupid*). Here are some PP passages, with the nominalizations in italics. In the rewrites, I've turned the nouns into verbs, adjectives, and adverbs:

> He investigated various studies to conclude if improving *articulation of production* of speech sounds can aid in developing spelling skills.
> Rewrite: *He wondered: If a person learns to articulate better, will he spell better?*

> Meaningful material that can be related to what the child already knows is necessary for *the development* of learning to read.
> Rewrite: *To learn to read, a child needs material he can relate to what he already knows.*

> When talking about elementary aged children there is a broad spectrum of *variability* to understand concepts and integrate them.
> Rewrite: *Some elementary-school children can understand and integrate concepts at a younger age than others.*

Most nominalizations are marked by easily spotted suffixes: *-ion, -tion, -ation, -ity, -ment, -y, -ance, -ence*. To no one's surprise, all these suffixes are Latinate.

The word *of.* When you nominalize, you inevitably get *of*'s:

"The building is tall" becomes "The height *of* the building."

"He ran fast" becomes "The rapidity *of* his running."

So if you count your *of*'s you'll get a good idea of how nominal your writing is, and if you deny yourself *of*'s, PP will be almost impossible.

The verb *to be.* When you nominalize, you're taking the meaning out of the verbs, so they tend to turn into forms of *to be: is, are, was,* *were, been, will be, may be, could be.* So these verbs are another measure of your PP level—the more there are, the worse the problem.

Don't replace *to be* with any of the dead verbs that appear more meaningful but aren't: *occur, result in, effect, cause, achieve, create, accomplish, further, develop.* Instead, go find the nominalization in the sentence and turn it back into a verb.

Of and *to be* are like Latinate words: You need a few of them; you just don't want to *cultivate* them.

Vitality

Wordiness and pretentiousness are things you take out. Vitality is something you put in.

Trying to teach someone how to be alive is like trying to teach someone to be funny. Memorizing rules for liveliness is as counterproductive as memorizing things to say in social situations to prove you're sincere. Rules can't tell you how to be alive, but that's okay, because you probably already know how. Almost all of my students write lively prose just fine—*as soon as I convince them it's okay to do so.*

If you need more than permission, go back to our basics: talking and modeling. Start with your talk and try to hold on to its virtues when you write. And read lively, energizing writers, and write like them.

If this holistic approach fails, you can *construct* vitality by adding to your own work four vitalizing devices:

Lively verbs

People

Concretions

Particulars

Use Lively Verbs

If you want to know how alive your writing is now, circle all your verbs and read them by themselves. Few verbs, dead verbs, passive verbs, and forms of *to be* mean trouble; lots of lively verbs mean health. Lively verbs have punch, movement, emotional color: *swill, scrape, hover, smother, twist, despise, pucker, slaughter, sashay, grow, touch, sniff, drool.* Dead verbs don't: *is, are, continue, accomplish, effect, affect, consider, involve, proceed, utilize, initiate, remain, influence, alleviate, obtain, result in, develop, determine, produce, enable, constitute.* Don't smother lively verbs with dead ones. "She is causing her kids to feel intimidated" smothers the one lively verb *intimidate* with three dead ones (*cause, is, feel*). Cut straight to the action: "She intimidates her kids."

Humanize

Humanizing means populating your writing with signs of human life. Dehumanized writing talks about phenomena without reference to the human beings who are experiencing them, as if the sight of them were in slightly poor taste:

> Parking decals for the spring semester will be available for purchase at the times and places shown below.

Who will do the selling and the buying? Let the people step forward:

> If you want a parking sticker, Doris will be selling them at . . .

In these dehumanized passages, notice the absence of people and watch them reappear in the rewrites:

> This allows the application of self-experience to enhance writing skills.
> Rewrite: *This way, the child can use her own experience to help her write.*

> The usage of a dictionary should also be instructed, so that the specifics of word spellings may be self-corrected.
> Rewrite: *A teacher should teach children to use a dictionary so they can teach themselves how to spell.*

People are what make writing matter. You can hardly have too many of them. *Peter Pan* begins with this note:

> Do you know that this book is part of the J. M. Barrie "Peter Pan Request"? This means that J. M. Barrie's royalty on this book goes to help the doctors and nurses to cure the children who are lying ill in the Great Ormond Street Hospital for Sick Children in London.

People appear in those four lines eight times: you, J. M. Barrie, Peter Pan, J. M. Barrie, doctors, nurses, children, and sick children. Take the people out, and the loss hits you like a chill wind:

> All royalties from the sale of this book are donated to further medical research in pediatrics and to help defer the cost of indigent pediatric medical care.

You don't have to be writing about people to have lots of people in your writing; any material, however impersonal and abstract, can be humanized. If you look at the informative and argumentative essays in Chapters 15 and 17, you'll see that a remarkable number of them have found ways to bring signs of people into their first paragraphs. The most obvious way is to mention people by name: *my mom, Madonna, parents, the average math teacher, my daughter's Girl Scout troop leader Beth, Joe College.* But there are lots of others:

Narratives: little stories, real or fictional.

Quotations and dialogue: You can use quotes from real people, or imagined quotes from the reader ("I bet you're asking yourself . . .") or invented characters ("The typical high school English teacher would say . . .").

Direct acknowledgments of the reader's presence: "Don't get me wrong"; "I know that sounds screwy, but . . ."

You and *me:* They're the two words dehumanized writing most meticulously avoids, so they're the two words you should try the hardest to use. Take this dehumanized example, written by John Lyons in *An Introduction to Linguistics:*

Linguistics may be defined as the scientific study of language. This definition is hardly sufficient to give the reader any positive indication of the fundamental principles of the subject.

Rewrite: *I would define linguistics as the scientific study of language. But that probably doesn't tell you very much.*

Contractions: Dehumanized writing says *cannot* and *they are;* humanized writing says *can't* and *they're.*

Two syntactic constructions make people disappear, so avoid them: *nominalizations* (p. 208) and *passive constructions.* When you nominalize a verb, you can dispense with the doer: "George destroyed the house completely" becomes "The destruction of the house was complete." Passive constructions do the same thing. In a sentence with an active verb, the doer is the subject: "George broke the chair." A passive verb construction—a form of *to be* plus a past participle—doesn't need to mention the doer at all: "The chair was broken." Therein lies the danger:

In teaching spelling and reading the method of phonics is questioned.

Who questions phonics? The writer? Some unnamed authority figure? The teaching community? The writer's friend Pete?

Passivity is a stylistic issue, but it's also a moral one. We live in a passive world, where everybody wants to avoid having to say who's *responsible.* The air is being polluted, our food is being poisoned with pesticides, and our water supplies are contaminated—by whom? No one's saying. Passive constructions let us off that hook.

There is one large exception to the "avoid passives" rule. In scientific and technical writing, if you are describing a process—a step-by-step series of events—then *what was done* is all that matters and *who did it* is honestly a distraction. In this instance the passive is efficient and the active is cumbersome. Write "The surface liquid was drained off and the residue transferred to a sterile Petri dish"; don't write "One of my lab assistants, Pippi Carboy, drained off the surface liquid and Lance

Credance, a post-doctoral fellow who shares the lab, transferred the residue to a sterile Petri dish."

Be Concrete

To be concrete you fill your writing with concretions, things you can see, touch, smell, taste, or hear. The opposite of a concretion is an abstraction: anything that can't be perceived by our senses.

Abstractions	*Concretions*
hope	door
faith	daisy
concept	crash
jealous	poke
hate	Bernaise sauce
abstinence	Pepsi
dishonest	slimy

If you're writing a recipe or an account of a car accident, you'll use concretions all over the place. The trick is to find concrete ways of talking about abstractions. Here's what we're trying to learn to do—four sentences rewritten from abstract to concrete terms:

People who buy handguns for self-defense are almost always inexperienced in the use of a handgun, and this leads to accidental firings and a great possibility of injury or death.

Rewrite: *People who buy handguns usually don't know how to use them, and so end up shooting themselves in the foot or plugging their spouses during a family argument.*

Does a short jail sentence really penalize a person for his "crime"?

Rewrite: *Do a couple of boring days staring at blank walls and two nights on a cot really penalize a person for his "crime"?*

The only really good persuader for using seat belts is a serious accident.

Rewrite: *The only really good persuader for using seat belts is a cranium through a windshield.*

She can't imagine not looking perfect.

Rewrite: *The words* pimple *and* split end *aren't in her vocabulary.*

If concretizing doesn't come easily to you, here are three concretizing devices: the metaphor, the simile, and exemplification.

Metaphors. A metaphor is an implied comparison. Instead of saying to your roommate, "Your living habits are filthy and revolting," you say, "You're a pig." You can't articulate clearly on a sleepy Monday morning, and instead of saying, "My mental processes are impaired," you say, "I can't jump-start my brain." Instead of saying, "That rock band is out of date," you say, "They're dinosaurs." In each case you're assuming the listener will know you mean an implied *like* or *as:* Your roommate is like a pig in some ways; your brain feels like a dead battery; the rock band is as graceless and anachronistic as the dinosaurs.

Everyday English is stiff with metaphors. In the world of sports, for instance, teams lock horns, fold, choke, run out of gas, get snakebit, and look over their shoulder. Players press too hard, go flat, carry teams, get swelled heads, rest on their laurels, and coast. Quarterbacks pick defenses apart and have to eat the ball, and pitchers throw smoke, pull the string, and nibble at the corners.

Unfortunately, all the examples we've looked at won't help your writing much, because the metaphors are all *dead:* We've heard them so often they cease to energize our senses. We don't *visualize* a team running out of gas anymore. So metaphors must be fresh; you have to make up your own. The media are constantly introducing metaphors that get coined, overused, and discarded in a week or two. The first time I heard it said of David Souter, a nominee for Supreme Court Judge, that he "left no footprints," meaning no one could tell from his past performance on the bench where he stood on anything, I got a vivid image. Three weeks later, after I had heard the media use the metaphor five thousand times, I just went brain-dead when I heard it. The best metaphors seem utterly right and invented for the occasion. An interviewer once asked Charlton Heston what Cecil B. DeMille, the legendary Hollywood director, was like, and Heston replied, "He cut a very large hole in the air." I've never heard it before or since.

Similes. Similes (rhymes with "Tim'll sneeze") and metaphors are almost the same thing. A simile is a metaphor with the comparison spelled out with the word *like* or *as:*

> Writing unrhymed poetry is like playing tennis without a net. (Robert Frost)

> The boy touched his sleeve, cautious as a city man reaching toward a horse. (John Gardiner)

> While her mind had wandered, her eyes had gone on reading, dutifully moving from word to word like well-trained horses through a haylot. (John Gardiner)

An *analogy* is a simile that goes on to explain exactly how the things you're comparing are alike: You say, "Writing unrhymed poetry is like playing tennis without a net," and then you give a few reasons. A favorite analogy of mine is that writing is like athletics, and I've mined it throughout this book.

Exemplifications. An exemplification substitutes an *example* for an abstraction. On a TV show I heard Stanley Kramer, the movie director, talking about how he financed his first movie. Straight out of the army, knowing no one and nothing about getting financial backing, he walked into a bank and asked for the money. Kramer wanted to say, "I'd never been in a bank before except to conduct minor personal financial transactions." But being an entertainer, he knew how dull that would sound, so he said, "I'd never been in a bank before except to take out twenty dollars." He was really saying something like, "I'd never been in a bank before except to (do things like, for example,) take out twenty dollars." All the concretizing examples on p. 212 are exemplifications.

Be Particular

That doesn't mean be picky; it means use particulars. Particulars are the opposite of generalizations. Think of words as denoting categories of things: The more things there are in the category, the more general the word; the fewer things in the category, the more particular. There are more shoes in the world than there are loafers, so *loafer* is more particular than *shoe*. The more particular the writing, the more lively.

Imagine every word as existing on a continuum or spectrum from very general to very specific:

thing→vehicle→ car→ station wagon→ Ford station wagon→ 1964 Ford Country Squire station wagon

act→ move→ walk→ mince

thing→ sustenance→ drink→ soft drink→ cola→ Coke→ diet Coke

When we particularize, we replace words with words to the right of them on such strings:

He's strong as a *Clydesdale.* (instead of *horse*)

She went off to school with her lunch pail in one hand and her *Pee-Chee folder* in the other. (instead of *binder*)

So you're furious with your little brother for riding over your block castle with his *Big Wheel.* (instead of *tricycle*)

Particulars have an irrational persuasiveness, as every good salesperson knows: The more particulars, the more we're *sold* on what we read. When I read an ad for a powerboat that says,

Kurtis Kraft 10-inch runner bottom, blown injected, $1/4$-inch Velasco crank, Childs and Albert rods, Lenco clutch, Casale 871 Little Field blower, Enderle injection,

I don't know what any of that means, but I can't help thinking, "It must be a great boat!"

Since particulars are stirring, dehumanized writing avoids them. Police officers are trained to say, "Please step away from the *vehicle*" instead of *car*; military folk are trained to say, "I accidentally discharged my *weapon*" instead of *rifle*; and administrators talk about building a new *facility* instead of *hospital.*

Particularizing and concretizing are hard to tell apart, but you don't have to—just do both. Robin Lee Graham, who sailed around the world when he was sixteen and wrote a book about it, concretizes and particularizes when he explains why he loved sailing. He might have said, "Sailing was a chance to escape from all the meaningless busywork of school." Instead he said,

> It was the chance to escape from blackboards and the smell of disinfectant in the school toilet, from addition and subtraction sums that were never the same as the teacher's answers, from spelling words like "seize" and "fulfill" and from Little League baseball.

Final Tips on Vitalizing

Don't overdo. Writing can be too energetic in the same way that people can be too energetic. If you're bouncing off the walls, you'll make your reader nervous and exhausted. Also, any writing habit can be overdone until it becomes a tic so distracting your reader can't hear what you're saying. You never want to be so self-consciously stylish that the reader starts reading the style itself instead of the content:

> The Westclox went off like Fourth of July roman candles inside my cranium. I staggered to the bathroom, ran the Remington over my stubble, and held my head under the tap. Never again would I mix Smirnoff and Johnny Walker Red, I swore. Who's the blonde on the Sealy Posturpedic?, I wondered.

Don't count words. Count words to fight wordiness, but don't count them to fight lifelessness. Lively people tend to be chattier than dead ones.

Is Vitality Always a Good Thing?

Writing in some fields disapproves of almost everything I've encouraged you to do in this section. Humanizing, metaphor, contractions, *I* and *you*, and exemplification would all be called vices by most writers in science, technology, medicine, and law. Neither of us is wrong. Part of being a writer is having different styles available to you and making judgments about what is stylistically appropriate to which audience. You'll need to form your own personal guidelines for making those judgments. Here are some of mine.

Different kinds of writing have different priorities. If you're writing a will, the only concern is that it be utterly unambiguous—to get that, you sacrifice vitality, pith, ease of reading, everything else. If you're writing for medical technicians, you can't afford to be misunderstood. If a lawyer stocked a will with rich metaphors, she'd be fired. But if you're writing a poem, ambiguity is a virtue, so you pack your language with a thick, stewy suggestivity, like Emily Dickinson's description of meeting a snake:

> a tighter breathing
> And Zero at the Bone.

With poetry we expect every reader to find her own meaning—something we can't have in law courts and operating rooms.

You can't have everything. You can't be totally unambiguous and vital at the same time, any more than you can be a good courtroom judge and a good standup comedian simultaneously. Since you must make choices, make them consciously and with good reason: What do you want your writing to do? What kind of person do you want to be?

The most popular arguments against vitality are bogus. Fans of deadness like to argue that dead language increases understanding, but in practice it almost always obstructs it. And they like to argue that vitality involves a loss of dignity or a trivialization of content, but all the great populist communicators in the sciences and arts—Leonard Bernstein on classical music, Stephen Jay Gould on biology, Oliver Sacks on neurophysical therapy—have proved them wrong.

The idea that professional audiences demand dead prose usually vanishes the moment you take a chance and write with life. A friend of mine once told me that at every stage in his writing career his teachers told him, "Well, of course I love the vitality, but those other stuffy professors and editors will make you rewrite it." He's still writing his vital prose, readers are still appreciating it, and those mythical oppressors have never materialized. Most people, whatever their line of work or their terminal degree, would rather be alive than dead and stimulated rather than anesthetized.

If you strip your writing of its living pulse, you had better offer the reader something of value to take its place. Writing without life is like talking at a cocktail party with bad breath: People will still listen, *if* what you offer is worth the torment. You have to be that much more insightful, that much more useful, that much more knowledgeable. Medical researchers can write dry prose, because what they have to say will save lives.

You've got to enjoy yourself, or you won't bother. Be as lively as your boss, audience, and purpose will let you, for selfish reasons—because it *feels good* to write juicy, sensual stuff that uses our blood and guts as well as our brains.

THINGS TO DO

---

1. Cut the flab from the following passages. The number in parentheses is the approximate word count you want to end up with.

    a. Compared to most university courses, this course would be categorized as virtually basic and simple; however, what the course lacks in rigor, it makes up for by providing its student with an enriching learning experience. (10)

    b. In the United States, there are at least 15,000 murders a year. Most of the deaths are results from gunshot wounds. About 51 percent of all American murders have been committed with pistols or handguns. (17)

    c. My main objective here is to inform you of the reasons Proposition 11, the bottle bill, should pass and become a California state law. We all know that there are always two sides to a bill like this, the ones in favor and the ones against. By the opinion of most Californians I have gotten the idea that they believe there are more positive aspects than negative aspects and benefits. (15)

2. Write a wordy parody rewrite of one of the following sentences:

    a. Keep language plain.

    b. Writing is hard.

3. Rewrite the following passages without pretentiousness:

    a. It is not possible to make a realistic determination of the degree of fatness of your body by your weight.

    b. The use of the IBM 35P computer will result in a reduction of long-term costs for labor, space, and materials.

    c. The potential of large underdeveloped lands and the intensification of farming areas currently being cultivated are the sources of multiplying the output of the world's food supply.

4. Here are two very Latinate passages:

a. Academic excellence has been achieved through a distin-
guished faculty whose primary responsibility is superior instruction. While each campus has its own unique geographic
and curricular character, all campuses, as multipurpose institutions, offer undergraduate and graduate instruction for
professional and occupational goals as well as broad liberal
education.
b. The center's major objective is the construction of effective
theories that will result in significant conceptual and practical impact on composition pedagogy as well as stimulation
of further research.

Choose one of the passages above and do the following things
with it:

a. Calculate its Latinate percentile.
b. Rewrite the passage in as low a Latinate percentile as you
can.
c. Calculate the Latinate percentile of your rewrite passage.

5. Write a PP parody of one of these old saws, like we did on
p. 206:

a. Don't count your chickens before they're hatched.
b. Too many cooks spoil the pot.

6. Underline the nominalizations in the following sentences
and rewrite the sentences without them:

a. This is a splendid book to facilitate in the instruction of
reading.
b. There has been no increase of improvement in the student's
spelling skills.
c. Oral reading in the classroom is a primary cause of student
anxiety, which leads to a disliking for the reading function.

7. Vitalize the following sentences by adding lively verbs, people, concretions, and particulars wherever possible:

a. Drunk driving needs to become less socially acceptable.
b. The drug traffic should be ignored, so law enforcement can concentrate on more important matters.
c. Graduation from high school is almost mandatory for avoiding menial labor jobs in later life.

Chapter 12

EDITING

Finally, it's time to go over the text line by line looking for rule-following problems. This isn't just more of Chapter 11. There, we tried to make our sentences strong, pretty, graceful, effective; here we're just trying to make them *legal*. There we were trying to hone our running-and-passing game; here we're just trying not to be offsides.

Before we talk about what the rules are, we must prepare the soil. The trickiest part of editing is doing it with the right attitude and for the right reasons. So first we'll talk about how to approach editing, then about how language rules are learned. Then finally we'll get into the rules themselves.

Getting the Editing Attitude

Six Starter Principles

Editing is not writing. Mechanics are the part of writing most students think of first and worry about the most when they take a writing class. When I ask my students at the beginning of the term what they need to do to become good writers, the most popular answer is "Work on my grammar." That's like believing that if you get good enough at not being offsides, you'll be a great football player.

Writing is mostly creating, communicating, getting clear on what you believe, playing with language, and entertaining readers. Editing is one small task that follows those large ones. It's no more the core of writing than wax is the essence of a car. And don't think that rule-following will make your writing substantially better unless an instructor tells you it will.

Editing follows creating. You create first, correct second. The worst thing you can do to your writing is to worry about rule-following when you're trying to invent. Nobody drives fluently with a cop in the rear-view mirror.

Edit for readers. If you write something and decide it's worth showing to an audience, edit it to make it legal, like you'd make sure your attire was appropriate before stepping out in front of a large audience to give a speech. If it isn't worth showing to an audience, don't bother.

I call this the Résumé Principle. Students who can't get themselves to care about editing on-course assignments come by my office when they start looking for jobs: "Mr. Rawlins, I've proofread this résumé ten times and had all my friends proofread it, but I'd was just wondering if you could look it over for me."

Editing is trivial and vital at the same time. That's why it's hard to know how to feel about it. Language legalities have no worth by themselves. No writer ever got rich off his splendid spelling, and subject-verb agreement has zero market value. Writers are celebrities, but copy editors aren't. Yet mechanics are also vital: If you spell poorly or say "Go lay down" instead of "Go lie down," a large percentage of your audience will write you off as illiterate. Even though you shouldn't equate editing with writing, unfortunately a lot of readers do. When a university professor outside the English Department complains that her students "can't write," she almost always means they can't spell, punctuate, or avoid usage errors. Grammar and mechanics are like the rules to a football game: You can't win the game by following the rules; on the other hand, if you don't follow the rules they won't let you play, however well you execute pass routes and trap block.

Grammar usually isn't the problem. Most people use the word *grammar* to describe a whole range of writing problems that are better called other things: awkwardness, clumsiness, ugliness, weak sequencing, ambiguity, poor organization. None of these things is fixed by learning grammar rules. How many bad basketball players can get good by memorizing the rule book?

Rule-following is fun. No, really, it is. Board games, card games, treasure hunts, car rallies, scavenger hunts, codes, and ciphers are little more than exercise for our innate love of obeying a set of directions. If it's not fun for you, it can only be because of two things: You're afraid of being punished or ridiculed, or you aren't sure what the rules are. If you're afraid, go back to Chapter 5 for tips on handling fear. If you're unsure of the rules, you have to learn them. Nobody likes playing a game with umpires hovering over her, about to whistle her for breaking rules no one told her about.

How Language Rules Are Learned

How do you learn to write "Go *lie* down" instead of "Go *lay* down"? First, let's rule out some ways you *won't* learn:

By reading a grammar handbook. You can't learn language deductively, by reading a general principle and then trying to apply it, because you can't understand the book until you already know what you're trying to learn, and because language rules are so complex that they really can't be said in words.

By classroom lessons. There's too much to know. It would take a million lectures, and the term is only fifteen weeks long.

By having someone line edit your essay and return it to you with a bad grade. It hurts too much, you can't understand the hieroglyphics, there's too much feedback to process at once, and being shown corrections doesn't explain how to make them yourself.

By doing mechanics exercises and drills. Language skills learned by drill don't translate and become a part of your writer's brain. Doing apostrophe exercises only teaches you how to do apostrophe exercises.

What *does* work? Learn grammar and mechanics the way you learn everything else about language. First and foremost, you need massive exposure. Read a lot in the dialect you want to master. Listen a lot to people speaking it. You're not really trying to learn grammar, because you already know one—the one you're speaking and writing now. You're trying to learn *a second* grammar, and you'll learn it the same way you did the first.

Next, you need instruction, but only the kind that works. It must be instruction *on your own writing;* you need to learn how to punctuate your own sentences, not sentences in the exercise book. It must be non-punitive, intended to ready the manuscript for public viewing, not to show you how dumb you are. It must be slow, an item at a time, because learning language by instruction takes time. And it must include explanations. The editor has to tell you how he knows the apostrophe goes there, or you won't know where it goes when you're on your own and editing new text. That means sitting down with an editor/teacher and talking through the mechanics of your own essay, line by line, as slowly as it takes for you to say, "I see what you're doing."

Grammar and Usage

Grammar means different things to different people, but most people use it to lump together three different kinds of rules for word usage and sentence building: conventions, rules of logic, and rules of clarity. It's helpful to keep the three separate, since we master each in a different way.

Conventions

We talked about how language is conventional in Chapter 1 (p. 12). Conventions are rules that can't be figured out, explained, or justified—they're just "the way it's done." Conventions change with time and differ from group to group and place to place. The grammar of California isn't exactly the grammar of Boston, the grammar of 1990 isn't exactly the grammar of 1950, and we all know that the grammar of the university professor isn't exactly the grammar of the junior-high student or the Georgia farmer. Unless you're learning English for the first time, you already know at least one set of English conventions—the set used by your peer group—and the only question is whether you need to learn additional ones. Any convention is as good as any other as long as everyone in the group agrees to abide by it, so there's nothing wrong with the ones you know or better about the ones you're trying to learn.

Most of us know the conventions of colloquial English, but the conventions of formal Essay English are occasionally different:

CE: Everybody has to bring *their* own pencil and paper.
EE: Everybody has to bring *his* own pencil and paper.

CE: I hate people *that* can't remember names.
EE: I hate people *who* can't remember names.

CE: This line is for people with ten items or *less.*
EE: This line is for people with ten items or *fewer.*

CE: Try *and* get some rest before the big game.
EE: Try *to* get some rest before the big game.

CE: None of these sentences *are* incorrect.
EE: None of these sentences *is* incorrect.

CE: Write on things you know *about.*
EE: Write on things *about which* you know.

Many people label these alternatives wrong and right or bad and good, but those are misleading terms, and you should try to substitute better ones: accepted and unaccepted, standard and nonstandard, appropriate and inappropriate. Even these labels are misleading, because they suggest a consensus about what's accepted or what isn't that simply doesn't exist. *Every user of English has her own sense of what "normal" language use is,* the same way everyone has her own sense of acceptable rules for dressing or sexual conduct or dinner-table behavior. There are extremes. Almost everyone in the United States considers plunging a knife into the back of your dinner hostess bad form, and almost everyone agrees that "Him and me, we gone do it" is bad form in a formal essay. But almost everything else is a matter of what you're used to.

Some years ago, *The American Heritage Dictionary* set out to settle the question of what's acceptable and what isn't. They established a usage panel, and invited the big names in language—writers, journalists, grammarians, linguists, teachers—to be on it. They asked the panel questions like, "Is it okay to write 'Can I go?' instead of 'May I go'?" So what did the usage panel find out? That every member of the panel knew exactly what was acceptable and what wasn't . . . but nobody agreed with anybody else. Those who said "Can I go?" was okay called those who thought it wasn't snobbish and archaic; those who said "Can I go?" wasn't okay called those who thought it was slovenly and unprincipled. In short, everyone thought that "right" was equivalent to "the way *I* do it"—and so do we all.

The wonderful thing about thinking in terms of conventions is that it cuts through a lot of confusing, highly emotional rhetoric surrounding the learning of Standard English. You aren't learning good English or better English. There's nothing wrong with the dialect you've been using. You aren't becoming a better person. You aren't being asked to forsake your heritage or abandon your other dialects. You're adding a tuxedo or ball gown to your closet of jeans and sweaters, not throwing the jeans away or spurning them. Maybe most important, there's nothing shameful about not knowing the dialect you haven't been around. If you went to an Arab's home and didn't know the etiquette, would you conclude that you're stupid or depraved? No—you're just new in town. You'll learn.

You already know from Chapter 1 how you learn conventions: by surrounding yourself with people who use them and picking up their conventions without particularly trying. That's how grammarians, linguists, and your teachers did it. There is no other way. If you want to learn the conventions of Essay English, read a lot of essays.

Rules of Logic

Many people believe that grammar is logic applied to language use. It isn't, since conventions aren't logical. But there is a small pocket of grammar that is logic based, and some language cops care mightily about it and will cast you into hell for not knowing it.

All of the following examples are illogical. (The asterisk in front of the sentence, which you'll see throughout this chapter, means the sentence is illegal; something is nonstandard.)

*Q: Do you mind if I sit here? A: Certainly.

*To make your spelling more perfect, study morphemic structure.

*He won't do nothing about it.

*I could care less if he quits.

*I need alot of attention right now.

*I forgot I was suppose to prepare a class presentation last night.

Here are the logic problems:

1. *Certainly* means "yes," and since the question asked if one minded, the response must logically mean "Don't sit!"
2. *Perfect* is an absolute—something is either perfect or not. If your spelling is perfect, it can't get any more so, and if it isn't perfectly perfect, it isn't perfect at all.
3. Two negatives make a positive, so if he won't do nothing, then logically he must do something.
4. If you could care less, then logically you must care some.
5. *Lot* is a noun and *a* its article, so there must be a space between them.
6. *Suppose* is in an adjective position, but infinitive verbs can't be adjectives; past participles can. Logically the phrase must read "I was supposeD to prepare."

The heart of language logic is consistency, which grammar calls *parallelism:* Once you start doing it one way, you must keep doing it that way:

If you're making a list and the first item in the list is a verb, make all the items in the list verbs; if it's a participle, make all the items participles. The same goes for nouns, adjectives, full sentences—anything.

If you start telling a story in the past tense, stay in the past tense.

If you start talking about *parents* in the plural, stay in the plural.

If you start referring to a hypothetical person as *her/him*, continue calling her/him *her/him*.

The four most common parallelism problems are unparallel lists, tense changes, subject-verb agreement problems, and noun-pronoun agreement problems.

Unparallel lists.

*I gained organization and speaking skills, along with thinking quick.

The first item in the list is a noun: "organization and speaking skills." So the second item should be a noun too. But it's not; it's a present participle: "thinking quick." You could fix it by making the items all nouns, or infinitive verbs, or participles:

Rewrite: *I gained organization and speaking skills, along with the ability to think quickly;*

or

I gained the ability to organize, speak well, and think quickly,

or

I got good at organizing, speaking, and thinking quickly.

Tense changes. The law of parallelism says, Stay in the same verb tense unless your meaning has shifted tense too.

> *A spelling game *may* excite the children and make learning fun. The class *will be* split in half. The first half *will* continue reading and writing while the second half *plays* the game. The group playing the game *would* line up across the room. Each child *is* given a chance to roll a set of dice.

You could rewrite in present tense, past, or future. Here's a present-tense version:

> Rewrite: *A spelling game can excite the children and make learning fun. Split the class in half. The first half continues reading and writing while the second half plays the game. The group playing the game lines up across the room. Each child is given a chance to roll a set of dice.*

Subject-verb agreement. Subjects and verbs are supposed to agree in number—they should both be singular or both be plural. Most agreement problems occur when the subject and verb get separated by distracting business in between:

> *If a child is made to write on a topic of little interest to him, the *chances* of his learning anything from the experience *is* slim.
>
> Rewrite: *If a child is made to write on a topic of little interest to him, the chances of his learning anything from the experience are slim.*

> *The *price* of letter-quality printers *have* fallen dramatically.
>
> Rewrite: *The price of letter-quality printers has fallen dramatically.*

Pronoun agreement. Pronouns *refer to* nouns: In "George thought he could do it," *he* refers to "George"; *it* refers to something we can't see. The noun and the pronoun must *agree in number:* They must both be singular or plural. Colloquial English's conventions are illogical in two cases:

1. Pronouns like *anyone, anybody, everybody, no one,* and *nobody* are logically singular, so possessive pronouns that refer to them must also be singular:

> *Everybody has to bring *their* own juice.
>
> Rewrite: *Everybody has to bring his own juice.*

2. Anonymous single people ("a student," "a parent") need singular pronouns:

> *Putting a child in a situation where *he* has to write to participate in a game is a good way to encourage *him/her* to use *their* writing skills.
>
> Rewrite: *Putting a child in a situation where she has to write to participate in a game is a good way to encourage her to use her writing skills.*

*The key to writing success is choosing subject matter *the child* is familiar with and a vocabulary level *they* are familiar with.

Rewrite: *The key to writing success is choosing subject matter the child is familiar with and a vocabulary level he is familiar with.*

The Limits of Logic

The only problem with approaching language logically is that it often doesn't work—logic will talk you into error as often as it will help you out of it. Here are two examples.

1. Essay English disapproves of *"A crowd of people are outside," because *crowd* is a singular noun and requires a singular verb: We should write "A crowd of people *is* outside." But if that's so, then, since *a lot* is also a singular noun, it too should take a singular verb, so we must write *"A lot of people is outside," which is nobody's English.
2. Essay English disapproves of *"Hopefully it won't rain tomorrow," because *hopefully* is an adverb and adverbs are supposed to modify verbs, not entire sentences. But if that's so, then, since *luckily* is an adverb, we shouldn't be able to write, "Luckily it didn't rain today," and that sentence is correct in anybody's English.

Here's what's going on. English, like any language, works by a set of rules, but they're unconscious and beyond our power to express. Some people call it "the spirit of English." It isn't logical. The spirit of English says that double negatives just double the force of the negative, so everybody uses them, including Shakespeare. The spirit of English says that *they* is the sensible pronoun to use in sentences like *"If a person says they hate spinach, then they hate spinach," because *a person* is really a generic type and is neither male nor female. None of this bothers any English speaker, because we all have the real rules of English deep within us. It drives foreign learners of English crazy, because they want a language that follows simple rules so they can learn it fast.

Beginning around 1600, along came a group of people called grammarians who said, "English should be logical." So they started passing legislation: Double negatives are illogical, so they shall be wrong from now on; and so on. The logic was taught in schools, and we learned it there, or we learned English from people who learned it there. And because the logic rules are special to school, they come to matter very much to people who use language to determine membership in the educated elite. So you can lose more points for a double negative than for saying something stupid or for being dull or disorganized.

That explains why the logic rules often seem to run counter to what your gut tells you works. Consistency demands that you stay in the tense you start in; yet every user of English wants to begin stories in the past tense and shift into the present when things get exciting: "I was walking down the street, minding my own business, when suddenly—bam!—this car comes right at me!" That tense shift *works*—we all know it does—and the rule takes the life out of it.

Rules of Clarity

Some language rules try to prevent confusion and misreading. The two most cited are rules governing *pronoun reference* and *misplaced modifiers.*

Pronoun reference. Since pronouns refer to nouns, every time you use a pronoun the reader has to make her best guess about what noun it refers to. To help her guess well, follow these three rules: (1) The pronoun must refer to a specific *noun;* (2) the pronoun can't refer to a whole idea or clause; and (3) the pronoun must *follow* the noun (that's why the noun is called the *ANTEcedent*). Reference problems usually afflict the pronouns *it, this, that,* and *which:*

> *I placed my order at a counter *which* looks like a regular fast-food restaurant. (What looks like a restaurant?) *It* is partially blocked off so *it* didn't bother me while I was eating. (What is blocked off? What didn't bother you?) After I ordered and paid for *it,* I sat down. (What did you pay for?)
>
> Rewrite: *I placed my order at a counter which looks like the counter in any fast-food restaurant. It's partially blocked off so I wasn't bothered by sights of food cooking while I was eating. After I ordered and paid for my food, I sat down.*

> *He implied that I tried to make an illegal copy of the program, *which* he claims caused the defect. (What noun caused the defect?)
>
> Rewrite: *He implied that I tried to make an illegal copy of the program and he claims that my attempt caused the defect.*
> or
> *He implied that I caused the defect when I tried to make an illegal copy of the program.*

Misplaced modifiers. A *modifier* is any word, phrase, or clause that modifies (roughly, "tells you something about") a noun or verb. When words modify other words, make sure the reader is in no doubt about which words modify what. Most of the time it's obvious and there's no problem: If I say "As the sun was sinking in the west, the tall Texan slowly lowered himself onto the stool," we know that *tall* modifies *Texan; slowly* tells us *how* he lowered, *onto the stool* tells us *where* he lowered, and *as the sun was sinking in the west* tells us *when* he lowered, so they all modify the verb. But modifiers get unclear in two positions.

First, when a modifier follows a complex sentence, it can be hard to tell which preceding noun or verb the modifier refers to:

> *County Sheriff Wayne Hamilton this morning discussed the problems of lodging in the jail unconscious people suspected of being drunk with the Jefferson County Commissioners.

"With the Jefferson County Commissioners" is a prepositional phrase modifying some previous verb, but there are four candidates in the sentence: *discussed, lodging, suspected, being drunk.* We assume the modifier modifies the verb nearest to it, which is the last one: *being drunk.* So the sentence ends up falsely implying that the sheriff is arresting people for being drunk with the Commissioners. In fact, the prepositional phrase modifies *discussed,* and if we put the modifier right next to its verb all problems are solved:

> Rewrite: *County Sheriff Wayne Hamilton this morning discussed with the Jefferson County Commissioners the problems of lodging in the jail unconscious people suspected of being drunk.*

Second, when a modifier is an introductory phrase, it's often unclear what part of the sentence it refers to, so Essay English says it must always *refer to the subject of the sentence.* If the modifier refers to some other word in the sentence, the problem is called a *misplaced modifier,* and you just have to move the modified word to the subject position:

> *As a future teacher, censorship seems to me to be an overblown issue.
> Rewrite: *As a future teacher, I think censorship is an overblown issue.*

But if it's a *dangling modifier,* the modified word is nowhere on the page and is simply implied, and you have to add it to the rewrite:

> *Despite having spent $1.3 billion since 1982 on county jails, the need for more jail cells is still strong. (Who has spent $1.3 billion?)
> Rewrite: *Despite having spent $1.3 billion since 1982 on county jails, we still need more jail cells.*

Most dangling modifiers are participles (phrases with *-ing* verbs), so it's easy to proofread for them.

So how do you learn logic and clarity rules? Conventions you learn unconsciously, through exposure, and you follow them guided by your *ear.* That doesn't work with logic and clarity rules, unless you grew up around people who spoke Essay English. But these rules, unlike conventions, *have reasons,* so we can learn them through formal instruction and edit for them methodically. Luckily, there aren't very many, so it's a manageable task.

Stripping Down to the Skeleton

We usually think of grammar problems as springing from a writer not knowing the rules, but in fact most of us know almost all the rules, but write problematic sentences anyway. Sentences usually get in trouble because they're so complicated the writer can't see that she's violating a rule she knows perfectly well. Nobody would say or write *"It's a problem for I," but lots of people do say and write *"It's an ongoing problem for my husband Andy and I." The problem isn't lack of grammar knowledge, it's simple busyness, and you fix the problem not by studying the rules but by simplifying the sentence until you can see what is basically going on. Strip the sentence down to its skeleton—its basic framework—and ask if the skeleton looks good by the rules we already know. If *"It's a problem for I" is illegal, then *"It's an ongoing problem for my husband Andy and I" is illegal, and we fix both sentences the same way, by changing *I* to *me*. It's just a matter of clearing out the underbrush:

> *I'm not so knowledgeable about computers that when problems are presented to me that I instantly find solutions. (Skeleton: *"I'm so knowledgeable that that I find solutions.")
>
> Rewrite: *I'm not so knowledgeable about computers that when problems are presented to me I instantly find solutions.*

> *Spearguns come in two forms: the kind that you cock and fire by pulling the trigger (this kind has better range). The other kind is called a Hawaiian Sling, which doesn't fire by a trigger and is usually cheaper and more simple. (Skeleton: *"Spearguns come in two forms: the kind you cock and fire.")
>
> Rewrite: *Spearguns come in two forms: the kind you cock and fire by pulling the trigger (this kind has better range) and the kind called a Hawaiian Sling, which has no trigger and is usually cheaper and more simple.*

Which problems need an extra step. Take the *which* clause by itself, replace the *which* with an *it* or its antecedent noun, reorder the words if you have to, and see if the clause is a well-formed sentence by itself:

> *The Board has set two ground rules which only one must be followed by manufacturers. (Skeleton: *"Only one the rules must be followed by manufacturers.")
>
> Rewrite: *The board has set two ground rules, only one of which must be followed by manufacturers.*

Which constructions in prepositional phrases are especially tricky, but since they go wrong more often than any other *which*'s, you must master the trick:

> *Children aren't familiar with the print and it becomes a challenge to them, a problem in which they can and must make sense of. (Skeleton: *"They can make sense of in the problem.")
>
> Rewrite: *Children aren't familiar with the print and it becomes a challenge to them, a problem they can and must make sense of.*

To strip to the skeleton, you don't have to cite rules or label anything. You only need a sneaking suspicion that something in the original sentence doesn't feel right.

Punctuation

If there ever was a part of writing that was reducible to rule and formal explanation, it's punctuation, right? No. Even comma placement proves to be more than we can explain or learn by conscious directive; every rule I'll give you in this chapter lies by oversimplification. Consider the commas in these two pairs of examples:

A. I closed the windows, so I'd like you to turn out the lights.

B. I closed the windows so the seat cushions wouldn't get wet.

A. A tall, handsome, unmarried stranger

B. A typical pushy American tourist

Why commas in A. and none in B.? It's hard to say, but you don't have to say—just hear it and trust your ear. If your ear doesn't tell you these commas are right, read until your ear is tuned. This section isn't everything there is to know about punctuation, but just a few things most people need to add to the huge body of knowledge their ears have already given them.

Think of punctuation as three different signaling systems. It's a way of representing the inflections and pauses you make when you speak. It's a guide to syntax. And it's a set of conventions, things we do just because that's how they're done. You'll need to think in terms of all three at one time or another when you punctuate, or you'll go nuts.

Since punctuation is a guide to reading out loud, and we can choose to read in lots of different ways and at different tempos, punctuation is often a matter of a writer's choices and intentions. Here's a sentence punctuated four ways, each correct:

George the gardener was arrested yesterday.

George, the gardener, was arrested yesterday.

George—the gardener—was arrested yesterday.

George (the gardener) was arrested yesterday.

The first sentence reads very quickly, as if *George the gardener* was his name. The second has slight pauses around *the gardener,* as if there is an infinitesimal hesitation before including the additional information. The third sets *the gardener* off from the rest of the sentence with long pauses, as if it's a startling interruption. The fourth turns *the gardener* into a whispered aside, an afterthought. The only way to choose among the four is to decide how you want the sentence to *sound*.

First we'll talk about the punctuation marks that mark pauses or breathing places. The littlest pause is the comma; the biggest is the period and other sentence-ending marks. In between are the colon, semicolon, parenthesis, and dash.

The Comma

The comma is the all-purpose mark that says, "An infinitesimal interruption or pause goes here." It goes in lots of places, so it's the hardest to master, and it's the most common punctuation mark—ninety percent of all punctuation errors are comma placement errors.

Commas are largely a matter of taste. Some people like a lot because they make sentence structure clear. Others don't because they slow reading down, risk mistakes, and waste ink. You can in fact get by with almost no commas these days—newspapers use almost none—and a good rule is, "When in doubt, leave it out." The longer your sentence, the more guidance the reader will need not to get lost, and the more optional commas you should use.

Commas do four main chores:

The introductory comma. Commas mark when a long introduction is over and the main clause begins:

> After the town had been battered by high winds for seven straight days, the rains came.

> Like a sly thief in the night, fall arrived.

> Exhausted and bitter, I seriously contemplated dropping out.

> If I hear the sound of bagpipes, I'll know the castle has fallen.

If the introductory bit is short, the reader probably won't need the comma's guidance, and you can leave it out:

> After the dinner I went to bed.

The conjunctive comma. Commas mark when one sentence (strictly speaking, one independent clause) ends and a conjunction begins another:

> The rage swept through him like the angel of death, and he stooped and picked up the knife.

> The loss of Flanagan will certainly hurt our offense, but we've devised some trick plays to make up for that.

As with the introductory comma, this comma can be dropped if the clauses are short and the reader is unlikely to get lost:

The rage swept through him and he picked up the knife.

Parenthetical commas. Commas *surround* parentheticals, phrases or clauses that interrupt the flow of the sentence. They come *in pairs*, like parentheses:

He stood over Ragnalf, sword drawn, and exulted.

I backed the old Rolls, inch by inch, into the narrow parking space.

My friend, my best, my truest friend, just lied to me.

Parenthetical commas, like parentheses, are a question of intrusiveness, not length:

Sometime after 3:00 A.M. he staggered slowly across the lawn.

Sometime after 3:00 A.M. he staggered, vomiting, across the lawn.

Lots of little things are conventionally treated as interruptions even though they don't feel very interruptive, and you should just memorize the fact that they're usually surrounded by commas: names in direct address, states or countries after cities, years after days, exclamations:

Bill, will you tell Harry that, uh, that guy in Toledo, Ohio, needs that stuff by March 13, 1993, or we're in trouble. Well, like, thanks a lot.

Dialogue usually needs masses of such commas.

The series comma. Commas punctuating a series of three or more go between each pair, including the last one:

Slowly, sensually, and seductively, he turned.

The three keys to academic success are studying hard, keeping a clear sense of one's goals, and using time efficiently.

Generations of students were taught to leave that last comma out, and newspapers don't include it, but most people still say formal essays should, so put it in.

Things Commas *Don't* Do

Beyond putting commas where they go, you have to make sure you don't put them where they *don't* go. Here are some popular misuses of the comma, most of them places where we pause when speaking but for some reason don't acknowledge it with punctuation:

First, commas do *not* go between a very large subject and its verb:

*The reason why I didn't tell you about cracking up the car and having to spend the night in chokey, is that I simply forgot.

Rewrite: *The reason why I didn't tell you about cracking up the car and having to spend the night in chokey is that I simply forgot.*

Second, commas do *not* go after conjunctions:

*I never showed up because, my parents wouldn't let me have the car.
Rewrite: *I never showed up because my parents wouldn't let me have the car.*

Third, commas do *not* go between two sentences with no conjunction; you need a semicolon, colon, or dash:

*The teacher cannot teach children to read or write, this can only be learned through doing it yourself.
Rewrite: *The teacher cannot teach children to read or write; this can only be learned through doing it yourself.*

*Go to the top row and carefully remove the plug wire, the little cap just pulls off if you put enough effort into it.
Rewrite: *Go to the top row and carefully remove the plug wire—the little cap just pulls off if you put enough effort into it.*

That no-no is called a *comma splice*—the splicing together of two sentences with a comma. It gets a huge amount of attention in school, and from some readers outside school, so it's worth learning to avoid. Say to yourself, "A comma isn't *big* enough to join sentences by itself; I need *more." Don't rewrite the sentence*; it's a problem with punctuation, not with wording. Replace the comma with a semicolon, colon, or dash, or add a conjunction.

A special kind of comma splice committed more by good writers than bad ones is the *however* comma splice:

*I'd really like to come, however my scheduling just won't allow it.
Rewrite: *I'd really like to come; however, my scheduling just won't allow it.*

However (and words like it—*nevertheless, therefore*) is really an *adverb.* Since it's not a conjunction, it and a comma can't join independent clauses. You need a semicolon.

Fourth, commas do *not* go between pairs joined by conjunctions, except pairs of sentences:

*He stooped with an air of graceful insouciance, and picked up something shiny from the gutter.

That comma separates the two verbs, *stooped* and *picked,* so it's wrong.

Rewrite: *He stooped with an air of graceful insouciance and picked up something shiny from the gutter.*

Finally, commas do *not* surround "anything that can be taken out of the sentence," as some of us have been taught. If you do that, you'll surround with commas everything but the main subject and verb. Put parenthetical commas only where there's a sense of interruption or turning aside:

> The Boston Red Sox, who are my favorite team, seem determined to break my heart.

> The Boston Red Sox who trashed that reporter's car should be heavily fined.

Do you put a comma "where you breathe"? Yes and no. Sometimes that rule works, in places where commas go and words have trouble explaining why:

> Andrew, my ex-husband, has really been a good dad.

> My ex-husband Andrew has really been a good dad.

> He said, "He already left."

> He said that "he already left."

But the rule will lead you astray more often that it will lead you right. For every true comma it will talk you into, it will talk you into three false ones. That's because the rule is circular: It really means, "Put a comma where *an essayist* pauses"—and most unpracticed writers don't know formal prose breathing patterns any more than they know formal punctuation. It's a rule better left alone.

The Semicolon

The semicolon does three things:

The antithetical semicolon. This semicolon joins sentences that are halves of a balanced pair—an *antithesis*. It says, "Don't think the thought is over just because the sentence is over. Keep reading; you're really only half done." The first sentence is the setup, a crescendo; the semicolon tells us to wait for the punch line, the decrescendo:

> Personal writing isn't trying to sell you anything; it's just trying to share a part of the writer's life.

> If it's above 70 degrees, it's too hot; if it's below 70 degrees, it's too cold.

A period between the sentences feels wrong, because you don't want the reader to stop. A comma is wrong because commas joining sentences make comma splices (p. 235). So you need the semicolon. You're using it correctly if what's on either side of the semicolon is a whole sentence; if not, it's wrong.

The semicolon will be a godsend to you if you've been told you write comma splices. In most cases, simply put a dot over the comma and make it a semicolon.

The series semicolon. Sometimes semicolons join a short series of sentences that have this same feeling of "read me all at once":

Nobody came. George was too tired; Suzy was held up at the office; Leroy forgot.

The postcolon semicolon. Semicolons show up in lists following colons, when the items in the list get so large that they have punctuation of their own:

They arrested three of our boys: Bill, Lars, and Sven.

They captured three of our boys: Bill, whose leg wound had started to bleed again; Lars, the one with the eye patch; and, worst of all, Sven.

What Semicolons *Don't* Do

Semicolons do *not* join sentences and following fragments—*colons* do that:

*There is only one reason why the new sex education program will never succeed; parental objections.

  Rewrite: *There is only one reason why the new sex education program will never succeed: parental objections.*

The Colon

The colon comes *after a sentence* and announces that what follows will list or enumerate something the sentence referred to but didn't specify. When you see a colon you say, "What is it?" or "What are they?"

Every time we try to make it work, we run up against the same two obstacles: my personality and her personality.

She knew what she needed: chocolate.

He suddenly had a wonderful idea: Why not hold the show right here?

Things Colons *Don't* Do

Colons do *not* follow sentence fragments. When you feel the urge to do that, either use no punctuation or rewrite the opening so it's a sentence:

*The three main problems facing the Middle East today are: poverty, Iraq, and religious fanaticism.

  Rewrite: *The three main problems facing the Middle East today are poverty, Iraq, and religious fanaticism.*

or

The Middle East today faces three main problems: poverty, Iraq, and religious fanaticism.

The Dash

The dash is nothing more than a big interruption. Use it when you come to a halt in the midst of a sentence and neither a semicolon nor a colon fits:

> He either had to say yes or tell her why not—a no-win situation.

> It's already raining outside—pouring, in fact.

If you write a lot of *sentence fragments,* put dashes between the fragments and the sentences that precede them and you'll probably be legal.

If the interruption is in the midst of the sentence, use dashes in pairs before and after, like parentheses:

> Suddenly there was a noise—it sounded more like a cannon than anything else—and the south wall disappeared.

> It was Shakespeare—or was it Madonna?—who once said, "All the world's a stage."

Almost everyone mistypes dashes. Type a dash with two hyphens and no spaces before or after, like so: "word--word." Many word processors will now make a real dash for you.

Dashes are informal, and they can encourage sloppy syntax, so some schools of writing instruction say they're unacceptable in formal essay writing—a pity.

Parentheses

Everybody knows that parentheses indicate a whispered aside, but punctuating around them can get confusing. Punctuate the sentence without the parentheses; then put the parentheses in, leaving all other punctuation alone:

> He was tall and mean looking.

> He was tall (very tall, in fact) and mean looking.

> He was tall, but his legs were so short he could touch his toes without bending over.

> He was tall (very tall, in fact), but his legs were so short he could touch his toes without bending over.

Question Marks

We all put question marks on the questions that feel like real questions, but lots of questions don't—the rhetorical questions to which you already know the answer—and they need question marks too. Put question marks on anything that is syntactically a question, whatever it feels like:

Could you please shut up for one minute?

Who is to say that wouldn't be a hindrance to him in the future?

Business and journalism are getting more and more comfortable with omitting the question mark in disguised requests, though I'm not:

Will you be kind enough to reply as soon as possible.

Now let's look at two punctuation marks that are less stage directions than grammar guides.

The Hyphen

The hyphen is a word-making tool. It lets us combine words and morphemes to make three kinds of words.

The compound adjective hyphen. The hyphen adds words together so they can be used as adjectives.

five ten-gallon hats
a nine-to-five job
the never-to-be-forgotten day
a soon-to-be-fired-for-his-incompetence employee

In practice it's hard to tell if a familiar two-word adjective should be written as two words, a hyphenated word, or simply one word: is it *red hot, red-hot,* or *redhot*? Just look it up in a dictionary. If it isn't there, hyphenate.

The verb-phrase noun hyphen. This hyphen adds a verb and its following adverb together so they can be used as a noun:

We were on a stake-out.

The car needed a little touch-up.

Both these hyphens say, "Take this group of words and think of it as a single word." The words have been taken from their natural position in a sentence and used in a slightly unnatural way. In their natural positions, they have no hyphens:

The hat held ten gallons.

I worked from nine to five.

The employee was soon to be fired for his incompetence.

We were going to stake out the house.

I asked him to touch up the paint on the car.

The prefix hyphen. Hyphens join prefixes to words if the joining is an awkward one:

> ex-husband vs. extinction
> De-louse him vs. destroy him
> pro-choice vs. productive

What Hyphens *Don't* Do

Hyphens do *not* join verbs-used-as-verbs and their adverbs:

> *We were going to stake-out the house.
>   Rewrite: *We were going to stake out the house.*

The Apostrophe

There are three kinds of apostrophes:

The contraction apostrophe. This apostrophe marks places where letters have been dropped out in contractions and reductions:

> could not → couldn't
> I will → I'll
> I expect he is swimming about now. → I 'spect he's swimmin' 'bout now.

The apostrophe goes exactly where the letter dropped out, and you need one for each place a letter or letters used to be:

> Write *doesn't*, not *does'nt.*
> Write *rock 'n' roll*, not *rock 'n roll.*

The possessive apostrophe. This apostrophe, with its accompanying *s*, is hard to explain in words. It marks possession, which is a loose kind of ownership:

> The pitcher's absence forced the cancellation of the game.

> The men's room is locked.

> The book's disappearance remained a mystery.

Sometimes it helps to think of the *-'s* as meaning *of:* "the pitcher's absence" equals "the absence of the pitcher." You've got the logic of possessives when the following sentences feel right:

> The Dodgers' uniforms look stupid.

> We're going to the Dodgers game.

Once you know you need a possessive apostrophe, the rules for where you put it are inflexible. If the noun is singular, add *-'s:*

the dog → the dog's collar.

Do this even if the noun ends in -*s* already:

the dress → the dress's hemline.

If the noun is plural and is pluralized with an -*s,* add the apostrophe after the -*s* that's already there:

the two dogs → the two dogs' collars
the two dresses → the two dresses' hemlines

If the noun is an irregular plural, add -*'s:*

the men → the men's department
the two octopi → the two octopi's mittens

If the possessive noun is a *pronoun,* use no apostrophe at all: *his, hers, theirs, yours,* and especially *its.* Memorize it: *Its* means "belonging to it"; *it's* means "it is."

If the noun is singular and ends in -*s,* sometimes the possessive looks funny, in which case some people give you permission to drop the second -*s:*

Ted Williams's batting average
            or
Ted Williams' batting average

These rules produce some odd-looking plurals, but follow them any-way. If I want to say "the place where the Jones family lives," I have to pluralize (*Joneses*), then add the possessive (*the Joneses'*). All those signs in front of people's houses saying "the Jones," "the Jones'," "the Jone's," or "the Jones's" are wrong.

Never let the -*'s* change the noun's spelling the way a pluralizing -*s* can:

The commitment of the University → The University's commit-ment, *not*

    *The Universitie's commitment.

The odd plural apostrophe. This apostrophe separates a plural noun from its pluralizing -*s only if* the noun is made of letters or numbers or if it would be confusing to the eye to use a normal plural form:

I love the Oakland A's.
Give me two 10's.
How many *e*'s are there in *separate*?

Don't let this apostrophe get out of hand. Use it only where you know it's very wrong without it. Otherwise you'll end up writing things like

*I'll have two pounds of tomato's.
    Rewrite: *I'll have two pounds of tomatoes.*

*I saw the Smith's last week.
    Rewrite: *I saw the Smiths last week.*

The apostrophe is the hardest punctuation mark to learn because we see it misused in print and on signs as often as we see it used correctly. As long as we're all surrounded by shop signs that say "McDonalds" and fruit stands advertising "tomato's 4/$1," you'll have to learn by *ignoring* all those wrong models.

Quotation Marks

Quotation marks do four things. First, as everybody knows, they surround someone else's exact words when you quote them:

I can still hear Monique saying, "But I didn't *mean* it!"

Her exact words were that she "hadn't a clue" about his whereabouts.

Use quotation marks even if the speaker or speech is imaginary:

I can just imagine what my father would say: "How are you going to pay for that?"

Nobody ever said, "Have a lousy day."

Second, they surround language you use but isn't really your own—language representative of the way others talk:

Doctors never like to talk about pain. When I'm sick, I don't "feel discomfort"—I *hurt!*

He's so out of date he still wears "groovy" clothes and smokes "tea."

Unions are always talking about "parity."

The quotation marks disown the language; they say, "That's not me talking; it's the people I'm talking *about* who are speaking there."

Third, they surround minor titles: titles of little things or parts of things, like chapters from books, songs, essays, short stories, or newspaper articles. The titles for the big, whole things (books, anthologies, newspapers) are <u>underlined</u>.

"Editing" vs. <u>The Writer's Way</u>

"The Telltale Heart" vs. <u>The Collected Works of Edgar Allan Poe</u>

"Man Bites Dog" vs. <u>The New York Times</u>

Fourth, they surround words as words:

How do you spell "necessary"?

I hate the phrase "special education."

Some formats, especially academic ones, use underlining or italics to do this job.

What Quotation Marks *Don't* Do

Quotation marks don't surround the title at the head of your essay. There are no quotation marks around "Editing" on p. 220, for instance.

They don't give emphasis to words or suggest heightened drama:

*Win a free trip to "Paris"!

*"Special" today, broccoli 35 c./lb.

The grammar rules for working quotations into sentences are complicated. See p. 422 in Chapter 19 for a primer.

Spacing and Positioning

If you're in doubt about spacing, sometimes picking up a book and looking will help you, but typing often uses different spacing than book printing does. When you're typing, follow periods and all sentence-ending punctuation marks with two spaces, commas and semicolons with one. Follow colons with one, unless what follows the colon is a complete sentence, in which case you can use two spaces. Don't space *inside* parentheses, like this: *(word). Dashes and hyphens have no spaces around them—not on either side. All punctuation marks except parentheses and quotation marks follow the preceding letter without a space. Quotation marks always come outside commas and periods; they come inside colons and semicolons; and question marks and exclamation points go wherever the sense dictates: If the question or exclamation is a part of the quotation, put it inside (He said, "Why?"); if the question or exclamation is the whole sentence, put it outside (Why did he say "ragmop"?).

Spelling

I have bad news. First, the world has decided that spelling matters enormously. If you can't spell, most readers will conclude you're illiterate, stupid, or both. Second, the world's spelling standards are very high. Two misspellings per typed page is considered poor. Third, spelling English is fiendishly hard, and nothing can make it easy. Fourth, spell-checker computer programs won't save you, because a misspelled English word often looks just like another word spelled correctly (*their/there, to/too, vein/vain, planning/planing*), and because most of what you write in your life will be handwritten things of the moment, and the world will judge you by them too. The only good news is that spelling is one of the world's most fascinating games.

The four most common ways people try to learn to spell don't work. Let's rule them out now:

1. *Don't* try to spell by rule. There are a few rules that help you spell (pp. 244–46), but they'll only solve one problem in a hundred.
2. *Don't* try to spell phonetically, by sounding words out. The majority of English words aren't spelled according to the phonics rules, and the more common the word is the less likely it is to follow the rules.
3. *Don't* spell by mnemonic devices, except now and then. A mnemonic device is a trick, jingle, or story to help you remember something: "the princi*pal* is your *pal*"; I shot *par* on two se*par*ate golf courses." Mnemonic devices work, but they're slow and cumbersome, so you can only afford to use them on a rogue word or two. I learned to spell *receive* via the famous mnemonic "*I* before *E* except after *C*," and thirty years later I still have to stop and recite the jingle every time I write the word. You can't do that a thousand times an essay.
4. *Don't* try to learn to spell by reading. Good readers are often terrible spellers, because reading well depends on *not* focusing on the letters.

So much for what doesn't work. What does?

Begin by caring in the right way. Most poor spellers just don't value spelling. If you don't, retrain yourself, not by lecturing yourself about how spelling will get you a good job, but by learning to love language and words and taking an interest in how they work. Read books about words. Become fascinated by etymologies. Play spelling games like Scrabble, Boggle, Password, Perquacky, and crossword puzzles.

Spell by recognition, the same way you remember faces or the names of movie actors. You look at *doesn't* and say, "That looks right" and you look at *dosen't* and say, "That looks funny." This method is effortless—you don't really work at it at all—but you can't do it the night before the test. It's a lifelong activity, and it starts to happen when you get interested in how words look, how they're built, what makes them tick.

Spell by using the dictionary. As my friend Steve Metzger puts it, "You spell with your arm"—the arm that reaches for the dictionary on the shelf. Good spellers look up words; bad spellers don't bother, then tell themselves the good spellers know some secret.

Spell morphemes, not words. A morpheme is a piece of meaning. Words are made out of them. *Unlisted* has three: *un-* (which means "not"), *list*, and *-ed* (which means "past tense"). The vocabulary of English really isn't a million unrelated words; it's a million recombinations of a few morphemes. If you can spell the morphemes, you can spell the words. If you can spell *-ment*, you can spell the last syllable of thousands of words.

Once you learn the morpheme *syn,* meaning "together," you've learned the tricky part of spelling *syndrome, symphony, syndicate, synchronize, syntax, synagogue,* and 450 others!

If you're unsure of a word, break it into its morphemes and spell each morpheme:

> *familiar = family + ar* (so *fimiliar* must be wrong)
> *vicious = vice + ious* (so *viscious* must be wrong)

Or think of other words using the same morpheme, words you can spell. The second syllable of *separate* is *par,* a morpheme meaning "equal." If you can't remember the *a,* remembering any of these words using the same morpheme will remind you: *par, pair, parity, disparate, compare, disparage, reparation.*

Get hints from other forms of the same word. Often what we can't hear in one form of the word sounds distinctly in another:

> circUit: think of *circuitous*
> musCle: think of *muscular*
> mouNtain: think of *mount*
> douBt: think of *dubious*
> siGn: think of *signal, significant*
> exHibit: think of *inhibit*
> condemN: think of *condemnation*
> critiCize: think of *critic*
> grammAr: think of *grammatical*
> utIlize: think of *utility*
> definItely: think of *definition*
> sentEnce: think of *sententious*
> relAtive: think of *relation*
> corpOration: think of *corporeal*
> benEfit: think of *beneficent*
> illUstrate: think of *illustrative.*

Make your own list of demons. Most of us only misspell forty or fifty words. It wouldn't take long to make a list of them; then you can master them the hard way.

Memorize a few rules. All rules have their exceptions, but four are worth knowing anyway:

1. *I* before *E* except after *C,* or when sounded like *A,* as in *neighbor* and *weigh.*
2. In stressed nonfinal syllables, vowels before double consonants are short; vowels before single consonants are long. *Matting* must sound like *at* and *mating* must sound like *ate.* This explains why *writting* has to be wrong.

3. Final *-e*'s disappear before suffixes starting with vowels; they don't disappear before suffixes starting with consonants: manage → managing, management; consummate → consummation, consummately.
4. Final *-y* becomes *-i-* when followed by a suffix, and it *never disappears:* pity → pitiful, rely → relies, controversy → controversial, family → familiar, they → their. Exception: *-y* before *-i-* or after a vowel stays *y:* pity → pitying; stay → stayed.

A Last Word on Grammar and Mechanics

The worst reaction you can have to language rules is to try to avoid breaking them by writing elementary-school sentences you're sure you can punctuate and spell. Probably three quarters of my students avoid misusing semicolons and colons by writing sentences that never use them at all. True, almost all rule problems disappear if the sentence gets short enough and the language gets basic enough. But that solution makes no more sense than not playing golf so you can avoid bogeys. No one writes to avoid error, except in school. Write the way racing drivers drive around the track: pushing the edge of the envelope, challenging yourself, taking risks, seeing just how much you can get away with. But the faster you drive, the more technique you need and the more time you must spend in the shop making sure the little things are just right. In theory it shouldn't be labor, because it's fun to fuss with things you love.

Following Format

A format is a set of rules about how an essay is laid out on the page: how big to make the margins, whether to type the title in full capitals or not, where to put the page numbers. Some students consider such matters too trivial for their attention, but editors and publishers don't. A friend of mine worked hard on an article for submission to a magazine. "Find out the magazine's format and use it," I said over and over. He had more important fish to fry. He submitted it in a format of his own invention, and they sent it back with a copy of their format sheet asking him to please use it if he wanted them to read his work.

There are no universal format rules, so the only way to know what the rules are is to ask the boss. Here's a safe format to use if your boss hasn't mandated one:

1. Use only one side of standard size ($8^1/2'' \times 11''$) paper of medium weight (20 lb.) or heavier.
2. Type or use a printer. Make sure the letters are dark and clean. Don't use erasable paper.
3. Proofread carefully, and make all corrections or additions in neat black ink.

4. Keep a margin of one inch on all four sides of the page. Approximate the right margin, breaking long words with hyphens to get close to the one-inch border.

5. Center each line of your title. Don't underline it or put quotation marks around it (unless it's a quote). Don't use full capitals; capitalize only the first letter of the first word and all important words: all nouns, verbs, adjectives, adverbs, and anything over four letters long. Put more space between your title and the text than there is between the lines of text themselves: If you're double spacing the text, triple space between title and text. Don't have a separate title page unless you're told to or the essay is more than thirty pages long.

6. For schoolwork, put in the upper right-hand corner of page one the following information: your name, the course *number* (not title), and the date.

7. Connect the pages with a staple or a paper clip in the upper left-hand corner. Don't fold the pages or dog-ear them.

8. Double space if the text is going to be edited; single space if someone's just going to read it and give you general reactions. If your printer has $1^{1}/_{2}$ spacing, use it instead of double spacing.

9. Indent the first line of each paragraph five spaces. Don't put extra vertical space between paragraphs.

10. Number all pages after page one. Put the page numbers in any one of three places: upper right corner, top center, or bottom center.

11. If your computer printer has lots of eye-catching fonts and type sizes, resist the temptation to dazzle with them. Be simple, conventional, and understated.

As you write, you'll realize there are thousands of questions that aren't answered here—questions about handling footnotes, charts and tables, bibliographies, poetry (do you indent a single line of quoted poetry or just put quotation marks around it?), and a hundred other subjects. Most style manuals and handbooks lay down policy on all such questions; wait until you need an answer, then look it up.

Some word processor users use the machine to excuse themselves from format responsibilities: "That's just the way the machine does it!" they plead. Students tell me their software can't double space, paginate, double strike, or adjust margins. It's rarely true. And I *know* that every word processor printer on earth will accept a new ribbon.

Proofreading

Proofreading is reading over the text to look for places where your fingers silpped and you typed *natino* instead of *nation*. It's the very last thing you do before handing the essay in or running the final printout.

To the writer, typographical errors (typos) don't really matter much. So what if you hit the wrong key by accident? But for the reader, an unfixed typo transforms the author from a seer to a buffoon. It's impossible to read about "fist graders" or "shot stories" without breaking up. How would you react to an essay beginning, "Censoring textbools for children is . . ."?

Proofreading problems are different than spelling or punctuation problems, and you fix them differently. Spelling and punctuating are usually problems of *knowledge,* and you fix them by *learning;* proofreading is a problem of *seeing,* and you fix it by *looking.*

You may be telling yourself, "I don't need to proofread—I have a spell checker on my computer." Not so. Spell-checking programs help you *spell,* but they make typo problems *worse*—precisely because they lull you into thinking they've fixed the problem for you when they haven't. A spell checker can't see when you've written "he" for "the" or "shot" for "short." The program will catch all the "hte" typos and leave all the ones that produce familiar but wrong words. And since you know the computer cannot err, you'll proofread cursorily and end up with more typos than you had in the pre-spell-check era. I've watched computers steadily improve people's spelling and erode their proofreading for years, and I've seen it happen to me. If you write on a computer, you'll have to proofread *even harder,* to overcome the complacency.

To proofread well, you must unlearn everything you've learned about reading. You have to go back to reading like a six-year-old, and stare at every letter. Here are some principles to guide you:

1. Ignore content. As soon as you start listening to what the text is *saying,* you'll start assuming and stop looking. Proofreading is like refereeing a basketball game: You're looking for traveling and charging violations, and you have to give up watching the game to see them.

2. Assume there's at least one typo. If you don't, you'll never find any. Tell yourself if you don't find any you'll reread until you do.

3. Forget what you meant. Since you wrote it, you know exactly what it's *supposed to* say. But you must forget that, or you'll never notice when you meant one thing and accidentally typed another. Read it as if you never saw it before.

4. Read it backwards to destroy comprehension and prevent guessing. If you still can't help reading for content, make a large card with a word-sized hole in it and move it over the page.

5. Set aside a time for nothing but proofreading. Since proofreading is a unique way of looking at writing, you can't proofread and do any other writing task at the same time. It's hard to stop tinkering with style or cutting that last needless word, but if you don't, you can't proofread.

6. Take your time. Any attempt to hurry or press and you'll start guessing and skimming. And of course that's exactly how we usually proofread: exhausted, up against the deadline, harried. We

say, "I'll proofread this thing quickly before I hand it in." That doesn't work.

7. Proofread a second time, this time listening to content. There are typos that reading backwards won't touch. They reveal themselves only when you proofread with a sense of the word's surroundings:

*I would explain that in our society there correct and incorrect forms to use.

*The little cap just pulls off it you put enough effort into it.

*After two weeks, it is evident that the that the consistent and continual printing errors are the result of a defective printer.

You'll only proofread well when it becomes a game. For me, finding a good typo is like watching a wonderful TV blooper. I once wrote that a good way to get started writing was to "write a letter to a fiend." I howled when I proofread it and shared it with all my colleagues, most of whom begged me to leave it.

Chapter 13

PUBLISHING

What, Me Publish?

I know what you're thinking: Publishing is for the grown-ups and the career writers. Publishing is what people like Stephen King and Tom Clancy do. You could never do that.

But you can, and what's more, you must. But hear me out—publishing isn't what you think it is, and you can publish the kinds of things you're writing now. I'll show you how.

You Must Publish

Think of the writing process as an electric circuit. The purpose of any circuit is to get juice to the end of the line. In writing, the end of the line is when the text reaches the hands of an audience. In the line are four on-off switches. They are (1) discovering something to say, (2) drafting, (3) revising, and (4) publishing. The switches are either closed or open (you do them or you don't). If they're open, the current stops; if they're closed, the current can continue.

There is no way for the current to get around the switches or compensate for an open switch by working really hard at the others. If any switch is open, there is nothing at the end of the circuit. Not a weak current or less than ideal current—nothing. If you think well, draft well, and revise well, then let the manuscript sit in a drawer, you've accomplished nothing.

Publishing is what we do all the work of Chapters 1–12 for. Writing without publishing is like spending your life training for a sport but never getting in the game. We should learn to call writing "pre-publishing," the way we call brainstorming "pre-writing."

We deny this truth constantly. Because the idea of publication is so daunting, composition classes rarely even suggest to students that they might publish their work. But only teachers think like this; a teacher may be impressed if you build three quarters of an electric circuit, but the lightbulb, which only cares about results, doesn't give a damn.

I know one instructor who tries to bring this reality into the classroom. He tells his students that anyone who publishes something more substantial than a letter to the editor—anything with a byline—gets an A in the class, automatically. Logically, he should add that anyone who *doesn't* gets an F, but we all have to live in the real world.

How Hard Is It to Publish?

Publishing is in one sense the hardest step in the writing process, because only one writer in ten ever manages to do it. But in another sense it's the easiest, because it takes no writing talent, no brains, and little labor—everybody knows how to mail a letter. It's just terrifying. But most of the fear is based on misunderstanding. So the first thing we have to do is understand what publishing is, and that it's something we can actually do.

When we think of publishing, most of us think of writing novels or full-time career freelancing, where you support yourself selling articles to magazines. With rare exceptions, none of us is ever going to do either of these things. Publishing in fact means nothing more than *making something public.* We will "publish" every time we show our work to readers not hand-picked by us, strangers whose goodwill we can't count on.

So publication means writing a letter to the editor of the local newspaper, or writing a news article for your club's newsletter, or writing an op-ed piece for the campus newspaper about how the library should open earlier and close later, or even posting a thoughtful response to someone else's posting on your electronic bulletin board. Scary, perhaps—but not impossible.

You don't have to be a career writer to publish, any more than you have to be a full-time professional speechwriter to talk at a public gathering; you just have to take part in that never-ending conversation among citizens that we've talked about a lot in this book. The ongoing public debate is about everything, from What does it mean to be a man? to What's the best way to recharge Ni-Cad batteries? From How can we bring peace to the Middle East? to Where's the best burger in this town? You listen; you occasionally contribute. And you don't just share your contributions with your friends, with whom you feel safe because they like you; you share them with everyone who can profit from your input. That's all publishing is.

Here's how it looks. My brother Eric is in middle management with a computer software company. He has never thought of himself as a "writer," and no one has ever called him one, but he goes public with his writing regularly and in a number of ways. He's a member of an electronic net, and he takes part in exchanges on a number of topics there several times a week. He once got an idea for a parody of military board games that he called Squab Leader, and he wrote it up and sent it to a newsletter for people who play such games. And twice in his life he's gone uptown: Twice he had something to say about public issues, wrote it down, and sent it to the local newspaper, which published it as a guest commentary in the Sunday essays-and-criticism supplement. No writing career followed, but that wasn't the point.

Getting Off the Bench and Into the Game

The best thing you can do, if you want to become a published writer, is to sit down with five published writers and ask them how they got in the business. It will dispel a lot of myths and save you from wandering down a lot of blind alleys. Here's one writer's story.

My friend Steve Metzger was an English major who wanted to be a writer. In 1980 he converted his clawfoot bathtub to a shower, realized others might be interested in how he did it, and queried the magazine *Mother Earth News* by letter asking if they'd be interested. They said yes and sent him a copy of their writer's guide. He followed it carefully, wrote the piece, and they bought it for $160.

In 1983 he took a trip to Spain, wrote up his experiences, submitted them to the San Francisco *Chronicle*'s travel section, and it hit the news-stands before they even told him they had accepted it.

All the while Steve had been doing his "real" writing, a novel about a young man discovering himself while skiing. He located an agent, who could interest no one in the project—of course. Steve finally wrote to *Powder*, a small skiing magazine, asking them if they'd be interested in serializing the novel; the editor said no, but invited Steve to write an article. He wrote a personal essay about returning to downhill skiing after being away for fifteen years. They bought it.

A year later, *Powder* called Steve and asked if he'd like to cover the World Cup ski races in Colorado. Steve jumped on an airplane, but once he got to the races he discovered there was nothing interesting to say about the races, so he boldly asked *Powder* if he could write something else: a story about an organization he had encountered at the ski resort that had brought 40 terminally ill children to the slopes as a last-wish present. *Powder* agreed, Steve wrote it, and readers loved it. Steve was now someone *Powder* would call when they had work—a regular contributor to the magazine.

Powder began asking Steve to accompany tour groups to European ski resorts and write articles on the trips. Every time Steve went on assignment for *Powder*, he met six or seven other journalists writing similar pieces. Those journalists knew of other jobs, or knew editors who had work needing to be done, or later became editors themselves. Steve's name became known in the business as someone who could produce a good product on time. People began calling him with assignments, and he stayed busy.

In 1985 Steve answered an ad in a newsletter calling for writers to work for an unknown small press named Moon Publications. The editor called Steve up and said he knew Steve's name through another editor

Steve had written for—what kind of book was Steve interested in writing? Steve thought fast and suggested a guide to California ski resorts. The book was a disaster, but Moon learned and Steve learned, so when they tried it again, with a guidebook to New Mexico, the book did well. The book was so profitable Steve quit article writing to concentrate on books. His guidebooks now bring in a steady enough income that he can afford to indulge his dream: He's writing screenplays.

What lessons can be learned here? First, you can just slip a manuscript in the mail and get published, but it tends not to lead to a career. Second, work comes when you get attached to a particular publication, so the editor thinks of you when there's work to be done. Third, steady work comes through contacts, so hang out with other writers. Fourth, you'll never sell that novel about a young man discovering himself. See what other lessons you can learn from Steve's career; then talk to other writers and learn from them.

Ways to Go Public

Let's talk about eight ways to get into print, roughly in order of difficulty.

Publishing in the Classroom

When you hand around copies of your writing in your composition class and ask for responses, you've gone public—you've let people who don't have a stake in telling you what you want to hear see your work. For many of us, that's enough to give us sleepless nights. Start here and work up.

Next, take the work to other classrooms. Exchange essays with another writing class for feedback and criticism. Organize an anthology of best essays from all the writing sections in your department, appoint an editorial board, and submit your work.

Publishing on Campus

Everybody at a college likes to argue, and everybody constantly needs answers to factual questions. So there is a lot of publishing going on, as people try to further the arguments and answer the questions. On my fairly small campus there are

- a weekly student newspaper, printing informative pieces, student essays, music and movie reviews, personal pieces, and letters to the editor;
- a twice-yearly campus journal, printing essays about the academic life of the campus—How is the General Studies program working? Is grade inflation a problem?;

- a literary magazine, printing poems and short stories by students;
- a student academic journal, printing the best work students are doing in their class writing projects;
- a magazine, published by the Women's Center, addressing women's issues;
- several student-edited counterculture periodicals, devoted to all the things the establishment publications ignore;
- a handbook for incoming students;
- an alumni magazine, to keep graduates in touch with their alma mater;
- a university press, devoted to printing books and monographs relating to the campus or the region; and
- countless newsletters for individual programs, like the English department's Writing Center newsletter, where composition instructors, tutors, and teaching assistants share their classroom experiences and insights gained from them.

Some of these have specific readerships so they aren't for you, but others will be, and they will be delighted to get a manuscript in the mail from you, astonishing as that may sound. Nonpublishing writers assume that all editors and publishers scoff at manuscripts from unknowns. Some do, but lots don't. There are three kinds of editors: those who happily read anything they're sent, those who want you to send them a query letter first describing the project so they can decide whether to look at it or not, and those who work only with writers they hire themselves and won't look at unsolicited manuscripts. If you're publishing locally, the easiest way to find out which kind your editor is is to phone and ask. But I promise you, if you're writing for a local newspaper or anything less pretentious, the editor is somewhere between merely eager for text and absolutely desperate. These editors have to fill their pages.

The actual logistics of submitting a manuscript for publication, whether to the campus newspaper or a national magazine, are fairly easy: You get an address (usually published in the publication itself). You mail off the manuscript to that address, with a very simple cover letter that says, "Please consider this for publication in your (whatever section, column, or letters to the editor section you have in mind)." Describe the piece in a sentence or two, but don't try to sell, or defend either the piece or yourself—let the editor read it for herself. Include a self-addressed, stamped envelope (a SASE, in the trade) and ask the editor to return the manuscript if she rejects it, but don't count on her doing so—always keep a copy. And remember, even small publications are usually made up of many sections and may have many editors; be sure to have a specific department in mind when you submit, send the piece directly to the editor who handles that section, and tell him exactly what you have in mind in your cover letter: "Please consider this for publication *in your spring supplement's 'Out and About' section*."

If you want to publish every week and think writing might be your career, you can join the campus newspaper staff. They'll be delighted to have you—every newspaper is as short of good help as it is of good submissions—and they won't ask you to be good right away; they'll train you.

Self-Publication

Self-publication means just what it says: You publish the piece yourself. More and more, authors are circumventing the publishing rat race by making their own texts and selling them. Before computers this was almost impossible because anything you produced looked amateurish, but no longer. Desktop publishing software (Quark Xpress is the acknowledged leader in the field) and a good printer allow you to do everything short of the binding, with professional results. Any small print shop will be happy to bind and cover the product. Now you're ready to walk into a bookstore and talk the owner into putting your work on the shelves, or to just set up a table in the student union.

Here's how it works. A colleague of mine asked his freshmen what students would read. There are some standard answers: a broke student's restaurant guide; a guide to classes and professors; an introduction to the campus and community for incoming freshmen. His students chose the guide for freshmen. They wrote it and, since no one in the class was a whiz with Quark, they talked a graphic design instructor on campus into making the designing of the book a class project for her students. Then they got some money from a grant for special student projects and hired the campus print shop to print the book. They set up a card table in the student union and they're still selling them to this day.

This is not easy. You (or someone) needs to be good with desktop publishing software, graphic design, bookkeeping, and marketing and salesmanship, well-enough funded to pay the printing costs, and—most of all—motivated enough to organize the project and see it through. The student project I described took a year and a half. It's definitely nicer to have an editor/publisher do it all for you. But it can be done. A book that will help you through it is *The Publish It Yourself Manual.*

Self-publishing used to be shameful—they called it "vanity press"—because it meant you couldn't find a publisher who liked your work. All that has changed. Now it means you're on the cutting edge, in too much of a hurry to get to market to wait for stodgy old editors.

Community Publications

There is a long list of local off-campus publishing opportunities, and they're good places to start because they tend to be user-friendly. Obviously, there is the daily newspaper, with its insatiable appetite for letters to the editor, travel tips, book reviews, rock concert reviews, human interest pieces on the man who built a house out of discarded cassette tapes, and essays on issues of the day. And there is more than one newspaper, each a distinct market. Even in my small town there is the politically conservative daily, a politically liberal and arts-oriented weekly, an arch-conservative weekly, a holistic health weekly, a sporting news devoted to area hunting and fishing, and a weekly devoted to the local rock music scene—all happy to take you on as staff (if you're willing to apprentice) or print the occasional piece you submit.

They will pay you, sometimes. You won't get rich, but on the other hand some newspaper journalism is dead easy to do. In my town there's an old mansion with tour guides in period costumes. No one looks at it twice, because it's always there, smack in the middle of town. Except a friend of mine, who thinks in terms of publication, took the tour, wrote down what he saw and heard, and sold it to the travel section of a newspaper in a far-distant state for $200—because he realized that old house was everyday stuff in Chico but was exciting travel news in Rhode Island. Then he sold the same piece to three or four other newspapers in other states.

Besides newspapers, there are many other opportunities to publish in town. Newsletters are probably the easiest, because they are so plentiful and so desperate for copy. I have no social life, but I get nine local newsletters in the mail: from my scuba diving club, the American Heart Association, the local yacht club, the local small-boat racing organization, the organization for owners of my particular sailboat, the in-town chapter of the Sierra Club, and the regional Sierra Club office, for the alumni of a personal growth seminar, and from the marina where I rent a slip. Someone has to fill them all. And the audience is congenial: There's no one easier to talk or write to than a fellow enthusiast.

There is a time-honored way of breaking the ice if you've never published before and you're nervous: the letter to the editor. It's easy, it's short, the standards aren't too high, and they'll print your name so you'll get that boost. Do it and be proud of it. I love an old cartoon in which an upper-class woman is on the phone saying, "We're having a few friends over—Herbert's letter made it into the Times," while Herbert beams in the background. That's how it should be.

You can get involved with your newspaper at different levels of commitment. You can hire on as a reporter. You can go to the editor, show him samples of your essay writing, and say you want to write a regular column. You can become an intern, an apprentice who exchanges work for experience and learns the trade by hanging around the plant. Or you can submit a piece whenever you have something to say.

Magazine Writing

In the myth of the freelance writer, you spend your life "on assignment" writing articles for glossy national magazines (writers call them "the slicks"), jetting around the globe, and earning thousands of dollars for each piece.

It can be done. The money is real. *Newsweek* will pay you $1000 for a 1000-word opinion essay. *Reader's Digest* will pay you $450 for a joke about campus life, for heaven's sake. And the slicks will look at your work, even if you're a nobody with no publishing record. A glance at recent *Newsweek*s shows guest essays by "nonwriters" like a female orchestra leader, a merchant seaman, a truck driver, an octogenarian struggling with advancing age, and an owner of a family winery; recent *Runner's World* noncareer authors include a high school teacher, an attorney, and a bartender. Many of the biggest women's magazines are 75 percent to 100 percent composed of unsolicited freelance submissions, and they pay well.

Now for the bad news. First, the competition can be fierce. Popular magazines like *Redbook* may publish only one article out of several hundreds received. Second, the editorial process can be grueling. Typically the editors will ask you to revise thoroughly anything they accept at least twice, and some publications have review processes that can drag on for several months, so by the time your piece sees print you've forgotten you wrote it. Third, freelance writing as a lifestyle burns you out. A thousand dollars sounds like a lot for an essay, but try selling fifty pieces a year, or even writing them. The average freelance writer makes about $1200 a year writing, and you have to do a lot of bowing and scraping. So by all means submit to the slicks now and again for the fun of it, but don't make a career of it.

To freelance, you need to do six things:

Buy a copy of *Writer's Market.* There are dozens of clones covering the same territory, but WM is the industry standard. This paperback, owned by every freelance writer in the world, will tell you everything you need to know about the logistics of submitting to specific magazines. You look up *Sports Illustrated* and it tells you things like, Will they read manuscripts from people they don't know?; What's the editor's name and address?; What's the desired manuscript (MS) length?; What's their editorial philosophy?; How many copies should you send?; How much do they pay?; How many pieces they accept per issue or per year?; and so on. It will tell you about publications you didn't know existed: If you want to write about your experiences snowboarding in Colorado, WM will list for you every publication interested in snow sports, snowboarding, Colorado, or Rocky Mountain recreation and tourism. If you have the money, also buy *The International Directory of Little Magazines and Small Presses*, which will tell you about markets too small or too specialized for WM to notice, and which may be just the kind of markets you're looking for.

Listen to what WM says: If it says a magazine doesn't read unsolicited manuscripts, don't bug them with yours.

Study the customer. Don't write a piece, then decide to send it to *Woman's Day*; instead, as you write, read *Woman's Day*, soak up its editorial philosophy until you know how they think and what they buy, and tailor the piece to suit them. Publications don't buy what's good; they buy what fits in with their program. *Sports Illustrated* only prints *Sports Illustrated*–type articles, and if you send them something else they'll just say no.

Send for the writer's guide. Many magazines, even low-key ones, have manuals for submitters, greatly expanding on the information in *Writer's Market.* They're free if you write and ask for one, and they'll tell you all about what style to use, what approach they favor, how to format the text, and so on. Some of these guides are invaluable mini-courses in good writing, and with some book publishers they're book-length volumes. Since they're telling you exactly how to make them buy your work, you'd be a fool not to listen.

Decide whether to submit a finished piece or query first. Sometimes, as with a short op-ed piece, it only makes sense to write it completely, then submit the finished MS; other times, as with in-flight magazines, you don't want to write the piece until someone buys the idea, so you send a query letter: "Would you be interested in a 1500-word piece on farmers digging out from last year's Mississippi River flooding?" You can query a dozen editors at once. Back before it happened, a friend of mine had the idea of writing a piece about the fiftieth anniversary of San Francisco's Golden Gate Bridge. He queried twenty editors. Some said no; some said it's too early, ask again later; some said it's too late, we've already assigned it to someone; and some said do it. So it goes.

Concentrate on the easy markets. Some markets are hungrier for material or friendlier to newcomers than others. *Playboy* is a brick wall. Small magazines devoted to specific sports and recreations (like bow hunting) are easy. Here are some popular places to start out:

1. In-flight magazines—the slick magazines you find in the seat flap in front of you during any commercial flight. But remember, they're extremely specific about what sort of thing they want— only cheerful, happy pieces, please.
2. Guest spots. Most national magazines have reserved a spot for one outsider essay per issue. In *Newsweek*, it's "My Turn"; in *Time* it's simply called "Essay"; in *Ms.* it's "Guest Room"; in *Runner's World* it's called "The Finish Line"; in *Cosmopolitan* there's one for women, "On My Mind," and one for men, "His Point of View."
3. Travel and tourism. The market for personal reports on trips and vacations is an insatiable maw. Almost any vacation is worth reading about to travelers who haven't been there, and no newspaper can afford to send staff reporters globe-hopping all the time, so most of it has to be done by freelancers.

4. Sporting and hobby magazines. Partly it's because the budgets are small so standards are pretty low (they're happy to get anyone who can write) and partly it's the spirit of fandom—enthusiasts love to read about the experiences and thoughts of other enthusiasts. You don't even have to know the territory—I just read a nice piece in *Runner's World* by a nonrunner about his feelings watching his daughter run in her first competition.

Basic math will reveal what your chances of getting accepted by a particular publication are. *Writer's Market* will tell you how many pieces a periodical accepts per issue and how much it pays. With a magazine that appears quarterly, accepts only two unsolicited pieces per issue, and pays well (so it gets two hundred submissions a quarter), your chances of getting accepted are $(2 \times 4) \div (4 \times 200)$, or one in a hundred; with a magazine that appears weekly, accepts twelve unsolicited submissions an issue, and pays adequately (so it gets twenty submissions per issue), your chances are $(12 \times 52) \div (52 \times 20)$, or three out of five. Play the odds.

Keep sending it out. Freelance writers get rejected a lot, so you have to learn to take the manuscript out of the return envelope, glance at the rejection slip, and slip the manuscript with a new cover letter into a new envelope and mail it off to a fresh editor.

You'll have the strength to do this if you remember the basic truth of publishing: Your piece wasn't rejected because it was bad; it was rejected because it didn't fit that particular editor's needs today. When you find someone who needs what you're doing, he'll buy it. Publishing is like falling in love: It's not about having everybody love you, it's about finding the right fit. True story: A friend of mine sold a story to a prominent home repair magazine 16 years ago. It was paid for but never printed, and the editors are *still* saying they will print it, as soon as it fits an issue's theme. Even book publishers think this way. They don't say, "Written anything that's good?"; they say, "We want to do something on the history of women's sports this year—done anything like that?"

Academic Publishing

Academic publishing is done in professional journals. Every discipline has them—your campus library probably subscribes to several hundred—and usually no one outside the discipline ever sees them. They generally come out quarterly (four times a year) with around ten articles per issue. Any professor can tell you which ones specialize in your area. In my field there are journals devoted to literary periods, genres, geographical regions, feminist criticism, particular authors, teaching approaches, classroom activities, literary theory . . . on and on. Most journals try heroically to read everything that's sent them if it's in their province, so you should at least get read.

You may wonder why I'm talking about academic publishing so late in the chapter. After all, you're already writing academic papers in your courses; what could be more natural than to send off the best of them to the journals? But I don't encourage you to, because the journals are the hardest nut in the publishing world to crack, and the rewards are slight. Every professor in the country is trying to get into those same journals, and there's little room, so the competition is fierce. Typically, journals are booked years in advance, so if you did get accepted your piece wouldn't see the light of day until you had graduated. They won't pay you a dime. If you do publish, no one but professors and graduate students will ever know. And the review process is long, convoluted, and agonizing. I once submitted an article to a prestigious journal and it worked its way through three separate boards of review, each producing lengthy critiques requiring major revisions, before it was finally rejected. Compare this to my experience writing an essay for *Newsweek*: I sent it to them in the mail on Monday, they phoned me Wednesday and said they wanted to print it in next week's issue—could I do some revising over the phone? I say, submit to the journals only when your instructor writes "Publish this immediately" at the top of your paper.

Electronic Publishing

I've put this one off not because it's the hardest but because it's the newest. It is in fact the easiest and most rewarding of all the forms of publishing in this chapter, and it's where the world is headed. More and more, even conservative scholars are simply refusing to wait the two years it may take for their work to see print in the professional journals, and are getting their texts into their colleagues' hands in seconds and hearing their reactions in hours.

You do it on your computer, and it never leaves the electronic network—you ship it by E-mail or electronic network link to everyone on a mailing list or everyone who checks the bulletin board (BBS, to hackers—"bulletin board service"). There is every level of polish, from the most casual chitchat to professional conferences sharing lengthy, formal academic papers, and topics run the gamut from requests for basic information (Where can I find a differential for a 1959 Chevy Impala?) to the weightiest philosophical questions (Why are relationships so hard?). There are even conferences (called "newsgroups" by users) for people who hate Barney the dinosaur (address: *alt.barney.dinosaur.die.die.die*) or people who want to discuss Spam.

To take part, you need three things: a computer, a modem (the box that connects your computer to other computers via the telephone line), and an account with a network or a service. A network is just an electronic linkage, like our national phone linkup but without a company owning and running the system. Networks tend to be unhelpful and chaotic because no one is in charge, so they are hard on beginners. The granddaddy of nets is the Internet, a mishmash of over 30,000 smaller networks jury-rigged together. To use it you'll need a tutor or a guidebook like *Internet for Idiots.*

Vastly more user-friendly are the services, which are like TV cable companies. They're much smaller than the Internet (the Internet has 35 million members, a typical service around a million), but because they're owned by companies and they're selling you something, they're slick, pretty, and winning. They'll welcome you and lead you by the hand. Big-name services are America Online, CompuServe, Prodigy, and GEnie. You can't predict ahead of time what topics a net or service will have conferences on, so about the only way to find the conversation you want is to hear about it from someone else in the field who already knows: Other sailors can tell you that the Internet has a conference on recreational boating *(rec.boats)*, and other screenwriters can tell you that GEnie has a screenwriter's forum.

The joys of electronic publishing are its ease, its speed, and its energy level. Once you join, no one can screen you out—everybody gets heard. You're communicating in real time, so you feel like you're talking, and you can get back cheers or jeers in minutes or seconds. As a result, there is an exuberance about this new form of publishing that's a refreshing alternative to the ponderous formality of much print media; people are having fun, and it shows.

The only downside is electronic publication may not *feel* like publishing, because you don't get the superiority rush of having an editor pick you over others, and it doesn't have the physical permanence of printed text. But you'll get over that as it becomes more the norm. And the first time you send out a message and your screen lights up with conference members saying, "Man, that really touched me . . . I've been thinking about your last posting . . . Thanks for the info—it worked!" you'll know it's real.

Books

Books are tough, because the publisher's investment is so great that she has to be very cautious about what she publishes. A newspaper editor can print an article by you and lose nothing but the time it takes to set the type; a book publisher, to print your book, has to commit tens of thousands of dollars in editorial and marketing costs.

The odds against you can be staggering. I heard a publisher of mystery novels say recently that his house publishes about thirty titles a year and receives several hundred submissions *a week*! Many writers slam their heads against book publishers' doors to no avail, then get wise, put their book manuscript in a drawer, and begin selling freelance articles or writing for newspapers.

But it's not impossible, since some fifty thousand books are published every year and someone wrote each one. If you want to try, here are three tips:

Write to fill a need. Write a book because you know people need it and it hasn't been written, or because the books that are already out there are clearly not doing the job.

Don't write the entire book. Write a chunk big enough to give publishers the idea, and a detailed description of the project (with an outline, a statement of intentions, and an argument for why the book is needed) and submit the whole proposal to publishers.

Seek out small presses. Major publishing houses have to sell 20,000 copies or more of a book to make back their huge costs, so they print what they think will sell; little presses, run by friends on a shoestring for the love of it, are often happy to publish books because they're interesting, for the love of the art. *The International Directory of Little Magazines and Small Presses* will help you find them.

THINGS TO DO

Of these activities, only the last involves actual submission of a manuscript for publication. But they all assume that publishing is the eventual outcome. Any "pre-publishing exercise" that lets you stop short of submitting a MS is worse than useless. The current either makes it all the way to the lightbulb or it doesn't.

1. Interview a well-published author. Ask her how she got into the business; how her career developed; what advice she has for beginning writers. Write up the interview and write a list of lessons learned: What insights did you gain that will be helpful to you in your publishing progress?

2. Make a list of all the publications on your campus. Brainstorm about what you might write for any three of them.

3. Look at your campus newspaper and identify three areas of the paper where your writing might appear: in the letters to the editor section, perhaps, or the "Just My Opinion" guest editorial.

For each of the three areas, brainstorm one writing project you might work up for it.

4. Make a list of all the organizations you're interested in that have newsletters. Brainstorm a piece for one of them, contact the editor, and query him whether and how he would like the piece submitted.

5. Do Exercise #3 with the biggest newspaper in your area.

6. Brainstorm three desktop publishing projects your class could do and sell on campus.

7. Submit a letter to the editor (a) to your campus newspaper or (b) to your community newspaper.

8. Look into *Writer's Market* and find three national periodicals that might be buyers of your work. Answer the following questions for each:

   a. Does the periodical read unsolicited MSS?
   b. Does the periodical want you to send a query letter before submitting?
   c. What is the name and address of the editor you would send the MS to?
   d. What are the length limits?
   e. How much do they pay?
   f. Guesstimate the odds of being accepted by dividing the estimated number of submissions by the number of published pieces, in the manner of p. 260.
   g. Are there any other guidelines or directions that will help you shape the piece to their taste?

9. Write to the three periodicals in #8 asking for writer's guides.

10. Write a half-page on each of the three periodicals in Exercise #8, defining the magazine's philosophy and style and listing for yourself the features that will make a piece attractive to it—for instance, what is the political tilt of the magazine? How does it feel about nontraditional roles for women? What's its expertise level? How informal is its tone?

11. Write query letters to the three periodicals in Exercise #8.

12. Pages 259–60 lists four easy markets. Using *Writer's Market* or other sources, find two possible buyers for your work within those markets. Be specific: Exactly where, in what publication, are you planning to publish? Brainstorm a piece for each buyer.

13. Choose an academic paper you've written recently for a college course and find two academic journals that publish articles in the same field.

14. If you're active on the electronic networks, bring a transcript of an online conversation into class; if not, observe a friend as she takes part in one and bring a copy to class.

15. Prepare one of your pieces for publication:

a. Format the MS according to the format instructions of your chosen place of publication.
b. Print two professional-quality copies.
c. Write a cover letter.
d. Make up a stamped, self-addressed envelope (and ask in the cover letter that the MS be returned to you).
e. Mail off the MS, with cover letter, to the editor or publisher, in a full-size manila envelope—keep the second copy for yourself.

Good luck.

Part Four

MODES OF WRITING

Chapter 14

PERSONAL WRITING

When you're doing personal writing, the basic rule is the same as for all writing everywhere: *You can't do it if you haven't read a lot of it.* So the easiest way to write a good personal essay is also the most pleasant: Read all the personal essays in this chapter and then *write one like them.*

There are two kinds of "personal writing." The first is writing you do for yourself, and keep to yourself, like a journal. Here "personal" means "private." I value such writing highly, but we won't study it, because there is only one lesson to learn: suit yourself. The second kind of personal writing is writing to share a part of your personality with your reader. That's what we'll practice here.

Personal writing doesn't teach the reader something utilitarian, like how to crochet or what to do with bored children on a rainy day. It doesn't argue her into buying an intellectual thesis, like "We should immediately offer economic aid to the Soviet Union." Instead, it's a sharing of the self. It says, "This is me"—here's a part of my life, here's a glimpse inside my head, here's something that really happened to me.

The difference is in how the reader uses the writing. When Kris Tachmier wrote the wonderful personal essay about how much she hated eggs (pp. 43–44), she didn't think you would learn anything new about eggs that you could put to practical use, and she wasn't trying to convince you that you should hate eggs too; she was just saying, "If you know how I feel about eggs, you'll share a part of me." And we love the essay not because we've learned or been persuaded, but because we feel so close to Kris—we've looked inside her emotional life and are delighted to discover that we're partners in the human experience. Personal writing is just a written version of our answers to the questions people ask us in our daily conversations when we're just keeping in touch: How was your date last weekend? Found a place to live yet? What are your roommates like? I heard your mom is ill—how's she doing? How are you handling your divorce?

For many of us, personal writing is the easiest writing we do, because we've trained for it every day in our talk and we believe that readers are interested. So we can often do it the moment we really want to make ourselves known—or we start writing to someone we believe really wants to know us. One student spent the term turning out acceptable but joyless writing addressed to me, until in the end I said to the class, "Go home and write the essay your classmates would most like to read." In one draft he dashed off this splendid "This is me" essay:

CITRUS HOOPS

RYAN CURRY

I lace up my Chuck Taylor high tops in a New York basket weave—not the normal straight style for me. I want to stand out and show the world that they shouldn't mess with me. I pull down my socks so that they crumple atop my highs, put on my gray shorts—pull 'em down so that my jock strap is seen on my back—and slip into a T-shirt that says "In your face, I do it with grace." Ya see, I'm goin' back ta Citrus—ta Citrus—ta Citrus.

To many, Citrus is just an elementary school located at Citrus and 4th Avenue, but to many others it's the ultimate place to play roundball. The three full courts all have baskets of different heights: one at eight feet, one at eight and a half, and one at nine and a half. From dawn to dusk on weekends and from 3:00 to 8:30 on weekdays, games are played. In Chico there is no better place to hoop.

Ya see, on eight-and-a-half-foot baskets everybody can create. Pretend that you're Larry Bird, Charles Barkley, Magic Johnson, Cheryl Miller, and, of course, Michael Jordan. Anything is possible: twenty-foot fadeaways, reverse gorilla dunks, alley oops, and sweet drives down the lane. It's the place where fantasies become realities: top of the key, jab step, cross over, down the gut, split the D, rise to the occasion, double pump, 360-degree right hand "slam jam bam" as Dick Vitale would say. It's a game of fast breaks, quick shakes, pump fakes, and talking trash in your face.

But before you decide to go play at Citrus, ya gotta have an understanding. If you're new you're gonna have to prove yourself. And if people start talkin' about Sir Ronald, understand that Sir Ronald is the only man known to have completed a Double Dip. No, it's not at Baskin-Robbins. A Double Dip is when a player dunks the ball and before it hits the ground takes it out of the air and dunks it again. Understand and respect the veterans and you'll stand a chance.

I finish lacing my shoes, step through the wire fence and call "winners." Everybody looks, nobody argues. When you're a Citrus veteran no-no-nooooobody will mess with ya. ❖

I later found out he was the leading scorer for the varsity basketball team, the team star. He had simply assumed I wasn't interested in hearing about any of it.

In some ways, personal writing asks little of you as a writer. You don't need a strong thesis, fancy title, disciplined structure, or clever conclusion. Here's a great character sketch with none of those things.

DAD

MICHAEL CLARK

I remember he used to take forever in the bathroom. Some mornings I could get up, eat breakfast, get ready for school, and leave without ever seeing him. I'd hear him, though: coughing, spitting, and gagging himself. Anyone else hearing him in the morning would probably think he was going to die. But he had always done that, and I figured it was just the way all grown men got up in the morning.

When he came home in the evenings you could tell he was glad not to be at work any more. It was always best not to ask him questions about anything or make any kind of noise. Mom would ask him a couple of things while she was fixing dinner. He'd answer her. Otherwise he'd just sit at the dining room table with his martini, reading the newspaper.

At dinner, Mom would make most of the conversation. He generally reserved his participation for when we kids got too light-hearted or proud or disrespectful or something and needed trampling.

When I played in Little League, he'd drive me. The Conservation Club was next to the park. He'd hang out there until practice was over. Once he ambled over a little early. He interrupted the coach and insisted on explaining the infield fly rule—not just once but three times. He'd have gone on like a broken record if the coach hadn't stopped him and thanked him and quickly dismissed the team.

I always hated riding home with him after he'd been at the Club. Winter was the worst. We'd take our trash to the town dump. The dump was also right next to the park, so naturally we'd stop in at the Club. We'd always stay past dark. On the way home I always wanted to tell him you shouldn't drive so fast on a day's accumulation of ice and snow, but I never did. The couple of times we slid off the road didn't convince him. He'd just rock the car out, get back on the road, and drive on as if nothing had happened.

As time went on, he'd come home later and later in the evenings. Often he'd come through the door all red-faced and walk straight into the bedroom, where we'd hear him moan a little and talk to the dog. Then he'd pass out and we wouldn't see him again until he came home the same way the next evening.

With my brother in the Army and my sister at college, I was the only one around to see that Mom was spending her nights on the living room couch. Though it didn't surprise me, the divorce came as kind of a blow.

I've seen him a couple of times since then. He's remarried. I think I called him last Thanksgiving. ❖

You don't even have to be explicit about what you mean. Michael never *tells* us that his father is pathetically isolated from his family and the human race by his alcoholism. And strict structure can be a curse. Imagine "Dad" rewritten to an *outline:* "Alcoholism made my father difficult to live with for three reasons. First, . . ." Personal writing craves an air of authenticity and genuineness, so a little chaos, a little meandering can help by giving the illusion that what's on the page is just what's coming into the writer's head as she talks to us:

Well, the big news is I'm pregnant. Boy, do I hate that word—PREG-NANT, sounds so harsh. "With child" sounds positively smarmy. "Expecting" always makes me want to say, "Expecting what?" It's not that I'm not pleased about this—I just don't think I'm comfortable with the jargon yet. And oh boy, is there jargon! La Leche League, Bradley, Lamaze, LaBoyer, transition period, episiotomy, and baby blues. In my naive way I assumed I'd have this baby, take a week off, and then jump into student teaching. Then I read the books, became acquainted with the terminology, decided to take the whole semester off. What I'm slowly realizing is that I'm not just PREG-NANT, I'm having a BABY—that books about the next twenty years. This is going to CHANGE my lifestyle! AAAGGGHHH! ❖

Burn out. I've been doing this for too long, and it seems like everyone around me feels the same way. I want to go beyond bitching this semester, so like the last three semesters I've told myself I'm going to take it easy. This time I mean it. I really do.

I can already see I'm lying. I want to audit the modern poetry class. And I want to keep tutoring. And I need to keep a few hours on the job. The money will be nice, and if I stop I'll have to start at $3.35 a hour when I go back. Then there's the newspaper. That ought to take a couple hundred hours. And I want to save time for my own writing. I've told myself I need to keep Tuesday and Thursday afternoons free. I'll probably have to tutor at one of those times, but if I'm lucky I'll be able to keep the other one free.

Planning. That's the key. I've got to stop bitching and start planning. If I'm still bitching two weeks from now, I'll have to say it's hopeless. ❖

So if you don't need all the traditional essay parts, what makes personal writing good? Two things. First, dramatic intensity: The reader feels he's in the scene, living it along with the writer, feeling the wind in his hair and catching the tang of gunpowder in his nostrils. Second, dramatic focus: The reader senses that everything in the essay adds up to one strong effect and takes us to the same emotional end point. Let's look at ways to get each one.

Show, Don't Tell

There's a paradox about drama: The worst way to communicate to the reader how you're feeling is to tell him. Ryan wouldn't strengthen "Citrus Hoops" by saying "I'm really proud of being one of the Citrus gang"; he would weaken it. Michael wouldn't strengthen "Dad" by saying, "My father was a pathetic drunk, and I feel like I lost out on having a father as a result"; he would weaken it. Instead, Ryan puts us on the court and lets us *feel* his pride; Michael lets us watch his father act out his life and witness his isolation.

Writing teachers traditionally express this insight by the ancient incantation, "Show, don't tell." These are just different words for the basic lesson of the "Vitality" section of Chapter 11: To get life, concretize and particularize. Avoid generalized abstractions: "He was really weird"; "It was the most exciting class of my life"; "She was really nuts about cars"; "I was so scared." Replace them with *things:* smells, sounds, specific gestures, objects, physical features. Let the particulars create the feeling you want—then don't bother to tell the reader to feel what he already knows. Listening to a writer *tell you about* someone is like listening to someone tell you about a movie she saw: It can be fun, but it's always a poor substitute for the real thing.

This can be a hard rule to obey, however many times teachers recite it to you, because it goes against something else school has been asking you to do since you started writing in classes: Say exactly, completely, and explicitly what you mean; avoid being misunderstood at all costs; summarize; generalize. "Show, don't tell" reminds us that the make-everything-explicit principle doesn't work for all writing. Here's a passage from a "telling" first draft:

> She was impulsive, funny, and highly irresponsible. I liked her because she did things I wouldn't do. I was reliable, down to earth, and boring. She was spontaneous. I looked up to her. In my eyes, she was a leader because she did things I was afraid to do. In many ways, she was immature. She took it for granted that life was one good time after another. She had no concept of responsibility. She would upset me because she wouldn't commit to anything. I loved being with her, though, because she was fun. Being with her was like being on a vacation. It was an escape.

We understand perfectly, but we feel nothing. Peer readers gave Cathy, the writer, the time-honored advice: Show, don't tell. Get out of the way and let us *meet* your friend. How about some for-instances? So Cathy rewrote. The essay now began,

> "Hey, Cathy, I'm dying for an In-N-Out burger and fries and, you know me, I don't want to go alone. I'll pick you up in ten minutes." "But Nikki, it's . . . CLICK . . . ten o'clock at night," I respond to a dial tone.

The rest of the essay was filled with lovely details like this:

> During the freshman initiation ceremony in high school, our friendship was born. We were dressed in costume (unwillingly) and instructed to do something totally silly and asinine in front of the entire student body. Nikki, dressed as Pinocchio, was told to tell a lie. "I love this school," she blurted out emphatically. Everybody booed.

Now Cathy doesn't have to tell us what we just saw.

Once you're in a showing mode, the next task is to *look close*—to tune the eye and ear for the little details that distinguish this scene, this person, from all others. A writer told of a friend of hers who "went crazy." First she exemplified, then she specified: "For two years she lived in a cabin with a chiropractor, slept with goats, and quoted Ewell Gibbons." Somehow living in a cabin *with a chiropractor* is more gripping than merely living in a cabin. Here's a beautifully specified description of an eatery:

> I was living in Laguna Beach and working at Tip's Deli. Tip's served beer and wine, chopped chicken liver, lox and bagels, pastrami on Jewish rye, and imported cheeses to a colorful clientele. Wally Tip was a short, plump, balding Jew originally from Toronto who claimed to have been a pimp in Las Vegas and made one believe in the possibilities of a Jewish Mafia. I liked him a lot. On Sunday morning he cooked breakfast himself, sweating and swearing over his tiny grill as he made his Tip's Special Omelet, which he served for a ridiculously low price to local business-men and hippies and outsiders from Los Angeles who bitched about the fat on the pastrami, compared the place unfavorably to Ratner's, and left looking pleased. There was usually a long wait. Every time an order was turned in, Wally looked dismayed and muttered that the bastards would have to wait.

This deli doesn't just have "customers"; it has "outsiders from Los Angeles who bitched about the fat in the pastrami, compared the place unfavorably to Ratner's, and left looking pleased."

You can practice the art of looking close by asking, "What kind . . .?" after your nouns: If she wore jeans, what kind of jeans? If he made himself midnight snacks, what kind of snacks? If he made the snacks with cheese, what kind of cheese? *How?* will do the same thing for verbs: If he walked, how did he walk?

If you take "Show, don't tell" to its logical extreme, you get an essay that's like a movie, where the writer stays out of the way while the scene unfolds and the reader watches and listens.

FORGET HOMEWORK

JENNIFER WISSMATH

"Jen please!"

"Geez, Darron, relax; I'm coming."

"I called you three times; this food has been sitting here forever!"

"I was taking an order and it hasn't been here that long. Where's the ticket for this order? I don't know where it goes."

"Table three. Hurry up . . ."

Man, he gets on my nerves. This plate is really hot. Hurry up, lady, move your stupid salad plate. "Here you go. I'll run and get you some Parmesan cheese. Do you need anything else?"

"Is our bread coming?"

"Oh yes, it should be right out."

Okay, Parmesan, water—whoa! I almost slipped. There's a puddle in here the size of Lake Michigan. This whole station is a mess!

You could never guess that there were two other waitresses who were supposed to do sidework before they left. I'm going to be here until way after ten—shoot, it's 9:45 right now. I guess my homework will just have to wait. "Here you go. Enjoy your meal—I'll be right back with your bread. Darron, I need the bread for Table 3."

"I already sent that out!"

"Well, Table 3 didn't get it. Hurry, the man on that table has been waiting forever."

There's the door—oh shoot, more people. Why are they coming in so late? I'd love to tell those jerks to leave—we could all get the hell out of here a little sooner. Let's see: Table 3—bread; Table 2—eating; Table 11—almost finished, they'll leave first; Table 8—okay; Table 16—take order.

"Hello, how are you doing this evening? Are you ready to order?"

"Yes. Honey, you go first."

"Um, okay. I think I'll get the eggplant."

"Oh, I was going to get that. Hm, I guess I could get lasagna and we could pull the old switcheroo."

("Jen please!")

"But, hm, I'm not sure I really feel like lasagna."

Oh God, could you please hurry up?

"Okay, she'll have the eggplant and I'll have the raviolis."

"Honey, I don't like raviolis."

"How about . . . well, I'll just stick with the lasagna."

What a revelation. Don't waste my time or anything. I don't think I'll ask them if they want salads. "Would you like any garlic bread?"

"Oh yes—Honey, let's get it with cheese?"

"I don't like it with cheese . . ."

("Jen please!!!")

"Will that be all for you?"

"Honey, don't forget the wine."

"Oh yes, we would like a litre of White Zinfandel."

Oh, please, make my night longer. I don't have anything else to do. I don't really need to read those three chapters for my history quiz, and I'm sure my teacher wouldn't mind my handing in a late paper. This job is too much. If I didn't need the money so badly, I would probably get straight A's.

"JEN PLEASE!!!"

Damn. Let's see—this goes to Table 8. Oh my gosh, they don't even have their drinks. I just love getting a late rush. "Here you go—I'll be right back with your drinks. Do you need some Parmesan cheese?"

Okay—drinks, Parmesan. Then deliver food, check water, pick up plates, pour coffee, add tickets, clear tables, be civil, do sidework, fill Parm holders, fill sugars, clean station, clean salad bar, mop floor, go home, *forget homework*, go to bed. ❖

Use Concretions As a Starting Point

You can follow the rule of "Show, don't tell" after the fact, in revision. Scan the first draft for generalizations and abstractions, and exemplify (p. 213) them, the way Cathy did for Nikki: "She was impulsive, funny, and highly irresponsible" becomes the anecdote about "I love this school." Every time you see an abstract generalization in the essay, ask yourself, "What did I see/hear/smell that led me to that conclusion?" Write out the exemplification, then see if you can't cross out the original telling statement as unnecessary.

But it's easier to work concretely from the essay's onset. Don't prewrite by asking abstract questions ("What sort of a person is he?"); begin by listing objects, gestures, or fragments of dialogue that capture the spirit of your subject. It's probably counterproductive to ask yourself at first to say precisely what they mean, and you may never have to; all you need is that sense that the way he says "It's your nickel" every time he picks up the phone is a big clue to who he is. Ask yourself questions like these:

What does she wear that reveals her personality?

What are her personal catch-phrases?

What objects does she surround herself with and treasure?

What were her most revealing moments?

What is she famous among her peers for saying or doing?

When you see or hear her in your memory, what is she saying? What is she doing? How does she look?

"Dad" might have begun with a list like this:

Coughing and spitting in the bathroom
Explaining the infield fly rule to coach
Talking to the dog
The Club
Sliding off the road in the car

Next, write out descriptions or mini-scenes of these prompts, denying yourself all authorial commentary: Just describe and narrate. Let the sense of the person emerge from the details, without you telling the reader what conclusions to draw. Here are two examples:

1. One day my father and I were working in the woods. We began to talk about rattlesnakes. What do you do if you run into one in the wild? I asked. "You just hit it with your shovel," he replied.

2. A student of mine once went with his grandmother to buy a Christmas tree at a lot. The salesman said, "You wanna stand on that?" and she climbed up and stood on the tree.

Now build the essay around the best items in the list, or start the essay with the best one. Of course, in the essay your reader may need some help drawing the necessary conclusions. She may not see that my father can't imagine anyone not having a shovel in his hand, since there's been one in his for the last thirty years at least. She may not see that climbing up on the Christmas tree summed up the grandmother's naively dutiful nature. But even if you have to explain a little, if you work from the concretions outward the essay will always be grounded in showing.

Let People Talk

The easiest way to capture the flavor of human experience is to let the reader hear your people talking. It's amazingly efficient. When former president Reagan said, "If you've seen one redwood you've seen them all," we knew everything there was to know about him. When you learn that overweight women in a sixties "figure salon" exercised to the chant of "Oh dear/I fear/I've overdeveloped my rear," the entire tragicomic scenario seems laid out for you.

Here are some of the voices I've met through my students' essays:

Herb out to dinner:

> *Let's get some beers going here while we decide. Where's our waitress?*
> *Miss? . . . Miss? . . . Michelobs for everyone. Put it on my tab!*
>   "What are you getting, Jean?" Tom asked me.
>   "Oh, I don't know . . . Fish maybe. I'm kind of in the mood for something light. What about you?"
> *How about it—steaks all round? I'll tell the waitress. Miss? . . .*
> *Miss? . . . We'll have steaks all round.*

Susan on the state of her life:

> I'm going insane in this town. I mean totally insane. My mother just thinks I'm totally irresponsible for quitting my job. I'm forty-some-odd years old. I'm tired. And I have been *so* psychic lately, Val. Did you see the full moon last night? I've been so psychic it's exhausting. My brain is working overtime, picking up all these vibes, going *wha wha wha*. And every man I've seen in the last five years has called me this week. It always goes in waves. Val, the men in my life are nauseating. I hate

middle-aged men. I quit answering the telephone because the worst ones haven't called yet, and they will.

Joe leaving a message on the answering machine:

> Hey hey hey, girl! Whassup? What choo doin' not bein' home when I call, huh? Dis is Big Daddy Joe, doncha know it, and we're kicking like chicken at Jay's wonderin' what been *up* with you, girl? You better call me back, 'cause things just ain't hap-pen-nin' if you get out of touch with the boy. We'll be here till like eleven, yep, so *call* me, girl! I be chillin' like a megavillain, catch you later, aw right?

In "Dad" Michael Clark never lets his father speak—a great example of breaking a rule for a good reason. His dad's silence preserves the wall between him and us, to dramatize his isolation from the human race. The central fact about him is that he won't let himself be known.

Find a Dramatic Focus

So now you have a lot of good concretions to work with. How do you know which to use and which to throw away, and what order to put them in?

Avoid outlining and other rigid structuring tools, because they'll just drive away the spontaneity we liked in the passages on pregnancy and school burnout on pages 272–73. Outlining is also a subtle encouragement to tell instead of show, because we usually outline ideas, not concretions.

Instead of outlinable structure, think about dramatic focus: What, overall, is the effect you're trying to have on the reader? You can call that focus by many names—a tone, a point, a purpose, a point of view, a thesis, a moral, a mood, a feeling—but you have to be able to say to yourself, "*That* is what the essay as a whole is trying to achieve."

Your focus can be pretty vague: "I'm trying to capture what it feels like to play in a rec-league softball tournament." It can be very specific: "I want to show how heartless and insensitive male doctors often are to female patients." But you need some principle of inclusion and exclusion, some rule that tells you "This goes in and that goes out."

Here are my versions of the effects sought by some of the essays in this chapter:

> "Dad": to capture the miserable alcoholic isolation my father lived with, and my inability to get near him.

> "Forget Homework": to capture how hysterical, frustrating, and dehumanizing my night-time job is, and to show how infuriating it is to have it ruin my schoolwork.

"Citrus Hoops": to capture the pride and cockiness of Citrus court life; to record the style and tone of that subculture.

Without a focus, you get a "core dump" essay, where you just write down everything you can think of to say about the subject. "Dad" does *not* contain everything Michael Clark can think of about his father; it contains only what furthers the specific task at hand.

You're performing a delicate balancing act here. On the one hand, you want the illusion of spontaneity and dramatic immediacy; on the other hand, you need a purpose, a reason for putting *these* things in *this* order. If you go too far in either direction, something fine is lost. If "Dad" seeks a more obvious order, we won't believe it as much. If the pregnancy passage gets any more spontaneous, it will feel like it's milling around. In fact it's probably only getting away with its present level of chaos because it's so short.

Once you have a focus, you can go looking for a Grand Design, a structuring principle:

> For "Forget Homework": Write the script for a typical scene near closing time at the restaurant, intercutting between dialogue and Jennifer's internal monologue.

> For "Citrus Hoops": Describe my getting girded for combat, then describe the combat, then return to the beginning scene, ending at the moment when I'm entering the arena.

Is a Focus a Thesis?

You can call your dramatic focus a thesis if you want. You could say that "Dad" 's thesis is "My father was cut off from the human race and his family by his alcoholism." The thesis in "Forget Homework" might be, "My wage-earning job often prevents me from being the best student I can be." But I avoid using the word *thesis* because to most people it implies argumentation, lessons, formal essay style, outlinable structure, and all those ponderous things personal writing joyously frees us from. Don't think about thesis if the word inhibits you, but don't be surprised if, when the essay's done, you find you can look back and discover that a thesis has emerged during the writing.

Does Personal Writing Have a Moral?

Usually not. Personal writing is sharing of the self, and we usually don't try to instruct our listeners while sharing. If we're chatting with a buddy on the sidewalk and suddenly sense that she's trying to *teach us* something, we'll probably feel condescended to or preached at. Essays like "Forget Homework" and "Dad" don't have morals.

But they could—because lessons can be drawn from experience. We could *use* "Dad" to make the argument that our culture teaches males to deal with their emotional pain through silence and self-inflicted isolation. We could *use* "Forget Homework" to make the argument that it's to society's advantage to support student aid programs, so worthy students can concentrate on getting the most out of their education. That's not what our authors chose to do, but it would be legitimate if they had. If you'd like to see it done, the Writers' Workshop section of Chapter 17 has two essays that use narrative in this way (beginning on p. 374), "Given the Chance" and "Why?"

WRITERS' WORKSHOP

Concretizing Abstract Generalizations

Let's look at how a writer revises a character sketch guided by the "show, don't tell" principle. Here's the first draft:

MY MOTHER

LORI ANN PROUST

She is understanding and always there for me. She listens and is full of positive support. I am lucky to have someone who is both a close friend *and* a mother. Not everyone has this kind of a relationship. I could find endless words in the thesaurus to describe my mother, but the one word that stands out above the rest is "incredible." She has cared for me and my family throughout my whole life. When I was growing up, she always did my laundry, took me to dancing lessons and the orthodontist for eight years, made me breakfast and my lunch for school every day without fail, took my sister to field hockey, sewed my clothes, typed my papers, cooked for the family, cleaned the house, did all the yardwork, and was happily married. I don't know how she managed to do all of these things so well and still have time for herself.

My mother is my sole support system. Whenever something exciting happens or there is a crisis in my life, she is the first person I turn to. I have seen many friends come and go in my life, but my mother is different. For eighteen years of my life she has always been there for me. No matter the distance in miles between us, we are always close. She understands me and knows me better than anyone else I know. She doesn't make demands nor does she pressure me with school and my future. She has complete faith and trust in me that I am doing the right thing with my life. I make her happy by letting her know I am happy and like who I am and where my life is taking me.

Every day I count my blessings and think about how grateful I am to have a mother who loves me. Not once do I take this for granted. I cannot imagine my life any differently without her. One thing is for certain: it just wouldn't be the same. ❖

Lori Ann's peer editors focused on three things in the draft. First, the generalities kept them from meeting the mother herself. Second, nobody *believed* the essay, because the generalities were impossibly simplistic and sunny. The essay felt like a sales pitch. Third, the essay was short, and since mothers and daughters usually have complex relationships, they felt that a lot must be missing. In the rewrite we encouraged Lori Ann to start from concretions. She said, "Well, I just had a phone conversation with her that was pretty typical— maybe I could use that." She did, and this is what she got.

MOTHERS . . .?!!

"Hello?"

"Hi, Mom. How was your day?"

"What's wrong?"

"Nothing is wrong, Mom. I just called to tell you I found an incredible place to live next year! It's an apartment in an antique house. It has hardwood floors, high ceilings, it's close to school, has lots of potential, and the rent is *only* . . ."

"Does it have summer rent?"

"Yes."

"Forget it then."

"Fine, Mom."

"I already told you that neighborhood is dangerous and full of rapists."

"Mother, I've lived on this street for the past *three* years now."

"And what about the fraternity boys across the street? Do you know what you're in for?"

"Mother, these guys are my friends and I have also lived across the street from a fraternity house before . . ."

"Forget it."

"Fine, Mom. Would you rather pay $225 a month for me to live in a two-bedroom apartment instead of $150 a month? You'd also have to buy me a car because the only apartments available in September are five miles from campus."

"Does your friend Denice know what a slob you are? Does she know *you're* the reason why you had cockroaches in your apartment last year?"

"Mother, that's because I lived in a *dive!* I found cockroaches before I even moved in . . ."

"Oh, are you suddenly scrubbing floors now? I just don't see why you can't wait until September to find a place to live. I'm *not* paying summer rent."

"Fine, Mom. I just thought you might *appreciate* my consideration in letting you know what I am doing with my life before I sign the lease."

"Well, it sounds like you're going to do it anyway."

"Thank you for your support, Mom."

"Bye." Click.

"Good-bye, Mom; I love you too."

To think that mothers are understanding is the world's ultimate illusion. I had to sit in the bathroom as I was talking to my mom because there were thirty screaming girls in the hallway; stereos were blasting, and if this wasn't enough, the smoke alarm was going off because the cooks were burning dinner. I had to control myself from sticking the phone down the toilet and flushing it. That's how understanding she was being.

My mother can be full of positive support but not when you need to hear it the most. "I'm sure you can find something cleaner, can't you? You're such a slob—I guess it wouldn't matter anyway." Right, Mom. To my mother's dismay, I am an immaculate person— just ask any of my friends. She is practically married to the Pine Sol man. She thinks her house is as sterile as the hospital. Well, I have news for her . . .

Whenever something exciting happens in my life, my mother is usually the first person I turn to. I don't know why because she always shoots down my dreams. I sent her flowers and a poem I wrote myself for Mother's Day and what does she do? She acts irrational over the telephone. "Why can't you wait until September to find a place? I'm not paying summer rent." Right, Mom. I already told her twice I would pay summer rent myself. Anyone with common sense would realize that it's an advantage to find the best place *now*. That way you don't have to pay storage over the summer.

For eighteen years of my life she has raised me. She knows me better than anyone else I know. It just doesn't make sense why she can't be more sensitive and supportive of my dreams. All I wanted was to hear her say, "It sounds great!" But it was obviously too much to ask.

The phone rang as I was finishing this paper tonight.

"Hello?"

"Hi. I've been talking to your father about that apartment, and he said he would pay half your summer rent. That way we don't have to pay for storage." (What did I tell you, Mom . . .) "So go ahead and sign the lease." (I didn't tell you before, but . . . I already did!)

"I'll see you soon, Mom. I love you."

My mom will never know this, but I went ahead and signed the lease yesterday, without her approval or support. I felt good about it, knowing I did the right thing. Today's phone call reassured me that I had done the right thing. Although my mother can be irrational sometimes, she is still my mother and I love her dearly. ❖

Discussion

The phone conversation went a long way toward solving all of Lori Ann's problems. It brought the mom instantly to life. It gave Lori Ann lots to do; the new draft is three times longer than the first and could easily get longer, as Lori Ann tries to come to terms with the evidence she's provided herself with. And most importantly it brought Lori Ann to life as well, as the very title shows. The first draft was her *head* talking; the second draft is living experience, which she feels in her gut (remember "Writing from Rage" in Chapter 3, p. 51). She now has to reconcile the dissonance between the first draft (the good-daughter party line on mothers) and the evidence (the harsh reality). She's writing now to fight for her right to be herself, and the essay crackles with the energy of the conflict. Generalizations can be places to hide; the concrete facts of the phone transcript forced Lori Ann to come out from behind the clichés. "Show, don't tell" is more than just a way of making readers feel more; it's also a fundamental principle of critical thinking: No assertion or belief can be trusted until it's been illustrated by example.

Where might a third draft go? As it is, the essay intercuts between the bad-mom phone conversation and the good-mom of the generalized assertions ("She knows me better than anyone else I know"). We *see* the bad mom in action; we *hear about* the good mom.

Lori Ann could let us meet both moms, do even less generalizing, and explore even further the fascinating question of how one's mom can be both so good and so bad.

Your Turn

Write a first draft of a personal essay; then diagnose it for telling instead of showing. Highlight every sentence that contains an abstraction or generalization—a feeling, a mood, a judgment, an interpretation ("He was the coolest guy I ever met," "She was always ragging on me," "I was terrified," etc.). Then try to rewrite every highlighted sentence by replacing the abstraction with concretions—what can you see, hear, smell, taste, or touch that will lead the reader to that abstract idea or generalization without you having to tell her? Look for objects, gestures, verbal habits, specific anecdotes and events that reveal truths about your subject.

A TREASURY OF GOOD
PERSONAL ESSAYS

Here are six of my favorite personal essays by my students. They're for your pleasure and inspiration. Read them to get the hang of personal writing; enjoy them; get turned on to write by them. Imitate them and steal from them. After each essay I'll· say a word about why I like it so much.

TOP CHICKEN
KATIE JAQUES

The recess bell shrills and we are outside like so many pistol shots heading for the monkey bars. Out of the shuffling and shouting two distinct lines emerge, one at each end of the metal battleground which looms several feet above our collective heads. I glance cockily at the other team and begin counting. My match is the fourth girl down, Julie Grovner. She is a chubby brunette cry-baby who, for show and tell one Friday, brought in miniature bottles of eau de toilette for each of us girls. A complacent smile spreads across my face. Too easy, I decide.

We have won the first two matches and lost the third, and now it's my turn. I climb up the side ladder and take hold of the overhead bars, slippery as iron snakes, hanging like suspended railroad tracks against the cloudless ten o'clock sky. I methodically swing first to the right, then the left, wiping each opposing hand dry of accumulated sweat as I do so. The yellowed oval calluses gracing each palm attest to my huge success as a chicken fighter, and I note them with a quick sense of pride.

At an observer's terse shriek, *"Go!"*, I lurch forward, anxious for battle. Julie sways toward me more slowly, her stubby legs flailing wildly. I can practically smell her fear and see, from the corner of my eye, her black patent leather shoes as they arc widely in a feeble attempt to encircle my waist. Swinging broadly to the right, I escape her grasp and can hear the shouts from the other kids getting louder, fueling my desire to win even more. To be pulled down to the black playground surface at this point is to lose my reputation. I set my teeth and curl my toes up tightly inside my brown stained oxfords in anticipation.

Julie can feel the pressure too, and releases, for one second, her left hand in order to wipe it dry, grimacing with strain as she does so. Quickly, hand over hand, I close the gap between us and tighten my long legs about her thick waist, squeezing my victim like a merciless boa constrictor.

The shouts are deafening now. Julie's brown eyes widen in surprise as she attempts to return her free hand to the bar. Noting this, I instinctively lock my ankles together behind her arched back and begin to pull her downward, watching her one remaining hand slowly relinquish its grip, knowing all too well the Indian burn sensation the metal generously imparts to the loser's palm.

Emitting a loud squeal, Julie drops to the charcoal turf ashamed and slowly hobbles over to her own side unacknowledged. Amidst the hoopla, I quickly monkey-walk back to my own team, unable to repress a victory grin that stretches from ear to ear. Climbing down and taking my place at the back of the line, I casually pick at an old callus with a shaking hand, barely noticing my aching thighs, counting out my next opponent. ❖

I love how Katie captures the enormous importance of child-hood experience. The battle on the bars takes on the weight of D Day. Words count here: "Julie drops to the charcoal turf

*ashamed and slowly hobbles over to her own side unacknowl-
edged" is rich with resonant verbs, adjectives, and adverbs,
and the last word is worth more than most entire paragraphs.
"Too easy, I decide" is a wonderful example of the power of
the unexpected staccato sentence.*

WHAT WENT WRONG?

JEANETTE MAINS

My brother was born in 1965 and was named Duane Ellis, the first
son of his parents, the last of three children. He always hated his
name because kids used to tease him by saying, "Dwain the bathtub,
I'm dwowning!" He changed it to "Alex" in his early twenties.

He was a pretty boy with hazel eyes, thick brunette hair, and
an oval head the shape of an egg. In pre-puberty he got hefty and
wore those thick, black-rimmed glasses that look so dorky on little
boys. He wore polyester shirts and pants and leather loafers, looking
like a chubby little business man. He was imitating my mom's
boyfriend, who also dressed like that. Our dad was gone someplace,
divorced when Alex was two.

Somebody called my brother a queer when he was still in elementary school. Somebody told him he was gay and he thought it
meant "happy."

Alex stayed in his room most of the time. Watched TV a lot.
Avoided the hassles and emotional rantings of mom. She let him do
whatever he wanted and always bragged about how brilliant he was
because he had memorized all the capitals of the world, all the
countries, and all the major rivers. He had taught himself beginning
French. He drew intricate designs and painstakingly colored in minute details on pictures. I just knew he would be an architect or
somebody important.

On Saturday mornings he and I used to sit at the breakfast table
and make up silly cereal commercials, believing ourselves to be
outrageously funny. My favorite game was to tell him he was adopted
because it made us both laugh. Mom would say, "Jeanette, don't tell
your little brother such things!" I could always see the tiny smile
about his mouth even though he tried hard to act mad. "Mom only
tells you that so you won't get your feelings hurt," I'd say. And the
whole thing would start over again.

One time Alex did something wrong and, quite typically, mom
didn't do anything about it so he went and stood in the corner to
punish himself. I slapped him upside the head and told him how

stupid he was. The night she cut her wrists in the bathroom he was hysterical, so we got down on our knees in my bedroom and prayed real hard.

Alex dropped out of school in the 9th grade. Mom was so preoccupied with her own problems that she didn't have the strength or time to fight with him or make him go back. While she was at work he would watch cable TV or listen to the stereo, study a map of the world. Somewhere he started smoking cigarettes and pot (which he probably got from our dad on one of his parental drop-overs—it gave them something in common). Mom smelled the pot coming out of his bedroom, but she thought it was incense. She was shocked when I told her it was marijuana. "Absolutely no drugs in my house!" He started drinking her beer on the sly.

He overdosed on pills at fourteen. Before Alex was twenty he was in and out of the county's mental facility for cutting his wrists and slashing his arms so often. They said he was a hazard to himself. That he needed counseling, needed to quit drinking. He took to wearing long-sleeved shirts, even in the hot summers.

Alex was an incredibly hard worker, often having two and three jobs at a time. Women often liked him because he was friendly, courteous, and did the work of two people. Guys usually ended up making fag jokes about him or tried pinching his butt. Sometimes he would quit. Sometimes he got fired for coming to work drunk.

Eventually he wound up on the Eastern seaboard after hitching a ride with some gay fellow from New Jersey. Alex lived in a Rescue Mission. Broke his leg when a few gay-bashers pushed him down a flight of stairs. He didn't even realize it was broken till he sobered up. In a bar he met two lesbians and had sex with one of them so she and her partner could have a baby. Aidan Andrew was born nine months later. Alex was drunk when he told me about his son. "It was a fluke . . . A total game . . . We were so drunk . . . I never thought she'd really get pregnant . . ."

He cut his arms, again, over the affair.

My brother lives in Vermont now with a lover. He's working two jobs—one in a factory and one in a deli. He called not long ago and asked for photographs of us all. He saves everything my kids make him—every card, picture, and letter.

Sometimes he calls mom. He's always drunk when he does. He parades the details of his private life before her; gets mad when she doesn't condone him; gets obnoxious; and she hangs up. He does the same with dad.

When my parents are alone they do a lot of grieving over Alex. Mom cries and tries to take some solace in Bingo games at the Catholic Church. My dad takes very long walks and gets lost in novels. When they are feeling vulnerable she will hold my hand and he will hang his head, never look up, talk to the ground. "Tell me," each will ask, "what went wrong?" ❖

This essay has guts. It tackles a touchy and complex issue for Jeanette, and it doesn't cop out by offering simplistic judgments, stereotypes, or solutions. It doesn't really want to fix anything—it just seeks to share the life. Which is quite enough.

COLORS

AMY JANSEN

The most enormous crush I've ever had was on a mean, irresponsible bastard I met in my first year at college. His name was Harvey, and I met him on the muggy August day when I tried out for the University Color Guard—he was destined to be my new guard instructor. I arrived on the scene after try-outs had been completed, but Harvey gave me a flag and asked me to do a few spins and a toss or two, and I was allowed to take my place among the others. As a guard member I would now attend practice four times a week and perform with the band at all home football games in front of 50,000 cheering fans. My first day of practice was like a dream with the excitement of the upcoming season gleaming before me, and I knew I'd learn a lot under the instruction of this talented instructor who seemed aloof and easy-going.

Harvey was, for lack of a better term, dumpy. He was about thirty pounds overweight, and it hung on him like a lead apron. When he walked he would drag his feet, his horrible posture transforming him into an old man, tired of moving, unlike the twenty-seven-year-old he was. I never wore my glasses to practice because the snap of the spinning flag would often rip them off my face, but even with my blurry far-away vision I could always tell when Harvey was walking into the stadium, his slow, turtle-like movements making him recognizable in an instant. After that first day of try-outs, he rarely spoke more than a few words of instruction unless a question was addressed to him, and in answering his voice was a low, scowling southern mumble that sounded as tired as his decrepit body looked.

Although he was our instructor, Harvey rarely showed up at practices, despite the $4,000 salary he was getting for the season. One afternoon in September he skidded into our practice area, stubbing out a cigarette as he heaved himself out of the car. We all stopped what we were doing and watched as he hurried through some instructions, teaching us a flag move that we "might do someday." He did the whole thing so quickly that many of us had no idea what we were supposed to do. I asked him for help and he waved me off, whining to our guard captain to show me, and then he sped off as quickly as he had arrived. Incidentally, we never used the move.

One afternoon later in the season he showed up near the end of practice when we were all marching on the field with the band. I was chewing gum, and when I looked at Harvey (whose eye contact I usually avoided), he was smacking his mouth around as if his cheeks were stuffed with tobacco. I gave him a questioning look, and as I realized that he was making fun of my gum-chewing he replied sarcastically, "Very sexy," and then more seriously, "You look disgusting." The rest of practice was void of any color but black.

On the rare days that he did stay for an entire practice, he never even stood with the guard. Instead he'd be up in the stands or off in some corner with his flag, obviously making up more difficult routines to teach to his high school guards who actually competed, unlike our just-for-fun college guard.

It was at these moments that my heart began to pound a little louder despite my resentment and my mind wandered—for when Harvey touched a flag or rifle, a metamorphosis came over him. His head remained snapped in a high angle, his eyes staring into an invisible audience. Harvey's back straightened and he was light on his feet, his tired body forgetting about those thirty extra pounds. It was as though someone coated his flag pole with pixie dust.

I watched him, oblivious to what was happening about me. I could find Harvey wherever he was within my vision's range, and even when he was behind me I could feel the electric currents as they flowed from his arms through the flag pole like a wand. He was a magician—a master. I was mesmerized by this strange and wonderful being. The more I was exposed to his talents, the more I wanted to see. I bought a rifle, and somehow convinced him to stay after practices to teach me how to perform with it. When we were alone in the band room together everything was color guard and everything was heaven. I would sit and watch with awe as he made music with his flag or rifle, and every minute I fell deeper.

On some days I would not have my car with me at practice, and Harvey would give me a ride back to my dorm, which was about a mile from the university. At these times I was taken from my Elysian fields and placed into the harsh reality of a cruel world. Harvey would contradict everything I said, having returned to his bitter old self now that the flag was stashed in the back seat of his smoke-filled car. After the first two sentences we would sit in silence for the remainder of the drive.

At the end of the season we had a celebration banquet where all of the band and color guard members got dressed up and had a wonderful dinner at the stadium club, an expensive hall on the top of a ten-story building with windows that looked right over the stadium walls and onto the green where the magic had occurred for all of us that season. When we arrived, Harvey had placed a long-stemmed rose on each of our plates, and I wondered if it was to make up for all of his absences and cruelty. He didn't sit with the guard, however, and after he had presented the award for the most honored color guard member he said a hurried good-bye and left, never to be seen or heard from until basketball season.

Last night I gave Harvey a call at the old school. We spoke for about ten minutes and I told him about my accomplishments here as the University Color Guard's flag captain and everything. He said he was happy for me, but he took a five-second pause before beginning each of his sentences as if he wasn't really paying attention to the conversation. I hurried off the phone so as not to take up any more of his precious time, but after I hung up I couldn't help but gaze long and hard at the picture above my dresser of the dumpy man with the smirk on his face and the disillusioned little girl cradling her long-stemmed rose. ❖

> *This essay demonstrates a grand principle of personal writing: The writing is always about individual people or experience . . . and the bigger issues they represent. Amy writes about Harvey, but she's also obliquely dealing with a lot of big, important life questions: How do we judge people who are talented but mean? What is a teacher's obligation to her students? Which is more important, to be nice or to be gifted? Are the two mutually exclusive? Amy still has Harvey's picture on her dresser—that's the answer she found to such questions.*

DR. PAYNE

TRICIA SWEET

When my dad, an M.D., comes to visit my husband and me, he hands me a bag full of birth control pills. "I'm a firm believer in population control," he says.

. . .

When I was twelve and my sister was fifteen, we proudly but shyly sunned our developing selves in our two-piece bathing suits. Our father stole upon us, his new tennis shoes kicking through the sand, and announced, "I've never really been into breasts. Really they're just globs of fat."

. . .

My dad always has had new tennis shoes, and he is always taking walks in them up big mountains that used to kill me when I was little. He always brings plenty of water on those trips, plenty of water and about twenty saltine crackers. Once I kept falling asleep as we were walking along and he carried me like a fireman. But then that was only once.

. . .

My dad's jaw muscles are huge. As a girl, I used to watch cautiously as those muscles grew tighter and tighter, more and more set. And he used to tell us about how the jaw muscles are the strongest muscles of all, stronger even than leg muscles.

. . .

For days, he would go without speaking. Sometimes, for days, he would speak only to my sister and leave all of my questions and all of my entreaties without response, without even acknowledging that he had heard my voice. Then it would be my turn to receive attention, and for days he would pretend that my sister was not there.

. . .

When I was four and my sister was seven, we went on a vacation with my dad to Twin Lakes. I got food poisoning from eating raw trout. My dad took my sister on an all-day hike and left me vomiting all alone. It was dark before they came back, and I lay under the bed crying and pressing my stomach against the cabin floor and watching the window and the door. On that same vacation, my sister swallowed a bunch of pills. Previously, she had asked my dad how many pills she would have to take before she killed herself. He told her that she would have to take almost the whole bottle. My sister was rushed to the emergency room, and her stomach was pumped. My dad still refers to that vacation as his favorite.

. . .

Los Angeles County pays my father to care for poor pregnant women. He'd say, "I can't figure out why they keep having children. These ladies are really uneducated. Really they all ought to be sterilized." Population control.

. . .

When I was little I wanted a Barbie, but Dad said that Barbie did not use her intellect, only her body. When I coddled my doll, my dad reminded me that mothering was not the only thing that a woman could do. "Girls can do anything that boys can do except for pee standing up." I got plenty of blocks and Legos and balls and bikes and race cars. At the Museum of Science and Industry, I liked to watch the chicks hatch best, but my dad always wanted me to be pressing the buttons at the exhibits where you could learn about the physical relationships of the universe.

.   .   .

Last year my dad told my sister and me that if we were to get sick he wouldn't be able to help us because he was spending twenty-two thousand dollars on the installation of used bricks around his pool.

.   .   .

After the recent Southern California earthquake, my dad called me from his home in Studio City to inform me that he was all right. I had left the lines free so that people who had loved ones in Studio City could reach them. ❖

> *This essay trusts us to read well. Instead of synthesizing and interpreting, it fragments its portrait into static images like snapshots and lays them out on the table one at a time, trusting us to assemble the pieces and see the whole picture. Sometimes we have to read passages like the last sentence two or three times to see the message behind the words. But everything fits, and we're horrified by Tricia's lack of emotionalism—a perfect demonstration of the power of showing over telling.*

POLLY

STEPHANIE MINER

The first time I saw her, she scared the pants off me.

Once a week she would come into the market where I worked, drawing attention every feeble step of the way.

"I'm here for my groceries, Eddie," she would yell out in her cracking voice, blowing an occasional drop of saliva out of her mouth as she worked to push the words past what few teeth she had left. Ed, my boss, would utter an irritated grunt of recognition. He was always bothered by her, so I usually took on the responsibility of waiting on her.

The old woman would take her grocery cart that doubled as a walker and shuffle up the aisles trying to find her groceries, yelling for assistance every step of the way.

"Where's the milk?" she would croak out. "Somebody help me find the milk. I don't see the milk." She looked at me with empty, cataract-covered eyes as I walked over to help her.

"Which one are you?" she would ask me. "Are you Lori?" She asked me this same question every time she saw me, and I'd politely tell her no, that Lori had quit working over a year and a half ago. She'd always laugh at her own mistake. "Polly's getting old, ya know. I can't remember all my kids' names." She'd then reach out and run a calloused, dirty, arthritic hand through my hair.

"I remember you now. You're my kid with the golden hair. Stephanie with the golden hair. Mine was like that." I tried to imagine her almost non-existent hair being full and golden blonde. She had once been a strong woman—almost as strong as the few silver strands of hair that still hung onto her scalp.

For almost two hours Polly would make her way around the store, yelling for this or that. Tourists would ask who the obnoxious little man was. I'd respond by telling them that the sweet old woman was a local who had simply gotten up in her years, all ninety-two of them.

Talking with Polly was always an experience. "I can't hear ya, Honey, gonna have to speak up. I need some bacon. Lotsa fat." I'd ask her how much bacon she needed.

"Bacon. Lotsa fat," she'd respond. I'd ask her how much again, this time louder.

"Bacon!" she'd yell. How much?, I'd scream in return.

Polly was very careful to keep track of her scant supply of money. She insisted that the cashier write a receipt for her, in addition to the cash register receipt, with the words PAID IN FULL written big so she could see it. After safety-pinning her money purse (a small, tattered fabric bag) to the lining of her clothing, she'd gather up her bags and yell for a ride home. "I'm ready, Eddie. Let's go."

Those were the last words I ever heard Polly say. She died twenty-four hours after authorities tried to force her to stay in a convalescent home.

"She loved you," an elderly customer told me when I returned to work over Christmas vacation and heard the tragic news. "She loved all her kids. Every person in this town is her kid. She loved her kids." ❖

This essay is a virtuoso performance. The subject is a cliché: the decrepit, crusty senior citizen who has preserved her personal dignity and really loves people beneath the crust. But Stephanie's technique makes the cliché come alive. It has a lovely opening hook. It has a fine ear for Polly's speaking voice. The timing of the "bacon" conversation is awesome. And the point of view is a stroke of genius. Stephanie makes everyone else fade into the background so Polly seems to move through the world in isolation. Polly is the only person allowed to talk, for instance.

SALAD WARS

AARON KENEDI

Elizabeth takes a bite of her sandwich and looks at me. I am grimacing. "You should try it," she says.

I look at this sandwich. It has what look like blades of grass sticking out of the side. Some sort of by-product of oats and soy is oozing juices onto the flowered plate.

"No, thanks," I reply.

"You're just afraid of food that's good for you," she says. "This is really tasty, I swear."

Elizabeth is my roommate. We share a refrigerator together. My side is full of butter, eggs, cheeses, an occasional meat patty, whole milk, and sour cream. I notice that most of her food is much more brown than mine. She says that's because it's full of nutrition and protein. I tell her it's because she doesn't cover anything up. She just smiles and eats a spoonful of tofutti.

Before we were roommates we used to go out and really dine: rich Alfredo sauces, fruity cabernets, tiramisu and ice cream, cappuccino. Now she says she needs to cleanse her temple.

Cleansing her temple means hummus. It means millet and barley and rice milk. Elizabeth eats like Gandhi now, and, though I love her, joining her is a sacrifice I can't force on myself.

Elizabeth has now made Udon noodles with tofu pesto sauce. She has sprinkled wheat germ on her spinach salad and is sipping ginseng tea by candlelight. "Come on, Aaron, try some," she urges me, smiling and looking at me over a fork full of . . . something. I am grimacing again. "No, thanks," I say again.

The next morning she is up early. From my bed I can hear her humming something. The juicer squeaks, the blender whirs, the oats roll. I turn toward the wall and go back to sleep.

When I finally wake up, there's a note for me: "Meet me at the cafe for lunch, love, Elizabeth." I grind the French roast into a gritty pulp and strain myself a thick mug of coffee. Then I pour a bowl of Cocoa Puffs into a mixing bowl and reach for the milk. It's sour and lumpy, so I mix a little half and half with water and eat my breakfast.

In my first class, I am a jittery wreck, at the same time exhausted and wired. My hands sweat and my eyes are heavy. In my next class I fall asleep.

When I see Elizabeth at the cafe she is smiling again. Her eyes are bright and she is sipping coffee. "Decaf," she explains to me before I can ask.

"So what's up?" I ask through a yawn.

"Well, this morning I finished that art project I've been working on, and then I did some research for a paper that's due next week, and after lunch I'm off to work."

"Sheesh," I mumble.

"How about you?" she asks.

"Oh, uh, I just woke up."

"Didn't you go to class?"

"I *was* in class."

She grins at me again. The waiter comes for our order. I've been eyeing that flap jack special, or maybe the four-cheese omelette. "I'll have the spirulina whip with a side of echinacia and a mung bean salad, please," Elizabeth says to the waiter.

I grimace, fold the menu, lean back in my chair, look around, tap my finger on the table, and smile back at her. "Me, too," I tell the waiter.

I feel better already. ❖

I like a lot of things about this essay. Aaron has a sweet light sense of humor about himself. The essay goes beyond the obvious "my roommate is a health nut" thesis—it has more to do—and it resists "telling" at every turn. The language is rich without flourishes: "Cleansing her temple means hummus" is a sentence I wish I had written, and the phrase "the oats roll" is worth savoring.

MORE THINGS TO DO

Obviously the thing to do now is to go write a personal essay of your own. If you want to hone technique first, here are some ways.

1. Choose someone in your life and make a list of objects, verbal expressions, and behaviors that capture the essence of him, like we did on page 277. How does he usually dress? What are his verbal tics? And so on. For three of the items on the list, write brief paragraphs showing how the item reveals a lot about the person.

2. Write a half- to one-page monologue or dialogue that reveals the character of someone in your life.

3. Write a two-page personal essay that uses the Grand Design (p. 280) from one of the essays in the Treasury beginning on page 285. Below the essay, describe the Grand Design in a sentence or two.

4. Write an essay which, like "Citrus Hoops" (p. 270), says most clearly and loudly to the world, "This is me."

Chapter 15

WRITING TO INFORM

With informative writing, the basic rule is the same as for all writing everywhere: *You can't do it if you haven't read a lot of it.* So the easiest way to write a good informative essay is also the most pleasant: Read all the informative essays in this chapter and then *write one like them.*

Convincing Yourself You're a Teacher

The purpose of informative writing is to get information to the reader. But all writing does that, so there must be more to it. Informative writing differs from personal writing in its purposes and in the way the reader uses the information. In personal writing, the goal is to share a part of yourself—if the reader knows Kris Tachmier by the end of "The Egg and I Revisited" (p. 43), the essay has done its job. In informative writing, the reader is going to go out and *do* something practical with the information: plant a garden, learn to waterski, get a good deal on a used car.

Since it's all in what you do with it, the same life experience can be turned into any kind of essay. My student Leo White wanted to write about his memories watching his grandmother slaughter chickens, but he couldn't decide if he wanted to focus on his relationship with his grandmother or teach the reader the practical ins and outs of chicken slaughtering. Why not write two essays, I said, one personal and the other informative? So he did. I like both of them.

Here's the personal version:

INVITATION TO A BEHEADING
LEO WHITE

When I was about nine, my grandmother came to visit us on our little farm in California. She was from Freeport, Long Island, and if you couldn't tell by her accent, the way she dressed would have given her away, in pleated polyester slacks and a loud plaid shirt, complete with long red nails and a sprayed coif like plaster of Paris. Thus attired, she turned to me one day and out of the blue said, "Ya neva know when ya might need to kill a chicken" and headed for the hen house. After a moment of reflection I decided she had a point, and so, partly horrified and mostly fascinated, I followed her. The chickens we raised were strictly for eggs, so it was all new to me.

She prepared herself like a Zen master—meditation, deep breathing exercises, and stretching. In her thick Hungarian/New York/Jewish accent, she told me, "Chickens aw de tastiest boid in de land when dey aw fresh. Yaw grandfathah loved de chicken in goulash, paprikash, you name it. Oy, dat he didn't have dose triple and double and God knows how many bypasses. It vas de cigars dat kilt him, lemme tell you . . . "

"Foist thing you do," she explained, "is get yourself a pair of gloves, an old shirt, a plastic bucket, a shawp ax, and some running shoes. Nikes are de best—dey got dat little swoosh on de side, makes you look fashionable. It's impawtant to always look good." When I asked her why running shoes, she looked at me blankly and said, "You ever tried to catch a chicken dat knows it's about to die?" I stepped aside and let Grandma limber up.

Next she stepped into the chicken coop, looking like some sort of lunatic surgeon—yellow gloves, black boots to her knees, and an apron reading "Party Animal." She propped a cardboard box up on a stick with a string tied to it, handed me the string, and gave chase. She was indefatigable, unyielding. It was a scene out of Monty Python, but it worked, I pulled the string, and finally the chicken clucked nervously under the box.

I brought the chicken over to the chopping block. Grandma felt the edge of the ax blade in her hands. I thought maybe I could see a slight grin on her lips when she declared it "not quite shawp enough" and proceeded to hone it with a stone until it glinted in the sunlight. She took some practice swings, saying, "Ya don't vant to botch de first try. Ya vant clean, quick cut right through de old neck. Nothing woise than a howling chicken." She didn't need to convince me.

She set aside her thick glasses and I held the bird carefully. Summoning all her might, she perfectly separated the head from the body. Before I realized it was dead, the bird got up, flapped its wings as if merely startled, and took off in circles around the wood pile. The blood spurted from its neck in thick streams, and it would convulse with each spurt like some avant garde modern dance student. "Dat's nawmul," Grandma said as she leaned on her ax and wiped her brow; "Dey usually jog around a bit afterward."

After the chicken fell in a heap in front of her, Grandma wound its feet together and hung it on an oak branch to let the rest of the blood drip out. "It's a bit like drip-drying the wash," she told me; "Only you vant to make sure the dogs and cats—or the flies—don't get at it."

We moved the operation into the house, and Grandma changed out of her bloody shirt and into an apron. She dunked the bird in a pot of boiling water, sat down on a stool on the front porch with a big garbage bag next to her, and began pulling out clumps of feathers like she was petting a shedding cat. "De hot water loosens up de hold de quills have on the feathers, just like a chuck key does a drill," she explained. Pointing to the now-naked bird, she said, "Heah's de tricky pawt. You see doze little bristles where de feathehs used to be? Well, ve don't vant to eat dem. So ve got to singe dem off." And she pulled out a Zippo lighter, flicked it on smoother than any movie gangster, and ran the flame lightly over the skin.

The next step was harder to take. Grandma set the bird on its back on the cutting board, took a cleaver, and hacked the neck off with such force that it flew across the room. Then she put on a rubber glove, gritted her teeth, and stuck her hand down the hole where the neck used to be. It sounded like mooshing a banana around in your mouth, which was bad, but the smell was horrendous, like a rotten deer carcass in the woods. She pulled out the heart, giblets, and liver and showed them to me like a Mayan priest at a sacrifice. Next came the gizzard. "Chickens swallow all sawts of crap," Grandma explained excitedly; "You never know vat you'll find in a gizzard. Once yaw great grandmother found a gold ring." We tore it open and there before our eyes were some roofing nails my dad had used to build the chicken coop, one of my Matchbox cars, and a penny.

I wanted Grandma to cut off the feet, but she insisted they were delicious to "suck on." "Now ve boil the whole damn thing and make soup—make the best chicken soup you've ever had," she said. "And tomorrow I'll show you how to make a zip gun." ❖

Here's the informative version:

YOUR FIRST KILL

LEO WHITE

Foster Farms no longer raises chickens. Instead, they raise large-breasted mutants so juiced on hormones they make Hulk Hogan seem normal. Armour raises its poultry in an environment so unspeakably inhumane that it makes you ashamed to be a human being when you hear about it.

You probably know all this—that's why you've decided to raise your own chickens. You're willing to do the work it takes to eat meat that's tastier, cheaper, healthier, and easier on your karma. But chickens don't come chopped up and packaged, so eventually (around the time of the summer's first barbecue) you're going to have to butcher a chicken yourself. Here's how. The method you're about to read is my grandma's, so you can rest assured it's quick and safe.

The first thing you need to know is that, unless you get emotionally attached easily, it will be easier to kill chickens than you think. Chickens aren't cuddly or adorable, and they aren't loyal— they'd do the same to you if the roles were reversed. And they can't cluck, poop, or peck when they're dead.

Roosters are okay to eat, but hens are better, because they're plumper and you'll have more of them in the coop. But before you grab your least favorite and start whacking, do some things first. Dress in old clothes you can throw away, because killing a chicken is about as dirty a job as it sounds. Wear comfortable shoes, preferably running shoes, because a chicken that senses doom is as difficult to catch as an Elvis concert. Consider laying a trap: tie a string to a stick, use the stick to prop up a box, and chase the chicken until she chances to pass under—then pull the string.

Now comes the icky part. You can do it two ways: either swiftly and violently twist the bird's neck until it snaps, or sharpen your trusty ax, have a friend hold the little bugger on a chopping block, and unleash a mighty whack on the bird's neck. Cut cleanly the first time, because a half-beheaded chicken makes a sound you've never heard before and will never want to hear again. Snapping is cleaner, but it takes some strength. Axing is easier, but the bird will run around for a few minutes. It's a shock at first to see a headless bird sit up and start jogging, blood spurting out of its neck causing it to shake and convulse, but you have to drain the blood anyway, so this method kills two birds with one stone (sorry).

After the chicken has exhausted itself, tie its feet together and hang it on a branch or clothesline over a bucket to let the remaining blood drip out—about two hours. Don't let dogs, cats, or flies get at it. Meanwhile, boil a large pot of water, prepare some table space, and sharpen your cleaver or largest knife. Put the carcass in the boiling water for about one minute *only*. This will loosen the quills and make picking the bird much easier. Pull out all the feathers, containing them immediately, while they're still wet, in a large trash bag or something similar.

Now you have a naked bird covered with little bristles where the feathers used to be. You can't eat them—it's like eating the rough side of those two-sided kitchen sponges—so you must burn them off. Light a gas burner or a cigarette lighter and, without cooking the chicken, carefully singe off each bristle. It's the most time-consuming step in the process, but it's essential for your gastronomic well-being.

Your chicken now looks a lot like the thing you buy in Safeway. Except on the inside. Now comes the other icky part. If you opted for the snapping method earlier, you first must chop off the head where the neck meets the body. You can also cut off the feet at this point, though Grandma swears they're the tastiest part. Now put on a rubber glove, take a cleansing breath, stick your hand down the hole where the neck used to be, and pull everything out. It's gross, it's messy, it smells like death, you'll feel like a brute, but it must be done. An alternative is to take your knife and split the carcass from the butt to the collar and pry the breast apart with your hands. This method is cleaner because you don't have to grab and squeeze any entrails, but the smell is just as bad. Once laid open, the inside of a chicken is practically designed for disemboweling—just remove everything. Throw the organs away like I do, or fry them up and eat them like Grandma does. The small thing that looks like a Hacky Sack footbag is the gizzard, where the chicken grinds to dust what she eats. If you're curious, cut it open and see what the chicken's been eating. Grandma insists her mother once found a gold ring in one.

Now rinse the bird under cold water and decide how to cook it. Chop it into pieces (that's another essay) and prepare a nice Kiev or marsala sauce, or plop it whole into a large pot, add vegetables, and make the tastiest, cheapest, healthiest chicken soup you've ever had. Grandma would be so proud. ❖

Informative writing is also different from argumentative writing, because in informative writing all or most of what the writer has to say isn't a matter of opinion, and again the goals are different: When you argue, you're trying to *move* the reader, talk her into giving up her opinion and accepting yours, and she doesn't want to go along, but in informative writing the reader usually grants that he needs what you're offering—a new owner of a VCR doesn't need much persuading to convince him that he needs help programming the thing. A rule of thumb: If you were to give the essay as a speech, what's the likelihood that more than a few people in the audience would stand up and say, "I disagree!"? If the likelihood is high, you're probably arguing, not informing. If I'm advising you on buying a used car and I tell you that Japanese cars have good repair records, I'm informing, since everyone in the know agrees; but if I tell you that the wonderful reputation of Japanese cars is a myth and Detroit cars are really better made, people in the know will not agree, and I have an argument on my hands. Leo's chicken-slaughtering experience could have become an argument—perhaps making the case that Americans have lost touch with the eternal verities like birth and death and need to get their hands bloody once in a while.

Informative writing should come easily to us because most of the writing in the real world—newspapers, directions, instructions, service manuals, cookbooks, business memos, technical and scientific reports, feasibility studies, encyclopedias, textbooks—is informative, so we're surrounded by models. But it doesn't, for one reason: *Most of us don't believe in ourselves as informers.* We think we "don't know anything," and so it seems dishonest if we presume to call ourselves experts. No one writes well in self-doubt. Step 1, without which everything else is useless, is to convince yourself that you are in fact a teacher and can inform with integrity. Here's how you can do it in stages.

First, realize you've been learning all your life. In a way we know that, but we tend to discount what we've learned as unimportant; we haven't learned how to split the atom or play tournament bridge. School is especially good at making us feel like we haven't learned anything yet. If we haven't learned school skills we call ourselves uneducated.

Second, to convince yourself that there's no shortage of things you know, make a long list of some of them. I can't tell you exactly what to put in it, but I can make some guesses. You've lived in some towns, attended some schools, known some teachers, dealt with parents, learned some crafts or sports or games. You may have been through a divorce, dated, traveled, bought and sold things, held jobs, applied for scholarships, worked for bosses, raised pets, and so on. Any such experiences teach you things, and they're all things worth knowing. Reread Chapter 3 (pp. 39–55) on finding things to write about if you're stuck.

Third, for any of the things you know, imagine people who don't know it and could use it. You might say, "I know how to survive in Mrs. Mercer's twelfth-grade English class. Someone coming into the class blind doesn't. I can help him avoid some scars." Or "I know basketball. Someone who's never watched the game doesn't. I can help a novice fan learn how to watch the game, help her understand what she's seeing."

Finally, write to that audience—that wonderful audience, deliciously ignorant and eager to learn. And notice how rarely the audience you invent is an English teacher.

Being a teacher doesn't mean you're smart or your student is dumb; it just means things have happened to you that haven't happened to her. So being an informative writer requires no more arrogance than it takes for you to say, "It's old stuff to me, but it's new to you; let me help." You've changed a tire or had your period or been to a dance or ridden the subway; they haven't. Here are openings by three writers who knew they didn't have to assume a position of godlike authority to inform:

> Okay, so your boyfriend dumped you, dirted on you, screwed you over, or just plain cut you. If your relationship was anything like mine, you probably feel like the lowest, most good-for-nothing human being on

earth. Well, that's how I felt, and I'm here to tell you that you can and will survive your breakup. Here are some things you can do to speed your recovery. (Jennifer)

It's that time of year again. School is ending, your bank account is low, classes are driving you nuts, and Friday night has arrived. Suddenly you realize your dilemma: you only have ten dollars to spend and you want to go out for a fun night. You don your economical thinking cap as you form a plan for having a good time Chico-style for only ten bucks. (Eric)

Is there central heating and air? Does the place have a dishwasher? Is the rent reasonable? Of course they're important considerations. But when looking for a place to rent, in our obsession with the inanimate, we often overlook one of the most important questions: What's the landlord like? If you're looking to rent, you should be asking yourself some key questions about your potential landlord, like, How close does he live? And, can he fix more than a bourbon and soda? (Kaye)

Using Paragraph One As an Attitude Checker

It seems odd to talk about writing paragraph one now, when we're still in the first thoughts and attitude stage. After all, I did tell you in Chapters 5 and 8 to write the introduction very late, perhaps last. But informative openers are in fact easy to write, once you've mastered the attitude we've been cultivating here, and so I'm going to encourage you to write the opener up front, as a way of diagnosing whether or not you're off on the right foot.

An informative introduction has four jobs to do:

Say who the reader is and what he already knows.
Tell the reader what he's about to learn and show him how he'll use the information.
Tell him why it's important that he have it.
Say, "Read me, read me!"

These four are just the informative writer's version of the three tasks Chapter 8 said any introduction must do (p. 140).

Say who the reader is and what she already knows. Define your audience, right on the page, so the reader knows that you know who he is. Jennifer's opener says, "I know you're a woman going through her first serious breakup." Tell the reader what level of expertise you're assuming on his part. Eric tells his reader, "I'm assuming you are familiar with Chico but have never focused on the cheap nightlife scene—what nights which bars have happy-hour specials, and so forth."

Tell the reader what he's about to learn and how he'll use the information. Everybody does the first part: Eric says he's going to tell us how to have a good time on the town with only ten dollars to spend, and so on. Not everyone does the second. Jennifer's audience will use the essay to heal their broken hearts faster; Eric's will be able to have a night on the town. Be specific; get good at saying, "I'm talking only to *you*; everybody else, go home." In "Europe and the Starving Student" (pp. 322–25) Andrew doesn't promise to tell everyone everything about Europe; he just promises to tell poor college students with a longing to see Europe what they need to know to make the trip happen: how to find a cheap airline ticket, get around on the trains, and find a place to stay.

Tell the reader why it's important that he have the information. If Kaye's reader doesn't have it, he'll rent the wrong apartment; if Jennifer's reader doesn't have it, she'll hurt longer after a breakup; if Eric's reader doesn't have it, she'll sit at home instead of going out for a good time.

If you're writing to real people for real reasons, the second and third jobs just happen. But when you're writing for fake reasons to no real audience—like when you're writing a term paper on Mexico only because it's required—they *don't,* and you can't make them . . . until you redefine your writer's purposes and find a reason to write about Mexico that matters to you and an audience that can put what you write to use.

Say, "Read me, read me!" (see p. 141). I know, jokes and personal anecdotes and slang are out of place in a lot of informative writing. But there are mature, sober forms of pleasure that aren't juvenile or boisterous or smart-alecky. I believe that all good writing, however gray, makes the reader say in his own way, "Oh boy!" Lots of informative writing gives itself permission not to do this, but I think it's usually wrong to do so. If the writing doesn't say "Read me, read me!" it better offer the reader plenty of reasons why it's important that he have the information.

Some kinds of writing seem to offer little room for personality—recipes, for instance—but don't give up without a fight. Here's a writer solving that problem by prefacing a fondue recipe with a personalizing introduction:

> My roommate and I are your basic health nuts. We never eat red meat or pork, and we try to stay away from sweets. Our main subsistence comes from rice cakes, fruits, and vegetables.
>
> Every once in a while, though, we break. This tremendous urge to eat something incredibly fattening seems to take over. Yes, the moment has finally arrived. It's fondue time.
>
> Cheese fondue is our favorite thing to pig out on. Not only is it delicious, but it's easy to make and fairly inexpensive. And even though it's high in fat, it really isn't all that bad for you.
>
> The first thing to do is make sure you have all the ingredients . . .

The four jobs, or messages, of an informative introduction are usually not *announced.* Rarely does a good essay begin, "In this essay I will show you how to . . . ," or say, "I'm assuming you're an eighteen-year-old Chico male . . . ," or "I figure you know what a tablespoon is but you don't know how to make fondue—am I right?" But the jobs get done nevertheless.

Want to make the four jobs easy? You'll do most of them without trying if you just do one thing, which our three opening paragraphs on pages 304–5 and all the essays in the Treasury (pp. 317–30) do: Use the word *you* a lot. Of course, if the conventions of your field won't tolerate the word, you'll have to do the jobs some harder way.

Warm Up with a Mock-Informative Essay

If you still can't convince yourself you're a teacher, become a teacher *as a joke.* Write a mock-informative essay, a parody of informative essays where you take something dead simple—putting toothpaste on a toothbrush or chewing gum—and pretend it's as complicated and arcane as building a hydrogen bomb. It loosens you up because it's a silly game; it takes the weight off. Mock-informative essays are also crowd pleasers, so it saves you (momentarily) from the informative curse of *knowing that what you're writing is boring.* Here's a masterpiece of the genre:

ERADICAT

PETER GERRODETTE

Putting out the cat can often be an emotionally trying experience. Cat owners are for the most part uniquely susceptible to feelings of guilt, frustration, and inadequacy. These feelings are normal and do not necessarily indicate an unhealthy cat-person relationship. Rather, dilemmas of this kind are often a direct consequence of the subliminal nature of what I term cat-to-people communication lines. Frequently it is the misinterpretation of signals on this network that leads to hardships and bad feelings all around. For a serious breakdown in communication, you should consider a competent cat psychologist. For more day-to-day concerns, I would like to offer some potentially useful strategies, the effectiveness of which is entirely dependent on the integrity of the cat-person relationship.

When first faced with a cat who is reluctant to exit, it may be best to try the traditional mainstay of the cat owner, the Here Kitty Kitty strategy. One stands poised at the door, radiating a sense of anticipation and singing "Here Kitty Kitty!" or a variation thereof. It's best to use the same intonations as when feeding the cat. Occasionally it may be necessary to extend your hand, loosely clenched, indicating the possibility of a tidbit, thus luring your cat out the door; however, use the subversive strategy sparingly, because cats will soon become wise and ignore your efforts.

Another strategy is the fall-back position of owners who do not or cannot reason with their cats. This is the Brute Force approach. Any time you have to bodily move or pick up your cat, you've lost. Applying this strategy means using your size and bulk to unfair advantage, like the playground bully you knew in third grade. In a new relationship, the Brute Force approach can be especially damaging, as cats are particularly sensitive to recriminations.

A third strategy is the ultimate synthesis of man's appeal to reason. I like to term this course of action the Descartes strategy, in honor of the thinker who gave us "I think, therefore I am." Cats always make a point of letting you know that they exist. Rubbing your leg and kick-boxing your shoe are examples of this behavior. A cat capable of philosophizing should be reasoned with. You must convince your cat that it's in his best interest to be put out. Maggie, for instance, is a lap addict. She understands that if she doesn't abide by the house rules, she doesn't get her fix.

Finally there is the Fred Flintstone strategy. At this point in your relationship you have accepted the possibility that your cat is smarter than you are and you sing to yourself, "Someday maybe Fred will win the fight! When that cat will stay out for the night!" ❖

Mock-informative essays are great fun, but you can't stop there, because they dodge the teaching challenge. Your audience isn't reading you to learn, and you're not writing to teach them. The joke lies in making simple things difficult, and so unclarity and needless complexity become virtues. Write a mock-informative essay to loosen up, then move on to real informative work.

Avoiding COIK Writing

There's something odd about informative writing. Most of it doesn't work—even the stuff written by professionals. Auto service manuals *fail* to teach you how to service your car. Insurance policies *fail* to tell you what you're covered for. The book on how to fill out your own income tax returns *fails* to teach you how to do it.

We're so used to that fact that we rarely even try to learn something by reading; if we want to learn chemistry or tennis or woodworking, we look for a live tutor. Even in writing classes, we assume that a written text by itself can't teach.

Informative writing fails to inform because of one problem. It's called COIK by tech writers, and it stands for "Clear only if known." COIK writing can only be understood if you already understand it before you read it. What's the point of that? you say. None at all. But think about it: Almost all the informative writing you see is COIK writing. You can't understand the auto manual unless you already understand auto repair; you can't understand the book on home wiring unless you already know how to do home wiring; only the practiced Macintosh users can understand the Mac manual. Again, we pretty much expect this, which is why school assumes you need a teacher in the room to explain the textbook.

So let's get clear on the challenge of informative writing. It's not to master the material, be clear, or be accurate, because professional informers do all those things, and professional informative writing usually fails. The challenge is to avoid the COIK trap. To put it the other way around, the only way to go wrong in informative writing is to lose sight of what the reader needs to know. Here's a writer having COIK problems in an essay for novices on how to change spark plugs:

> To begin, make sure that everything you need is handy. That means get out a socket that fits snugly over your spark plug, the new plugs, and a grease rag and put them within reach. Next, open your hood and locate the old plugs.
>
> Go to the top of the first row and carefully remove the plug wire— the little cap just pulls off if you put enough effort into it. Then put your socket over the old plug and turn it to the left until the plug is removed. Then take the new plug and carefully tighten it by hand in the hole left by the old plug. When you have tightened it as much as you can by hand, put the socket on it and turn it to the right until it is extremely tight. Be very careful while tightening the plug; it's made of porcelain, which cracks very easily. The plug is worthless if it's cracked.
>
> Put the wire back on the top of the new plug. Go on to the next plug in line and repeat the same process until you run out of plugs. The process is now complete, and even this mechanically inept person could do it, so you should have no problem whatsoever.

This is clear to me, since I've done it dozens of times, but if you've never worked on a car the first paragraph alone will leave you with many questions:

> What is a socket?
> What is a spark plug?
> What does changing a spark plug mean?
> Why change spark plugs?
> Where do you get new plugs, and how do you know what kind to get?
> How do you locate the old plugs?
> How do you know when plugs need changing?
> What's a grease rag?

This author unconsciously assumed that her reader really already knew about cars and spark plugs. Every informative writer does that to some degree. Your job is to minimize how much you do it.

Four Steps to Rid Yourself of COIK

Conquer COIK problems by keeping your readers in mind at all times and learning to read your own writing as if you were one of them. You can sneak up on the problem by stages.

Step 1: Realize why COIK happens. Accept it as an inevitability to be guarded against with eternal vigilance. Writing to inform is a real paradox: You need to have the knowledge of the expert and think like the ignorant audience at the same time. For instance, if you know about cars at all you know that "changing a spark plug" means removing it from the engine block, throwing it away, and replacing it with a new one. But there's no reason why a beginner should be able to figure that out, since changing something usually means altering it in some way, not replacing it. When my teenage daughter Molly says, "Stop trying to change me," she doesn't mean I'm trying to remove her and replace her with a new daughter. But it's hard to remember that you have to explain.

Step 2: Define your audience and their level of expertise precisely to yourself. They must know less than you do, or you have nothing to teach them. But nobody knows nothing; you must assume they know some basic English words at the least. In between knowing-next-to-nothing and your own level of expertise, you are free to define your audience's knowledge level as you wish (but be sure to tell them what assumptions you're making). This definition answers the basic informer's questions: Have I said enough? Have I said too much? For instance, does my spark plug audience know what a hood is and how to open one? If not, I've lost them when I say "Open your hood" unless I explain. If they do know, I've bored or offended them if I do explain. Chapter 4 gives you lots of practice in defining your audience.

Step 3: Once you've defined your audience, try to think like them every moment as you write. Read what you write from their point of view, and ask yourself over and over the basic COIK-avoiding questions:

Would this make sense to me if I didn't already know it?
What else would I need to know to understand?
How would I be likely to misunderstand?

What you're trying to do is carry on both sides of a teacher-student dialogue by yourself. There's a diagnostic to see how well you're doing: See how often you answer an imaginary reader's question or discuss an imaginary reader's reaction to what you just said. Here's a paragraph from an essay on wine tasting that does this:

As you're sipping, take in some air. It's a disgusting slurping sound, but the oxygen does have a purpose: it gets the wine to the back of the mouth and enhances the taste.

The first sentence is the teacher talking; the second is the teacher reacting to the reader's imagined "Yuck!" reaction. If we wrote out the dialogue, it would look like this:

WRITER: As you're sipping, take in some air.

READER: Ugh, that sounds gross.

WRITER: I know, it's a disgusting slurping sound, but the oxygen does have a purpose: It gets the wine to the back of the mouth and enhances the taste.

If you find you're often anticipating the reader's responses and writing from that "I know what you're thinking . . ." perspective, you've got COIK problems on the run. Many of the Eight Teaching Tips (beginning on p. 312) are in fact ways of responding to an imagined reader's reaction: giving reasons imagines a reader saying "Why?"; giving examples imagines a reader saying, "Like what, for instance?"; saying what *not* to do imagines a reader saying in error, "Couldn't I just do *this*?"

Step 4: Get yourself some real readers. All writers need peer feedback, but informers need it especially, to guard against COIK problems. It's hard to be an expert and remember what a learner needs, but it's easy for real learners to tell you. Just hand your draft to real people of your chosen level of ignorance who really want to know what you're teaching and ask them to tell you everything they still need to know, everything they didn't need to hear, and every place where they were in doubt about what you meant.

Narrow Your Topic

Avoiding COIK problems always involves saying more than you thought you had to, filling in blanks and answering questions, like the question-and-answer session after a speech. It can take a long time. So usually as you revise, you try to cover less. You begin writing about how to garden, realize you can't cover it all, decide to write about lettuce only, can't cover it, decide to write about pest control for lettuce, can't cover it, decide to write about organic pest management for lettuce, can't cover it. . . . Composition teachers preach this principle using the famous phrase "Narrow your topic," which my brother still frequently delivers in a high whine imitative of his high school English teacher, who said it daily. In other words, pick a job small enough that you can do it thoroughly. I had a student who had recently discovered the game of darts and tried to write an essay on darts—*everything* about darts. After listening to classmates deluge him with unanswered questions, he said, "Holy moley, I could have written the entire essay about choosing flights!" (Flights are the feathers that make the darts fly true.) Chapters 9 and 18 practice narrowing topics in this way.

Eight Teaching Tips

Now that you feel like a teacher, are aware of the ever-present COIK danger, and have your audience always before your eyes, here are eight teaching techniques that help people learn.

Give an overview. An overview is a summary, a simple map of the territory you're about to traverse. If I'm going to take you through the thirty steps of a tricky recipe, you'll appreciate knowing that overall you're going to (a) make the stuffing, (b) stuff the meat, (c) make the sauce, and (d) bake the meat in the sauce. Overviews often use lists or categories: "First, . . . second, . . . third, . . ."; "There are three things you must do. . . ."

> Planning is very important when it comes to saving money on a long trip. I divide my expenses into three categories: fuel, food, and miscellaneous.

If you're working from an abstract, an outline, or a grand design, that *is* your overview; you could just put a one-sentence version of it into your opener. If you're writing summary thesis sentences for your paragraphs, you can gather them together in paragraph one. If we were to collate the thesis sentences in "How to Audition for a Play" (pp. 315–16), we'd get an overview like this:

> Scoring at the audition comes down to four things: knowing what you're getting into, doing a little homework beforehand, dressing the part, and acting confident when you're on.

Give examples. No generalization or abstraction ever existed that isn't easier to understand with a following "for instance." A writer begins:

> A thesaurus, like a dictionary, is arranged alphabetically, but instead of definitions it lists words that are synonyms or antonyms of your source word. It offers alternatives to words you feel are used too often, are too bland, are not descriptive enough, or contain connotations that do not apply.

That would have been COIK writing if the writer hadn't gone on to illustrate:

> For instance, let's say you're writing about the desert and you realize you've used the word "hot" nine hundred and thirty-two times. Look up "hot" in the Thesaurus and it will give you a list of similar adjectives: parching, toasting, simmering, scalding, very warm, scorching, and blazing.

If you need a crutch, force yourself to write *for example* and *for instance* a lot, but in fact these links are usually needless and can be cut out in a late edit.

Use analogies. An analogy says that *X* is like *Y*. "A word processor is like a typewriter that puts magnetic impulses on plastic disks instead of ink on paper." Analogies are great teachers because they make what the reader is trying to learn familiar by translating it into terms she already understands. Here's an analogy for how to breathe while singing:

> To use the diaphragm correctly you must imagine your midsection is being pumped up like a tire.

Most analogies use the words *like* or *as if*, but not always: "Imagine your diaphragm is a tire being pumped up."

Tell the reader what not to do as well as what to do. Warn the reader away from common errors he's likely to make. Once you know you should do this, it's pretty easy: Just make a list of the five most popular ways to screw up, and tell the reader not to do them. Recipes almost always fail to do this, which is why I can't cook. "Leaving Nothing on the Table" (pp. 317–19) tells you how not to buy a car as well as how to buy one. "The Last Stop for America's Busses" (pp. 325–26) tells you not to expect air conditioning or bathrooms on Mexican first-class busses.

Tell the reader why. Once a dishwasher repairman came to fix my dishwasher. He told me three things: "Always rinse your dishes before putting them in the washer"; "Buy dishwasher soap in the smallest container you can find"; and "Run your sink water until it's as hot as it can get before running the dishes." I would have ignored all three instructions, since they sounded like he was just trying to get me to spend money, waste time, and increase my energy bill, but the repairman knew how to teach, so he told me *why* I should. Rinse the dishes, he said, because the dishwasher's drain pipe is small, so it clogs easily, and it's rubber, so it can't be cleared by drill or Drano. Once it clogs it's a major repair to clear it. Buy small boxes of soap, he said, because dishwasher soap is an unstable chemical with a short shelf life—it quickly begins to lose its clout, so you don't want it sitting in your cupboard for weeks and months. Run the water to hot, he said, because dishwasher soap is engineered to work in very hot water—less hot, and the soap doesn't dissolve. I understood; I've done as he suggested ever since.

Draw a picture. If you're describing physical things—how to tie a clove hitch, a typical backyard garden layout—you'll get into impossible verbal tangles trying to say the simplest things. Just draw it. That's obvious, but students often don't because they think it's cheating to make writing easy. Isn't the fact that it's hard to say the point of the exercise?

No. Writing isn't pumping iron; we don't have to feel the burn, and resistance isn't a sign that we're doing it right.

Use imperatives. Imperatives are commands: "Do this!" "Don't do that!" Shy writers find them pushy, so they avoid them with passives and other circumlocutions. Don't. If you want to tell the reader to do something, *tell* him:

> The plugs should be tightened. → Tighten the plugs.
> A deep mixing bowl and a pair of chopsticks are needed for mixing.
> → Get a deep mixing bowl and a pair of chopsticks for mixing.

Seek to persuade. Informative writing is almost defined by its lack of persuasive purpose—what's persuasive about how to change your spark plugs?—but we always write better if we're trying to sell something; it gives us oomph. It only takes a slight twist to recast a purely informative intent into a persuasive one:

Subject	*Thesis*
How to set up a backyard garden	A backyard garden will provide you with cheap, healthy food, good exercise, and a tan.
Picking the right landlord	Picking the right landlord may be the most important part of renting an apartment.

This is just another form of the third job of the informative introduction (p. 305): "Tell the reader why it's important that she have the information." A persuasive thesis helps you organize, too, because it converts you from a data sponge to a writer with a reason for putting things in a certain shape.

WRITERS' WORKSHOP

The Eight in Action

Let's read through an informative essay noting when and where the eight teaching tips are used. I've marked such places with numbers and labeled each in the right margin:

HOW TO AUDITION FOR A PLAY

STEVE WIECKING

You're standing in the center of a room. Dozens of people surround you, watching intently your every move. You are told what to do and you do it. Sound like the Inquisition? It isn't, but some might call it a close relative: the audition.

Every few months of every year your college's drama department offers every student the chance to audition for a part in a stage production. (1) As a theatre arts minor who was cast with no acting experience in a one-act play last October, I can tell you that auditioning for a play is a truly horrifying, but ultimately rewarding experience. Who wouldn't want to show their stuff up there behind the footlights? Auditioning is open to anyone, and the best way to go about it is to prepare thoroughly and go into it with a feeling of confidence.

1. Persuasive purpose

(2) Just as if you were going to a job interview at your local Burger King, (3) you have to know some practical information before an audition. First, what kind of an audition are you going to? If the audition announcement calls for a "cold reading," you're in for performing any given scene from the play unprepared. Well, almost unprepared—there is some accepted cheating. (4) Go to your main library or the Drama Department's script library and check out the play. (5) Find out what that Macbeth guy is up to or what's bugging Hamlet. (6) Don't try to memorize; just be happy with the headstart you'll have on the material because you know what's going on.

2. Analogy
3. Overview

4. Imperative

5. Example

6. What not to do

Instead of a cold reading try-out, you could be going to one that calls for a monologue. (7) In that case, prepare, *memorize,* a two- to three-minute scene of a single character speaking from any play of your choice (unless instructed otherwise). This requires some hopefully obvious rules. (8) Choose a character that suits you. Be as realistic as possible concerning age, sex, and situation. (9) Freshman girls not yet over the trials of acne should not attempt the death throes of Shakespeare's King Lear. (10) Avoid overdone roles like Romeo or Juliet—(11) to the directors, these have

7. Imperative

8. Imperative
9. Example

10. What not to do
11. Why

become (12) like hearing "Hello, Dolly" sung without cease. (13) And above all avoid Hamlet. (14) Each director has his own idea of what he wants Hamlet "to be or not to be," and it usually comes in the form of Sir Laurence Olivier—stiff competition at its worst.

> 12. *Analogy*
> 13. *What* not *to do*
> 14. *Why*

Once you know where you're going and what to expect, the proper clothing is necessary. Dress subtly and comfortably in something adaptable (15) like jeans and tennis shoes. (16) You have to be able to move well, and (17) you don't want to be so flashy and singular that the casting director sees only a paisley tie or psychedelic tights instead of a possible character. (18) I recently watched a girl audition in a red, white, and blue sailor suit with spiked heels. If the directors had been casting "Barnacle Bill Does Bloomingdale's" she would have been a shoo-in, but otherwise it was man overboard time on the Titanic.

> 15. *Example*
> 16. *Why*
> 17. *What* not *to do*
>
> 18. *Example*

(19) Once prepared, at the audition nothing is more important than confidence. Present yourself well. (20) Eye the surroundings as if to say you know where you are and have control of the room, and greet the directors pleasantly to show them you want to be there. Handed an unfamiliar script? Make a quick choice as to what you're going to do and stick with it. (21) *Don't glue your eyes to the script.* (22) I guarantee no one has ever been cast for having a wonderful relationship with a xerox copy. When your turn is over, exit graciously with a smile and a "thank you" that let people know the chance was appreciated.

> 19. *Overview*
>
> 20. *Imperative*
>
> 21. *What* not *to do*
> 22. *Why*

Of course, this all sounds easier than it really is, and you may say that I've left out one key requirement: talent. But talent you either have or you don't, and if you've seen many college drama productions you'll know that it isn't exactly a huge prerequisite after all. ❖

Steve doesn't draw pictures, because his subject isn't visual, but he uses the other seven teaching tips. He's particularly good at providing *don't*'s and *why*'s. He has just the right touch of persuasive edge in his introduction. His overviews are minimal—little more than thesis sentences heading occasional paragraphs—and the essay might profit from a road map in the introduction. There's a version of one on page 312.

Your Turn

Do to a draft of your own what we did to Steve's essay. Identify in the margins any places that do any of the eight teaching tips on pages 312–14. If there are any of the eight the draft hasn't done (and you should do most of them more than once), add passages that do them.

A TREASURY OF GOOD INFORMATIVE ESSAYS

Here are some of my favorite informative essays by my students. A word about how you might use them appears at the beginning of the Treasury in Chapter 14, page 285.

LEAVING NOTHING ON THE TABLE

HYMAN FEHR

The sun reflecting off his bright yellow pants blinds you. You find yourself chuckling at his jacket, a throw-back to the leisure suit era.

"How you folks doin' today? My name's Bob, what's yerz?" He dresses like a clown, but make no mistake, this man is probably the shrewdest pitchman you will ever encounter. He is your new car salesman. Over the next month, he will, or should, become your worst enemy. His goal is to bleed every penny out of you that he can. Your goal is to buy the specific car you want for as little money as possible.

You've selected the make, model, option, and even the color you want. What it comes down to, then, is the purchase price. Let's touch on two possible methods of pricing a car; then we'll investigate the strategy I like, the "Take this offer or shove it" approach.

The first method, which I don't recommend, is called "Take my wallet, please." It's the strategy my father uses. He walks into a dealership and, after deciding which car he wants, pays whatever price is listed on the window. This approach has its advantages: it's easy, the salesman loves you, and you can leave with a car in minutes. But you will probably spend thousands more for the car than you need to.

Then there's the "Take a few dollars off and I'll buy it" approach. In this scenario, you look at the price on the window, argue for hours, and arrive at a price of a few hundred dollars less than the sticker. You've saved yourself a few dollars, but you've expended all that energy and experienced all that frustration for a few hundred dollars. Armed with a few hours of research you could easily have quadrupled your savings. Allow me to explain how.

Remember Bob? He's going to show you two price stickers on the window. One will look like a computer printout; the other will look less intimidating and will probably be handwritten. It may include "Rustproofing = $200," "Dealer Mark-Up = $500." "This is the asking price," he'll pronounce; "That's what my boss will let me sell it for." He's lying. The printout is the manufacturer's suggested retail price (MSRP); it's required by law. He won't tell you that, nor will he tell you that the MSRP already has a substantial profit percentage built in. The other sticker is fiction, something the dealer uses to boost his profit margin. You can dismiss it.

To determine your purchase price, you need that MSRP. Copy down the base suggested retail price, at the top, and everything listed below it, item by item: for example, Automatic Transmission = $495, Sunroof = $520. Now drive your old clunker to the nearest bookstore for the latest edition of *Edmund's Car Prices.* There's an edition for foreign cars and another for domestics—make sure you get the right one.

You now have all the research materials you need for the "Take this offer or shove it" strategy. Your objective is to determine how much the car really costs the dealer, so *you* can decide how much profit to sign over to Bob.

Look up your car in your new book. Find the "dealer cost"— what the dealer pays the manufacturer for a car, also known as the "invoice cost." Even under threat of death Bob would not tell you this figure. Find the dealer option price for all options on the car. Add up all the figures and you're close to having the actual dealer cost of the car. You'll have to add a few more things: $50 for advertising (yes, they charge you for that), $20 for gas and oil, dealer prep charges, destination charges, and any taxes (listed in exact amounts on the MSRP).

The lone remaining item is the profit. Remar Sutton, author of *The Insider's Guide to Buying Your Next Car,* suggests three or four percent of the dealer cost is a fair offer. I've found five percent to be more realistic. One caveat: never, ever pay more than $1000 above the invoice. A friend recently bought a $40,000 Mercedes for a thousand over invoice. There is no reason to spend more.

You're now negotiating from a position of knowledge. Walk into the showroom, look Bob right in the eye, and tell him to "take this offer or shove it." Chances are good, after he's tried every angle to raise the price, that he'll take it. If he doesn't, the next dealer will, and he knows it. ❖

> *This essay does for me what all informative writing should do: make the reader feel powerful. I am terrified of dealing with car salespeople—or was until Hyman gave me the power of knowledge. It makes me want to run around shouting, "I can do it now! I can do it now!" I love the ending too—a lovely sense of finality and control.*

COLD TURKEY

JASON C. VORE

You say you're tired of smelling like a pool hall. You say you're tired of being out of breath from walking a flight of stairs. You say you're tired of being the center of people's animosity and scorn. Mostly, though, you say you're just tired of smoking. Good for you. That's a very hard decision to make. I know. I made it myself, a year ago.

I'm not here to advocate non-smoking; that's your decision. If you still enjoy smoking and don't really want to quit, I can't help you—nobody can. If you don't want to quit, you won't. But, if you do want to quit smoking, I can help.

If you've made the decision to stop smoking, the key to staying smoke-free is to remember three things: 1) it's a physical addiction; 2) it's also a habit; and 3) it's not curable, but it's controllable.

Smoking is a physical addiction. Your smoking isn't a character flaw. We all know by now that cigarettes contain nicotine, and that nicotine is very physically addicting. But physical addictions have lifespans. Nicotine only stays in the body for twenty to thirty days. During this period, you will be miserable—you will experience withdrawal symptoms such as irritability, loss of appetite, and anxiety—but if you can make it through the first month, you'll beat the actual "addiction." Now it's the habit that needs to be broken.

Smoking is also a habit. The habit is what most ex-smokers will tell you is the hardest part to conquer. My mother, a smoker for twelve years who quit fifteen years ago, says, "Once a smoker, always a smoker." For an ex-smoker, the urge to light up is a constant battle, like the battle against nail-biting or any other ingrained tic.

To break the smoking habit, you're going to have to break all the other "habits" that went along with your smoking. You need to get away from the things that you associate with smoking. This is probably going to entail a lifestyle modification or two. If you always smoke at bars, limit the time you spend in them, if any. When eating out, sit in the non-smoking section in restaurants. Don't go to the smoking area at school or at work. Basically, you need to stay away from other smokers, because if you don't, the urge will probably be too strong for you. If your spouse or roommate or family smokes, you are going to have to decide how to deal with that for yourself—move, put up with it, get them to quit with you, or whatever.

Avoiding the situations you associate with smoking isn't the only part of breaking the habit, however. You need to find a substitute, something that will meet some of the psychological needs that smoking met and keep your mind busy so you don't dwell on the fact that you're "not smoking." Chewing gum is good because it occupies the mouth, but eating isn't because overeating can be almost as bad for you as smoking. Things that involve both the mind and the hands, like hobbies and sports, are good because they leave no room for smoking. Exercise is great, because you'll feel good and "not smoking" won't feel like a punishment.

Finally, **smoking is not curable, but it's controllable**. The urge will probably return throughout your life—if you tell yourself otherwise, you're just setting yourself up for failure. But after a while, a habit of not smoking develops, and it gets stronger as the old habit gets weaker. And that's a habit you can live with. ❖

> *Here we see the power of the overview. Jason says there are three facts you must know about smoking—keep them in mind and they'll give you all the weapons you need to lick this thing. It seems so easy, so doable now.*

SURVIVING HOMELESSNESS

MICHAEL EGAN

You probably think that it could never happen to you. But suppose your house burns down and you never had enough money to buy insurance. You have no savings and no one to help you get back on your feet. All you have is the pair of pants and shirt you managed to throw on as you went out the door. Welcome to the ranks of the homeless.

Without clothes and a place to shower every night, you can't keep the job you had before, so you're forced to quit. You can't even apply for Unemployment Insurance for six weeks. You've got fifty dollars in your pocket. Life is looking pretty bleak. But you *can* survive. I did.

Though your first inclination might be to sit down on the curb and rail against fortune, this is no time for self-pity. Your ability to take quick action in the first few days can mean the difference between getting back on your feet and getting stuck in a hell you can't get out of. If it helps you to deal with the stress, think of it as a sort of urban camping trip.

The first thing you need to do is get down to the post office and rent a post office box. The seven-dollar investment will come back to you tenfold the very first day. One of the ironic little twists of this game is you can't even apply for Public Assistance without an address.

Next, go to the Welfare Office and apply for emergency food stamps. There are some forms to fill out, but you'll walk out with about fifty dollars in stamps. But don't expect Welfare to solve your problems. It's a fulltime job sitting in that office waiting for one of the slowest bureaucracies on the planet to act, and by the time you get your small subsistence check, you'll probably be so caught up in the system you'll never get out. Better to rely on yourself to save you.

There are ways to eat without doing the paperwork. Soup kitchens, like the Salvation Army's, and grocery-store dumpsters are the best known. But I find both demoralizing. Even in your sorry state, it's important to be able to tell yourself, "It could be worse."

Next you need shelter. If you own a car, park in a place where the police aren't likely to arrest you for vagrancy. Wealthy residential areas away from street lights are good, but park between houses and move out early. Never park in the same place twice. If you're on foot, woodsy areas along freeways are great. Try to find a place that's close to a public rest room so you can keep clean. You can take sponge baths in rest rooms, but it's nicer if you can find someplace to take a real shower. If your town has a college, try the gym's locker room.

You'll need to stay warm, so you'll need a heavy coat and some blankets, or ideally a sleeping bag. All these are readily available at the local Salvation Army Store for next to nothing—a sturdy coat can be had for as little as $2. While you're there, pick up some decent clothes for job hunting.

You want a job that won't care how you look. My personal favorite is dishwashing. The work is always easy to find, the customers can't see you, often a hot meal comes with the job, and you can make tips for walking-around money. Try to get the night shift, so you're free for job hunting during the day. If you can't find work on your own, every town has a Temporary Agency where you can obtain one- or two-day jobs.

Now you just have to save money like crazy. Don't spend a dime that isn't absolutely necessary. If you have expensive vices, give them up. A lot of people drink or take drugs in bad times like these, but if you do you may never escape the streets. If you scrimp, within six weeks you can save enough to move into an apartment and start putting your life together again. You may even find a new confidence in knowing that when the going got tough, you got going. ❖

> *This essay reminds us of two lessons about informing. First, informing is serious business. Knowledge can be life-or-death stuff. Second, the informer isn't smarter than the reader; he has just experienced things the reader hasn't. Michael's saying, "I've been through it; you haven't yet. I can help."*

EUROPE AND THE STARVING STUDENT

ANDREW ROE

If you think the prospect of traveling to Europe is out of the question because you're only a "starving student," then you've never been more wrong in your life. I went for five months and took only $2050.00, but still managed to see and experience the many wonders it has to offer. There was a lot of Europe that I didn't get to see, but still I can say, "I've been there!" Follow me closely, and I will show you just how easy it is.

The first thing you need is motivation. If you lack the desire, you'll never get there. If you really believe that on such and such a date, you'll be flying at thirty-five thousand feet above the Atlantic Ocean, destination London, you're halfway there.

Next, it's important to start saving money early. Don't keep going out every weekend; consider every single dime you spend here will be one less that you can spend there. Friends may try to persuade you to go out with them: "Hey, don't grow roots on that couch, man, let's drink some brewskis!" Let your "cultural alarm" take over and think about being in Europe. Tell yourself and tell your friends that you have other goals than just living for the moment. Smile, relax, and pop in a video. May I suggest "American Werewolf In London"?

There's a basic formula to figure out how much money you should take with you. If you plan on staying for six months, then save every penny you make for six months. This money is your "spending money." This will pay for your food (which you can purchase and cook in the youth hostel kitchens, as I'll explain), local transportation (which could be free if you use your thumb), and entertainment.

Now that you mentally know you're going, it's time to set up a plan for getting there. Airlines are obviously the most efficient in terms of time and money, but you must be careful to not get duped by purchasing the first ticket a travel agent offers you. Newspaper advertisements will quote airline fares running from $699.00 and up. Travel agents will sometimes quote fares as high as $2000.00! The key to finding a ticket for the starving student is to be persistent. You need to search in the classified ad sections of major newspapers in the large international American cities like Los Angeles, New York, or Chicago. Under the "for sale" column there is a section specializing on tickets. Don't be surprised if you see sporting events and concerts for sale in this section too. People sell either actual discounted airline tickets or travel discount coupons for up to 70% off. This is how I purchased a ticket on Pan Am and ended up paying only $400 round trip. You can also save money by traveling in the off-season—usually winter—when demand is low and the ticket prices drop. The places you want to visit will be less crowded then too. Remember, always buy a round trip ticket—it's cheaper, and some countries may not let you in if they think you're not planning on leaving.

Now your tickets are taken care of; where are you going to stay? This is the easy part. Pick up your telephone and ask directory assistance for the local branch of the International Youth Hostel Foundation. Call them! The IYHF was created in the early part of the century for people just like you, young people who want to travel but can't afford the ritzy hotels such as the Grosvenor in London. The cost for a night in a hostel ranges from about $5–$11. You sleep in dorms with anywhere from four to twenty people. Most dorms aren't co-ed, but some have "couple quarters"—if you're traveling with your significant other you'll have to reserve them far in advance. Hostels have lockers for stowing your gear, rentable for mere pocket change. Bring your own padlock—they don't provide them.

Hostels are an experience. You may not be like all of the people you're sleeping with, but you all have a few things in common: you're young and you're a traveler in a foreign land. Trust me, this will create some of the best and most interesting friendships you could ever hope for. IYHF requires a membership fee—somewhere between $20 to $30 dollars for a one-year membership. Buy the membership, or you may find yourself arriving at a hostel and hearing what Jesus heard: "Sorry, there's no room at the inn."

Where do you want to go? If you want to specialize in just one country you should get a train pass for that country only. For example, I purchased a Britrail Pass good for thirty days' travel throughout England, Scotland, and Wales. For only $200.00, this gave me unlimited train travel, anywhere, any time in Britain. If you want to travel all over Europe, the Eurail Pass is the one for you. Usually, the cost for Eurail is based on how long a term you want. Passes come in either fourteen-day, twenty-one-day, one-month, two-month, or three-month terms. A sixteen-day pass will cost you about $280.00, a three-month pass about $700.00. I know it sounds expensive, considering you can probably get your airline ticket cheaper, but remember: you want to "see" Europe. Trains offer you a relaxing windowseat on the countryside, where you can sit back and soak it in.

From my own experience, I think it's best to decide exactly where you want to go. Instead of buying a Eurail Pass, if there is one particular country you'd like to emphasize, get a pass only for that country and allocate some extra funds for buying train tickets to the other major European cities you wish to visit. The advantage of not buying a Eurail pass is that you don't have to be on any "schedule" when traveling. I bought my Britrail Pass for $200.00 and then spent only $300.00 on regular train tickets. After going through eighteen different cities and towns in Britain, I traveled direct to France (stopping in Paris and Reims), Germany (stopping in Cologne, Essen, and Berlin), Holland (stopping in Arnem and Amsterdam), and Belgium (stopping in Brussels and Ostend), and finally returned to England. This took five months. I was on my own schedule and didn't need to purchase the Eurail for $700.00. If you want to make a "whistle-stop tour," get the Eurail Pass, but remember: If you fall in love with the place you're in and decide to stay, your pass will expire and you will have wasted a lot of money. Don't forget to purchase the Eurail Pass here in the U.S—you can't buy one in Europe.

Eurail is a standard price, so it's OK to go to a travel agent for this. For a national pass such as Britrail, contact the Embassy for the country of your choice. They will provide you with the information you need. Once again, you must purchase the pass in advance.

Let's review: motivation, travel fund, airline tickets, youth hostel membership, and train passes. You, the starving student, are almost in Europe. It wasn't that difficult, was it? When you're about to leave, make sure to get your money in the form of traveler's checks so if your money is lost or stolen, you can get it back. Another helpful hint is to change your currency here before you leave. Get some traveler's checks in British Pounds, German Deutschmarks, French Francs, etc. You'll get a better foreign exchange rate.

I have left one item to the end so you won't forget: Get your passport! Without it you don't go anywhere. You can apply for one at your local post office, or passport office if you live in a big city—call US Customs if you're not sure where to go. It can take up to three months to process the papers, so start early.

These tips are for the starving student, the young traveler who wants to see the world as it really is. If you want to see Europe from the window of the London Marriott, then disregard this traveler's advice. If you are that open-eyed young one, then I say, "Happy traveling and bon voyage!" When you get back you too can say, "I've been there!" ❖

> *Andrew demonstrates the power of the narrowly defined audience and purpose. European vacation travel is a gigantic topic, so Andrew chops it down to manageable size by writing only about travel preparations, and only for the young traveler going to Europe for the first time on a shoestring.*

THE LAST STOP FOR AMERICA'S BUSSES

JOHN MERCER

After waving off my friends, I just stood there, dwarfed by the enormous message towering over me: "International Border, Welcome to Mexico." Taking a deep breath, I tossed my duffel bag over my shoulder and headed for the bus station. It was here that I was forced to make my first decision. A large blackboard displayed the names of various cities in alphabetical order. To the right of each name were times and prices. "Primero and Segundo," I read, thinking to myself, "First and second class . . . I wonder what's the difference?"

Mexico, like all countries, has its own system of bus transportation. To help you get started, I've summarized the functions of the four bus classes below. With a little time and a lot of patience, you'll soon be bussing your way across Mexico like a local.

The woman at the counter was helpful and fortunately spoke a little English. First-class busses have toilets, air conditioning, and fewer stops; second-class busses don't. Naturally, considering a thirty-six-hour bus ride, these items are no longer luxuries; they're necessities. Within fifteen minutes I had bought my ticket and boarded the bus for Guadalajara, first class . . . or so I thought. An hour later, I was fidgeting in my seat after four unsuccessful attempts at the restroom door. I remember thinking, "The poor bastard must really be constipated"; then I remembered I was in Mexico and knew that wasn't possible. Someone finally stopped me and explained the facts: the restrooms don't work; they never have worked; they never will work.

The same can be said for the air conditioning. In all fairness, the first-class bus does have fewer scheduled stops; however, due to the lack of facilities, it's always making those necessary unscheduled stops. Realistically, there's only one reason to travel first class: you won't normally find the crowds that plague the cheaper second class.

I probably wouldn't have ever tried a second-class bus if it hadn't been for the first-class bus strike which left me stranded in Puerto Escondido. Preparing myself for the worst, I was pleasantly surprised. Although the busses are uglier and lack the maintenance of the first, passengers have the comfort of knowing the drivers are first-rate mechanics. Second class has more scheduled stops, but they have little effect on arrival times. Like the tortoise racing the hare, the bus sputters along at a consistent pace, seldom far behind in the end. The atmosphere is pleasant, probably due to the open windows and fresh air.

It was this favorable impression of second class that led me to try third class, and for this I'll always be grateful. The third-class bus stations are separate from the previous two, and are normally found in the sections of towns best avoided by people with white faces. However, for those of you who have the time and aren't easily discouraged, you may find the heart of Mexico lies along the paths they forge. They're almost free, because they're government-subsidized. If you're in a hurry or trying to get someplace, forget it. But if you like the thought of listening to Bob Marley tapes through distorted speakers while traveling in a modified school bus so old it may have taken your grandparents to school, stay seated—you're in for a ride. The routes are treacherous, sending the bus bouncing and rattling up and down roads without signs to places without names. Along these roads, most of which are dirt, you will come face to face with people who have spent their entire lives camping out. I remember their stares, looking at me like someone might look at moldy food discovered in the back of the refrigerator. I suppose the story of the man with the white face who was seen on the bus that day may still be told at night by the fire or among the women doing wash at the banks of the river. I will always remember the people and places I found while riding the third-class bus.

The fourth and last class of busses are the city busses. They're the cheapest way to tour a city without getting lost. Like all city busses, they spend the day doing laps. So don't hesitate; jump on, toss the driver a C-Note (about five cents US), and relax. ❖

Here's a nice example of basic information enriched by a lively and complex personality. To John's simple informative message he adds the dramatic in medias res *introduction, the narrative structure, and rich physical details ("listening to Bob Marley tapes through distorted speakers"; "I suppose the story of the man with the white face may still be told at night by the fire . . ."). He portrays himself as a slightly inept gringo falling into this wisdom against his will. That helps with a problem all informative writers face: the reader's fear of the unknown. John is saying, "I blundered my way through, so you can do it."*

THE BASICS OF HANDGUNNING

COLBY C. MEYER

Handguns are currently an extremely controversial subject in our society. Half the people want to ban them and dump them all into the ocean, and the other half either own them already or are seriously contemplating the purchase of one. If you are a member of the first group, I recommend that you learn to shoot in order that you can make an informed judgment. If you fall into the second group, then you must learn the proper way to operate your firearm for the sake of safety and responsibility.

The first and most important thing to learn about your new firearm is safety. This is an area that leaves no room for error, and with a few simple rules it is not that difficult a process. There are five rules, and as long as you follow them the chances of you having an accident are extremely small. The first rule is to never point your firearm at anything you do not intend to shoot. It doesn't matter whether the gun is unloaded or not—you don't take the chance of an accident. The next rule is to keep your finger off the trigger until you have the specified target in your sights. As long as your finger is off the trigger it's impossible for the weapon to fire. The third rule is to never handle a weapon without physically determining that the weapon is unloaded. If you are not sure how to check this, have someone who is present show you how to determine whether the gun is loaded or not. The fourth rule is to always make sure of what lies beyond your target. If you are not absolutely sure that the bullet will be stopped harmlessly, do not fire the weapon until there is something solid enough behind the target to stop the bullet. The last rule is to keep the weapon out of the hands of children at all times. If this means you must purchase a small gun safe, do it. The death of a child because of an ignorant adult with a gun is deplorable and totally avoidable.

Now let's move on to the actual operation and firing of the weapon. Before you fire your weapon you must have some basic equipment and a base knowledge of the firearm. We'll first go over the equipment, then examine the firearm, and last we'll walk through the actual firing sequence.

First and foremost you need the actual gun. There are many types of weapons available on the market, but from viewing many shooters and having had a lot of experience with first-time shooters, I recommend a double-action revolver in either .22 or .357 caliber. The double-action revolver is the simplest, most accurate, and most controllable firearm available to the beginning shooter. The term "double-action" means that with one pull of the trigger the weapon will cock and fire itself. The other advantage to this design is that the beginner can also manually cock the weapon, putting it in single-action mode, which makes the weapon much easier to fire for the beginner. "Caliber" refers to the diameter of the gun barrel—the bigger the caliber, the larger the size of the bullet. The .22 is a favorite beginner's weapon, small and easy to handle. The .357 may sound like too much gun for you, but in fact the "kick" of a handgun comes from the amount of gunpowder in the ammunition you choose, not the diameter of the barrel, and if you ask your gunstore clerk to guide you to the less powerful loads you'll find the .357 tame enough.

Next you need ammunition. If you chose the .22 revolver, there is a multitude of standard to high-velocity ammunition available. This ammunition does not kick (recoil) hardly at all and is relatively quiet. This often has a big effect on how well the beginner can shoot because it is not intimidating to the shooter. If you chose the .357 revolver, I recommend low-velocity .38 special target ammunition. It's like the .22 ammo in that it isn't very loud and hardly kicks at all.

Now that you have your gun and ammunition you will need eye protection, consisting of polycarbonate safety goggles of the type commonly worn with power tools, and ear protection, either an earmuff-type unit or ear plugs. This safety gear will protect you from any unburned gunpowder particles in the air and from the noise of the gunfire.

Finally, you need a gun cleaning kit. Firing a gun coats the inside of the barrel with particles of lead, and they must be removed thoroughly after every shooting session. The kit is like a miniature chimney sweeping device, and it's not expensive.

Before we shoot, let's look at the weapon we have chosen and figure out how to make the bullets go where we want them to. For ease of explanation I will assume the shooter is right-handed; if you're left-handed, do yourself a favor and learn to shoot right-handed, since all guns are made for right-handed people. With your right hand grab the gun's handle firmly, as high up as you can while still having a comfortable grip. Then bring your left hand back, grasping your right wrist and hand firmly. Ideally you want to have seventy-five percent of your strength holding the weapon coming from your left hand. This frees your right hand from stress, allowing your trigger finger to move more smoothly and giving you better control of the weapon while firing. As you look at the top of the weapon you will notice some type of sighting device. In its simplest form this will consist of a square post on the top front of the barrel and a U-shaped notch on the top back of the weapon. When holding the weapon at arm's length, close your left eye and sight down the top of the weapon with your right eye. You want to position the square post in the center of the U-shaped notch and have the top of the post level with the top of the notch. As you're sighting down the weapon, focus on the front post. If you are focused on the target, you're sighting incorrectly. Once you have figured out how the sights are supposed to look, next concentrate on your trigger pull. This is a squeeze of the trigger, not a jerk, not a smash, but a gentle, controlled squeeze. This is where you want to manually cock the weapon, putting it in single action, and then, using just the tip of your finger, gently squeeze the trigger while maintaining the alignment on your sights. The hammer should fall with an audible click before you realize the gun was even going to fire.

Now it's time to go to the shooting range and try what we just did with real ammunition in the gun. At the range, there will be a rangemaster who supervises all of the shooters present. His commands are final—whatever he says, you do. He will specify when and how to put up your targets, then as you return to the shooting area he will give a command to the effect that it is okay to commence firing. At this point, make sure your eye and ear protection are on, and, with your weapon pointing downrange, load the ammunition into the gun. This procedure varies from one design of gun to the next, so unfortunately I can't tell you how but, as you already have been shown how to determine if the gun is unloaded, this should not be too difficult. Once the weapon is loaded, assume your correct shooting stance—feet a little wider than shoulder width, body facing the target, arms fully extended—manually cock the hammer, concentrate on the sight alignment and gently squeeze the trigger. If all goes well you will experience a mild surprise as the gun recoils with a flash and a bang and a little round hole appears right where the tip of your front sight was positioned on the target. And that is all there is to it. All you have to do now is practice so that you become more and more familiar with the process.

Now it's time to use that gun cleaning kit—if you don't, the lead residue in the barrel will rust and ruin your weapon. Clean the gun every time you fire it, the moment you get home. Never tell yourself you'll clean the gun later, and never tell yourself you only fired it once or twice so cleaning isn't necessary. The kit comes with instructions, but the idea is simple: you're going to run a bit of rag dipped in cleaning solvent back and forth through the barrel until you can look through the barrel and see only shiny metal.

Hopefully you will enjoy shooting. From my personal experience I have taken several "anti-gunners" shooting and made converts out of them. This wasn't because they were psychotic and liked the power trip, but because shooting is a fun, challenging sport that anybody who can see and stand relatively still can get good at. Shooting doesn't require great strength or size, and it provides you with steady feedback on your improving performance, as the scores on your targets go up. I believe that everybody should try shooting at least once; many will become shooting converts, and if you don't, well, at least you'll know what you're talking about. ❖

This essay reminds us that good informing needn't put on a show. Good writing rewards, but there are all kinds of ways to do that, and Colby's way is to bypass jokes and "look at me!" flourishes and just teach us what we need to know, quietly, with dignity and grace. We appreciate it.

THINGS TO DO

Obviously the thing to do now is to go write an informative essay of your own. If you want to sharpen technique first, here are some ways.

1. Chapter 15 lists Eight Teaching Tips for informative writing beginning on page 312. Pick any essay in the Treasury, see how many of them it uses, and note where.
2. Practice adding the persuasive edge to informative topics by rewriting the following informative topics as theses, the way we did on page 314:

    a. Shopping at garage sales
    b. How to sing
    c. How to survive divorce
    d. Where to take kids on a rainy day
    e. How to make one-pan lasagna
    f. What is cholesterol?

3. Write a one- to two-page mock-informative essay, to loosen up.
4. Write an expert/ignoramus essay with a collaborator. Sit down with a classmate and explore things each of you knows about

until you find a topic one of you is knowledgeable about and the other one knows next to nothing about, but wants to learn. For instance, one of you may have been in military service and the other one is considering joining up, or one of you may have taken a class the other one is thinking of taking and already knows the ropes. Try to find something the ignoramus can really *use,* not just something she'd kind of like to know about. Write the essay together, the expert being responsible for knowing things and the ignoramus being responsible for asking questions, alerting the team to COIK problems, and identifying gaps to be filled. Treat each member of the team as equally responsible for the essay; don't think of the expert as the writer and the ignoramus as an assistant.

Chapter 16

WRITING AN ARGUMENT, PART I: THINKING IT THROUGH

With argumentative writing, the basic rule is the same as for all writing everywhere: *You can't do it if you haven't read a lot of it.* So the easiest way to write a good argumentative essay is also the most pleasant: Read all the argumentative essays in Chapter 17 and then *write one like them.*

What's an Argument?

Argumentative writing is the only kind of writing I ask my students to do where we often disagree fundamentally about what the label means. When I show them argumentative essays I like they say, "But those aren't *arguments!*" And if they write arguments that are in any way personal, playful, or imaginative, they often write tremulously at the bottom of the essay, "Is this an argument?" So let's begin by talking about what an argument is and where my students and I differ.

In an argumentative essay you try to move people to agree with you. That's different from personal writing, because personal writing doesn't seek agreement; we can love eggs and still connect with Kris Tachmier's loathing of them in "The Egg and I Revisited." And it's different from informative writing, because informative writing allows little ground for *dis*agreement: When Andrew Roe tells us that international hostels are the cheapest decent lodgings in Europe (p. 323), if a substantial number of the readers say "I disagree," he's either factually wrong or he's arguing instead of informing.

An argument isn't just a belief or an opinion, like "I like the Beatles," because an opinion gives the reader no grounds to agree or disagree, and it doesn't urge the reader to join you. An argument is an opinion with reasons to back it up and intentions to sell itself to others. As soon as you say, "I think the Beatles are vastly overrated, and I'm going to try to get you to agree with me," some of us say, "The heck you say," and you've got an argument on your hands.

An argument isn't a sermon, because a sermon preaches to the converted. Its listeners don't need persuading; instead, it *celebrates* a message the audience has already accepted, allowing them to renew their faith by agreeing all over again. You may think the warning is unnecessary, since you're not a minister, but in fact arguments are always in danger of turning into sermons, because we'd all rather talk to people who already agree with us. Most arguments against gun control, for instance, begin by *assuming* that gun control equals gun prohibition, that the Constitution guarantees American citizens the right to own handguns, and that citizens' ownership of handguns is a deterrent to crime—exactly those things your reader *doesn't* grant and will have to be convinced of.

If you're in doubt about whether you're writing an argument, apply two tests. The first is the Should Test: Can the essay's thesis be expressed in *should* form?

> You should buy your groceries at a local market, not at a chain store, because the owner cares about you and your money stays in town.

> The United States should withdraw from the United Nations because it's a phenomenally expensive failed experiment.

> You should go see Steven Spielberg's latest movie—it's marvelous.

To avoid the sermon trap, administer the second test, the Stand-Up Test: How likely is it that a substantial number of the people in the audience will stand up after you state your thesis and say "I disagree"? If you can't imagine more than a scattered few doing it, you're either doing personal writing, informing, or preaching. Go find something that will make more people want to stand up.

Finding an Argumentative Prompt

That's easy—arguments seek you out every minute of every day. You've been handed an argument every time

> You eat in a restaurant and like it (in which case you can argue that other people should eat there), or don't (in which case you can argue that other people shouldn't);

> You see a movie and like it (in which case you can argue that other people should see it), or don't (in which case you can argue that other people shouldn't);

> A teacher does something you like (in which case you can argue that other teachers should do it), or something you don't like (in which case you can argue that no teacher should do it);

> The university frustrates you or betrays you or treats you shabbily (in which case you can argue that something should be done so you and other students don't have to suffer like that anymore);

> A politician says or does something incredibly dumb (in which case you can point out how dumb it was to those voters who amazingly don't see it); or

> A roommate, policeman, parent, best friend, shop clerk, or other human being does something to you that drives you crazy or makes you mad (in which case you can argue that they or people like them should be taught to be different).

In short, the world is constantly presenting us with evidence that Things Aren't the Way They Should Be. We are moved to try to Fix the Problem, and one ancient way is by arguing Those Who Don't See It into sharing our view of the problem and our solution. If you're still stuck, just keep a list of the times during the next few days that the world proves itself screwed up, wrong-headed, unjust, misguided, stupid, or cruel, and ask yourself, "What should be done about this?" Your argumentative theses are "THIS is what's wrong" and "THIS is what we should be doing about it."

A few rages don't lead to good arguments, because there's nothing to DO about them. A student of mine wrote a raging essay about being arrested by the cops for playing loud music in his apartment complex when in fact the noise was coming from someone else's room. His rage was well founded, but the neighbor who complained did so in honest error, the cops were just doing their job, and so there wasn't anything to "fix." All the writer got out of it was a personal essay. Similarly, if you rage at your parents for refusing to cater to your whims, the argument won't go anywhere, because you have no case—throw your hissy fit and get on with your life.

Keep in mind our basic principle for getting ideas: Ideas don't jump into your head to fill the vacuum, they come in response to (a) living and (b) reading. Consider the most tired issue in our society: gun control. What could there be left to say on such a worked-over topic that isn't cliché? If you just try to "think up something new to say," you're primed for failure. But I've read two marvelous pieces on gun control recently, both of them springing from personal experience. The first was by an ex-military man who argued thus: In the Army, we soldiers using firearms were subjected to the most stringent restrictions and training. We had to sign out for bullets and account for each and every one at the end of target practice, for instance, and weren't allowed to touch weapons until we had been indoctrinated in their dangers. Why, he asked, does the U.S. military think that professional weapons handlers need this kind of training and discipline in order to guarantee responsible use, while our society thinks that anyone who can sign his name and wait a few days can own a gun? The second was by a common citizen who owned a gun "for security." One night he heard an intruder trying to break into his apartment, got out the gun, aimed at the outline in the window, tried to pull the trigger and couldn't, and then discovered the figure in the night was his roommate's boyfriend trying to surprise her with an unannounced visit.

Neither essayist was necessarily a superior thinker—just a person who had lived through an experience with firearms most of us haven't had, and had thought about the implications.

If you haven't been living, go read something. I can't imagine reading your way through a contemporary newspaper without being outraged, bemused, astonished, and nauseated several times. You only have to turn the emotional response into argument.

Thinking It Through Versus Selling the Case

Let's assume you've found your argument. The work that remains can be divided into two stages. Stage one (this chapter) is thinking it through—what teachers call critical thinking—where you try to reason your way to a position you really believe and that holds water. Stage two (Chapter 17) is selling the case, where you take the thought-through position and find ways to sell it to your audience.

You want to have the first task done before you begin the second, for a good reason: If you try to do them together, or do the second task before the first, the second poisons the first. Selling keeps you from thinking clearly, because selling blinds you to the weaknesses in your argument. If you're selling a car, any sense of the car's weaknesses makes you a weaker salesman, so you blind yourself, and convince yourself that the car is a treasure. You can't seek to know the truth and persuade at the same time—the goals are contradictory. For the truth-seeker, discovering a flaw in the reasoning is a victory; for the salesman, it's a defeat.

Arguing before thinking cripples almost all the arguing writers I teach. They seize on a thesis, and, skipping the thinking stage, immediately begin setting out to strengthen their case by convincing themselves of its absolute rightness, stopping their ears to everything that doesn't reinforce that first position. Thinking is supposed to lead you from a first shaky thesis to theses wiser and more solid, but my writers' "thinking" only makes them more and more dug in and resentful in the face of change, because they began by defining letting go of the original thesis as failure.

How to Think

Talking about how to think is a confusing business, so let's keep it simple at the outset by remembering our universal rule for making writing easy: *Get a reader.* Draft the argument, give the draft to an intelligent person who doesn't entirely agree with you, have her read it, talk with her about how it looks to her, and try to incorporate what the conversation has revealed to you in your further thinking. Then do it again, with a different reader, and again, and again. . . .

Don't think, then write; draft something immediately, because you need a starting position to poke and prod and progress from. A position statement ("Something should be done about the constantly increasing fees students have to pay around here") and a reason or two ("Because it's unfair and anyway if something isn't done to stop it I'll have to drop out of school—I'm already working two jobs as it is") will do. If you've got a draft, you can divide the thinking process into three steps: getting the right attitude, forming useful assertions, and asking good questions of those assertions.

Getting the Right Attitude

Before we start looking at the draft, we have to rid ourselves of a hobbling definition: thinking equals error hunting.

Many people equate thinking with identifying and eliminating the flawed or fallacious ideas. The myth says, if you kick out all the fallacies, what's left will be the truth. Some logic textbooks encourage that kind of thinking by devoting all their pages to listing logical fallacies. That approach doesn't help you think, for the same reason that grammatical error hunting doesn't help you compose. Thinking and writing are both creative acts, and you can't create well by seeking to avoid error.

To think well, try thinking the way we practiced writing in Chapter 3: as play, a game, a risk-free discovery process without right answers. Thinking is like a free-form frisbee game on the lawn. Your frisbees are your ideas. The point of the game is to stretch yourself, see what the discs will do, test their limits. You try more and more outrageous things until you overreach yourself and you fall on your face or the Frisbee ends up in a tree. You laugh about it, but you've learned a lot. Nobody loses. Being careful defeats the whole purpose.

In practice, that means we won't count logical fallacies often in this chapter or point out examples of bad thinking to be avoided. Instead, we'll ask interesting, open-ended questions of our first-draft statements. We'll ask them of *all* our statements, not just the flawed ones, because you don't throw only the bent frisbees. The questions have no right answers, but trying to answer them will teach us a lot. And we'll avoid trying to think in steps or by rules. No good thinker ever said, "Now I'll apply the false analogy test." I'll have to talk in terms of steps because I can only say one thing at a time, but don't try to follow the steps like a child walking in her mother's footprints in the sand.

Forming Useful Assertions

The essence of critical thinking is asking questions about assertions: You make an assertion, then you poke it and prod it with questions to see how it stands up.

Our first draft is full of statements, of course, but lots of statements are almost impossible to think about. To solve that problem, do four things:

Turn statements into assertions.
Ask yourself, "Exactly what do I mean?"
Avoid loaded language.
Avoid clichés.

Turning Statements into Assertions

Our first thoughts are often fragments and hints of assertions: "Can you believe that? That's just so lame. Who does he think he is? I'm just so furious. I mean, give me a break." It's almost impossible to think further about these until you turn them into *assertions,* formal position statements consisting of a conclusion and a reason: "*X* is a bad idea because . . ." or "We shouldn't do *Y* because . . ." or "Do *Z* because . . ." or "Vote for *A* because. . . ." Assertions start conversations and invite scrutiny; exclamations, like "Give me a break" or "Enough's enough" or "That's just so stupid," terminate conversations and prevent scrutiny. Assertions may be unexciting, but clearing out the emotion is probably a good idea until you're sure that you are in fact taking a stand and that you have some reasons for taking it.

The two most popular assertion-avoiding devices are the rhetorical question and the reason as conclusion. The rhetorical question (p. 370) leaves you to construct the entire assertion yourself by inference:

Who are you to decide when someone should die?
(*Implied assertion:* Capital punishment is wrong, because no one has the right to decide when someone should die.)

Why shouldn't young people be allowed to have a good time and blow off steam once in a while?
(*Implied assertion:* The administration should stop trying to break up student parties because young people should be allowed to have a good time and blow off steam once in a while.)

The reason as conclusion gives half the assertion: It states the reason and assumes the conclusion is obvious. It's a popular ploy in conversation: "Sure, you're a man" means "You don't have any understanding of what women's lives are like and aren't qualified to speak on the subject, because you're a man." Often the conclusions we're expected to draw are unclear and we're left saying, "So . . . ?":

Policemen in England didn't even use to carry guns.
(*So what?—American police shouldn't either?*)

Almost all of the world's great chefs are men.
(*So what?—Women are inferior to men?*)

Most environmentalists are just ex-hippies anyway.
(*So what?—We should distrust them?*)

The key to forming assertions is the word *because,* and most state-ments will be easier to think about if you add it:

England has very few guns, and look at her crime rate.
(*Implied assertion:* England has a low crime rate *because* English people have very few guns.)

If they're so keen to save the forests, why do they live in wooden houses?
(*Implied assertion:* They're hypocritical *because* they support forest conservation and live in a wooden house at the same time.)

Many assertions contain the word *should*: America *should* give more money to its school system; the university *should* have longer library hours; the right to bear arms *should* be protected at all costs. When the word *should* appears, be sure there is a *because*—include at least one reason *why* the *should* is true.

Asking Yourself, "Exactly What Do I Mean?"

Once you've turned your first-draft fragments into whole assertions, ask yourself what they mean. "Of course I know what they mean," you say; "I said them, didn't I?" But oddly enough we have as much trouble understanding ourselves as we do understanding others. Language is am-biguous, which means that any sentence can usually mean several differ-ent things. Here are three sentences each open to a dozen interpretations:

American children are really spoiled, and the schools are encouraging it.

Multiple-choice tests don't test real understanding.

MTV prevents young people from understanding who they really are.

What does being spoiled really mean? What is real understanding? How do you understand who you really are? It isn't that I don't know the answers to these questions; it's that I know too many, and I have to elaborate to make sure I know which one I mean. I could say that a spoiled child is one who has been treated too nicely and thus has come to ask for things he doesn't deserve. But if I think about it I have to ask: How can you be too nice to someone? What does a child really deserve? How does being nice to someone harm him? Some people think it spoils a child to let him cry, listen to his complaints, or give him a voice in how a family or classroom operates. Others consider such things basic human rights and think it's unjust to deny them to children.

The more familiar and accepted the assertion, the more likely that your meaning will go unexamined. "TV is garbage" is a statement all of my students grant, but the more you think about it the harder it becomes to say what it really means. How can art or entertainment be "garbage"?

Is TV supposed to be doing something and failing? What is "good" art? Is TV garbage because it's stupid (in which case, what's the intellectual level of an hour spent playing basketball or gardening?) or because it's full of ads (in which case, is *all* selling garbage, or only highly manipulative selling, or what?)?

Avoiding Loaded Language

Loaded language implies or forces a conclusion. Like loaded dice, it predetermines outcomes and thus short-circuits the whole thinking process.

Language offers us the power to impose positive or negative judgments on almost anything we label: We can call cops "peace officers" or "pigs," women "ladies" or "broads," cohabiting "exploring alternate life styles" or "living in sin," teen sex "being sexually active" or "promiscuity." England calls the political viewpoint that opposes the government "Her Majesty's opposition," which implies they're doing something quite grand; some people call U.S. citizens who do the same thing "un-American"; some people call them "traitors" or accuse them of "giving aid and comfort to the enemy." You can train yourself to be sensitive to loaded language by making lists of such positive/negative pairs:

> *a woman's right to choose* vs. *killing unborn children*
> *development* vs. *environmental destruction*
> *affirmative action* vs. *reverse discrimination*
> *patriotism* vs. *jingoism*
> *family planning* vs. *abortion*

Loaded language will make up your mind for you. A student wrote an essay defending fraternity partying habits in which he said, "It's unfair of Andrews to slander greeks for doing what they like." Once he called the criticism "slander," the outcome of his thinking was settled: Andrews's criticism could only be wrong. A student wrote about trial marriage, "It offers people an easy way out and saves them from having to make a commitment." Having an easy way out sounds bad, and making a commitment sounds good, so trial marriage is damned at the outset. But in both cases there are rich, complex conversations the language is preventing. Should people be able to do what they like? Where does a person's right to do what she likes end and the rights of the community begin? Why does a fraternity exist? Should we make it hard to get out of a relationship? When do we have the right to dissolve commitments we're sorry we made? Is the purpose of a relationship to practice committing?

If you find yourself using words or phrases that get strong "yea" or "ugh" responses, either find less loaded substitutes or ask the loaded words hard questions: "Is this in fact slander? What does *slander* really mean, anyway?"

Avoiding Clichés

A cliché is a phrase you've heard so many times you don't stop to think what it means anymore. Clichés are like fast-food burgers, so familiar we inhale them without noticing we're eating anything: *dead as a doornail, until hell freezes over, the bottom line, dumb as a post, you can't fight city hall, tip of the iceberg, last but not least, how are you doing?, and so in conclusion, in the fast-paced modern world of today, farm-fresh eggs.* Anything we say over and over turns into a cliché, so political positions tend to get reduced to clichés: *law and order, pro-choice, no nukes, save the whales, read my lips, never trust anyone over thirty, show the politicians who's boss, tune in, turn on, drop out, remember Willie Horton.*

Clichés put your brain to sleep and prevent clear thinking by inviting a preconditioned reflex response, like waving the flag at a political convention:

> College students *have a right* to *have a good time* and kick back once in a while.

> We must support the soldiers *fighting for our freedom* in the Near East.

> (In support of environmental legislation): Why are people making such a big fuss about the money when our health and *our lives are at stake?*

In each of these sentences, we're expected to kick into automatic knee-jerk approval mode when we reach the italicized words.

Deal with clichés the same way we dealt with loaded language: Either replace the cliché with words of your own, or, if you can't, ask the cliché hard questions. Demand to know exactly what the cliché means to you:

> Where does the right to have a good time, or any right, come from?

> How do we know our soldiers are motivated by love of freedom, and not by all other possible motives—desire for the paycheck, lust for blood, sadism, love of power, stupid romantic fantasies about soldiering, loyalty to comrades, fear of court martial?

> Exactly who will die, and when, if we don't fund this bill?

A one-word cliché is often called a *buzzword,* meaning a word that thoughtlessly buzzes one of your mental buttons. If you're using any word that's kicked around a lot in public debate—sexism, racism, American, equality, freedom, liberty, rights, fascist, communist, socialist, liberal, conservative—you've probably stopped asking yourself what it means and it will take some work to pin down the meaning you've thoughtlessly assigned to it.

I've said to *avoid* ambiguous, loaded, and clichéd language, not *elimi-nate* it, because you can't. All language is ambiguous, emotionally loaded, and clichéd to some degree. So just do your best and keep the problems to a manageable level.

Asking Questions

Once you have a clear sense of what you're saying, you're ready to ask more questions:

> How do I know?
> Like what?
> What do I want?
> How will it work?
> What assumptions is this based on?
> What's the logical extension?
> Where do I draw the line?
> What's the philosophical antithesis?
> What are the alternatives?
> Is there an implied either/or?
> What are the other consequences?
> Is there an implied analogy?
> Am I using *post hoc* reasoning?

Most of the questions are open ended: They don't have yes/no or "right" answers. They aren't tests that your ideas either pass or fail. The process is more like brainstorming than courtroom cross-examination. Nor are these the only questions you might ask. Let them suggest others to you and help you form the questioning habit.

How Do I Know?

An assertion has to come from somewhere. Ask yourself where you got yours.

There are really only a few possible sources for a belief:

Authority: some teacher, parent, book, scientist, or other expert told us;

Faith: it's an unquestioned principle of your religion or worldview;

Instinct: you just feel that it's so;

Logic: reasoning led you to that conclusion;

Personal experience: "I know because it happened to me."

Of these five sources, authority and logic are vastly overvalued. We tend to believe anything in print and assume that all arguments should be settled by cold logic. But all beliefs and opinions, even the foolish ones, have authorities endorsing them, and logic leads you only to logic's kind of truth; so don't slight the other sources of insight.

Instinct and faith are venerable and grand, but they can be conversation stoppers. Once you've said, "I believe this because I just know it in my heart," the process of intellectual scrutiny comes to a halt.

The source most undervalued by students is personal experience. *The best reason for believing something is because you've lived it.* Once I asked a class to react to an essay by Charles Krauthammer that argued that American schools spent all their time making students feel good about themselves and no time actually teaching them anything. All 25 students gave back responses grounded in logic, objective fact, and authority: They quoted educators, cited statistics, and pointed out logical fallacies in Krauthammer's reasoning. Not one student saw her personal experience—thirteen years or more, seven hours a day, in school—as relevant. No one said, "I agree, because school made me feel good and taught me nothing," or "I disagree, because school didn't make me feel good." Students laid down generalities about school directly contradicted by their personal experience, and when I asked them, "Is that what school did *to you?*" they'd say, "Well, no, but. . . ." Your personal experience isn't the last word, because other people may be having experiences different from yours, but it's what you know best, you can count on it to be true, and it's what you care about. If it isn't the source you use most often, I'd suspect you were discounting it.

When you're asserting a matter of fact (which is really just another form of authority), realize that the conversation can't continue until the facts are in. You may have to go gather some data to see what the expert consensus on the matter is:

> Most welfare recipients would jump at the chance to get off the dole and support themselves.
> (Research question: *What percentage of welfare recipients say they would jump at the chance if they were offered a job?*)

> Animals only kill for food, and then they kill only as much as they can eat.
> (Research question: *Are there any animals who kill for reasons other than hunger, or who kill more than they can eat?*)

> I don't want to wear seat belts, because I don't want to be trapped in the car if there's an accident.
> (Research question: *How many people die in car accidents because they are trapped in the car by their belts, and how many die because they aren't belted in?*)

Like What?

If your assertion is an abstract principle, you can't trust it until you've concretized it with examples. Just ask yourself, "Like what, for instance?":

> Ads are unhealthy because they teach us to hate our bodies, which in turn causes lots of diseases.
> (*Like what diseases, for example?*)

Government in America has always been patriarchal, so our system of laws is inherently antifemale.
(What are some of those sexist laws, for instance?)

This often involves data-gathering research, but sometimes you can just ask yourself. If you say, "Schools should only censor books that are clearly harmful to children," ask yourself to make a list of clearly harmful books and argue with yourself about which titles belong on it and which don't. If you say, "Punishment in schools is never necessary and doesn't work," construct school scenarios in which students misbehave and teachers react. For example, you're a teacher and a student throws a book at you during class. How can you handle it without punishing?

What Do I Want?

If your assertion is an opinion or feeling, ask yourself, "OK, so I feel that way—do I want anyone to *do anything* about it?" And if so, what? If you assert "TV is a waste of time," ask yourself what you're trying to *get* by making the assertion. Do you want the reader to watch less TV? Do you want parents to limit their children's TV time? Do you want the networks to commit themselves to quality programming? Do you want Congress to legislate guidelines for children's TV? Do you want to plead with advertisers to refuse to sponsor violent or sexually irresponsible programs? If you assert that religious proselytizers who knock on your door Saturday morning to preach at you drive you nuts, what do you *want done* about it? Are you seeking a law prohibiting unsolicited door-to-door proselytizing? Or do you just want to gripe? If you assert that all men are sexist pigs, what do you *want done* about it? Are you asking men to understand women's needs better and be more empathic, or are you supporting castration laws for sex offenders?

Until you commit yourself to action—as long as you're just saying, "I feel this"—it's hard to really tackle the assertion. If you say, "Jehovah's Witnesses bug me," I can't do much more than say, "OK, if you say so"; as soon as you say, "And there should be a law barring them from my door," all the questions in this chapter suddenly begin yielding fruit.

I'm not saying that any argument without a call to action is bad; I'm saying that any argument without a call to action should be scrutinized to make sure you're not just writing a personal venting essay. A personal essay, like Kris Tachmier's egg essay, says, "I feel this way"; an argument says, "I feel this way, and you should get out of your chair and come over and join me, and here's why."

How Will It Work?

If your assertion says that something should be done, ask yourself how it will work in practical terms. The best principle in the world is useless if it won't work. If you say we should preserve the ozone layer, make the antagonists in the Middle East see reason, or prevent oil spills, how exactly are you going to do that?

> College professors should be hired and promoted on the basis of their teaching, not publication. After all, teaching is their primary job.
> (*How can we measure good teaching? Shall we test students to determine how much they learn during the term, or shall we ask them how much they like the instructor?*)

> Traditional women's jobs always pay less than traditional male jobs. Payment should be determined by the principle of comparable worth. Jobs that demand equal skills and training should pay equal wages.
> (*How do we determine the worth of a job? How does the worth of an English professor with ten years of college who writes critical articles about unknown dead poets compare with the worth of an unschooled baseball player who swings a piece of wood at a ball?*)

What Assumptions Is This Based On?

Every opinion or conclusion rests on basic principles or assumptions. Spelling them out is the rock on which all good thinking depends.

You'd think that the point is to discover which ideas rest on flawed principles and discard those, but it rarely works that way. Occasionally you do find an idea that's simply indefensible, but that's the exception. The norm is to discover that the assumptions start interesting conversations without right and wrong answers. In a discussion of European attitudes toward nudity, a student said, "I hope Americans never accept public nudity. It would rob making love of all its intimacy." The philosophical assumptions here are slippery and fascinating: that intimacy is dependent on hiding flesh, that clothes are necessary for privacy, that sex and nudity are dependent on each other. You don't just agree or disagree with such principles. A stimulating conversation is now ready to begin. If you see a stranger naked in public, does that mean you're intimate with him, or does it make later intimacy or intercourse less precious? Does a member of a nudist colony feel intimate with all other members? Does she find sex less special? Are Europeans uninterested in making love because nudity is ever present? Are we Americans better or worse off for living in a culture where skin is a semisacred mystery?

Here are other assertions, with some of the assumptions that underlie them and the conversations they start:

> The government has no right to tell me to wear seat belts. It's up to me if I want to kill myself.
> (Assumption: *The government has no business protecting citizens from themselves, and my death would affect only myself.* Discussion: *In one view your death is your own business. In another, your death affects other people in lots of ways, and the government may have the obliga-*

tion to protect them. And why shouldn't the government protect citizens from themselves? It already outlaws or penalizes self-destructive behavior in all sorts of ways, like banning cigarette advertising on TV; is it always wrong to do so?)

Meat is good for you. Why do you think we're carnivorous?
(Assumption: *Whatever we were designed by nature to do is good and we should do it. Discussion: There's a question of fact here: Are Homo sapiens really engineered to eat meat? Many vegetarians argue that we aren't—that our intestines are designed for the long-term digesting of carbohydrates. But there are philosophical issues as well: Isn't it possible that nature engineered us to function well in an environment that's been extinct for three million years and that, since times have changed, so should we? Don't we in fact alter nature all the time, by wearing clothes, for instance? Are morality and nature synonymous or antithetical? "Human nature, Mr. Allnut, is what we were put on this earth to rise above," says Katharine Hepburn in* The African Queen.)

What's the Logical Extension? Where Do I Draw the Line?

Philosophical principles aren't simply true; instead, we agree with them only up to a point—then we bail out. Everybody is for free speech . . . up to a point. Everybody wants to protect the environment . . . up to a point. The question isn't whether you believe, but where you draw the line. If you think Americans have a right to own firearms because the Constitution protects their right to bear arms, you probably don't think they have a right to own any and all firearms. Instead, you draw the line somewhere. Hunting rifles are definitely okay, handguns probably, machine pistols maybe not, assault weapons and machine guns no, and bazookas and grenade launchers definitely not. So a good way to understand your own position is to take the underlying principle, make up more and more extreme applications of it, and discover when you say "Enough's enough." Then ask yourself why you support the principle in some applications and not in others. Here are some other assertions pushed to logical extremes.

We need special university admissions standards for minority students. After all, they didn't ask to be born into disadvantaged environments.
(Principle: *Standards should be proportional to a candidate's advantages. Extension: Imagine a world where all criteria were weighted to take into consideration such advantages. Should graduate schools have higher admission requirements for graduates of "good" colleges, since they've had the advantage of a good undergraduate education? Should personnel officers have hiring criteria that rise as a job applicant's family income rises? Should ballet companies be less demanding of potential members who have been denied quality training in their youth? Should the university's special standards continue into the classroom, where disadvantaged students are graded on one more forgiving*

scale and advantaged students on another, more rigorous one? If you part company with the principle somewhere, where do you draw the line? Why should we admit disadvantaged students by a special standard but not grade them in the classroom by one?)

Women who pose in bikinis for calendars must have no morals.

(Principle: *All women who make money off their bodies or their sexuality have no morals. Logical extension: All models, cheerleaders, beauty queens, prostitutes, and many actors and entertainment figures earn a living off their bodies and their sexuality. Which forms of that are okay and which aren't? How is being paid to pose in a bikini different from being paid to look glamorous while you read the news on TV? How is being a cheerleader different from being a stripper? Is it not okay to pose for a calendar but okay to walk the beach in a string bikini cruising for pick-ups? Is it okay for women to get breast implants to further their careers, or to increase their attractiveness to their partners?)*

What's the Philosophical Antithesis?

Another way of discovering where you draw the line is to imagine your principle as one half of a pair of opposites—an antithesis—and ask yourself where you stand *between* them.

All absolute principles come in pairs:

Individual rights vs. social order
Sanctity of human life vs. law and order
Ethics vs. expediency and practicality
Preserving the environment vs. economic prosperity
Self-determinism vs. fate
Discipline vs. spontaneity and liberation
Equality vs. personal freedom
Cynicism vs. faith and optimism

Only zealots can pick one side of the antithesis and call it the right one; the rest of us find a working compromise, a spot on the spectrum connecting the two. We say, "I'm all for freedom of speech, but there are limits . . ." or "Sure, you have the right to live the way you want, but you have to consider your neighbors too." Like two magnets, the two ideals pull at us, and we move between them until the forces are balanced.

To figure out where your balance point is, think of examples where each principle rules. For instance, we all believe that people should be responsible for their own actions and that companies should be responsible for their products. When a boater ignores storm warnings, takes a dinghy out into the ocean, and drowns, and his family sues the boat manufacturer for "causing" the drowning, we cite the first principle—people should be responsible for their own actions. When a tire manufacturer makes a flawed tire, knows it, covers up the fact, and continues to sell the tire anyway, and drivers are killed when the tires fail, we cite the second principle. When does one principle give out and the other come into play? If someone trips over a pile of laundry in the middle of his living room and breaks his leg, are the clothing companies responsible? You never simply find the right place between the extremes; instead you keep weighing the pros and cons as each new test case arises. For instance, the courts have recently been trying to decide if tobacco companies are financially responsible for the lung cancer their customers get. On the one hand, the companies have done everything they can to seduce people into smoking; on the other hand, every smoker knows the health risks and chooses to smoke anyway. You decide. Here's another example:

> Random drug testing is wrong because it's an invasion of privacy and a violation of our civil rights.
> (The antithesis: *Civil rights versus a society's right to protect itself. We all like civil rights. We can also all think of situations where society's needs outweigh those rights. People don't have the right to drive drunk, for instance. Imagine situations where one principle outweighs the other. Does society's need to assure itself that air traffic controllers aren't stoned outweigh the controller's right to privacy?*)

What Are the Alternatives?

No proposed course of action is simply right; its worth can only be measured relative to the alternatives. If you say, "We should do *X*," what you really mean is, "*X* is the best of all the alternative solutions." So test your assertion by asking yourself what the other alternatives are:

> It's a crime to hand out condoms in elementary school classrooms. It just encourages the kids to have sex at that age.
> (*What are the alternatives? Kids are having babies at age fifteen. Unless you want to argue that nothing should be done about it, what can we do that will work better than handing out condoms?*)

> Nobody knows how to spell anymore. Schools should devote more time to teaching spelling.
> (*What are the alternatives? Maybe teaching spelling isn't the best way to teach spelling—maybe spelling is better learned by reading, in which case schools should devote* less *time to teaching spelling. And maybe the problem isn't in the teaching, but in the spelling system itself—maybe it's time to modernize English spelling so it's easier to learn. Anyone can learn to spell Spanish perfectly because the spelling system is simple and regular.*)

It's easy to go wrong here when you're arguing against something by thinking the question asks for alternatives to the thing you're against—you're arguing against boring TV, so the alternative is exciting

TV. That's not enough. The question also wants you to think about alternative *ways to get what you want.* If you want to enforce seatbelt laws to cut down on traffic fatalities, what other ways of cutting down on fatalities are there (airbags, law enforcement, stricter driver's license tests, electronic governors in cars that beep when they sense a car too close to your bumper?), and is your solution the best among them?

Is There an Implied Either/Or?

Either/or's are assertions that offer alternatives, but only two: You can do *A* or *B*; life is either *C* or *D*; there are two kinds of people, the *E*'s and the *F*'s. Either/or's are dangerous because they fail to ask, "What are the other alternatives?"—and there are *always* other alternatives. Sometimes either/or is called black-and-white thinking. Ask yourself, "Where's the gray area?"

Sometimes the word *either* or *or* is actually used:

> We can either suffer a little monetarily and live in a healthier environment, or we can let the world get worse and worse.
> (*What are the other alternatives? There may be ways to help the environment that don't cost money, and there may be better ways to spend our money than this bill.*)

> It's a pain having to pay $5 to enter a state park, but the parks have to charge user fees or they'll have to close.
> (*What are the other alternatives? There are other ways for the state government to fund the parks—taxes, for instance.*)

But typically the either/or is disguised and we have to learn to see the *implied* dichotomy:

> I was nauseated by the Homecoming Rally. Ten years ago those students would have been at an antiwar rally or something that really mattered.
> (The implied either/or: *Either you go to pep rallies or you go to antiwar rallies. What are the other alternatives? It's possible to do both.*)

> If he's so keen about saving the forests, why does he live in a wooden house?
> (The implied either/or: *People are either consumers of natural resources or supporters of conservation, so anyone who says he's a conservationist and lives in a house built of dead trees is a hypocrite. Since we all consume natural resources, either (a) no one is a conservationist, or (b) the either/or is false. There must be ways to help preserve the earth that don't require living in a mud hut.*)

What Are the Other Consequences?

If your assertion leads to a plea for action, remember that every act has many consequences, both good and bad. Plague eases overpopulation.

Recycling paper produces toxic chemical waste. If we resolve to do only those acts whose consequences are all good or not to do an act any of whose consequences are bad, we'll do nothing. Instead, we try to do the things whose good consequences outweigh the bad ones. So if you assert that we should or shouldn't do something, ask yourself what the *other* consequences are, and see if they alter the equation:

> Sex education is a bad idea because it undermines the authority of the nuclear family.
> (*It may, but it may also help stop teen pregnancies and save people from AIDS. Perhaps undermining the authority of the family is a price we're willing to pay. Are more people suffering from an unwanted pregnancy or a nonauthoritative family?*)

> High schools are graduating students who can't even read or spell. We desperately need a standardized national competency test for high school graduation.
> (*Such a test might mean that more graduates can spell, but what other consequences would it have? More students would drop out, more teachers would teach to the test, more time in school would be given to remedial education, student fear would increase tenfold, and vast sums of money would be diverted from teaching to testing, just for starters. In the long run, would we be better off or worse off?*)

Weighing pros and cons is laborious, so we like to reduce the workload by reducing decisions to single issues: "Vote for *A* because we need a strong military defense"; "Vote for *B* because he's pro-choice"; "Vote for *Z* because he's a newcomer and we have to show the incumbents we're fed up." Single-issue voting rarely works well, in the polling booth or in your mind.

It's easy to go wrong here if you're arguing *against* something by weighing only the negative consequences of the thing you're against. For example, you argue that TV rots your mind; you ask yourself, "What are the consequences?", and you say, "It also wastes time, hurts your grades, and makes you antisocial." OK, but the tougher question is, what are the consequences of *the thing you're trying to accomplish*—what do you want to do about TV, and what are the other consequences of *that*? If you say TV rots your mind, so Congress should pass legislation banning stupid programs, you can ask yourself if you're ready to live with the consequence: having the government decide what you can and cannot see.

Is There an Implied Analogy?

An analogy is a comparison: "*X* is like *Y*." We use analogies to draw conclusions: Since something is true for *Y*, it's also true for *X*. "Marijuana is like alcohol, a popular, low-intensity drug. Alcohol is legal, so pot should be legal too." If your assertion is based on an analogy, remember that *no two things are exactly alike,* so all analogies are only partly true. Ask, "In what ways are the two things alike, and in what ways are they different? When does the analogy break down?" For instance, George Will wrote an essay to express his outrage and disgust at the sexual violence of rap lyrics. He ended by saying, "America today is capable of terrific intolerance about smoking, or toxic waste that threatens trout. But only a deeply confused society is more concerned about protecting lungs than minds, trout than black women" ("America's Slide into the Sewer," *Newsweek,* July 30, 1990). That's an implied analogy: Minds are like lungs, people are like trout, only more precious, so we should treat minds and humans the way we treat lungs and trout, only more carefully. When does the analogy break down? We care for lungs and minds, trout and people in different ways, because they need different things. Smoke is bad for lungs, but what's bad for minds? We're not sure. Censorship may be worse for minds than sexually violent language. Similarly, we know what's good for trout, but we're not sure how best to care for humans. Some people think we do it by preventing them from hearing unhealthy thoughts; some think we do it by protecting them from well-meaning censorship.

The occasional analogy will use the words *like* or *as,* but usually the analogy is implied and you'll have to sniff it out:

> We teach kids to just say no to drugs. Why can't we teach them to just say no to premarital sex?
> (The implied analogy: *Drugs are like sex, so we can educate young people about them in the same way.* Where it breaks down: *Drug abuse ruins your health; sex improves it. So if we tell people the truth about drugs they may stop, but if we tell them the truth about sex they may not.*)

Am I Using *Post Hoc* Reasoning?

Any time you assert that something is good or bad because what followed it in time is good or bad, you have to watch out for the logical fallacy called in Latin *post hoc ergo propter hoc,* meaning "after this therefore because of this." Causation is hard to prove. If *X* happened after *Y,* we can't be sure that *Y made X happen.* There could be no connection: The Korean War broke out shortly after I was born, but my birth didn't make it happen. Even if there is a connection, it's hard to pick out one factor among the countless influences on an event and say, "That's the one that caused it." If I say, "We can thank Hollywood for the rising teenage pregnancy rate," I'm assuming that movies by themselves *cause* teen pregnancies. Movies may well be a factor, but so are sex education or the lack of it, the lack of a social consensus on moral behavior, the automobile, working parents, the decline of the church as mentor, peer pressure, teen boredom and spiritual malaise, alcohol abuse, laws limiting teens' access to birth control, the stereotype of female passivity, antiabortion campaigns, and the social stigma attached to buying condoms. Which of these cultural developments *caused* the others?

Most *post hoc* assertions don't blatantly say, "Since X followed Y, Y caused X," so you'll have to learn to spot the hidden logic:

> Trial marriage doesn't work because statistics prove that people who live together before marriage are more likely to get divorced than people who don't.
>
> (The *post hoc* assumption: *Since the divorces followed the trial marriages, the trial marriages caused the divorces.* The logical weakness: *It's also likely that the sort of person who is willing to flout society's customs by cohabiting also gives herself permission to leave a bad marriage.*)
>
> Of course, legalizing gambling leads to crime. In the sixteen years since they legalized gambling, New Jersey's crime rate has increased 26 percent.
>
> (The *post hoc* assumption: *Since New Jersey's increased crime rate followed the legalization of gambling, legalizing gambling caused the increased crime rate.* The logical weakness: *Though the gambling may have been a factor, countless other factors affect crime statistics. Maybe the population tripled. Maybe a new law was passed making tobacco smoking a felony.*)

WRITERS' WORKSHOP

Using All the Tools

I don't want you to think you use these questions like golf clubs, selecting the right tool for the right job and applying the appropriate one for the assertion at hand. Instead, approach every assertion with all of them, and slop messily from one question to the others. Here's a typical first-draft assertion followed by the kind of conversation you might have with yourself to think it through, armed with the tools we've practiced in this chapter. Whenever I've used one of the tools, I've italicized it.

The assertion: Capital punishment is wrong because we say murder is wrong and then we murder people for murdering. If we execute a criminal, we're as guilty as he is.

Discussion

What exactly do I mean? There's a question about *ambiguity* here: What does "murder" mean? It usually means "killing I don't approve of," which only postpones the question of whether I should approve of state executions or not. If "murder" means "illegal killing," executions aren't murder because they're legal—but should they be? The language is also *loaded,* since murder is inherently bad. "Execute" isn't much better, since it's a euphemism that obscures the graphic ugliness of the act, and is therefore loaded positively. Maybe "killing" is the only neutral word. The assertion's also a *cliché,* since the opinion has been expressed in these exact words a million times, so I might try to say it in fresher language or at least realize that it will be hard for me to be open minded about language so familiar.

There are a number of *underlying assumptions:* that all killing is wrong, that all killing is murder, that killing by state decree is the same as killing in passion and for individual profit, that performing an act to punish a guilty party is morally identical to doing it to an innocent victim for personal gain. I'd better *extend the logic* on all of these and *see where I draw the line.* Let's take the first one. Almost no one really believes that all killing is wrong, and neither do I. Killing is acceptable in some circumstances and under some kinds of provocation. Some people tolerate killing in battle; some don't. Most people grant police officers the right to kill, but only under the most strictly defined circumstances—what are they? Euthanasia is often favored precisely by the people least willing to grant the state the right to kill. Few people would call killing someone who was trying to murder you murder. So where do I draw the line? What are the features of acceptable killing that separate it from unacceptable killing?

It's not easy to say. Even if I decide that individuals can take life to protect themselves from danger, how immediate and life threatening does the danger have to be? Can I shoot someone who has just shot me and is reloading? Someone who is aiming a gun at me? Someone who is carrying a gun? Someone who has threatened to kill me? Someone who has tried to kill me, is now running away, but will probably try again?

I'm struggling here with a *philosophical antithesis* between two abstract principles: the belief that human life is sacred versus the belief that individuals and society have the right to protect themselves from grave threat. When does the threat become grave enough to justify killing the threatener? A few people say "never" and will die without raising a hand against their killers. I'm not one of them. Some people say that individuals never have the right to take life, and that when the state takes life in war or law that represents the collective will and is therefore okay. That may be a moral cop-out—maybe every soldier should take personal responsibility for every death he causes. At the other extreme are totalitarian states that execute people who might someday cause the state inconvenience.

If I claim that killing is justified when innocent parties are under immediate threat, there are *other consequences* to that logic that aren't pleasant. For one thing, a state execution that takes place two years after the crime is unjustified. For another, it puts victims in the same quandary women face when they're told, "If you're being raped, be sure you get severely beaten up so you can show the bruises to the police." So if he's holding a knife to my throat I have to make him cut me?

There's also an *implied analogy* here: Executing a convicted murderer is like murdering an innocent person. *Where does the analogy break down?* I see two significant differences between the X and the Y here: (1) The criminal has committed a heinous crime, which may terminate his rights as a human being; and (2) he has been judged by a supposedly impartial legal system, so there is no passion or personal gain influencing the decision. The *logical extension* of the analogy questions the whole concept of punishment: Since taking someone's money against his will is wrong, fining him for traffic violations is wrong; sending my child to her room when she breaks the house rules is as unjust as her sending me to mine on a whim. All these assertions are as open to questioning as the one I started with, of course: Does committing a crime cancel your rights? Is the legal system impartial? Is punishment a flawed concept, and is a disciplining parent as criminal as any other assailant? After all, lying to a liar is still wrong, for instance. But that's another *analogy*, and as suspect as any other.

If I abolish capital punishment, *what's the alternative?* I could lock murderers up for life, but is that really more humane? If killing criminals makes me no better than criminals who kill, doesn't imprisoning criminals make me no better than criminals who imprison? Lifelong imprisonment is certainly punishment, so if I convinced myself I didn't have the right to punish, I wouldn't like this any better than execution. If I resolve not to punish, what methods are left to me to deter violent crime? People talk about rehabilitation, but what does it really mean and *will it work?* ❖

This discussion, like all thinking processes, never ends. Neither will yours. Don't wait; just start writing, keep thinking, and hand in whatever you've thought your way to by the essay due date. Next week you'll have thought some more, and will want to write a new essay showing how far you've traveled.

If this conversation feels like work to you, imagine how much work it would be to ski a difficult slope or cook a complex meal if it wasn't play. Thinking must be play. If it isn't, go back to where this chapter started, with the frisbee metaphor. Chuck those ideas around. See what they'll do. *It's a game.*

Your Turn

Here's some first-draft thinking about a militant group of environmental activists. Ask the draft each of the thirteen questions on page 342; write out answers; then write a one-page response to the draft exploring the new stuff the answers have turned up. Remember, you aren't arguing with Kevin, fighting with him, or trying to shoot him down; you're helping him trouble-shoot the argument, see what's working and what isn't, and generally help the thinking go further. You're no more his enemy than your auto mechanic is your enemy when he tunes your car.

THE METHODS ARE INSCRUTABLE

KEVIN MATHIESEN

Are the Earth First people really doing the right thing? These people claim that they are doing what is in our best interests. But I don't feel that they are doing the right things. They are terrible people, terrorists to be exact.

The things these people do to help our environment are scary. Tree-spiking is a common one. They pound spikes into the trees so that the loggers can't cut them down. They claim they mark the trees so the loggers will know not to cut them, but a tree might not be marked and a logger could be seriously hurt. The logger might even cut through the tree without hitting a spike, and when the tree reaches the mill the man on the saw might be seriously hurt.

Earth First destroys equipment too. The leader of the organization has put out a book on how to destroy logging equipment. Now, you can't tell me that they will destroy equipment and never seriously injure a person. Give me a break. These people aren't mechanics.

They are also putting people out of work—people who have been loggers all their lives and don't know any other way to support themselves and their families. Earth First is taking food out of children's mouths when they put a logger who is a family man out of work.

Down with the Earth First terrorists. They should stop doing drugs, because that's the type of people they are, and catch a clue about the ways they are hurting people. They might be thinking about our earth first, but they sure aren't thinking about people first. ❖

MORE THINGS TO DO

1. Practice noticing the arguments the world brings you by recording your argumentative thoughts for two days in a small notebook or something you can keep with you. Look for the times when the world seems wrong-headed, out of whack, in need of work—then ask yourself what should be done about it.

2. For a week, keep a list of everything that makes you mad, irritated, frustrated. From that list, turn three items into argumentative theses by asking yourself, "What should be done about this?" Find two items that don't translate into arguments because there is nothing to do about them.

3. Pick any two of the following statements and write a half page of critical thinking about each. First, go through the four steps on page 338; then ask any of the thirteen questions listed on page 342 that help you see more deeply into the matter.

    a. Prohibition proved that you can't legislate morality—if people want to do something, they'll do it.

    b. Intelligence tests are racist. Blacks consistently score lower on them than whites.

    c. Boxing is brutal. It's incredible to me that in a society that bans cock fighting and bear baiting, we permit the same sort of thing with human beings.

    d. I didn't want to hurt him, but I had to say it or I wouldn't be honest.

e. Twenty-five years ago the public schools abandoned sound-it-out reading approaches, and the nation's reading scores on standard tests like the SAT have been dropping ever since.

f. Schools should return to teaching grammar. Most students today don't even know what an adjective is.

g. Asians do better in school because their families traditionally value schooling more highly than other minorities do.

h. Marijuana isn't so bad in itself, but it leads to heavier drugs. Most cocaine and heroin addicts started out on pot.

i. If my neighbors want peace and quiet, why do they live in a student neighborhood?

j. Female reporters have to enter male athletes' locker rooms. If they don't, they can't do their jobs.

Chapter 17

WRITING AN ARGUMENT, PART II: SELLING THE CASE

Now that you've thought through your position, it's time to think about ways of selling it to your audience. You have to do three things:

Define your objectives realistically
Establish a positive relationship with your audience
Find a dramatic structure

With each of these three, there's an easy way to go wrong, and we'll begin by learning to avoid them.

Define Your Objectives Realistically

How to go wrong: Set out to do impossible things.

It doesn't sound sensible, yet many writers do just that. They try to have the last word, say the pure truth that no one else has been able to figure out and that ends debate forever. That only gives you writer's block. So don't try.

Instead, set out to do something possible. Your job is to make a small contribution to the ongoing debate. The contribution isn't "truth"; it's a personal view of things. It doesn't end debate; it generates it by stimulating thought in other people. You aren't saying to your reader, "You're wrong; I'm right"; you're saying, "Here's something I see; maybe it can be a factor in your whole view of things." It needn't even be the only opinion you have on the matter, since it's a contribution to *your own* whole view of things as well.

Think of this as the Stew Theory of argumentation. In this theory, there is a gigantic pot of Argument Stew always cooking on the Stove of Our Culture. Every citizen is responsible for contributing something—a carrot, a potato—to this stew. And what makes a stew good? The abundance and variety of ingredients. The more varied the contributions, the better the stew gets. And which contribution—which potato—is the "true" one, the "right" one that makes all the other ingredients unnecessary? No such thing. In a stew, the potatoes aren't trying to shout down and silence the carrots. So don't try to toss in the potato that ends the stew; toss in *your* potato, add your piquant bit of flavor to the rich, complex mass. And what if you come up to the stew pot to make your contribution and just say, "I second the potato that other guy threw in"? That doesn't help the stew, so don't make an argument that simply agrees with someone else's argument—you must increase the argumentative mass.

It's hard to see this never-ending, constantly enriching conversation, because most of the arguments we see seem to stand alone. They're printed by themselves in newspapers or magazines, and we can't see all the stew ingredients that came before and will come after. But there are places where you can catch a glimpse of the process. In the "Letters" section of any issue of *Newsweek* or *Time* you'll see six or eight one-paragraph responses to a particular news article offering different viewpoints on an issue—six or eight ingredients being added to the stew by thinkers who were spurred by the original article's contribution.

But where the stew-making process really shows its true colors is on computer network conferences (for more on these, see Chapter 13's discussion of electronic publishing, p. 261). Here hundreds or thousands of users can be hooked up to the same bulletin board at the same time, reacting to the same issue simultaneously. You have a thought, post it, it appears on all users' screens instantly, and two hundred readers may grab their keyboards and send you their thoughtful reactions in minutes. In this environment, a single discussion can gather several hundred contributions and rage merrily for months. Nobody wins. Nobody shuts anyone else up. No one ever succeeds in saying it all. A day or two in this argumentative hothouse will cure you of any notion that arguments are solitary, final-word things.

Here's what it looks like. I gave my students a prompt on our English department's classroom computer network and asked them to react via their keyboards and then react to each other's reactions. Here's the first hour and a half:

The prompt. A California School Board member has suggested that the local schools ban homework. He has two reasons: (1) Homework is interfering with the family by taking the child away from family life in the afternoons and evenings and, more importantly, (2) homework is discriminatory, because students with PC's and other assists have an unfair advantage over students who don't, so homework rewards the advantaged and punishes the disadvantaged. The Board is considering the proposal. What do you think?

The conference:

Eric: If we can't have homework because some people have computers and some don't, how can we have anything? Lectures are obviously "unfair" because some people hear better than others.

Lindsay: I find it hard to believe that there are absolutely no resources for these children who lack computers or typewriters. If this is indeed the case, then the rules should be changed, so that assignments could be hand written.

Jill: I baby-sit a seven-year-old whose parents are poor and don't have the money for a computer—but the kid has a Sega system and dozens and dozens of games. So is it a problem of resources or priorities?

Eric: Trying to "fix" America's family or social problems by banning homework is like trying to clean up our toxic dump problem with a toothbrush. We're always looking for the quick fix, the regulation that will make our world a healthy, happy one. No such thing.

Lindsay: I loathed homework just like any other kid. But the plain and simple fact is, homework teaches responsibility. Every child is going to have to learn this sooner or later. Taking away homework will only teach kids that they will have more time to spend doing things that are fun—not more time with the family.

Aaron: The new family structure is part of the problem. My aunt is a single parent, and she cannot say no to her son. She tells him to do his homework, he begs to play Nintendo, and she gives in. It's emotional blackmail, and lots of single parents feel it.

Adam: I can see how it is unfair if one kid turns in a paper with amazing graphics and a pretty cover page and gets an A where someone with the assignment done on a typewriter gets a B. I have seen this injustice, and it must stop!!

Joan: Stop the discrimination, sure, but stop it by stopping grading, not homework.

Eric: Right—don't throw out the baby with the bath.

Adam: Classrooms are already over-crowded as it is and having no homework will make it worse.

Tricia: In what way?

Aaron: If families are worried about homework interfering with their together time, why don't they help little Timmy do his homework "together"? It's educational, it's potentially interesting, and it's much more productive together time than sitting around the old TV.

Dan: In this day of latch-key children and parents abandoning their kids to take vacations, is it really the homework that's causing this lack of quality family time?

Paula: Homework should be required to be done by hand—PC's are doing too much of the work.

Tony: Are people supposed to limit their academic development and wait for everyone to catch up before they can continue to learn? Is this called being "academically correct"?

Keri: No one in the real world is going to wait for them or eliminate all inequities so they get a fair start.

Hennie: Lindsay's right, homework is a form of learning discipline. You have to take something home long enough to think about it and work with it outside of structured school time. Parents can balance their check books, go through bills next to their children who do book reports. This way each can understand what each other is doing and work together.

Lindsay: Very few parents and children do bills and homework side by side. Is that a realistic hope?

Stacy: Homework keeps kids out of trouble.

Eric: How does forcing kids to waste time doing boring and meaningless tasks keep them out of trouble?

Keri: Homework isn't meaningless—it's practice for the real world. Students have to learn that most jobs demand time after working hours. When I get off work at 5, I go do all the off-the-clock chores that go with my job. Most professionals have homework.

Eric: But the motivation is different—your evening work is purposeful and productive.

Tod: Do you really think kids want to spend their free time with their parents, or would they rather go out with their friends or play Nintendo?

Ed: Definitely YES, if the parent is doing something the kid values.

Eric: It's easy to say that homework doesn't get in the way of the family, until you're a parent. When my teenager hit high school, homework used up all her at-home time—now she comes home, watches a little TV to relax, we have dinner, and she does homework until bedtime. Of course, that doesn't mean that less homework will make her choose to play Monopoly with the family.

Tony:	Homework should take 1–2 hours a day. Working parents get home 1–2 hours after kids get home from school. So what's the problem?
Eric:	Maybe the schools should have two hours of mandatory after-school group homework sessions every day. That way the homework will be done before dinner, and it will be done in peer groups, so it's not isolating or boring.
Jill:	Some schools are trying something like that.
Mark:	There go all the sports and after-school activities.
Keri:	Next they'll be asking professors to give those students who have to work (like me) a break because they have less time to study. Life is full of disadvantages and kids need to learn this. It's overcoming these disadvantages that makes you a stronger and better person.
Eric:	Uh, how is this different from the old argument that you should beat your children so they learn that life is cruel and learn how to take a punch?
Joan:	We're already behind the Japanese in academic skills—do you want to get further behind?
Mark:	If we don't get going, we'll all be working for them in ten years.
Eric:	No thanks. The Japanese are all working 12-hour days, racked with ulcers and committing suicide when they make a mistake, thanks to the wonders of the school system.
Lindsay:	I had a friend who went to elementary school in Japan. She came home with lashes on her back—they had beaten her for forgetting her homework. Is that the kind of discipline we're after?
Joan:	Eric, how much is "a little" TV? If your daughter watches TV until dinner time, I'd say that is about three hours that could be used to study. Maybe you should peek in there and see what she's working on. You could have some father-daughter time there. You could help her with her writing, or is it you that have no time?
Scot:	Homework is essential to brain activity and the well-being of our country.
Paula:	"The well-being of our country"? Expand on that, please.
Tricia:	Ditto.

Mark:	Right on, Joan. These so-called parents are so glued to the Simpsons they can't pull themselves away to help their child with their homework. Homework brings families together—as a parent, I know.
Eric:	So maybe we need a new kind of homework—one done by families, not individuals. My daughter has a class that gives her assignments like, interview your parent or cook a meal with him. Love it.
Scot:	This is another case of the American society whining. Who cares if the other kid has a computer? If we buy into this theory, we are admitting that education is only competition and we are then skirting the real issue—to learn.
Eric:	Bingo—if we're all here to learn, this whole issue of who's got the edge on whom disappears, and people just help each other.
Joan:	The competition is a fact of life. The school with the better test scores gets more Federal aid, right?
Stacy:	Right—we're all here so we can COMPETE in the job market.
Joan:	Extra-curricular activities interrupt both family and study time. If the student can't do all three . . . drop one.
Eric:	Which one, is the $64 question.
Stacy:	So, Joan . . . a student is punished because she's involved in activities?
Aaron:	I wonder how many of us are pro-homework because of tradition: we did it so they have to do it.
Tricia:	I did a lot of homework the teachers assigned just because they knew they were supposed to.
Eric:	Psychologists call that "dissonance reduction"—you're tortured as a youth, and you justify the pain by doing it to the next generation. I once heard a person who was a victim of childhood sexual abuse say she was glad it happened because it made her stronger!
Lori:	Why are we all assuming that homework is boring and unrewarding?
Hennie:	That's the real point. Homework isn't rewarding to the people doing it. Don't give less or more homework—work on making it pay off.
Mark:	I agree. The homework I give my students prepares them for the next day's class session. If they don't do it, they're lost the next day. They can see that.

At this point, I pulled the plug—but not because we had run dry. In fact, we had more things to say after an hour and a half than we did when we started. The more ingredients go into the stew, the more you discover you want to add.

Chapter 16 reminded us of why we can each find a personal potato to throw in the stew: we've all led different lives. My author on page 335 has a personal potato about gun ownership because he's actually tried to shoot an intruder and most of us haven't. Angela Coop (p. 385) has a personal potato about affirmative action because she has watched her husband deal with it and her sister change her mind about it as a result of her own experience. Melissa Schatz (p. 374) has a potato about at-risk teens because she's volunteered at a halfway house for such people and has worked with, cared about, and had her heart broken by them.

Establish a Positive Relationship with Your Audience

How to go wrong: Try to convince everyone at once, adopt a debater's persona, or assume your reader is your enemy.

Writing to everyone has the same problem in arguments it has throughout this book: It's too hard (see p. 62 for a reminder of why). So you don't write to everyone—you don't even write to everyone concerned about the issue. You write to a specific group with two qualities: (a) The issue matters to them, so they can use what you're offering; and (b) they have a definable set of values, beliefs, interests, and wants. This guarantees that you're writing for real reasons, and it allows you to answer the Writer's Questions: How do I talk?; What do I say?; How much background information is enough?; and so on. So you write an indictment of the inadequate child care available in your community, and you choose whether to write to parents struggling with the problem, or city administrators in charge of funding, or voters who don't have children and must be convinced that this concerns them too. You write a scathing indictment of the tenure system that allows burned out, out-of-date professors to keep teaching at your school, and you choose whether to address students (who suffer), administrators (who enforce the rules), other teachers (who unwisely defend tenure), citizens (who elect the legislators who make the laws), or parents (who foot the students' bills).

Once we know exactly who we're talking to, we have to create a relationship with them. Many writers set out to create precisely the relationship that will prevent success. They write from the persona of the Pure Thinker—emotionless, academic, super-rational, inflexible, absolutist—the better to impress their readers with their arguing credentials. And they treat the reader like an enemy, a fool, or a villain—the better to pressure her into yielding. Both approaches make the reader less willing to hear us, not more.

Who Are You?

When you argue, what kind of person do you want to be? The kind of person people are convinced by, the kind people like to agree with, obviously. And are you moved to agree by thinking machines, inhuman spewers of facts and figures? Hardly—any more than you most want to date the person who marshals the best reasons why you should. People are moved to agree by warmth, understanding, wit, sympathy, drama, energy —by personalities we like, in short. Most writers of arguments worry too much about their logic and evidence, and not enough about their relationship with their reader. If arguments were won by the quality of the thinking or the evidence, the president would be the best thinker in the country, and every TV ad would be chock full of logic and footnotes. If you doubt this, wait for the next televised debate between presidential candidates and ask people for their reactions afterward. For every one person who will judge the candidates on their reasoning and evidence, a dozen will react to their personal affect: Did they sound shrill, did they exude confidence, did you like them?

We'd like to think this isn't so. We want to believe we bought the car because of its objective virtues, not because the salesman made us feel good. Certainly argument should be different from advertising, where affect is everything and content is nothing. But we're also not like *Star Trek*'s Mr. Spock (or Commander Data, depending on which generation you prefer). All of which is why we talked about how to think elsewhere, in Chapter 16.

It's not easy to be likable on command, but some things are obvious: People don't like stuffy, boring, inhuman, and rigid. So stay witty, dramatic, playful, and daring. Writing is always a *performance*—arguing doesn't change that. Give the audience a good time. Instead of beginning a movie review of the film *Problem Child* with a thesis plop like "*Problem Child* is a hackneyed film that offers the viewer little more than a rehash of previous films in the genre," you begin like this:

> *Problem Child* is the story of a misunderstood and unwanted boy who finds love from a caring adult who discovers a side of himself he didn't know as he deals with the child's painful struggle to be accepted.
>   Vomit.

You embrace the personal, because people are convinced by people, not by arguments. You take a stance that says openly, "This is *my* view of things; *this* is what's happened to me to make me feel this way."

Whenever my students read their arguments out loud, the power of the personal reveals itself. A student reads out a conventional argument. We listen politely. Then, as soon as the reading is over, the writer begins to explain the essay: what he was trying to say in it, why he wrote it, why it matters to him, what he really felt, what didn't quite get done in the essay or what never got said with enough force. And it's great. He's passionate and free, and the class is riveted, full of questions and infected with his desire to be heard. When the discussion is over, I say, "Wouldn't you love it if he put all that in the essay?" Everybody says, Yeah, oh yeah, that would be great.

For example, a student wrote a conventional essay on American military involvement in South America. We had heard it all before, so everybody went on automatic pilot. Immediately afterward, the writer said, "I really care about this because I think most Americans don't really know what's going on down there. My brother is in the Service and he's been down there for three years, and you wouldn't believe the things he tells me. . . ." Suddenly the room was alive, the argument mattered, the speaker had enormous credibility, and we listened rapt to anecdotes from the front . . . none of which the writer had put in the essay. We chorused, "Put it in, put it all in!"

The personal focus grips the reader in a moment. One student turned in an essay that began like this:

> Attempts to correlate murder to punishment rates have been made for a long time. Most of these studies were full of errors because they were showing the correlation between murder rates and the presence or absence of the capital punishment status, not to the actual executions, which are what really matter. Others failed to properly isolate murder rates from variables other than punishment, even when these variables are known to influence murder rates.

So it went for three pages. I said to her, "Why are you writing about the effects of incarceration anyway? What's it to you?" She told me, I said, "Wow! Put it in the essay!" and the next draft began:

> I was in prison for four years. True, I was an officer there, but at eight hours a day, sometimes more, for forty-eight weeks a year . . . well, I put in more time than most criminals do for their serious crimes. My opinions certainly did change while I worked there.

Now we're ready to listen.

Tuning Your Persona

Here's a question to test-drive your argumentative persona and shore up weak spots:

> How is the reader likely to dislike me for saying what I'm saying?

When you have an answer, put something in the essay to deflect the negative response.

When you try to talk people out of their beliefs and into yours, they frequently don't like you for it. If you ask yourself what form that dislike will take, you can often talk them out of it. For instance, if you're defending a thesis that says, "Formality is a dying art; people don't know how to dress up and be formal anymore," the most likely negative image your reader will get of you is that you're a snob. So you add a disclaimer: "I'm not one of those people who think Levi's or pants on women is a crime against nature. I love being casual, and I live in jeans most of the time. I'm not saying formality is better than informality; I'm saying that every once in a while knocking out a really fancy recipe, getting dolled up, and inviting friends over for grown-up time is *fun.*"

All this does not mean you should always be nice when you argue. Some of the essays in this chapter are deliciously nasty. Be as nasty as you want (a) when you're attacking one group and talking to another, as in "Dear Governor Deukmejian" (p. 378), or when you're talking to the *student body* about the outrages of the university *administration;* or (b) when you decide to use confrontation as a tactic—in effect saying, "I'm going to shake things up and be a little rude on purpose." That often works with issues of great seriousness, like child abuse or the conspiracy of silence surrounding family alcoholism.

Now that you've made yourself into someone someone else would like to buy from, the next task is to make the reader into someone he wants to be.

Are You Talkin' to *Me*?

The Chair Theory of arguing says your reader is in a room full of chairs, each chair representing an argumentative position. She is sitting in the chair that represents her opinion. Your goal as arguer is to convince her to get out of her chair and move to your chair, or at least to a chair closer to it. What makes a person willing to move from one chair to another? Does a person get more willing to move if you tell her, "You're an idiot for sitting in that chair. I can't comprehend how anyone with the intelligence God gave a mutt could sit in that chair. You must be evil or heartless or cruel to sit in that chair"? No—yet many arguers attack their readers in exactly this way. We begin by laying down the premises: I can't fathom how any decent person could think the way you do, and you'll have to confess how wrong or bad you've been in order to agree with me. It just seems so obvious that the harder we push and the more completely we demonstrate the reader's wrongness, the more he'll have to give in and agree with you. *You* don't respond that way, but you assume *he* will. But all we're really doing is hardening the reader's heart against us.

So, since the assault approach doesn't work, you go the other way. You assume that the reader is human like you and that what works in arguments on paper is the same thing that works arguing with a roommate at home about whose turn it is to do the dishes. For instance, *you* don't like being pressured or attacked, being made to look stupid or forced to give in, feeling unheard or misunderstood; neither does the reader.

Most people feel agreeable when they think the other party understands them, sympathizes with and accepts them, is one of them, has their interests at heart. So you want to send messages like:

I respect your viewpoint.

I understand what you're feeling; you have good reasons for feeling ·that way.

You're not the enemy.

I don't know all the answers.

We really want the same things; let's work together.

Few arguments have an audience diametrically opposed to their thesis. Of the essays in this chapter, "Consider Nuclear Energy" (pp. 386–87) is probably the only one. All the others have different, less contrary audiences: people who haven't made up their minds, people who agree with you completely and enjoy watching you bash the enemy (as in "Dear Governor Deukmejian" on p. 378), people who agree with you but aren't as passionate as you and need to be prodded to action, or—the most popular audience for an argument—people who haven't shared your experiences and so lack your personal insight into the matter. If you write a movie review damning the latest *Friday the 13th* sequel, you're arguing, but you are *not* writing to wrongheaded people who have all decided the movie is great.

At those rare times when you are writing to people who hold opinions you violently oppose—when you're trying to talk the National Rifle Association members into gun control or convince radical environmentalists that loggers should be allowed to earn a living—it's hard to treat them civilly, because they're so obviously *wrong*, but the distance between the two sides only means you have to do all the conciliatory tasks we're talking about *even more*.

Two Questions to Keep You Reader-Sensitive

Keep the reader's needs in mind by asking yourself two questions:

What would my reader most like to hear me acknowledge about him?

What is my reader's most likely fear in response to my argument?

When you have answers to these questions, put them in the essay to show the reader he's known to you. Here's an example of the first question. You're writing an essay addressed to the university administration, defending the thesis that the threatened fee hike for university students is unfair and shouldn't be enacted. What would your reader (the university administrator) most like to hear you acknowledge about him? Probably that administrators aren't cruel fiends who just like to rip off students. So you add a passage reassuring her: "I know that administering a university isn't easy, especially in these hard times. You aren't raising fees just for the fun of it. And I know students like to cast you as the villain, which just makes things worse. We both want the same thing: to see the university be as good as it can be. I think we can avoid student hardship *and* keep educational quality high."

Here's an example of the second. You're writing an essay arguing that The Green Tortoise, a counterculture, low-rent bus line, is an attractive alternative to planes, trains, or conventional bus lines. What is my reader's most likely fear in response to my argument? Probably that the busses are full of winos and creeps and driven by ex-hippie dopers who aren't safe on the road. So you add a passage reassuring her: "I know everyone's image of bus travel: being sandwiched between a wino in the seat to your left and a pervert in the seat to your right. But the Green Tortoise isn't like that. The customers are people like you and me: relatively clean, sober, normal people just trying to get somewhere without spending a fortune. Nor are the drivers and other employees your stereotypical hippie flakes, though my driver did wear a tie-dyed T-shirt; every employee I dealt with was sober, professional, and competent."

Writers often ask, "Do I have to rebut the opposition's argument in my essay?" The Chair Theory gives us the answer. You don't "have to" do anything, but if your reader is happy in her chosen chair, she probably isn't going to get up and move, however attractive you make your chair, until you talk her out of her reasons for staying. Until you do, she'll say to herself, "He's right, sitting over there is good, but sitting here is good too."

Two Last Audience-Minded Tips

There are two verbal tics that arguers love but readers don't: rhetorical questions and all varieties of *I think*. If you keep your reader in mind you'll see why they don't work the way you expect them to.

Rhetorical questions. Rhetorical questions are questions you already know the answer to, ones you ask for effect. Here are some from the essays in this chapter:

Is this what we want education to accomplish? To teach students how to cram? ("Why I Never Cared for the Civil War," pp. 383–84)

But do we really think we can right past wrongs by creating new ones? ("A Moral Victory?," pp. 385–86)

Doesn't Stacey deserve the chance? ("Given the Chance," pp. 374–75)

A rhetorical question always implies its own right answer—the answers the reader is supposed to give to the questions we just listed are "No," "No," and "Yes."

Rhetorical questions aren't to be avoided entirely. They're fun to write, they're dramatic, and they show you know the reader is out there, since questions imply listeners. But there are three reasons why you should use them sparingly. First, they're like potato chips—the more you use, the more you want to use, until your argument becomes a series of questions without answers. Second, they allow you to avoid saying anything; since they *assume* and *imply* answers, they allow you to weasel out of ever having to take a stand and make an assertion. But third and most important, they rarely get the answer you expect, unless you're writing a sermon. Readers have an infuriating habit of giving their own answers to your rhetorical questions, and when they do you're simply drilling them in how they really *don't* agree with you after all. If Melissa Schatz asks, "Doesn't Stacey deserve the chance?" and the reader answers, "No, she's had a dozen chances and wasted them all," Melissa loses face. So use rhetorical questions, but as an occasional special effect. Two per page is a lot.

I think. This includes *in my opinion* or *it's my belief that* or any of the formulae that tell the reader you believe what you're saying. At first glance such locutions would seem to be good strategy because they'll make the writer seem flexible and nondogmatic. But their effect on the reader is always negative. First, they're an insulting waste of space, since the reader knows the difference between opinion and fact. Second, they undermine his faith in you, since protestations of integrity always lead people to doubt it. Third, they don't make you sound understanding, they make you sound cowardly and passive. Fourth, they sound like a substitute for reasons and evidence. *In my opinion* often translates into "It's just something I believe, for no particular reason." Almost never use them.

Find a Dramatic Structure

How to go wrong: Decide that, since an argument is won by error-free logic, you want a structure of stiff, outline-inspired rigidity, with the thesis plopped at the end of the first paragraph, the supportive arguments in numbered series following (the most important last), and a restatement of the thesis at the end—so the reader can't misunderstand.

Since that doesn't work, do the opposite: look for energetic alternatives to the five-paragraph, thesis-plop format; find alternatives with some drama to them. Experiment with personal narrative, dialogue, satire, and letter format. How about writing the argument in the form of a parable:

EXACTLY HOW WE WANT IT

SCOTT THOMPSON

Marvin was almost finished. He was on his way to his final depart-ment: Body Parts and Functions. He followed the shadows into the arena. There were different lines for each piece of the human body. His first stop was Facial Features. Marvin selected two squinty eyes, a big nose with a mole on the end, a mouth with large loose lips and extreme overbite. This was perfect because it exposed the crooked teeth he carefully selected. Marvin looked in the mirror: "Ah, yes, exactly how I want it."

Next stop: Torso Department. After studying the different choices he selected Number 1: fat. Marvin looked in the mirror: "Ah, yes, exactly how I want it."

Off Marvin went to the Limbs Department. Here he chose a couple of chubby weak arms and legs. The legs he made sure were short enough to make his height under five feet, four inches. Marvin looked in the mirror: "Ah, yes, exactly how I want it."

As Marvin walked to the Externals Department, all he could think about was how perfectly everything was working out. He chose pale, mottled skin and lank, greasy hair. Marvin looked in the mirror: "Ah, yes, exactly how I want it."

Marvin was now on his way to the final department, Afflictions and Diseases. Marvin was undecided between cerebral palsy and muscular dystrophy. He figured that since he already had almost everything he wanted, he would leave the good diseases for others. He just took acne and poor eyesight.

Marvin took a good long look in the mirror: it was all exactly how he wanted it. In a few days, the paperwork was completed and he returned to his school. As he walked on campus, he was greeted with "Hi, Shrimp! Here's Dumbo! Hey, Four-Eyes, how many fingers am I holding up?" The day continued with pretty much the same treatment. Marvin came straight home from school, went to his room, lay on his bed, and, with a tear in his eye, whispered, "Ah, yes, exactly how I want it."

Doesn't make sense, does it? So why do we act as if it was true? People don't come into this world with a choice of how they look or what physical problems they have. Why treat them as if they're responsible and it's their fault? Next time, think about it and refrain from the stares, the gestures, the funny comments. ❖

Since you're trying to escape the five-paragraph curse, avoid *outlin-ing*, since it encourages rigidity, and cultivate *abstracting*, because it encourages flow. Good arguments often look horrible when they're outlined. For instance, here's an outline for the wonderful essay in the Treasury called "Where Did Louise Go?" (pp. 388–89):

I.   The question of what happened to Louise still burns in my brain.

    A.   I wasn't the only one bothered by the silence.

    B.   Louise chose the easy way out.

    C.   I rationalized my silence.

II.   Other ways to avoid participation

    A.   Focus on the social scene

III.   Discussion classes

    A.   Make the problem more noticeable

    B.   Have greater potential

IV.   Three ways you can tell a class is "rich"

V.   But you have to take the risk

VI.   Class can be a scary place, but it requires intimacy, so we avoid the danger.

    A.   I notice a general lifelessness and distancing in classrooms.

VII.   Have we chosen to do what Louise did?

The outline is a disaster, but we'd be wrong to think that proves the essay was. So if you let outlines judge your arguments for you, you'll never write arguments like "Where Did Louise Go?"

"Do I *Have* To?"

All my advice on arguing isn't something you *have to do* or you're doomed. It's possible to write a good argument that deals with a gigantic issue like abortion, addresses a national audience, stresses impersonal, sober reasoning, and uses an outlinable structure. Cliff Podbielski's "Consider Nuclear Energy" (pp. 386–87) does it, and it's great. Yes, it's possible. It's just harder, and you have to be very good, as Cliff was.

Alternatives to Five-Paragraph Structure

We agreed on page 371 that we would strive to find more energetic alternatives to the thesis-plop grand design. But what if it's the only structure you know? Here are two alternatives, both familiar friends of ours by now: writing from narratives and modeling. Since we already know how to do both of them, I'll just show you some results to prove they work.

Arguing from Narratives

We all arrive at most of our opinions by experience, so we can write the essay in experience form: Tell the story of what happened to you that led you to that opinion. How much of the essay is narrative is up to you. You can write a narrative hook of a sentence or two:

> Standing in line at Thrifty's the other day, I overheard four teenage boys talking about women.

> This week I've been reading the assigned book in my literature class, *The Education of Little Tree.* I don't know exactly why, but I always feel uneasy reading this kind of thing. I mean, we always read books about American Indians, and there are no American Indians in the class.

Or the narrative may be a long lead-in to the argument itself:

GIVEN THE CHANCE

MELISSA SCHATZ

I met Stacey three weeks ago, when she came to live at the Group Home where I work as a counselor. I liked her immediately. She's a bright, friendly, attractive sixteen-year-old. She's on probation for two years for petty thefts, and she has a two-year-old son. But her biggest problem is that she's a speed freak—she's addicted to shooting methamphetamine directly into her blood stream.

After spending a month in Juvenile Hall, where she went through withdrawals, Stacey came to the Group Home in fairly clean condition. But she has run away from here twice since then, staying out several days each time. She admits that she was "using." She says she's been an addict for several years now. Her parents are drug addicts too. Stacey wants to quit, but she needs help. She says she needs to go through a drug rehabilitation program. I believe her.

Unfortunately, I can't get Stacey into one. I've tried, but every-where I've turned I've run into a wall. You see, drug rehabilitation programs cost big money—two to three thousand dollars for a one-month stay. And absolutely no one will pay for Stacey to go into a program.

Of course Stacey herself doesn't have any money. Nor do her parents. And addicts don't have medical insurance. This doesn't surprise me. What does surprise me is that the State, which has taken custody of Stacey, placing her in a group home in the first place, refuses to pay for drug rehabilitation. It makes me angry. I feel as if the State has said, "Here, hold on to this," and then chopped my hands off.

Now, I know that drug rehabilitation programs aren't cure-alls. It takes more to kick a drug habit and keep it kicked, especially a mainline habit. It's a day-to-day struggle. Yes, I've known addicts who make their annual trip to the drug rehab. But I have also known addicts who *did* turn their lives around on such a program. Doesn't Stacey deserve the chance? While the State has her in custody, the opportunity is perfect. We're at least obligated to try. And isn't it money well spent, if it saves us from having to support Stacey in prison in the years to come?

Given time, the Group Home could help Stacey work through her behavior problems, get through high school, and learn some social and emancipation skills. But the fact is that unless she kicks her drug habit, she probably won't stay long. Her probation officer told me the next time she runs away he'll put her back in Juvenile Hall to clean out. We both know this doesn't work. Just taking the drugs away isn't the answer. But apparently the State has decided the real answer is too expensive. They tell us to fix these kids, but won't give us the tools. They're not giving Stacey or me a chance. ❖

But often the essay is almost entirely narrative, and the thesis is only implied in the telling or lightly sounded at the very end:

WHY?

DANA MARIE VAZQUEZ

I looked forward to it for months. I began the countdown in March. Only thirty-five days, only twenty-three days, only fourteen days. As the days passed and it got closer, my excitement grew. Finally it was the night before. I counted down the hours, minutes, and even seconds. "The time is 11:59 and 50 seconds—beep—the time is 12:00 exactly," the recording said as my friends yelled, "Happy birthday" and I popped the cork on my bottle of champagne. It finally happened: I was now twenty-one years old. My friends insisted that I drink the entire bottle of champagne myself. Why? Because it was my twenty-first birthday.

As I was guzzling the champagne, my friends were encouraging me to hurry because it was already 12:15 and the bars would be closing at 2:00. Oh yeah, I just had to go to Safeway and contribute to the delinquency of minors by buying for my twenty-year-old roommate. Snapping pictures the entire time, my roommates cheered me on until I reached the finale at the check stand and the clerk ID'ed me and announced to the entire store that it was my twenty-first birthday.

After a round of applause and much cheering in Safeway, I was dragged out the door and shoved into a car. "We've got to go to Joe's," they exclaimed as we raced towards my downfall. Once inside, I was given a drink that contained every alcohol known to Man. As I sucked mine down, my roommate kept refilling it. Why? Because it was my twenty-first birthday.

"It's her twenty-first birthday," my roommate shouted to a guy across the room she knew. "Then come join our game," was his reply. This dice game was quite easy. The rolls of the dice were counted and whoever reached twenty-one drank a shot. Lucky me—I was chosen to drink a shot of vodka and a shot of a Russian apple. Did my dice roll equal twenty-one? No. Then why did I have to drink? Because it was my twenty-first birthday.

"Yeah" my roommates shouted as I barely downed the vodka. "Let's go to Riley's," they laughed as we ran down the street. "Just a beer, all I want is a beer," I pleaded as we entered. Why was I still drinking even though I didn't want anything, even a beer? Because it was my twenty-first birthday.

So we all chugged a beer and raced on to the Top Flight. "It's her twenty-first birthday," they shouted at the doorman as he checked my ID and I swayed to the pounding music.

"Go tell the bartender and you'll get whatever you want," he screamed at me. I followed his command and ordered a Long Island iced tea. This wasn't a very wise choice because it also had many different types of alcohol in it, but at that point I really wasn't thinking. They were getting ready to close the bar, so I pounded my drink and we left.

About a half hour later—BOOM—it hit me. I began removing everything I had put in my stomach in the last three days. I did this, I'm told, for close to two hours. I was so hung over the next day that all I wanted to do was crawl into a hole and die. But did I go out to the bars still? Yes. Why? Because it was my twenty-first birthday.

I've thought about my birthday a lot lately, and I don't understand the rationale I and everyone else used that night. I don't like it, but I don't think it will change. You'd think I would be the first to want to change it ... but it was my roommate's twenty-first birthday three days ago. We took her out to the bars and made her drink and drink. She got sick at Riley's, puked at Top Flight, and vomited at Shell Cove. She could barely walk, but we still took her to the Bear's Lair. Why? Because it was her twenty-first birthday. ❖

Your Turn

Search your life for an experience that teaches a lesson or proves a point. Write an argument using the narrative of the experience as the organizing principle for the essay. You may either make the case explicitly, as Melissa does in "Given the Chance" (pp. 374–75), or make it implicitly, as Dana does in "Why?" (pp. 376–77).

Using Models

Chapter 3 showed how to use models to open doors and inspire yourself to experiments you'd otherwise never think to undertake. Nowhere is that as useful as in arguing, where our internal paradigm can be so constipated. Go read the joyful, creative arguers. Don't take your models from high school debate class, courses in logic and critical thinking, stereotypes of courtroom trials, panel discussions on educational television, or newspaper editorials; take them from Jimmy Breslin, Alice Kahn, Russell Baker, George Will, Bob Greene, Calvin Trillin, Mona Charen—the columnists who have to hold readers' interest day after day or they don't get paid.

Here's how it looks. My student Cinnamon Kern read an essay by Steven Reddicliff called "The Politics of Eating at McDonald's," in which Reddicliff, in a letter to then president Ronald Reagan, teases Reagan for not knowing what to order during a visit Reagan's entourage made to a McDonald's in Alabama during a campaign tour. Cinnamon was inspired by the fictional letter device to make a point about another politician, the former governor of California:

DEAR GOVERNOR DEUKMEJIAN

CINNAMON KERN

Yesterday when I was lured into the local Family Planning Clinic by promises of free birth control and easy sex, I was saved by your brave decision to cut their State funding.

The lobby was full of misguided souls like myself with leering faces. We oozed promiscuity like cheap perfume. We sat and watched as other brainwashed victims left, clutching their brown paper bags with lewd expressions as they hurried to cheap encounters with strangers.

When I went into the accounting office, the woman there told me in a sad voice that they would be unable to provide me with State-funded birth control and I would have to practice abstention. My dreams of romantic half-lit encounters with all those delicious young men crashed to the floor. I knew that without birth control, I couldn't have sex. With that den of iniquity shut down, people will have to stop their disgusting sexual behavior and behave in a chaste, pure manner. I know that this brave move will help generations after us lead clean lives.

Thank you so much for your faith in mankind's ability to control their fleshly urges. It saved me from a life of degradation and filthy promiscuity.

Sincerely yours,

Cinnamon Kern

Sometimes all you need to do is read the model and try to "make it sound like that"; sometimes it's good training to list the features of the model worth imitating. Lizette Strohmeyer found inspiration in an essay by Stanley Bing:

TWENTY GOOD REASONS TO CRY*

1. Your team has just lost the seventh game of the World Series.

2. Your stockbroker is arrested for insider trading, and you realize the guy never did one single unethical thing for you.

Esquire, June 1987, p. 225.

3. Your wife has run off with Marvin Hamlisch.

4. You decide to forgo your designer clip joint and have your hair cut by Rocco at the local barbershop. Six dollars and fifteen minutes later, you emerge with a kind of abrupt, vertical look currently sported only by military men and recently deinstitutionalized mental patients.

5. Indoor soccer.

6. You shave off your mustache and remember that you hate your face.

7. You forget to preorder the vegetarian meal on TWA and, famished, eat two stuffed bell peppers in marinara sauce before you realize what you've done.

8. You spend $540 on a state-of-the-art compact disc player, only to find out the next day, in the current issue of *Audiophile*, that digital tape has suddenly become the decreed format of choice.

9. Twenty-four-year-old MBA's who earn in excess of a million dollars a year and complain their lives are empty.

10. Two weeks with your parents at their geriatric enclave in Sun City, Arizona.

11. You hear from your dermatologist that the only way to save your hair is to have injections of estrogen.

12. Your wife absolutely refuses to let you buy that personal helicopter you saw in the window at Hammacher Schlemmer.

13. In the course of a schmooze with a bright and frisky young woman you thought understood you, she inquires, "Woodstock? You mean Snoopy's little bird friend?"

14. Fatty corned beef.

15. You find yourself actually paying attention to Dr. Ruth Westheimer.

16. You don your seersucker suit for the first time since last summer and find that, while you can still button the trousers by forcing every bit of air from your lungs, the fly flares so radically your zipper shows.

17. In New York City today, the only legal place to light your post-dinner Monte Cruz is at home with your wife or in the middle of Central Park—and you don't feel all that safe in either location.

18. You enter a room filled with intelligent, dynamic, slender women, and realize that you will never know a single one except at exorbitant personal cost.

19. You are stuck on an elevator with Siskel and Ebert.

20. Your dog, Rags, with whom you shared every confidence and crisis for more than seventeen years, can no longer control his bodily functions. You make that last, inevitable trip to the vet. Afterward, you stand on the sidewalk in the bright sunshine, alone for the first time since your youth, wondering where life goes and, in your heart, knowing. ❖

Lizette and I talked about what she saw in the model that she valued: most obvious, the essay in the form of a numbered list, but also the sudden shifts and surprises in tone and style from item to item— Number 13 to Number 14, for instance—and the big surprise at the end, where the last item dwarfs all the other items. She set out to write an essay reproducing all those virtues:

SIXTEEN REASONS YOU CAN'T START YOUR ESSAY
LIZETTE STROHMEYER

1. You had a power failure and now your Macintosh won't work.

2. You haven't bought the footnote-and-bibliography program yet.

3. Can't find a pencil.

4. You found a pencil but it's not sharp enough and you don't have a pencil sharpener.

5. Your thesis isn't ready to talk to you yet.

6. The moon is in Scorpio, Capricorn, Aries, whatever.

7. Speaking of astrological signs, your horoscope tells you that today is the day for romantic liaisons and you need to go shopping for a new outfit.

8. You need to clean your room first and you can't do that until you do your laundry, and your boyfriend's, and since you've got the washing machine warmed up you might as well do your room-mate's too.

9. The moon is full.

10. The moon isn't full.

11. Though you've never done it before, you suddenly have an urge to walk the family dog.

12. Still can't find a decent pencil.

13. You broke a nail.

14. You left your lucky writing shoes over at a friend's house.

15. Ever since you watched *Annie* you've always held on till tomorrow.

16. You set the alarm clock for four in the morning. When it goes off in a piercing frenzy, you open one eye, look around blearily, and marvel at how dark four in the morning is. You flop one leg out from under the covers, feel the icy chill, and retreat under the down comforter. You remember that interrupting sleep cycles can cause lasting physical and psychic damage, and as a health measure you go back to sleep.

Your Turn

Read the model essay below. Find inspiration in it to write an argument unlike one you'd think of yourself. List the features of the model you admire and want to reproduce in your imitation. Finally, write the essay you most want to write that's like the model.

PROTECT YOUR INALIENABLE RIGHT TO STEER TANKS

ADAM HOCHSCHILD*

Certain misguided elements in Washington are now arrogantly questioning the constitutionally guaranteed right of Americans to possess assault rifles. This outrageous attack on our liberties hits at the very foundations of everything our Founding Fathers fought for.

And it's a creeping attack as well. First the do-gooders went after the "Saturday night special." Now they're going after the assault rifle. Tomorrow they could very well be going after the tank. Surely no other example shows so clearly the dangers in this new un-American mania for banning weapons.

Tanks have an honored place in our history. Their indisputable ancestor, the horse, was enshrined in the fabric of American life even before the Constitution. If today's ban-everything liberals had had their way two hundred years ago, Paul Revere would have had

San Francisco Chronicle, "Sunday Punch," May 7, 1989.

to walk on his famous journey, perhaps taking days or weeks. And could the mail have been carried across the West by a Joggers' Express?

When tanks came along, it was the cavalry who sent them into battle. And just as an earlier generation of Americans in peacetime enjoyed the right to collect horses or use them for sport, so, too, do we enjoy the same rights with the tank. Today, no foolish restrictions prevent law-abiding sportsmen from enjoying the thrill of target shooting with the splendid machines. Serious collectors can freely compare the technological capabilities of American tanks with historical models and German, Chinese, or Israeli imports. And all of us living in this increasingly dangerous society can rest secure in knowing that we enjoy the age-old right to defend our homes and property with a turret-mounted 105-mm cannon.

What if the ban-everything do-gooders, claiming that these weapons might fall into the hands of drug gangs, attempt to ban tanks? An American right and tradition, stretching back to the frontiersmen and beyond, would be irrevocably lost.

Most important, the do-gooders fail to understand that tanks don't destroy cities, people destroy cities.

The drug scourge is indeed a terrible menace. But the way to deal with it is not by banning weapons that have a long and honorable history in the hands of sportsmen, collectors, and citizens defending their homes, but by getting these drug people off the streets. For good. Preventive detention is one solution. Mandatory capital punishment for all crimes is another. Capital punishment for all residents of drug-infested areas is a third.

In fact, with bold and imaginative tactics such as these, the tank itself could provide a useful tool in suppressing the drug problem once and for all.

And we who know and love these weapons would be glad to offer our services. ❖

```
┌─────────────────────────────────────────────┐
│  ┌───────────────────────────────────────┐  │
│  │                                       │  │
│  │           A  TREASURY  OF             │  │
│  │                                       │  │
│  │      ARGUMENTATIVE  ESSAYS            │  │
│  │                                       │  │
│  └───────────────────────────────────────┘  │
└─────────────────────────────────────────────┘
```

Here are some of my favorite argumentative essays by my students. A note beginning the Treasury in Chapter 14 (p. 285) suggests ways you might use them.

WHY I NEVER CARED FOR THE CIVIL WAR

SHAWNI ALLRED

I got mostly A's and a few B's all through high school and have managed, for the most part, to do the same in college. I'm sure that most people, when they hear that, are thinking, "That means she's really smart." Well, I'm not stupid, but I don't know near as much as people think I know. I just learned how to pass tests. I got an A in history, but I couldn't tell you where the first battle of the Civil War was fought. I got an A in geometry, but I couldn't in a million years tell you the area of a circle. There are many things I "learned" that have vanished from my memory, thanks to some flaws in the teaching system.

The set-up is always the same. The teacher lectures, and the students take notes. I'm thinking of one class in particular, a history class. We went from the Pilgrims to Harry S. Truman in twelve weeks. I was bored out of my mind. I tried so hard to care about the soldiers in the Civil War, but with the teacher outlining the lecture on the board and citing facts as though he were reading from a cookbook, my passion for them was lost. As a result, I remembered what I needed to remember to pass the test, but then it was gone.

The tests reinforce the problem. Comprehensive, timed tests encourage short-term memory. The students, knowing all along their grades will rest heavily on tests, study for the sake of passing the test, not for the sake of learning. They stay up late the night before, cramming as much information into their minds as they can. And it works. They pass the exams and get rewarded. Unfortunately, that A or B is often only a measure of the student's ability to cram.

Is this what we want education to accomplish? To teach students how to cram? Or to teach them to remember the Civil War like it was a recipe? I hope not. I hope the aim is to teach students information they will remember, that means something to them, information they can teach others and use themselves for the rest of their lives. The first step to improving the quality of education is for educators to agree that these are their primary objectives. From there, the solutions to achieving these goals are exciting and endless.

Controlled discussions could be used in place of lectures. For example, if my history class could have had us sit around in a circle and bounce ideas off one another, I might have gotten to the heart of what the Civil War was all about. We could have asked each other questions like, Why did we allow slavery? How do you think the slaves felt? What would you have done if you were one of them?

Even more creative is the idea of using experience as the basis for learning. A friend once had a class where the students acted out the Salem witch trials. Some were judges, some townspeople, some witches. He says he'll never forget that part of history. Another friend had a philosophy class where students walked into strange classrooms and stood inside the doorway until they felt the stares of the other students, in order to understand what Sartre meant by "the Look."

Finally, we could grade, not on timed tests, but on class involvement, homework, and maybe take-home exams. Students would feel they were being rewarded for getting involved in their education, not for becoming experts in test taking.

The question remains whether teachers are willing to step out of old ways of teaching. Some already have. It's because of one teacher I had in the fifth grade that I remember the names of the microorganisms that live in a drop of pond water. We went to the far end of the playground and scooped up the muddy green water all by ourselves and took it back to the classroom to look at it under a microscope. There were paramecia, volvoxes, and amoebas. I remember. ❖

I love the way Shawni respects her personal experience. She says to herself, "I know that much of my schooling was a waste of time, because I was there." She trusts her ability to tell which teaching approaches work for her and which don't. And the conclusion is a work of art. "I remember." It gives me a little chill every time I read it.

A MORAL VICTORY?

ANGELA COOP

In 1984, a group of white male police officers brought suit against the city of San Francisco, alleging that they were the victims of reverse discrimination. They maintained that they had been passed over for promotion in favor of less qualified women and minority officers because of the city's affirmative action policy. The U.S. Supreme Court has recently refused to hear their case.

This action is seen by some as a victory for women and minorities, but, if the allegations are true, isn't it really a loss for us all? The law prohibiting discrimination is intended to ensure equal opportunity for everybody. No group is exempted. It doesn't mean equal opportunity for everybody except white males.

I'm not a white male, but I've been married to one for fifteen years, and I've seen a lot through his eyes. My husband is a mechanical engineer. He's a professor now, but he worked in industry for seven years, and he had a consulting business for six years while he taught, so he has a good understanding of his place in the professional world. Unfortunately, reverse discrimination is nothing new to him. It's a fact of life. Employers are forced by federal equal-opportunity quotas to give preference to Hispanics, blacks, and women.

My sister is also an engineering professor. Although she teaches in the same system with my husband, her experience has been vastly different. Basically, what she wants she gets. It's that simple. It has to be that way, because the quota system makes her a sought-after commodity, and her employer can't afford to lose her.

It took my sister a long time to appreciate the injustice of this. For years, she felt like she deserved everything she got, even though other professors actually quit working in her department because she was treated so favorably. Somehow she felt like she was rectifying the problem of sexism in the workplace, a goal so virtuous as to be worth any cost.

When I talked to my sister last week, she was excited because her department was interviewing the wife of one of my husband's friends. The department doesn't actually have an open position, but the University has funding for a certain number of faculty who meet "specific criteria." As luck would have it, this woman, who normally wouldn't be considered because of her lack of experience, is black. She's irresistible!

We feel an awful sense of collective guilt in this country for what we've done to women and minorities, and we should. We've behaved inexcusably. Affirmative Action policies were developed in an attempt to make up for those past injustices. But do we really think we can right past wrongs by creating new ones? It's said that those who forget history are condemned to repeat it. I would never propose that we do that. But I think it's time to forgive ourselves and move on. ❖

I love the way this essay moves through its material with complete sureness but no sense of thesis plop or wooden out-line. It's an anticliché essay (p. 394), or was when it was writ-ten, and it sets the reader up for the surprise thesis nicely in paragraph one by inviting the clichéd response. The conclusion is a lovely lesson in how to end without summary restatement.

CONSIDER NUCLEAR ENERGY

CLIFF PODBIELSKI

Electricity is a part of everyday life for virtually every Californian. Since the Seventies conservation measures have enabled the power producers to supply more and more households with power using mostly existing hydroelectric capacity, and generating capacity has been increased by use of geothermal steam, wind, solar, some small new hydro projects, and cogeneration. But it isn't enough. Californians should look into expanding the use of nuclear power.

"Blasphemy!" you say; "Didn't Earth Day have any effect on you?" Yes, Earth Day had an effect on me; it convinced me that intelligent, informed choices must be made now to ensure environmental quality and future energy needs, in that order. The call to conserve, eliminate waste, reduce consumption, and recycle is noble. But, however well we are able to implement those virtues, consumption by ever-increasing numbers of power users will continue to grow.

Even our attempts to help the ecology will require more energy. Urban areas trying to improve air quality need to provide transportation options that reduce dependence on the automobile, and electric-powered light rail is one of the best alternatives. Industries that are burning fossil fuels need to convert to electricity. New home construction needs to incorporate more energy-saving features, which ironically are almost always electricity-based.

The energy has to come from somewhere. Where do you want it to come from? We all want energy from the inexhaustible sun. However, current solar technology can only supplement our needs. Which river do you wish to dam for a hydro project? Will a coal-fired plant be your choice? A poor choice—the burning of fossil fuels is causing acid rain and global warming. Wind power is unreliable, and a wind farm is not a thing of beauty. Nuclear power is the only alternative that's non-polluting, efficient, and proven.

Oh, I hear what you're saying: "Nuclear power, how can you consider it? I mean, after all, what if . . . ? Even the engineers who design them admit they aren't 100% accident-proof."

How great is the risk? We don't give a thought to driving down the highway with ten gallons of highly explosive liquid attached to our behinds. It's just a matter of understanding the gas tank and trusting the engineering. We live with risk every day that requires us to trust engineering. Planes occasionally fall out of the sky, but we don't require that engineers give us a 100% guarantee that there will never be another plane crash. Instead, we sensibly decide that the risks are outweighed by the rewards of driving and flying.

"Ludicrous analogy," you say; "If a plane crashes it's tragic but the damage is done; it's not going to injure entire populations and damage future generations like a nuclear accident would." That's true, it's different, but the designers and operators of nuclear power plants recognize the danger and act accordingly. The likelihood of a nuclear accident is infinitely smaller than the chance of a plane crash, and the safety factors designed to prevent one have back-ups on the back-ups.

And what if the back-ups fail? Our worst nuclear accident so far is Chernobyl, where something like the worst-case scenario came true: a cloud of radioactive gas spreading cancer across Europe. And how many deaths do even the pessimists predict will be the result? Fewer than we slaughter on our nation's highways every year. The fact is we are always living with a sense of an acceptable level of mayhem.

And what about the waste disposal problem? Presently the majority of spent fuel is recycled to be used again and again. The remains—the volume of a small car every six months from each plant—will eventually be sealed at the bottoms of deep wells drilled into stable rock formations. It's crude and expensive, but it will work.

I know the issues are complex and the price of error is high. But many people just hear "nuclear energy" and have a knee-jerk emotional response. That's too superficial an approach to the difficult technical decision we have to make. Ask yourself: Do you in fact *think* about nuclear power any more? ❖

Cliff does a great job of taking a tired, huge issue with an audience of everybody and with which he has no personal connection and making it fresh and alive. There's the keen pleasure of watching a good mind work its way through logical processes with sureness. Cliff is conscious at every moment of the imagined reader, predicting her responses and dealing with them: "Oh, I hear what you're saying. . . ."

WHERE DID LOUISE GO?

TARA GILLIGAN

The question still burns in my brain. Haven't you asked it too? It was hard not to notice when the most vocal person in class stopped coming one third of the way through the semester. Louise left us after our "why no one talks in this class" conference, a fifteen-minute discussion on the agony of silence. Someone finally said, "The silence is killing me." I breathed a sigh of relief—I thought I was the only one who noticed it. But then the instructor said, "Something's got to change." My guard went up. I usually draw the line at intimacy. I don't think Louise liked it either. But this was a class set up for dialogue, and we were either going to take the plunge or perish in silence.

Louise chose the easy way out—she stopped coming. I, being a more practiced non-participator, chose a more subtle tactic. I convinced myself that I was just there for the grade. Why should I put myself on the line for a lousy B? That was my safeguard against vulnerability. Anyway, couldn't everyone just tell that I was a good student, since my silence was so obviously pensive? (God, can I really be that pompous?)

That was my way of avoiding participation. There are others. A common tactic at this university is to focus on less threatening issues outside the classroom, like social activities. The cry for the right to party is deafening, while the silence on the course material is roaring. To be sure, not all the learning at college transpires in the classroom. But some of it does, as we try in our embarrassment to ignore.

All these tactics become glaringly noticeable in a classroom set up for dialogue. The silence is agonizing because these are the classes with the potential for making a difference. I know it has been a rich class when questions linger (What the hell was J. Alfred Prufrock looking for?); when doors are opened (There's philosophy behind mathematics?); when connections are made (How about coffee after class so we can, uh, explore this a little further?). But the rewards only begin when students take a chance, make a commitment, trust a little. The last thing on earth I wanted to do was allow a bunch of strangers to peer edit my first essay on my father and observe a personal dissecting of my life. But that class session turned out to be the most rewarding one for me in the entire term.

The classroom can be a risky, terrifying, and exhilarating place, but only if the thoughts of grades, job skills, and degrees are left behind. A kind of intimacy is called for. It's hard enough to give that to one person, let alone twenty foreigners. So we avoid the experience, even at the cost of learning. And every day we practice the arts of silence, distance, and denial.

Louise's absence sticks in my mind as we struggle to avoid the learning experience that can be terrifying. I keep noticing splintered dialogue, edginess when asked to share, a general joylessness. It's always easier to just stay out. Paul Simon says there are fifty ways to leave your lover. Likewise, there are as many ways to leave the classroom. Louise chose one. Have we chosen others? ❖

> *Here is writer's courage. Tara began the essay, not with a simple thesis she knew she could defend easily, but with doubts and questions: Why did the disappearance of Louise haunt her so much? What did it mean? She knew the answers wouldn't be simple or safe. Her role in the essay—she is as guilty as anyone of the charges she brings—is a powerful device for defusing the reader's resistance to her message.*

This next argument requires some historical background. In 1994, California residents voted on Proposition 187, which proposed that the state stop providing illegal immigrants with nonemergency medical care and schooling. The following essay argues the merits of the proposition:

HONEY ON THE BREEZE

JOAN BASSLER

The magpies dart and dance about between the rows of Kiwis. The early morning sun has already sipped the dew from the grass blades stretching away from the edge of the porch. I can smell the distant sweetness of the bee hives.

Every spring, when the weather warmed, the kids swarmed into my grandparents' yard to climb in our trees. We had some of the oldest trees on the block, and some of the best peaches and apricots. Grams used the lemons for her lemonade. In the fall, the kids played in our leaf piles.

Terry's voice breaks into my serenity. "Hey, did you vote yet? You have to do your duty and vote."

"I know." I pray for a slight breeze to blow the trail of smoke away before it corrupts the smell of the nectar. Too late.

"Oops," she sings, flying through the door. "I got out of there as quick as I could when I realized. Very little smoke got in there, honest. Now, promise me you're voting, because I don't want that awful Prop 187 to pass."

"Well, I promise, but I'm afraid I'm voting *for* 187." I force a smile, knowing what's coming.

"No way! You, the voice of the people . . . you supported Cesar Chavez." She smothers her cigarette on her boot heel and drops the butt in the flower pot nearby. "You can't. 187 is totally discriminating, it's racist, it'll cut off the farm laborers from education and medical care."

The children raced across the open fields of waving grass. I saw them approaching. For years I watched them race from the school yard—at first no more than six, but soon their numbers doubled and tripled.

At first it was good. The kids climbed in the branches and picked fruit. But when the numbers grew, the limbs would get overloaded and crack. The kids threw apricots at each other and at the porch, stomping on the ripe fruit on the ground. Then it wasn't as pleasant as it had been.

"Actually, I think 187 will *help* the farm workers. It only targets illegal immigrants." I cross the porch to reclaim the fresh scent of the morning. "If there are fewer illegals, there won't be such a large reserve labor force waiting in the wings to take the place of any legal worker who stood up for his rights. The legal immigrants will end up commanding decent wages for a change."

Terry plops herself down in the chair, feet on the table. "But Prop 187 doesn't provide for any additional border patrols, so what's to keep the illegals out?"

"That's my point—this isn't about 'keeping them out,' it's about making the system work better so they have less reason for coming. Policing the borders hasn't worked anyway."

Terry shakes her head. "Americans are so greedy. You just don't want to share. And we have so much."

"No, we don't—not all of us. Lots of American citizens are poor and rely on the public health clinics, and the clinics are swamped by the flood of illegal immigrants."

"So all those immigrants should be denied medical attention? What good will kicking kids out of doctors' offices do?"

My grandparents enjoyed watching the kids climb the trees. Sometimes Grams and I put out lemonade for them. But when the numbers grew, it got too hard. One day little Jonny Jamison was swinging on a limb of the apricot tree, the limb broke, and he fell and scraped his arm badly. His parents were furious—they didn't know he was climbing in our trees, and they blamed us. Later the apricot tree died of a fungus that got into the bark through the broken branches. Grampa built a fence.

My eyes follow the path of a golden butterfly. "The point is not to deny people medical care. The point is to take the shine off our apples."

"How'd we get to apples?" Terry sips from her coffee mug.

"If the U. S. doesn't look so appealing, maybe fewer people will come over illegally."

"But it's going to cost us billions of dollars." Terry starts tapping her cigarette pack on her knee. "Federal funding for schools and public health programs will be cut, because the proposition is in violation of federal laws." She pulls the cigarette from the pack. "It's in violation of the Constitution!"

"I'm not a Constitutional lawyer, so I don't know about that. If the proposition is unconstitutional, the Supreme Court won't let it take effect. But let's not dump a good plan because some lawyers *might* decide to block it somewhere down the road."

Terry shakes her head. "I don't know. The prices of produce are going to skyrocket, since they're all harvested by illegals. We're cutting our own throats."

I had heard this line before, and I grinned. "So, you're comfortable exploiting the farmworkers whether they're illegal or not. What's your real concern here, human rights to medical care or your right to cheap lettuce?"

At first the fence seemed like a good idea. Two weeks went by. The fruit began to fall from the branches. Grampa and I picked as much as we could; Grams made pies, preserves, and fruit roll-ups. But there was too much fruit. It was rotting on the ground. We needed the kids to help us like they had done for years before.

Grams invited six kids to play in the yard after school, ones we knew well. We taught them how to care for the trees and shared the fruit with them and their families. The other children saw, and they came back, eager to throw fruit pits, squash peaches on the ground, and swing on the tree limbs. When they found out that these things were no longer allowed, they went away.

The click of Terry's lighter draws my attention. She says, "What about the disease and crime 187 will cause? We'll be turning loose a population of uneducated, sick outcasts who will spread disease and have no alternative but to turn to crime."

"There's a safety net—emergency medical care won't be refused. And as to crime, that's plain blackmail. Anyone can argue that if society doesn't take care of them they'll be 'forced' to turn to crime. People are still responsible for their actions. They have alternatives to crime—they can go back to their homeland, for instance. The simple fact is, we shouldn't reward people for lying and cheating. If the liar says, 'But if I can't lie I'll have to steal,' you just have to call his bluff."

The flame on Terry's light sputters and disappears. She flicks it again and again. "Damn, thing's dead. Isn't Prop 187 pure racism—an anti-Latino movement pure and simple?"

"The people against Prop 187 keep saying that, because that's what they want us to think. If they can convince us that 187 is racist, they automatically win. But it isn't about race; it's about citizenship and economics. The illegal immigrants deprive Americans of needed government services and help perpetuate a subculture of below-poverty-level drones to do the grunt work in our society. That's not a Latino issue, just a human one. No supporter of 187 has ever suggested that we have too many Latinos in California or that Latinos should go back to Mexico or that 187 should apply only to Latino immigrants."

"Don't get off track! We're talking about cutting off health care for pregnant women here!" Terry jumps off the table and struts into the house. I reluctantly leave the sunshine and follow her into the kitchen.

Gramps got the idea for the Sunday picnics. All the tree-climbing kids brought their families. We got to know all the parents, and found out which kids had permission to climb the trees and which were allowed to stay late into the afternoon. Grams invited all the families to come pick fruit on Sundays. The picnic turned into a weekly ritual.

Other tree owners in the neighborhood had been having similar problems. They heard about our system and set up ones like it. People got to know each other. Parents knew what their kids were doing, and felt safer. It brought the community together.

"Terry, it's not a pleasant thought, but the resources are limited. Maybe if we deny prenatal care to the people who are here illegally, the legal immigrants and other needy Californians will be able to get better, faster care."

"It's going to lead to endless hassling—every brown person in the state will be constantly asked to prove he isn't an outlaw. The skinheads created the whole proposition, I know it."

"Terry, every law is accused of 'curtailing people's freedoms.' The seatbelt law, which is saving thousands of lives, was going to lead to a police state where cops invaded people's cars, we were told. The motorcycle helmet law was an invasion of privacy. And what does the NRA say every time someone tries to pass a law taking their assault rifles away?—that the police will start kicking in the doors of honest citizens. It doesn't happen."

"Well, I just don't think this proposition is going to get us anywhere." Terry closes her eyes stubbornly.

"Did I ever tell you about my grandparents' house?" I ask.

"Yeah—a bazillion times."

"Well, those kids were like the immigrants. Finally my grandparents had to separate the kids who obeyed the rules from those who didn't. And in the end there were too many kids and my grandparents had to choose between living in harmony with the ones who followed the rules or watching the yard be destroyed.

"You know, even if the Supreme Court shoots down Prop 187, it sends a wake-up call to the government—it says, we need to set some limits, before all the trees are broken down.

"Don't you think, Terry? Terry?"

Leaning forward, I see that Terry is asleep.

Every spring, when the weather warmed, the kids would return to the yard, to climb the trees and play in their branches. Every summer, the families would return to gather the fruit. We had some of the oldest trees in town. ❖

> *This essay demonstrates how far from thesis-plop a good argument can get. The interpolated fable about the grandparents' orchard, the dialogue format, and the rich attention to details of character and the natural scene all keep the discussion alive, personal, captivating. Terry is a wonderful foil, speaking the opposition's case with convincing badness and damning herself with her cigarette butts and acrid smoke.*

THINGS TO DO

Obviously the thing to do now is to write an argument of your own. But if you'd like to approach it by steps, here are some things you can do.

1. Find a good model on your own and imitate it. Read the arguments that surround you, in the newspapers and elsewhere, until you find a piece that excites you by doing things unlike what you usually do. Then write an argument that uses, in your own ways,

some of the techniques of the prompt. Attach a copy of the model to your essay when you bring it to class.

2. Write an argument in the form of a parable, a fictional tale like "Exactly How We Want It" (p. 372).

3. To prove that good arguments aren't last words (p. 334), find an argumentative prompt among the essays in this chapter, in the newspaper, or anywhere else in your daily reading, and write a one-page argumentative response to it. Remember, you're not necessarily agreeing or disagreeing with the prompt, you're not saying the prompt is simply wrong, and you're not saying you have the last word; you're just saying to the prompt, "Thanks for your contribution to the public debate on this issue; now here's mine."

4. Write an anticliché—an essay that argues *against* a trendy belief people hold without thinking about it. Make a list of thoughtlessly held beliefs. People's heads are full of them: Save the whales, affirmative action is good, we should balance the federal budget, everyone should have access to high-quality medical care, help the homeless, give to charity, teachers should care about their students as individuals, people should accept responsibility for their actions, free speech is good, discrimination is evil, men are thinkers and women are feelers, hunting is cruel, etc. Pick one you find particularly facile, and make a case for questioning it. "Consider Nuclear Energy" (pp. 386–87) is an anticliché, and so was "A Moral Victory?" (pp. 385–86) when it was written.

Remember the fallacy of the absolute truth: You don't have to decide that the belief is wrong to argue that there are alternative points of view worth holding. And don't turn the anticliché into a joke, which is a great temptation—don't write things like "Nuclear war is good because it will help solve the problem of traffic jams."

5. Write a short draft of an argument and do the following tasks with it.

    a. Write a description of your audience. Be sure to include a statement about why they want what you're giving or how they will use it, and a description of their position—what they believe and why.

    b. Write out their argument—what would they say if they were arguing with you? The goal here is not to make their case look weak, but to understand how sensible, caring humans like you can hold such views. Respect their position.

    c. Write a rebuttal of their argument: now that you understand and respect their position, how would you talk them out of it and into yours?

    d. Ask of the draft the three questions that test-drive your persona and relationship with your reader (pp. 367, 369):

What would my reader most like to hear me acknowledge about him?

What is my reader's most likely fear in response to my argument?

How is the reader likely to dislike me for saying what I'm saying?

Write out answers to the questions. Then incorporate the answers in some form in the draft.

Part Five

THE RESEARCH PAPER

Chapter 18

DATA GATHERING AND COMPOSING

A research report is like a lab report, except that the answer is found not in the lab but in the library. It gathers information primarily from written materials to answer a question or solve a problem, and it's usually long. It's often called a term paper because it's traditionally assigned at the end of the term, as the culmination of the semester's work, and it's a test to see if you can do a lot of reading, synthesize it, and bring it all to bear on a complex problem of a substantial size over an extended time—a very different kind of talent than the one the lab report tests. A research paper can be any length, but we'll talk about the typical term paper: one about ten to fifteen pages long that takes approximately three to six weeks to do.

Since the topic is large, we'll divide it into two chapters. Chapter 18 will talk about the discovering and creating parts of the task: going to the library, gathering information, writing drafts. Chapter 19 will talk about putting it all into conventional term-paper form: handling quotations, citing sources, making bibliographies and graphs and title pages.

In a sense, Chapter 18 has nothing new to say. Term papers are just like other essays, only bigger, which means to write them you do the same things we've done in earlier chapters, only they're harder. Since four weeks of pointless labor is worse than two days of pointless labor, you must work even harder to make sure that you're writing with a real purpose to real people. Since beginning twenty pages is more terrifying than beginning two pages, you must work even harder to ward off writer's block. Since organizing four weeks of reading is harder than organizing a day's reflections on eating vegetables, you must work even harder to outline, abstract, and use the other organizing crutches we've practiced. Since remembering four weeks of thinking is harder than remembering two days of thinking, you must work even harder to write down everything that goes through your head.

Purpose

When I was in the seventh grade, I wrote my first term paper, on Russia. I slaved over it. I paraphrased lengthy passages from articles on Russia in several different encyclopedias and collated them. I cut out dozens of pictures of Russians farming from back issues of *National Geographic.* I traced maps with little hay ricks indicating grain-producing areas. In the report I always referred to Russia as "the Union of Soviet Socialist Republics," because it filled more space. I got an A. And at no time was I or the teacher bothered that I didn't know what Russia was. A few years later I was mildly surprised to discover it was a country, like the United States.

That first term paper was my initiation into all the academic writing vices this book has lobbied against: writing to no purpose, writing to get a grade, writing to fill space, writing to impress, writing as fakery and plagiarism, writing as pointless information pushing. And for most students, that's what a term paper is. If you must write one, realize you're walking into a Disneyland of temptation, and guard yourself.

The risks are all at the beginning, when you decide what it is you're trying to do. Definition of purpose is almost everything in a research paper: Set out to do something worth doing and within your powers, and the battle is largely won. Unfortunately, that turns out to be difficult.

Setting Yourself a Good Task

A good term-paper task has six features. First, like all good seeds, it is a job to be performed, a question to be answered, or a thesis to be defended, but *never* only a topic.

Information gathering is such a large part of research that researchers commonly fall into the error of thinking that it's *all* of research. Not so—research is information gathered *to some end.* Here's a test to make sure you haven't forgotten this: If you're reading sources and you aren't sure if what you're reading is pertinent or not—if you find yourself unsure whether or not to take notes or are simply taking notes on *everything* on the chance it's pertinent—you've probably lost sight of your task and slipped into topic thinking. If you know what you're trying to do, you should be able to say "That helps; that doesn't" pretty easily as you read.

Second, a good term-paper task is primarily achieved through *information gathering,* not opinion or argument. Seeds that break this rule sound like seeds from the argument chapter: "The democratic process prevents the best person from achieving office"; "The United States should get out of Central America"; "Men are so sexist"; "Ross Macdonald is the greatest American novelist of our time." Your task can have a thesis and an opposition, but the argument must be primarily settled through facts. The thesis "Routine infant circumcision serves no purpose and should be discontinued" is a good task because the basic questions are all factual ones: What does circumcision supposedly accomplish? Why did doctors start doing it? Why don't other countries do it? What are the results of their not doing it? What are the drawbacks to infant circumcision?

Sometimes the difference between objective and subjective tasks is in how you phrase the question. If you ask, "Why do people rape?" you're probably not going to get hard answers, since no one really knows; if you ask, "What are the accepted psychological theories on why people rape?" or "What cultural factors produce a rape-prone society?" you're on more solid ground. If you ask, "Why can't people read anymore?" you're going to have a harder time than if you ask, "How has the schools' approach to teaching reading changed in the last ten years, and has it made any difference in students' reading performance?"

Third, the task is something you know enough about to ask intelligent questions. Sometimes people (including teachers) think the point of the term paper is to learn about something you're totally ignorant of, but if you do that you'll be almost forced into writing to cover your ignorance, writing on topic instead of task, pointless information gathering, and plagiarism. The good topic is one you know well enough to know what still needs knowing: I've sailed for a few years, bought a couple of sailboats, and dreamed of buying others, so I know that recently a number of new alternatives to outright buying are being made available to the family sailor: mainly chartering, joining a sailing club, and buying, then leasing back to the seller. What are the advantages and disadvantages of each of the four? I don't know the answer, but I know the question needs asking.

Fourth, the task is something no other source has quite done for you. If you find a book or article that simply does your task, beautifully and finally, you're out of business. You must find a new task, or you'll have nothing to do but plagiarize the source. This is a ghastly and common problem—how many issues are there that have never been written about?

You can hope that when you find that article the research is poorly done, incomplete, or outdated, in which case there's still room for a contribution from you. But there's a surer way: personalize. If you've got a real audience with real needs, it's highly unlikely that someone else will have written to precisely those needs, since everybody's needs are unique. If you set out to write on alternatives to fossil fuels, a host of writers will have been there before you. If you're writing on the comparative virtues of different kinds of home heating for someone who's building a small cabin in Trinity County, California, considering the area's peculiar wood fuel supply, power company rates, and building codes, and your audience's floor plan and budget, it's unlikely that it's been done. If you write on anorexia, everything seems to have been said already; but if you write to freshmen anorexics attending college away from home and talk about the special pressures of that environment on that particular personality type, you're more likely to find new ground to break. You don't need to gather new information; you need only find a new question to use old information to answer. Engineers don't reinvent math and physics when they build a new dam, but they certainly do new work.

Fifth, the aimed-for product is something your reader can *use.* Students hate term papers because they're pointless. I won't hate writing on sailboat buying versus chartering because I believe potential sailboat buyers are out there waiting for the information—at least I know *I* am.

The audience whose needs you care about the most is you, so the research paper that's easiest to write is one that finds an answer *you* can use. The term paper on home heating alternatives was in fact written by a student who was building his own cabin; he spent four weeks happily comparing brands of stoves. Of course, it needn't be something utilitarian: If you *just want to know*—how dictionaries are made, how Legionnaires' Disease was conquered—you'll research well.

And finally, the task is neither too big nor too small. "The term paper *must* be twenty-five to thirty pages," the instructor says, and you just know what's going to happen. Either you'll pick a topic that runs dry after eight pages and you end up padding and stretching, or to prevent that you'll pick an umbrella topic like U.S. foreign policy and never finish the background reading. How can you find the task that is neither too long nor too short?

First, any *topic* is too large, because all topics are endless, however narrowly defined: There's an endless stream of information on Russia, but the stream on Moscow is equally endless, and so is the stream on the Kremlin. Second, any almanac-type question is too small: "How many people in this country actually escape prison via the insanity plea?" Interesting question, but after you write down "On the average, thirty-five a year," the report is over.

Beyond that, any task that fits our other criteria will prove to be the right size, *if* you master the skills in Chapter 9 for making a prompt expand or shrink as the need arises. You *don't* define a thirty-page task at the outset. Rather, you pick a task and begin; as you read and write and think you say, "This is getting to be too much—I have to cut back," or "I'm getting to answers too quickly—I've got to enlarge my scope." And you shrink or expand to suit. If my buying versus chartering versus leasing paper proves too much, I can write about the virtues and vices of chartering only; if it proves too little, I can write about all possible ways to get sailing, including crewing for others, or discuss the cost of sailing, including insurance, maintenance, and hardware options. If I'm writing on how effectively the FDA monitors drug testing and marketing and that proves too large, I can write on whether the FDA dropped the ball on Nutrasweet; if it proves too small, I can write about whether federal regulatory agencies generally do their jobs and whether they do more harm than good. I'll do however much I have room to do.

Getting Things Organized

A term paper is organized like anything else, but because the stack of things to be shaped is higher, you have to use your organizing tools more. You may be able to organize a short essay in your head, but a term paper will probably have to be organized on paper, and organized several times. So now is the time to go back to the organization chapters and use all those things they offer you.

You need a system for handling bits. Bits are pieces of information: facts, figures, quotes, thoughts from you, slips of paper with insights written on them, titles of works to be read. You need to be able to find a bit in your notes, cluster and recluster bits quickly, tell whether or not a bit has been used in the report yet, and footnote the bit in the final draft.

If you have a word processor you must decide early on, will you do your clustering in the machine or on your desk, with pieces of paper? There are advantages either way. The word processor's advantages are that it encourages you to think in terms of categories and labels, since you need to create and title files, and it makes reshuffling bits and pieces easy, so you're less reluctant to experiment with restructurings. You can write yourself a note and move it from file to file, trying it out in any or all groupings, without recopying. Its drawbacks are that you can only see one screen's worth of data at a time, so it's harder to get the big picture; and some programs make getting into a file, locating a particular spot, and getting out again time consuming, and you'll be doing it a thousand times. Also, much of your note-taking will be done while you're reading, perhaps in the library. It's difficult to read at the keyboard, and difficult to smuggle your computer into the library reading room unless you have a laptop.

More and more, I find myself working on the computer instead of on paper. In the beginning, I did everything but the drafting on paper; then I began note-taking on the computer, then organizing. One stubborn hold-out was researching in the library—I still would write down lists of sources to be read. But even that has gone electronic, because on-line databases will now print out your chosen citations for you or save them to your disk. In a year or two, I'll be ready to yard-sale my pencils. All that's left are the pen and notepad sitting by my keyboard as I write, to catch the irrelevant thought that crosses my mind and hold it until I can get it into the file where it belongs. I encourage you to go the same route, and push yourself to computerize your work style. It may seem foolish at first, when a good idea strikes you, to go to the Mac and open a "Notes" file when a pencil and notepad are right at hand, but the payoff down the line, in ease and quality of work, is enormous.

Whichever approach you choose, you'll probably use the following principles in some form.

Record all bibliographical data as soon as you begin to take notes.
Write down the authors' full names, the complete title of the work, the
publisher and place and year of publication if it's a book, the volume
number, issue number, and date if it's a periodical, and the page number(s)
where the things you're taking notes on appear. Record anything else you
suspect you might need later, like edition number, subtitle, editor, serial
number, and so on. Don't figure you'll do it later—you won't. Record the
library call number as well.

**Invent a system for marking bits you've used in the report and bits
you haven't.** You must be able to look at a dozen bits and say, "Those
seven I've used; those five I haven't." But don't check off the used bits
by wiping them out or throwing them away—keep your data intact so
you can rethink it, use it elsewhere, and proofread it later. I like those
highlighting pens that write right over the ink: I line out bits as I use
them, so anything that isn't highlighted remains to be dealt with, yet a
week later I can still read what I've lined out. A computer makes this
easy because it offers you a dozen fonts—highlight the used bits in italics,
boldface, or gothic print.

Invent a cueing system for your notes. You need a way of labeling
your notes so you can tell what they're about without rereading them.
Some people use keywords: When they've taken notes on an article, they
head the notes with a few keywords (or phrases) identifying the article's
main issues. If you're writing on alternative heating sources, you might
read an article hostile to wood-burning stoves and end up with a list of
keywords like:

wood-burning stoves

air pollution

shrinking resources

health hazards

In theory, if in three weeks you come to a point in the first draft
when you want to deal with the health hazards of indoor open fires, you
simply make a stack of all note cards bearing the *health hazards* keyword
and your data are ready to go. Word processors are great aids to this
because they don't admit that a body of data exists until it has a label.

How do you know what "keys" to use? You aren't sure when you
start, because you can't be sure which issues will turn out to be the "real"
ones. So you guess, and as the research proceeds the real keys emerge and
you revise your keyword system accordingly, just the way you reoutline.
By the way, trying to get content or thesis into the keywords is probably
asking too much; pure topic should be enough.

Build cubbyholes. These are locales to house notes according to topic or keyword. Again, a computer forces you to do this, because you have to house each bit in some chosen file, but if you aren't using one, do it anyway. Set up manila folders or shoeboxes or wastebaskets.

Put each bit on a separate piece of paper if you're not working on a word processor. You want to be able to cluster and recluster your bits as the paper grows and changes—to move them from one cubbyhole to another. And you may have hundreds of such bits. You can't do it in your head, and it takes forever to move bits of information by recopying. So don't take notes on full-size pages; take notes on sturdy little pieces of paper, like 3 × 5 or 5 × 8 cards. Here's where the computer, with its wonderful ability to move small blocks of text from place to place, really shines.

Never let the bit and its bibliographical data get separated. As you move a quote or a stat from cubbyhole to cubbyhole, keep all info on where it came from attached to it. *Don't* tell yourself you'll cluster or write first and then later figure out where the bits came from.

But don't go too far in using these principles. It's easy to get *too* organized and try to tie the creative act down to a strict schedule: On day 1 you'll formulate a working thesis, and draft a statement of purpose and audience; on days 2 through 4 you'll scan indexes and bibliographies and form a working bibliography; and so it goes, until the day before it's due, when you proofread.

What's wrong with that? The same thing that's been wrong with it throughout this book: Writing is a messy, recursive business, and you never quite know where you're going until you get there. You need a long leash so you're free to wander and discover—the opposite of the calendar method.

Here are just two common ways that approach cripples you:

1. If you divide the researching process into steps, you'll probably decide to do background reading first, then think, then write a first draft. What could be more obvious? Or more deadly? Reading is when you think best, and writing is how you think, so you don't want to separate them. Begin writing and thinking from the beginning of the project, and keep reading until the report is finished.
2. You'll probably decide to make a list of sources by scanning the bibliographies, then read them. It would seem you have no choice—you can't read the stuff before you find it—but in fact there is a better way: Find two or three things worth reading, go read them right away, and *let their references guide you to other good readings.* The best source of material in your area isn't a bibliography; it's a heavily footnoted book or article. In research,

the more you read, the more the reading puts you on to more things to read. Postponing your reading until you finish your working bibliography is just putting off the discovery.

So you need a balance, a writing approach that is organized enough to handle the data avalanche and give you a sense of where you are, yet loose enough to let you do the serendipitous wandering that leads to the really good stuff. It's tricky.

Using the Library

Term papers are often in large part exercises in learning to use the library. The library, like all monolithic institutions, is a tough place to hold your own. Many graduate programs devote an entire course to the art of going in there and finding something. Even a reference librarian, a hard-core library lover who has spent his career learning its ways, doesn't know every nook and cranny. I won't try to tell you everything there is to know, but I can help you get started.

Assume you're writing a report on the environmental impact of wood burning for home heating. Somewhere in the library you assume are perhaps two books and seven articles with the information you need to find your answer. How do you find them?

Texts and Search Tools

Think of the library as being made up of two things: the texts—those books, articles, and encyclopedia entries that contain the actual stuff you're looking for—and search tools, instruments like catalogs, indexes, and bibliographies that help you scan the texts and find which ones have your stuff. We'll talk about each in turn.

Library texts. Libraries traditionally divide their holdings into five sections: books, references, newspapers, government publications, and periodicals. You find your way around each by means of its own search tools.

Books are the part of the library we think of first. They reside in the *stacks*, and you find your way around them by means of the *main catalog*, which used to be called the "card catalog" when it consisted of banks of card files, but more and more these days is computerized and accessed through a keyboard and terminal. You can look in the main catalog under the author's name, the book's title, or the subject. Sometimes that's three separate catalogs; sometimes they're all run together. Unless you seek a specific title or author you'll be most interested in the *subject catalog*. You can look under subject headings at random (you might try "Fuel," "Wood Burning," "Home Heating," and so on), but it's more efficient to consult the nearby *Library of Congress Subject Headings*, a big book that will tell you what subject headings the main card catalog recognizes. For instance, if you look under "Home Heating," it may tell you to look under "Heating—Home."

Books are the easiest part of the library to find your way around in, but they're usually a poor source of information, for two reasons. First, since it takes years to write, publish, and catalog a book, any information in the book stacks is at least several years old. If your project is a matter of current interest, anything in a book is probably out of date. Second, books, because they're large, expensive things, have to be pitched at wide audiences, so they're usually broader in scope than a journal article. You'll do a lot of time-consuming winnowing and get less out of it per hour than with the periodicals.

When you're taking a book from the stacks, roam the shelves—examine the titles on either side for a couple of feet at least. Libraries shelve books on related topics together, so the book next door may be as useful as the one you came looking for. In theory, the subject catalog should do this for you, but subject catalogs, like everything made by the hand of Man, are imperfect—don't rely on them.

The *reference* section of the library houses all the encyclopedias, dictionaries, almanacs, and other volumes devoted to amassing core information. There you can look up the mailing address of your favorite author, find out how to say hello in Swahili, get a list of all the works Beethoven composed, see how many times Shakespeare used the word *liquid*, get a quick plot summary of *Moby Dick*, or find out the side effects of the drugs the doctor prescribed for you. Many of the library's book-form search tools will be housed here as well. Everything in the reference section should be listed in the card catalog, but again don't rely on it—ask a reference librarian to point you to the section housing books in your field, and then browse.

The reference section is fun. But it's of limited use to researchers, and most beginners try to make it do too much. Encyclopedias and such things have the same problems as books, only in spades: Since they're for an audience of everyone and are intended to last through the ages, they have no focus and hardly try to be up to date. So the reference section is great if you want almanac-type facts—the average rainfall of Brazil—or if you want a very brief, focusless introduction to a topic—What is socialism?—but beyond that it's only a guide to where to go among the books and periodicals.

We all know about the general encyclopedias and dictionaries, like the *Encyclopedia Britannica* and dictionaries of contemporary English, but there are specialized encyclopedias and dictionaries—encyclopedias of psychology and mythology, dictionaries of music and black magic— and they will have the space and expertise to treat your subject more thoroughly.

The *newspapers* usually have their own section in the library, and they take up so much space most libraries reduce them to *microform*.

The virtues of newspapers are obvious: They're up to date, and the articles are about very specific topics. But the vices overwhelm the virtues: (1) They're cumbersome, or they're in microform, which is clumsy in its own way; (2) they're undocumented—you can't always tell who wrote something or where the data came from; and (3) they're usually unindexed, so you can't find anything. I suggest you use newspapers only if you're looking for something you know is there—if you know that the *Los Angeles Times* had a big article on stoves near the front page in early April of this year—or if the newspaper has a good index. There are indexes for four major newspapers: the *New York Times*, the *Christian Science Monitor*, the *Wall Street Journal*, and the *London Times*.

Governments produce a constant stream of publications on everything under the sun. These *government publications* are usually a world unto themselves in the library, a maze of pamphlets, fliers, commission reports, and the like, often without authors, dates, or real titles, identified only by serial number, usually catalogued only in their own card catalog and not in the main catalog. Using them is a rare and difficult art. But for those who master it, the government publications are a rich store of up-to-date data on the workings of the world. Often one reference librarian specializes in the government publications; start with her help.

I've found fault with the books, the reference section, the newspapers, and the government publications as research sources. So what's good?

The *periodicals*—the magazines and journals. Almost all research is done primarily in this part of the library. The very recent issues are usually out on racks somewhere where people can browse in them, but the older ones are collected, usually all the issues from a single year or two together, bound as books, and shelved in their own section of the stacks.

With each passing year, more and more of these materials are no longer macroscopic, physical text on shelves; they're electronic files summoned up on computer screens. Journals, which are bulky, expensive, and of interest to a select few, especially are going this route, but even books are beginning to exist only in cyberspace. But since accessing electronic journal articles is much like using the electronic databases, we'll talk about how a little later.

Search tools. The best article or book in the world is useless to you if you don't know of its existence. The library knows this, and it works hard at providing you with tools to help you find what you're looking for. Search tools have been revolutionized by computer databases, so we have to talk about two kinds of searches, the old-fashioned kind done with books and other macroscopic texts, and the newfangled kind done with a computer and an electronic database. Your library will probably have a mix of both. We'll talk about four kinds of macroscopic tools: bibliographies, indexes, abstracts, and research guides. Then we'll talk about computer-based (also called on-line, virtual, cyberspace, or electronic) tools.

A *bibliography* is a book or a section within a book that lists titles of works on a subject and how to find them (often indexes are called bibliographies, which makes things complicated). A bibliography is supposed to list only *books*, but that rule is broken as often as it's followed.

An *index* is like a bibliography except it lists sources in *periodicals* and it's usually a multivolume, on-going project with a new volume every year or so—the 1991 volume lists publications in the field for 1990. If you want to know what's been published in home heating over the last ten years, you'll have to look in ten separate volumes—ugh.

An *abstract* will do more than just give you titles and bibliographical data—it will also give you a one-paragraph summary of the work. This will save you from reading works with promising titles and useless substance, so use an abstract whenever one is available.

Bibliographies, indexes, and abstracts, like encyclopedias, have subjects, and they range from very broad to very specific. The broadest are bibliographies of everything, like the *Readers' Guide to Periodical Literature.* (Since I can't list all bibliographical sources, please assume there are always other works like the ones I name.) It will tell you what has been published on your topic in any given year in any of several hundred popular magazines and journals. Use it if you want to know what *Redbook* or *Esquire* published on your topic. It's easy to use, and is the beginning researcher's favorite source.

There are bibliographies devoted to the broad academic areas:

> *The Humanities Index*
> *The Social Sciences Index*
> *Business Periodicals Index*

Other bibliographies are devoted to specific disciplines:

> *Music Index*
> *Art Index*
> *Index Medicus*
> *Biological and Agricultural Index*
> *Education Index*
> *Child Development Abstract and Bibliography*
> *Psychological Abstracts*
> *Chemical Abstracts*
> *Abstracts of English Studies*
> *MLA International Bibliography of Books and Articles in the Modern Languages and Literatures*

There are bibliographies in subdisciplines, like Victorian poetry, movie reviewing, and neuroenzyme chemistry. Often the leading journal in a discipline publishes a yearly index of work in the field—see if yours does.

A *research guide* is a book that gives you even more help than an abstract; it's a real instruction manual on doing research in the field. It may summarize, discuss, and critique the sources it lists, review the bibliographical materials available, give an overview of what's being done in the field, and even suggest fruitful new lines of inquiry. Research guides are sometimes on very specialized topics: There's one on the minor nineteenth-century novelist Elizabeth Gaskell. If you can find a reference guide to your subject, lucky you—begin your research there. But look at the publication date—reference guides get out of date like all books.

A *citation index* is a special kind of index, and it's the most underused research tool in the library. It lists for you every time one author or work has been referred to by another—that's all. That doesn't sound powerful, but it is. When you find a work that is useful in your research, look it up in a citation index, and the index will hand you in effect a list of all other researchers who found that work useful too—in other words, a bibliography of everyone working on your research question. Glorious. If you want a one-sentence lesson in the art of research, it boils down to: *Ask an expert, browse the stacks, use the bibliographies in the backs of your sources, and use the citation index.*

The search tools help you find the articles, but how do you find the search tools?

1. Bibliographies are listed in *The Bibliographic Index.*
2. All bibliographic materials should be in the main catalog under your subject—look for a heading like "Home Heating—Bibliographies."
3. Do my favorite: Ask a researcher in the field.

Searching in cyberspace. With each passing year, the reference materials we've been talking about are less likely to be *books*, and more likely to be *computer databases.* This means that, instead of flipping through a book to find your sources, you'll be sitting at a terminal following the instructions of a software program.

On-line databases have lots of virtues. They're fast, thorough, and comprehensive. A database at my library called UnCover will search back issues of 14,000 journals—over five million articles—and list for me every article that refers to Charles Dickens or A-frame architecture in about ten seconds—then, if I see something I like, it will give me a short summary, tell me what the call number of the journal is if my library has it, and arrange for a fax of the article to be sent to me immediately if my library doesn't have it. An on-line database will print out any information you want to keep or save it to your disk, so you are spared all that copying. Many of them (the "full-text" databases) will bring the entire article or book to the screen for you, so you can do your searching and your reading without moving from the chair—without leaving the house, in fact, since many databases are available over phone lines now. And they're up to date the way a book can't be; a printed bibliography is lucky to be redone every year, but many databases are updated *daily.*

But they have some vices. Foremost, they're terrifying at first, like any computer interface, a blur of meaningless key commands and cyber-babble. Accept the fear (it's a reality), and deal with it:

1. Ask for help. Reference librarians spend almost all their time now leading novices step by step through their first experience with databases.
2. Find and use the manual. Since libraries are flooded with panicking novices, they usually work hard to put plain-English user's guides right at hand. The guides have helped a thousand klutzes do this, and they'll help you.
3. Take a class. Most libraries run orientation classes for people in your shoes, and as always we learn best by talking with real people and taking the wheel under a tutor's eye.
4. Don't wait till you need results. Computers are fun to noodle around on, but they're loathsome if you need to know how to work them NOW. So go to the library twice, once when nothing is due, to toy with the databases and look up articles about your favorite actor, then a second time when the assignment is made and you have work to do.

The second vice of databases is they are too big and have no judgment, so they give you too much. This may seem like a blessing in the comfort of your home, but in reality it's a curse. You ask the machine for articles on your paper topic, and it offers you 1200 of them. It would take you a week to review them and pick the ones that are useful. Since the machine can't think, it can't make a wise decision about what's useful to you and what isn't, and it dumps everything on you. The art of using any database, then, is the art of defining the search task well, so you get all the articles that are truly useful—and no others.

You tell a database what you're interested in, and it goes looking, in two different ways. Some databases search by *subject*—someone has cross-referenced the entries so when you tell it you're interested in A-frame architecture it pulls everything that has been tagged for that subject. These databases are the easiest to understand, and you get less junk, so you might start with them, but you are dependent on the cross-referencer—if you and he disagree about what the article is "about," you won't see the article. Other databases search for *keywords*—you ask for every article that contains the word "A-frame," and that's what you get, whatever the article is about. I once asked a database for everything it had on *Rickey Jay,* the magician, and it gave me hundreds and hundreds of articles on Toronto Blue *Jay Rickey* Henderson. Keyword databases come with detailed instructions about how to define the search terms to avoid this kind of problem, and that makes them initially harder to use but better in the long run, since you can control the search more precisely.

Databases tend to come in two forms. They're either on a disc owned by the library (often called CD-ROM, meaning "compact disc read-only memory") or they're over-the-wire, like the Internet or the phone company, where you call into a central database over which the library has no control. CD-ROMs are usually free and user-friendly, because someone has carefully packaged them for sale. Over-the-wire services can be larger databases and more up-to-date, but they can also have severe restrictions on their use: They may charge by the minute for their use, require that you be authorized to use them, or require passwords or access codes. Your library will tell you.

Databases, like the computer industry itself, are in chaos and constant change. None of the electronic search tools my library used five years ago exists today, and none of the ones we use today will probably exist two years from now. No database has established itself as the market leader, so I can't predict which ones your library will own. You'll just have to go to your library and see what's there.

When you get there, you may find a lot of databases, because the field is exploding and companies are scrambling for a piece of the market. My library has twenty-one databases for students. Which one should you use? Ask five questions:

1. What's the coverage? Each database chooses to cover a certain territory. Some are very narrow, which is a good thing if you know what you want. The Biological and Agricultural Index covers only 220 journals, all in agriculture, biology, ecology, and nutrition; CINAHL (Cumulative Index to Nursing and Allied Health Literature) covers only nursing journals; PSYCHLIT indexes only psychology journals; Newspaper Abstracts abstracts ten major newspapers only. Some databases are vast, which is good if you're just browsing. Lexis/Nexis attempts to cover almost everything. UnCover indexes a staggering 14,000 journals and magazines.

2. What's the expertise level? Some databases cover only the highly technical literature—academic journals and such. Some cover only newspapers. Some try to do it all. Judge your own sophistication level, and look for a database that will find you sources that talk in your own language. Lexis/Nexis will give you hundreds of citations on almost anything, but the bulk of them will be newspaper articles—will newspapers get deep enough to satisfy you?

3. How user-friendly is the database? You have to talk to this machine, which means you have to speak its language. Each database has its own. Some (like ASAP) are almost comically user-friendly: You sit down, the screen greets you, and you start answering simple questions about what you want. Others are cryptic hodgepodges whose logic and command system are completely counterintuitive (Lexis/Nexis is pretty bad) and you spend half your time staring at the user's guide. Your librarian can steer you toward the user-friendly ones. And not to worry—they're getting easier to use with every passing week.

4. How much text will I get? Some databases are only indexes—they'll give you the title of the article and the bibliographical data so you can find it. Some give you abstracts or brief descriptions. Some give you full text—if it looks good, you call up the complete article right now and begin reading. Flashy systems give you a choice: Do you want the title, a quick summary, or the whole thing? The more complete the text that's provided, the better for you, whatever kind of research you're doing, so look for a full-text database.

5. How far back in time does the database go? In the old days, the problem with bibliographical tools was they were usually months or years out of date. Now databases can be updated daily, but we have the opposite problem: Since the amount of data is so vast and is coming in constantly, databases often chuck older information before it's really old. Unless your research question is brand new, make sure the database goes back far enough to cite the good research done five or ten years ago.

The perfect tool for you is a full-text database that covers the field you're working in and not much else, at your level of expertise, and is very user-friendly. Good hunting—and remember, if there is no such thing, there will be shortly.

Last words on using search tools. First, *use them.* Don't just look in the card catalog or wander the stacks hoping the right book will fall on you. Indexes and such are intimidating, but you need them. Assume there's a bibliography or index on your subject, and find it; two hours spent finding a great bibliography can save you a week's research.

Second, *choose your level of expertise.* If you're just learning about mastectomies, scholarly articles in medical research journals are going to be over your head, so the *Index Medicus* is probably the wrong place to start; an article in *Newsweek* or *Ladies' Home Journal* is probably just what you need, and the *Readers' Guide* is the bibliographical tool for you. On the other hand, if you're a medical student doing research in state-of-the-art surgical techniques, the *Readers' Guide* is a waste of time. In general, use the most specialized material you can understand. If you're working on mastectomies, an encyclopedia of medicine will be more helpful than the *Britannica* and an encyclopedia of cancer or surgery more helpful still. If you're working on the novelist Elizabeth Gaskell, why work with a bibliography of general literature when there's a 430-page reference guide to Gaskell alone?

Third, *watch publication dates.* You can save yourself a lot of time by not bothering to look at sources that are too old to be useful. In most sciences, five years old means archaic.

Fourth, *don't reinvent the wheel.* If you are putting together a bibliography of works on racism among northerners during the Civil War, probably every scholar who has written on the topic has already put together her own, and it's in the back of her book. Instead of spending thirty hours collecting sources, find one or two good books on the subject and use their bibliographies. This is not stealing; it's common sense.

Finally, *ask someone who knows.* Let's face it: There's too much bibliographical resource material for anyone to know it all. If you're doing research on Christina Rossetti, the British Victorian poet, you'll need to know that

1. The *MLA Bibliography* is the standard bibliography in literary studies.
2. There is a standard yearly bibliography of Victorian literature, *Bibliography of Studies in Victorian Literature.*
3. There is a database on Victorian culture, the LITIR database.
4. There is a standard yearly bibliography of Victorian poetry, *The Year's Work in Victorian Poetry.*
5. There is a reference guide to Victorian poetry: *Victorian Poetry: A Guide to Research.*
6. There is a reference guide to Christina Rossetti: *Christina Rossetti: A Reference Guide* (G. K. Hall and Co.).
7. Of these six, only items 1 and 3 are on-line, so they're easiest to use.
8. Items 5 and 6 are probably too old to be very useful.

A reference librarian can be expected to know only the first one of those eight. But any Victorian poetry scholar knows it all like she knows her own name. She probably wouldn't mind sharing it with you.

Going to the Library

Follow me as I pick a project and walk through the basic research steps, from the library front door to the source on the table or the computer screen before me ready to be read. Since I know nothing about bibliographical materials in medicine, I pretended I was writing a paper on "What alternatives are there besides radical mastectomy for women with breast cancer, and how well do they work?" Twice I walked over to the library and began to research, once using the traditional macroscopic search materials and again using databases. Here's what happened.

Research, In Ye Olde Style

The first thing I *would have* done ordinarily is call up my colleague Mary Memmer, who teaches nursing, and ask her for a five-minute course in medical research materials. But I wanted to see if I could master the library without her help, so I didn't.

I found the *Library of Congress Subject Headings*, which told me that materials on mastectomy would be listed in the subject catalog under "Mastectomy," "Mammectomy," and "Breast—Surgery." It also told me materials were shelved under call number RD 667.5 ("Cancer Surgery"), so I could have gone directly to the stacks and browsed the shelves, but I chose not to.

I looked under "Mastectomy" in the card catalog. There was one entry: *A Woman's Choice: New Options in the Treatment of Breast Cancer.* That sounded so good that ordinarily I would have gone to it immediately to see if it had a bibliography, but I wanted to see what the other tools could do first.

I asked the reference librarian to direct me to the medical section of the reference department and browsed the shelves. I found no bibliographies, but *The Encyclopedia of Common Diseases* gave me a five-page introduction to breast cancer, and *The Encyclopedia of Alternative Medicine and Self-Help* summarized alternatives to traditional surgical treatment and offered a short list of works cited, including titles like *Laetrile Control for Cancer.* None of the works cited seemed promising enough to run to.

I looked in the latest volume of *The Bibliographic Index* to see what was there under "Mastectomy." Nothing looked useful, and I didn't bother to look at earlier years. Under "Cancer" I found something called *Advances in Cancer Research*, two bibliographies on chemotherapy, one on cancer prevention, and one on the psychosomatics of cancer. None of it looked worth pursuing.

I decided to explore the resources of the subject catalog more thoroughly. Under "Breast—Tumor" I found *The Breast: Its Problems, Benign and Malignant, and How to Deal with Them.* Under "Breast Cancer" I found seven entries, several of which looked good. Especially attractive was *Carcinoma of the Breast: A Decade of New Results with Old Concepts.* But the date—1968—said forget it. "Breast Cancer—Surgery" and "Breast Cancer—Treatment" yielded nothing helpful. "Medicine—Bibliography" yielded six entries, including the *Index Medicus* and the *Quarterly Cumulative Index Medicus*, the basic medical indexes.

I asked a librarian where the *Readers' Guide* was and looked under "Mastectomy" in the most recent yearly volume. It said to see "Breast—Cancer—Surgery." There I found "Alternatives to Mastectomy" (*Newsweek* 101.69 My 23, 83) and "Good News for Women! No More Mastectomies" (*Ladies' Home J* 100:34+ Jl 83).

Such sources won't have footnotes, but they might put me on to big names and works in the field, and they'll be solid readable introductions to the topic. If this were a real project I would then have looked at the volumes of the *Guide* for the last six years or so, then turned to the front of the *Guide* to find out how to translate the bibliographical code (101.69, etc.).

I figured the *Index Medicus* would be over my head, but I had to look, so I inspected the latest year's volume under "Mastectomy." I was right: Most of it was on cancer rates in gerbils under laboratory conditions. I did find "Total Mastectomy Vs. Partial Mastectomy and Radiation Therapy" in "J Med Soc NJ 1984 Mar 81 (3):247–8"—I'll have to get help from the front of the *Index* to translate all that. I looked under "Breast" and found the big entry under "Breast Neoplasms," which was broken into several categories, including "Drug Therapy," "Psychology," "Radiotherapy," and "Surgery." Some things did look interesting even to the lay reader: Under "Psychology" I found an article called "Psychological Reactions in Younger Women Operated on for Breast Cancer. Amputation Versus Reaction of the Breast with Special Reference to Body-Image, Sexual Identity, and Sexual Function" (Dan Med Bull 1983 Dec; 30 Suppl. 2:10–3). Under "Surgery" I noticed "Female Sexuality and Crisis of Mastectomy" in the *same issue,* so that may be a key source—perhaps a series of articles on my topic. But I knew the *Index* was the wrong place for me.

I think I'm on my way. It took two hours. I'd start my reading with the book *A Woman's Choice* and the two articles I found in the *Readers' Guide,* and hope they show me where next to go. I have two tasks left: (1) Take the book's call number, find a guide to the shelving system, and find where the book is shelved in the stacks; and (2) find the library's periodicals filing system and find out where they shelve *Newsweek* and *Ladies' Home Journal.* Where's a reference librarian?

Research, The Next Generation

Back to the library—same research question, five years later. I ask a librarian where the databases are, and she directs me to a bank of computers. Two years ago I would have had to hop from machine to machine, since each machine was linked to only one database, but my library has linked the main databases together, so a single keyboard will access any one of them.

I sit down and read through the library's handout on databases (all twenty-one of them) with brief descriptions of their coverages and what information they provide. I'm looking for user-friendly full-text databases covering medical information at a not-too-technical level. I choose three that look good: ASAP, very user-friendly with occasional full-text coverage of scholarly and professional journals generally (probably too technical, but worth a look); Lexis/Nexis, a gigantic full-text database that offers technical and nontechnical databases within it but uses a difficult command language; and Un-Cover, moderately user-friendly and covering 14,000 journals and magazines, both scholarly and general-interest. UnCover isn't full-text, but it offers abstracts—good enough, and the coverage is too good not to use.

I select ASAP from the screen menu and simply answer the plain-English questions the screen asks me until it asks me to identify the topic I'm researching. ASAP searches by topic or by key word, so I choose a topic search—it's easier to program. I type in "mastectomy" and it lists subtopics: among them is "Alternatives—see Lumpectomy," so I select "Lumpectomy" and in seconds I have a screen list of twenty-nine titles—every article in the database under that heading. One looks good, an article from *Prevention*, June 94, titled "No-Lose Breast Treatment." The list gives a two-sentence abstract: "A study where patients had a higher survival rate with lumpectomy. . . ." If I'm interested (and I am), the full text follows immediately on the screen: "The fifty-five women who fit the criteria for lumpectomy actually fared better than the 103 who had the whole breast removed," and so on.

I decide to see what the keyword search produces, so I go back to ASAP's search menu, select "Key Word," type in "mastectomy," and get a list of forty-four titles. The eleventh looks interesting: an article in the *New York Times* headlined "Flawed Cancer Study 'Devastated' Women." The summary tells me what it's about: It was recently revealed that much of the research "proving" that lumpectomies were as effective as radical mastectomies used doctored data. ASAP doesn't have the full text of the article, but it tells me where the newspaper is shelved in my library—smart database.

If I wasn't practicing, at this point I would initiate new searches using new keywords like "fraudulent" to get more information on this exciting new development. But I want to see what the other databases will do for me, so I return to the database menu and choose Lexis/Nexis.

Lexis/Nexis is leased by the university, so its use is tightly controlled. I have to show my ID card to prove that I'm a member of the university, and I have to work through two layers of security by typing in ID numbers and security codes, which I got earlier from the librarian.

This database is enormous, so I have to do a lot of work to not be awash in citations. First, L/N offers me a long list of "libraries," databases within the database. There are three medical libraries—one called MEDEX for medical emergencies like accidental poisonings—and I play it safe by choosing GENMED, for general medicine.

L/N then asks me what kinds of sources I want searched: journals, newsletters, product guides, the Society of Pharmacists drug information? I pick journals.

L/N now asks me to define my search request. Here's where L/N separates the sheep from the goats. L/N searches by keyword: it will cite any text in which the keywords I select appear even once. So the challenge is to select combinations of words that will call up only those articles that are useful. To prove that this isn't easy, I type in "mastectomy" and L/N balks—it says I've asked for over a thousand articles; would I please narrow the search? It takes a long time to get good at tailoring a keyword search, but I keep it simple. I study the user's guide for five minutes and type in "mastectomy and lumpectomy," which will give me all articles where both words appear. L/N tells me it has found 199 articles—do I want just the citation, the short text, or the full text? I choose short text, and the screen lists the first citation and the sentence or two in which my key words appear.

It's a 5,000-word review in the *Journal of the National Cancer Institute* from 1994 titled "Statutory Requirements for Disclosure of Breast Cancer Treatment Alternatives." The excerpt tells me that the state of Pennsylvania now has a legal consent-to-surgery form that includes the phrase "I have been informed of the current medically acceptable alternatives to radical mastectomy." Interesting. But the search is still too broad, so I redefine it, asking for texts using "mastectomy and lumpectomy and radical." That helps a little—I get 131 citations, the first of which is the same review from the NCI journal.

I flip through the next few citations. The fifth is from the *Journal of the American Medical Association,* 1994, a 1600-word editorial titled "Breast Conservation Operations for Treatment of Cancer of the Breast," and the quoted sentence says, "The results of breast conservation were as good as the more radical operations." Might be useful. But this database is too technical, so I type ".cl" ("change libraries") and select a new database: NEWS for general news of the day. I'm offered twenty-five databases—one is called SIMPSN and is devoted to news of the O. J. Simpson trial—and I choose General News and type in the same key words.

I get 270 citations. The first is about a pro golfer who had a mastectomy and wanted to become a role model for other women by publicizing the fact. Not useful. But the second could be a gold mine. It's an obituary for Dr. George Crile, a doctor who spent his life trying to wake up the American medical establishment to the advantages of alternatives to radical mastectomy. Crile worked on the mission from the early 1960s till his death, and he wrote some books, so I might do an author search, find Crile's work, and see if he could hand me some useful bibliographies.

Now I encounter one of the frustrating things about computers: They give you more than you can use. The next eight citations are duplicate Crile obituaries from other papers.

It's time to try UnCover. Here for the first time I meet with interface problems—I can't understand the choices I'm offered. I have to choose among seven databases and twenty-one library catalogs. I choose what seems most innocuous, and now I'm asked to choose from a list of smaller databases called some very strange things. I'm just guessing now, but I choose "Article Indexes." Another list of databases follows, this time with headings like Metro Denver Facts! Nothing looks remotely useful, so I swallow my pride and ask a reference librarian. She calls in the "UnCover expert" on the staff, who explains to me that, way back among the twenty-one library catalogs, I had to choose my own university library to access the general-interest journal articles. Don't ask why, just do it. She refers me to the user's guide at my elbow, and I promise to use it.

I've finally gotten to a search menu, which asks me if I want to search by author or keyword, or browse tables of contents of journals. I select keyword and type in "mastectomy"; I get a list of 194 abbreviated titles. The eighteenth looks good: "Therapy update: controversies, choices, and conclusions." I call up the abstract for the article. It tells me it's from *Consultant* magazine, March 1, 1994, and gives me a summary: "Which option—lumpectomy, radiotherapy, chemotherapy, mastectomy—will afford your patient the greatest chance of beating the disease?" This sounds good, and the entry tells me it's in our library, gives me the call number, and also offers to fax me a copy of the article for $7.75.

This seems like enough progress for a first day. I've been at the terminal for an hour and a half. I go to exit the database, and—dang!—I can't figure out how to tell the program to shut down. I flip madly through the user's guide, determined to crack this case without assistance, until finally the program reverts to the main menu all by itself, having been programmed to know when its user is hopeless. I leave the library, my cheeks burning with embarrassment.

Chapter 19

FORMATTING AND
MECHANICS

Let's assume you've gathered all your materials and your thoughts and have written out a draft or two. Now it's time to think about the proprieties of presenting it to the reader. When do you quote, and how do you punctuate the quotations? When do you need footnotes, and how do you format them? How do you lay out the title page? All that is the business of this chapter.

Using Other People's Thoughts

Before we talk about how to reference your sources, let's talk about why and when. The art of graceful term-paper writing is in part the art of smoothly weaving other people's writings into your own. If you do it well, your references will support and strengthen your ideas, like a rhythm section supporting a lead guitarist. If you don't, the paper will turn into "My Reading's Greatest Hits." Your references should always assist you in doing something that's your own; they should never become the thing you're doing. Hog the spotlight. Relinquish the microphone for brief seconds only.

There are three basic ways to work someone else's text into your own: summary, paraphrase, and quotation. I list them in order of difficulty—it's easiest to quote and hardest to summarize—but you'll do best to rely on your words as much as possible by summarizing most, paraphrasing next, and quoting as a last resort.

Summary is brief restatement, which we've used at every stage in the writing process, especially in the abstract. Professionals summarize a lot, often reducing a large article or report to a single sentence. If you read Patrick Hartwell's 22-page essay in *College English*, February 1985, called "Grammar, Grammars, and the Teaching of Grammar," you might sum it up in the term paper this way: "Formal grammar instruction has no positive effect on language performance [Hartwell]." That style will allow you to bring in a dozen or more sources in a single paragraph.

Paraphrasing is saying someone else's content in your own words. It's what you do when you tell a friend what another friend told you. Patrick Hartwell writes, "In 1893, the Committee of Ten put grammar at the center of the English curriculum, and its report established the rigidly sequential mode of instruction common for the last century." If I was going to say it, I might paraphrase: "American schools have assumed that education should center around grammar instruction ever since 1893, when an influential report by a U.S. government committee decreed that they should."

Why paraphrase when it's easier to quote? For two reasons. First, Hartwell's purposes and audience aren't exactly mine, so his words shouldn't exactly suit me; I should be able to do my own thing best in my own words. If you consistently find that others say what you want to say better than you can, worry that you've lost sight of a narrow and personal purpose. Second, I'm not sure I understand the quote until I can say it in my own words. Paraphrasing does run the risk of getting the meaning wrong, but quoting runs a greater one: It frees the quoter from having to understand her source.

Quotation

Why and When to Quote

Quoting is a healthy thing, for several reasons: It makes you stick close to your sources; it reminds you that the project should be more than just collecting the thoughts in your head; it keeps you in the habit of backing up your claims with hard evidence; and it honors the scholars on whose shoulders you're standing.

But it's easy to quote too much. A paper should never be more than about a fifth quotation by volume. If you're quoting more, worry that you've fallen into the overquoting trap. It comes in three forms. In the first, you think that when you use a writer's substance you must use his words too. Not at all. Quote only when the *words themselves* are of great value. Never quote just for the content.

In the second, you find that quoting is much more fun and much easier than writing, and the paper turns into a pastiche of other people's good lines. Don't let quoting become a substitute for having your own say. Holding tight to your personal purpose and thesis should solve the problem.

In the third, you quote far too much when you quote, reproducing a paragraph when all you need is a splendid word or phrase. *Quote often, but quote little.* Quote only the words you absolutely need, the words that pay for their space. How much of the following quotation really pays its way:

> Hoffmeister captured the essence of Lang when he said, "When the dust has settled and we can see him standing clearly before us, we see that the real Lang is not really comic, but tragic."

Perhaps you need only the last phrase:

> Hoffmeister captured the essence of Lang when he said, "Lang is not really comic, but tragic."

Maybe you can get by with the single word:

> Hoffmeister captured the essence of Lang when he called him "tragic."

If you learn to quote only the telling words, you can easily quote three or four times per paragraph and still have the text be 90 percent your own.

To quote only the few words that pay, you need the *ellipsis*, the row of three periods that shows something's missing (. . .):

> Hoffmeister said, "The real Lang is . . . tragic."

People often try to use the ellipsis every time there is significant text preceding or following the quotation. That doesn't work, simply because there is *always* significant text before and after, so you end up using the ellipsis all the time:

> *Hoffmeister captured the essence of Lang when he called him ". . . tragic. . . ."

You don't need that. Use the ellipsis in only two places: when you've cut words out *of the middle* of your quotation, as in "The real Lang is . . . tragic," or when the quotation is seriously misleading unless you indicate there is text before or after. Since the reader will *assume* there is text preceding and following in almost every case, that second situation is so rare it approaches never.

How to Quote

Running a quotation into the midst of your own sentences without getting into grammatical or mechanical trouble is a challenge. There are two basic principles for doing this.

First, *make the quotation match the grammar of its surroundings.* Make sure the quotation has the same number, tense, and person as the text around it. If the sentence is in past tense, the quotation will probably have to be in past tense. If the sentence begins by calling Hamlet *he*, the quote will have to call him *he* too, even if the quote is spoken by Hamlet. This rule is just a version of our general rule about parallelism on page 227. Here's a quotation that goes awry by ignoring it:

> *When George sees his mother, he doesn't know "how I can tell her of my pain."

To check yourself, read the sentence without the quotation marks:

> *When George sees his mother, he doesn't know how I can tell her of my pain.

If a sentence is grammatically flawed without quotation marks, it's flawed with them. You can solve the problem in three ways:

1. Use less of the quote.

> When George sees his mother, he just isn't able to tell her about his "pain."

2. Rewrite the quotation slightly to make it fit. Surround the changes with square brackets (not parentheses):

> When George sees his mother, he doesn't know "how [he] can tell her of [his] pain."

3. Introduce the quotation with a phase like "He says" or "Hernandez put it like this":

> When George sees his mother, he can't talk; he says, "I don't know how I can tell her of my pain."

Second, *have transition between the quote and your preceding text.* There must be *something* beyond a period between the quotation and the sentence preceding it. Here's a passage that goes awry by ignoring the rule:

> *Everybody knows that drinking and driving don't mix, but a lot of people still insist on getting behind the wheel of a car while under the influence of alcohol. "Alcohol is a drug that confuses the mind and slows down the reflexes."

Sometimes it only takes a single word, like a conjunction:

> Everybody knows that drinking and driving don't mix, *since* alcohol "confuses the mind and slows down the reflexes" (Willard, 1980; p. 34), but a lot of people still insist on driving drunk.

You can fix the problem by replacing the period with a semicolon or colon, adding a conjunction or a phrase like "Willard said," or quoting words or phrases instead of sentences. One way *not* to fix this problem is with a comma splice, the illegal punctuation where a comma joins two whole sentences by itself:

> *My opinion is that they think in another frame of mind, "I've got mine, to heck with you, Jack."

Documentation

Why and When to Document

Scholars care greatly about the *sources* of your insights and your information. The daily paper or *People* magazine almost never tells you where its facts come from because no one seems to care very much, but to a researcher, your facts are only as good as the place where you got them and your conclusions only as good as the facts they're based on. You *must* tell your reader where the raw material came from. Scholars call doing this documentation, citation, referencing, or, loosely, footnoting.

What needs to be documented? There are things in your head you owe to no one: personal feelings, opinions, memories. Those things don't need documentation, because their source is inside you. Everything else you write or say you owe to some outside source: You heard it somewhere or read it somewhere or saw it somewhere. Those things aren't yours; they belong to the people who first thought or discovered them. You're borrowing them. You acknowledge the owner in a citation.

Besides the stuff in your head, the only stuff you *don't* document is data that's common knowledge or easily verifiable. If you claim that Tierra del Fuego is at the southern tip of South America, you needn't document it because your reader can verify the fact in any atlas. But if you assert that Tierra del Fuego has tactical nuclear weapons, you'd better tell the reader where you found out. It's like shopping: If I encourage you to buy Levi's, I don't have to tell you where to find them, since they're in any clothing store; if I encourage you to buy Guatemalan chamois yak-riding culottes, I'd better give you the address of the store that carries them. By this logic, *all* quotations must have their sources identified, since it's never obvious where a person's words came from.

Document for two reasons. First, to have accountability. If your reader doesn't know where the information came from, he can't evaluate your sources or see if you're using them well, and thus he can't trust you. Second, to avoid plagiarism, the number-one pitfall of the research paper. If you're not sure what it is, read the next paragraphs carefully. Most plagiarism by students is innocent: They think they're *supposed* to do it.

Plagiarism is scholarly stealing: taking someone else's data or words or thoughts and peddling them as your own. In the academic world, our ideas, words, and data are our most prized possessions—they're what we make, the way GM makes cars. Stealing them is taking our life's blood. Most universities expel any student caught plagiarizing, and faculty members caught doing it find that their careers are over.

Sometimes it's hard to tell what you owe to whom by the time the writing is over because no one writes alone. You must do the best you can. Documenting only the hard facts and specific insights isn't enough;

you owe an acknowledgment to those who helped you with basic approaches, philosophical premises, and the like.

People sometimes plagiarize out of dishonesty, but usually they do it as the result of two kinds of bad reasoning. The first says, "Since I don't know anything and the books in the library know everything, I don't need to acknowledge sources because my teacher *assumes* that everything I say I got from somewhere else." If you're writing with a personal purpose and thesis, you won't fall into that error. The second says, "I don't want to admit that none of this is mine—it looks like I didn't do anything." To avoid that error you must realize that acknowledging sources isn't any more shameful than saying "Thank you." We do ourselves honor by honoring our debts to others. We're all *supposed* to read our colleagues' work and use it in our own.

Students are often shocked by how rabid researchers are about documentation; they say, "But if you do that you'll be documenting every other sentence!" That's right. Some scholarship has a citation after every paragraph, telling you where the information in the paragraph was found. On the other hand, if you're documenting everything you write, that's a sign that you've become a data sponge. Your sources should always be used to accomplish a task or answer a question that's your own.

How to Document

Let's assume you've just quoted from one of your readings and you want to tell the reader where the quotation came from. If you're like most people, you think of *footnotes*, those references at the bottom of the page cued to raised numbers at the ends of words in your text. In the text you see, "In fact, Earth has been invaded three times by aliens[1]," and you look at the bottom of the page and see the footnote:

> [1] Smith, Jolene, <u>Aliens Among Us</u> (New York: Vanity Press, 1991), p. 12.

That format is extinct, killed by its own incredible inefficiency. We'll practice the three most common citation formats that have taken its place: MLA citations, APA citations, and numbered citations. All three systems use short-hand parentheses in the text as cues to bibliography entries at the end of the paper. You write, "In fact, Earth has been invaded three times by aliens ( )," and between those parentheses you put just enough information to let the reader find the fuller information in the bibliography. The three systems give different cues, and consequently they format the bibliography differently as well.

MLA citations. The Modern Language Association has established a citation system used by scholars in literature and allied fields. It puts in its parentheses the author's last name and the page number. That's all—no punctuation, no "p.," no nothing:

> In fact, Earth has been invaded three times by aliens
> (Smith 12).

Now the reader knows to look through the bibliography until she gets to a work by Smith; there she'll find out the author's full name, the work's title, the publisher, date of publication, and anything else she needs to find a copy of the source herself.

In any of these citation systems, the basic rule is, put in the parentheses the minimal information the reader needs to find the bibliography entry. So if your text tells the reader the author's name, the parentheses don't have to:

> Smith showed that Earth has been invaded three times by
> aliens (12).

But if there is more than one Smith in the bibliography, you'll have to tell the reader which one you mean:

> In fact, Earth has been invaded three times by aliens (J.
> Smith 12).

And if Smith has more than one title in the bibliography, you'll have to tell the reader which one you mean by including an abbreviated version of the title:

> In fact, Earth has been invaded three times by aliens (Smith,
> Aliens 12).

It's often easier to include that sort of information in the text itself:

> Jolene Smith, in Aliens Among Us, argued that Earth has been
> invaded three times by aliens (12).

If you're working with plays, poems, long works divided into books, or any text where the page number isn't the most useful way of directing the reader to the spot, give her whatever is. For a play, give act, scene, and line numbers; for a poem, give line numbers; for a long poem divided into books, give book and line numbers:

> Hamlet blames himself for his ''dull revenge'' (4.4.33).

> The people on Keats's urn are ''overwrought'' (42) in more
> than one way.

> We're reminded by Milton that Adam and Eve don't cry for very
> long when they leave the Garden of Eden (12.645).

Hamlet's line occurs in Act 4, scene 4, line 33, Keats's comment in line 42 of "Ode on a Grecian Urn," and Adam and Eve's tears in line 645 in Book 12 of *Paradise Lost.*

When you find yourself in a situation not quite covered by the rules, just use common sense and remember what citations are for: to get the

reader to the bibliography entry. If the work has no author, you'll have
to use the title as a cue:

> In fact, Earth has been invaded three times by aliens (<u>Aliens
> Among Us</u> 12).

If the title gets bulky, it's cleaner to put it in the text:

> ''Studies of UFO Sightings in North America, 1960-1980''
> offers strong evidence that Earth has been invaded three
> times by aliens (12).

Or use a short form of the title, if it's unambiguous:

> In fact, Earth has been invaded three times by aliens
> (''Studies'' 12).

In the MLA system, at the end of the paper you write a list of all
the sources you've cited and title it "Works Cited." Each source is listed
once, and the sources are in alphabetical order by authors' last names.
The sources are unnumbered; the first line of each entry is unindented,
but all other lines are indented five spaces. In the entry you include all
information the reader might need to locate the source itself (*not* a particular page or passage in the source). Here's a typical entry for a book:

> Smith, Jolene. <u>Aliens Among Us</u>. New York: Vanity, 1991.

Here's a typical entry for a magazine article:

> Smith, Jolene. ''Aliens Among Us.'' <u>UFO Today</u> 14 Jan.
>   1991: 10-19.

The title of the article is in quotation marks, the title of the whole volume
is underlined (or in italics). All information about volume numbers, issue
numbers, seasons (for example, the fall issue), days, months, and years is
included. The page numbers are the pages the article covers, not the pages
you used or referred to in the citations.

APA citations. The American Psychological Association has a citation system that is used by many of the social sciences. Sometimes called
the name/date or the author/year system, it gives the author *and the year
of publication* in parentheses, and usually omits the page number:

> In fact, Earth has been invaded three times by aliens
> (Smith, 1991).

APA encourages you to put the author's name into the text, put the year
in parentheses immediately following the name, and put the page number
(*with* the "p.") at the end of the sentence if you choose to include it:

> According to Smith (1991), Earth has been invaded three times
> by aliens (p. 12).

Because the APA scheme asks the reader to find sources by author and year, you must structure the entries in the bibliography (which the APA calls References instead of Works Cited) so the year of publication immediately follows the author:

For a book:

        Smith, J. (1991). <u>Aliens among us</u>. New York: Vanity
    Press.

For a magazine article:

        Smith, J. (1991, January 14). Aliens among us. <u>UFO To-</u>
    <u>day</u>, 10-19.

There are lots of little ways in which this format differs from MLA's, beyond the location of the year. For instance:

1. Only the author's first *initials* are used, not the whole first name;
2. Only the first letters of titles and subtitles and proper nouns are capitalized, but, just to make things hard, names of *periodicals* (like *Science Weekly*) are capitalized conventionally;
3. Titles of articles or chapters, which have quotation marks around them in MLA style, have none here.
4. APA uses "pp." before the page numbers for newspapers, but not for articles in professional journals (no joke!); MLA never uses it.
5. MLA uses punctuation differently, in several little ways.
6. APA indents the reverse of MLA: APA's first line is indented, and all subsequent lines are flush to the left margin.

In an author/year scheme, if you have several works by the same author, list them in chronological order, the earliest first. Distinguish between items in the same year by assigning letters: 1990a, 1990b, etc. If the source has no author, begin the entry with the title and alphabetize it as if it were an author.

Numbered citations. In some sciences, you simply number all the entries in the bibliography and cue the reader with the number and a page number in parentheses:

    In fact the Earth has been invaded three times by aliens
    (3:12).

The "3" means you're citing the third entry in the bibliography. The "12" is the page number. The numbers free you from having to order the bibliography in any other way, but typically the entries are alphabetized anyway.

The numbering system is super-easy, but unpopular—probably because numbers are proofreading nightmares: They easily go wrong, and once they do the error is hard to spot.

As soon as you start making citations, you realize you have a thousand unanswered questions about format. Does an editor's name go in front of the title or after? Do you write the date of a magazine "December 2," "Dec. 2," "2 December," or "12/2"? Do you underline record album titles or put them in quotation marks? If you have four authors, do you list them all or just list the first and write "et al."? Don't try to memorize answers to all such questions; instead, follow a few common-sense principles:

1. Use common sense and blunt honesty. If you're entering something weird and you're not sure how to handle it, just tell the reader what it is. If it's a cartoon, write "Trudeau, Garry. 'Doonesbury.' Cartoon," then the usual newspaper information. If it's an interview, use "Interview" as your title. If it's an editorial, add "Editorial" after the title. If it's a review of *Gone With the Wind*, write "Review of *Gone With the Wind*." If it's a private conversation or a letter, write "Private conversation with author" or "Personal letter to author."
2. When in doubt about whether to include information—a government pamphlet's serial number or a TV show's network—err on the side of helpfulness and put it in.
3. Be consistent. Once you do it one way, keep doing it that way.
4. Get a style manual or research guide. Citation format is pure convention, so you can't deduce it, and it's complex, so it takes the better part of a book to cover it. Find the manual in your field and imitate it scrupulously. For literary writing, it's *The MLA Handbook for Writers of Research Papers*; for psychology and other social sciences, it's *The Publication Manual of the American Psychological Association*. Biology uses *The CBE Style Manual* from the Council of Biology Editors. There are many others.

Here are templates for common bibliography entries, in MLA and APA format.

A book with an edition number and multiple authors:

MLA: Tremain, Helen, and John Blank. Over the Hill. 10th ed. New York: Houghton, 1946.

APA: Tremain, H., & Blank, J. (1946). Over the hill. (10th ed.). New York: Houghton Mifflin.

A book with an editor:

MLA: Blank, John, ed. Over the Hill. New York: Houghton, 1946.

APA: Blank, J. (Ed.). (1946). Over the hill. New York: Houghton Mifflin.

A book with an author and editor or translator:

MLA: Blank, John. Over the Hill. Ed. Helen Tremaine. New York: Houghton, 1946.

APA: Blank, J. (1946). <u>Over the hill</u>. (H. Tremaine, Ed.) New York: Houghton Mifflin.

MLA: Blank, John. <u>Over the Hill</u>. Trans. Helen Tremaine. New York: Houghton, 1946.

APA: Blank, J. (1946). <u>Over the hill</u>. (H. Tremaine, Trans.) New York: Houghton Mifflin. (Original work published 1910).

A government pamphlet:

MLA: United States. Dept. of Commerce. <u>Highway Construction Costs Per Mile, 1970–1980</u>. #32768. Washington: GPO, 1981.

APA: U.S. Department of Commerce. (1981). <u>Highway construction costs per mile, 1970–1980</u>. (DOC Publication No. 32768). Washington, DC: U.S. Government Printing Office.

Anonymous article in a well-known reference work:

MLA: ''Alphabet.'' <u>Collier's Encyclopedia</u>. 1984 ed.

APA: Alphabet. (1984). <u>Collier's Encyclopedia</u>.

Anonymous newspaper article:

MLA: ''Man Bites Dog.'' <u>New York Times</u> 25 Dec. 1984: D3.

APA: Man bites dog. (1984, December 25). <u>New York Times</u>, p. D3.

Television show:

MLA: <u>Company's Coming</u>. ABC. KZAP, San Francisco. 13 Oct. 1983.

APA: (1983, October 13). <u>Company's coming</u>. San Francisco: KZAP.

Computer software:

MLA: <u>The Last Word</u>. Computer Software. Silicon Valley, CA: DataBase, 1986.

APA: The Last Word [Computer software]. (1986). Silicon Valley, CA: DataBase.

Lyrics from a record album or compact disc:

MLA: The Ruttles. ''Company's Coming.'' <u>Live Ruttles</u>. CD. RCA, 1964.

APA: The Ruttles. (1964). Company's coming. On <u>Live Ruttles</u>. [CD] New York: RCA.

Format

Since a term paper is bigger than an essay, the format may be more elaborate, with several parts that shorter papers usually don't have:

1. A *title page*, on which you give title, your name, the date, and usually the course name and number and instructor's name;
2. A *table of contents*;
3. *Appendices*, where you put the raw data the average reader won't want to read;
4. *Graphics*—pictures, tables, graphs—either in appendices or throughout the paper;
5. A *list of illustrations* following the table of contents, if you have graphics throughout the work;
6. A *letter of transmittal* on the front, addressed to the receiver of the report, saying in essence, "Here's the report";
7. An *abstract* before page 1, summarizing the paper for the reader who only has a minute.

Of course you include some citation system, with citations in the text and a bibliography at the end. You may divide the report into formal sections with formal section headings like "Introduction," "Conclusion," or "Discussion," or you may title the sections of the body of the report in some revealing way: "History of the Problem," "Three Possible Solutions," "Recent Advances," or whatever—your outlines should hand these divisions to you, and they should simply be the heads of your Grand Design. *Don't summarize the report in the conclusion.* Summary conclusions don't work any better just because the paper is a little longer. The conclusion is for discussing, drawing conclusions, making recommendations, none of which is restatement of what's gone before. If there is to be summary, the place for it is up front, in the abstract or perhaps the introduction section.

Don't fall in love with format for format's sake. Keep apparatus to a minimum. Many beginning researchers see format as an easy way to look like a big deal. I've seen reports where every paragraph is given its own splendid heading and the list of illustrations is a bigger piece of work than the illustrations themselves.

Graphics

If your research involves numbers, you'll probably find yourself using *graphics:* charts, tables, graphs. There are lots of regulations about how to handle graphics, but they're all variations on one rule: Remember your reader, and make things easy on him. In other words, present data so they're easy to read, understand, and put to use. News magazines like *Time* and *Newsweek* are masters of that art, so study their graphics for lessons in effective presentation. Here are some principles to follow.

First, graphics are *not* self-explanatory. Be sure to tell the reader exactly what he's looking at and what it means. Title the graphic informatively, label its parts clearly, and explain whatever needs explaining, in footnotes below the graphic or in the report's text *right above or below* the graphic.

Second, avoid overload. A graphic's power is in its ability to dramatize and clarify a point or show the relationships between a few bits of data. If you try to make a graphic do too much, its power is lost. Better three graphics making three points clearly and forcefully than one spectacularly ornate graphic making three points at once and obscuring all of them.

Third, number all graphics, unless you have only one.

And finally, we understand *pictures* better than *numbers,* so whenever possible express your data as a drawing, not as columns of numbers—use *figures* instead of *tables,* technical writers would say. Let's pretend we're reproducing the results of an agricultural experiment on the relationship between fertilizer application rates and plant growth. The experiment took five groups of identical plants and gave each a different amount of fertilizer, then measured the growth after a month to see what dosage produced the most. Here are the data expressed in a table:

Group #:	1	2	3	4	5
(mg/gal)	(10)	(20)	(30)	(40)	(50)
Growth (in inches)	1.2	3.1	5.0	−1.1	−3.7

Here are the data expressed in a figure:

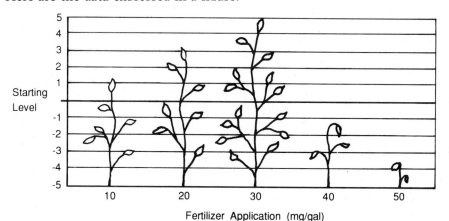

Fertilizer Application (mg/gal)

Isn't it easier to see the point in figure form?

A Model Term Paper

Let's see the lessons of Chapters 18 and 19 at work. Here's a lovely term paper. Notice how much its prompt matters to the author, who was tutoring college students in writing at the time and had great use for an answer to her own question. Notice also how the author's scholarly apparatus hasn't stripped her of her personality, her vitality, or her critical judgment.

Is There a College Literacy Crisis?

by

Eunice Cunningham

for Jack Rawlins

English 221

November 12, 1985

''Why Johnny Can't Write,'' proclaimed <u>Newsweek</u>'s cover. It was December, 1975, and America found itself at the height of its most recent literacy crisis. The cover photo shows a collegiate Johnny at his desk, pen poised above paper, a couple of false starts discarded to the side of the desk. Consternation besets his brow. The assumption underlying the caption is that Johnny can't write. The accompanying article focuses on this ''fact'' of widespread illiteracy among college students, with the implication that we're in the midst of an appalling literacy crisis.

A 1973 announcement of a decline in Scholastic Aptitude Test (SAT) scores provided hard data for the claim. Many blamed it on the changes in education during the ''unshackled Sixties'' (Fadiman 10). Some saw connections with the unhappiness due to Watergate, the anti-war protests, the loss in Viet Nam, the economic recession, and a growing suspicion of schools because of the ''New Math'' and ''New English'' (Judy, <u>ABC's</u> 26).

Some literary types were eager to jump on the literacy crisis bandwagon. Edwin Newman, John Simon, and even such solid old-timers as Mario Pei made mileage out of the ''crisis'' in interviews, book sales, and articles. Even Richard Lanham, a composition specialist, wrote, ''We face in America, there is no doubt about it, a genuine and frightening crisis in literacy'' (''Literacy as a Way'' 10).

I will examine the truth of that statement. After a look at definitions of literacy, I will examine the SAT scores so often

Cunningham 2

used as proof of the crisis. Many blame the supposed literacy decline on television, so a look at it is in order. Finally, after examining literacy crises in their historical and linguistic contexts, I hope to offer an informed answer to the question, "Is there a college literacy crisis?"

If we could analyze literacy objectively, statistics could show us if there was a crisis or not. However, literacy doesn't come in such a tidy package. Definitions of literacy itself are rare among believers in the crisis, who are more apt to make statements like Edwin Newman's: "Language is in decline" (17). To substantiate such claims, they are likely to object to certain current usage patterns. Newman doesn't approve of the use of <u>thrust</u> in the sentence "What is the thrust of the report?" (17). <u>Newsweek</u> defines literacy by examples like "It's obvious in our modern world of today theirs a lot of impreciseness in expressing thoughts we have" (60). Literacy is defined by implication in these examples as the language that you and I (read, "the elite") use and speak, and illiteracy is in evidence whenever we can spot error by others and prove them wrong.

Those who don't believe in a crisis are perhaps less anxiety-ridden and have time (since there is no crisis) to put forward more helpful definitions of literacy. Hillerich, in "Toward an Assessable Definition of Literacy," describes a "continuum of 'degrees of literacy,'" and points out that the idea of a continuum helps us rid ourselves of the "literacy/

illiteracy dichotomy'' (54). In his comprehensive <u>The ABC's of Literacy</u>, Judy adopts Hillerich's ''dimensional literacy'' definition as a broad pedagogical base:

> For education to become dimensional we must overcome
> our obsession with basics, minimums, standards, and
> norms, to concentrate on something much broader, and
> at the same time much more fundamental: helping each
> child on an individual basis extend his or her use of
> language in as many directions as possible, so that he
> or she can participate fully, creatively, and inde-
> pendently as a literate member of society. (20)

These are lofty and, at the same time--as Judy shows--attainable aims (53).

Since 1973, when the College Entrance Examination Board announced declining SAT scores, those who had suspected that education was getting worse have had statistics to back them up. <u>Time</u> magazine published ''Bonehead English'' in 1974, and <u>Newsweek</u>'s landmark ''Why Johnny Can't Write'' appeared in 1975. The SAT scores were the green light for these doomsayers. How reliable are they?

Clifton Fadiman in his book <u>Empty Pages</u> does believe in a literacy crisis, but he knows SAT scores alone don't prove it. He understands that writing competence isn't necessarily linked to a high verbal aptitude score on the SAT (16). But he concludes that other measures do prove that literacy is in a state of emergency: sixty percent of a large California high

Cunningham 4

school, he asserts, "couldn't write a single sentence . . . [and] couldn't maintain and develop an idea" (17). Still, Fadiman doesn't define what "writing a sentence" means or offer comparative evaluations from the same high school from years past, so one can't be sure what his "evidence" proves.

Fadiman calls people who don't agree there is a crisis "non-alarmists." These people (e.g., William Angoff, Stephen Judy, Kenneth Goodman) are more apt than the alarmists to be aware of the complexities of interpreting the SAT scores. They're also more apt to be English teachers. Angoff wrote "Why the SAT Scores Are Going Down" in March, 1975. He argues that, more than anything else, these scores are "idiosyncratic to the changing nature of the SAT population" (10). Angoff is Director of the College Board Program for Educational Testing Service, the outfit that prepares the SAT. He lists many sociological and economic factors governing the self-selection process of the SAT-taking group. Federal Financial Aid was getting into full swing; one could no longer be denied a college education due to lack of funds. The Education Opportunity Program shepherded into college many students who came from educationally deprived backgrounds. These students had to take the SAT if the college of their choice required it for admission, but it didn't matter what their score was; they only had to take the test. Thus their motivation level was very different from those taking the test in former years. Private schools felt the pinch of the economic recession and lowered their SAT cut-off

scores in order to attract more students. Thus academically
poorer students who previously would have attended junior college first were now taking the SAT. Judy poetically sums up these
trends: "In casting the net wider, the colleges naturally at-
tracted students from less and less literate backgrounds"
(ABC's 29).

Other data besides SAT scores from the same era suggest the
existence of an illiteracy crisis isn't so obvious: Shrader's
tests show a rise in reading performance from 1955 to 1965, high
school juniors show a rise in PSAT (Pre-SAT) and National Merit
Scholarship Qualifying Test scores, and Flanagan and Jung's
tests of high school seniors from 1960 to 1970 show a rise in
reading performance (Angoff 11).

It's popular to lay the blame for the supposed crisis on
television. Lois DeBakey argues that the diversion and immediate gratification of television cause children to reject reading
and writing, which "require prolonged effort for mastery"
(qtd. in Fadiman 30). Even Columbia University's renowned phi-
lologist Mario Pei thinks that television is the culprit:

> To the extent that modern man takes his fiction on TV
> and radio rather than out of books and magazines,
> there is an impingement upon the written language.
> (42)

The negative effect of television on literacy, nonetheless, hasn't been proven. Goodman notes that per capita sales

and circulation of printed matter have increased in our television era (3).

Many English composition teachers see the literacy crisis as a media invention. Gary Tate writes:

> Composition teachers have always known that most freshmen don't write well. But now that the media have discovered it and told the public, we're suddenly acting as if we had never known it. (Qtd. in Baum 34-35)

Judy sees Americans as linguistically insecure and thus susceptible to the doomsayers' message of crisis. We worry about saying the wrong thing (is it _lay_ or _lie_?). Years of proscriptive grammar have made us self-conscious about the way we write, to the point of being close-mouthed and literarily constipated. Our insecurities feed into the media's literacy crisis. We are only too ready to believe that when a college graduate uses _who_ after a preposition, the nation is in a state of literacy red alert.

The "crisis" has resulted in a deluge of writing about language by a group of "experts" who don't teach writing, upholders of the holy mother tongue who resist change in education and in language and call for a "back to basics" movement. To them "basics" means ignoring all the insights and advances of composition teachers and linguists in the last fifty years. John Stewart writes that "those who today insist we go 'back to basics' yearn for the rigidified forms of discourse of the 1890's and, above all, for superficial correctness in writing" (50).

He views this as ignorance of the advances in compositional pedagogy's movement for meaning. One charge that <u>Newsweek</u> makes,
and Suzette Elgin forcefully counters, is that the new English
teachers have adopted an "anything goes" attitude towards language. This, <u>Newsweek</u> claims, is due to the idea that every dialect has its own correct grammar. True enough, Elgin argues; we
do now understand that "Standard English" is only the dominant
culture's dialect. Few have argued, however, that it be ignored.
All teachers understand that it's important for students to
learn to use this dialect successfully, at least for upward mo-
bility in our culture.

The cry for "back to basics" is based on the assumption
of a crisis; if there is no plunge in students' ability, there's
no imperative to change teaching methods. Even the claim that
spelling and punctuation are at an all-time low is unfounded.
The National Assessment of Educational Progress studied written samples from seventeen-year-olds for a five-year period from
1969 to 1975. They concluded:

> In general, . . . mechanics . . . (<u>e.g.</u>, punctua-
> tion, capitalization, agreement, spelling, word us-
> age, and so on) are being handled adequately by the
> vast majority of students, and there is no evidence of
> deterioration in their use. (1)

"Back to basics" proponents also clamor for an emphasis
on grammar instruction, but Patrick Hartwell argues that

Cunningham 8

grammar instruction has no relation to writing ability. He

reviews the literature of the last century and concludes that

there is no "relationship between a knowledge of technical

grammar and the ability to use English and to interpret lan-

guage" (126).

Judy notes that "every outcry of 'back to basics' has fol-

lowed on the heels of a major expansion of the educational sys-

tem" (<u>ABC's</u> 36). He quotes periodic outcries over the "new"

illiteracy from 1841 to 1975. From 1841: There is "almost en-

tire neglect of the art of original composition in our common

schools." From 1917: "Our freshmen can't spell, can't punctu-

ate" ("Who Resurrected"). Harvey Daniels, in response to

<u>English Journal</u>'s Forum question "Is there a decline in liter-

acy?" points out that Jonathan Swift in 1710 "announced in the

<u>Tatler</u> that the degeneration of the English language was quickly

proceeding" (17), and that Landor in 1824 blamed the newspaper,

then a new thing, for language deterioration (19). One can't

help but think of the modern analog, television. Judy puts the

historical record of literacy crises in perspective: "If the

complaints about the decline of English over the years were even

half true, literacy would have hit rock bottom generations ago,

and we would be communicating with grunts and hand signals"

(<u>ABC's</u> 36). Maybe the public and the colleges are just slow to

admit what a 1964 <u>Harper's</u> editorial makes no bones about: "Ev-

ery businessman knows that it is a rare day when he can hire

either a woman or man who is capable of writing reasonably competent English" (Fischer 16). And that was before the "crisis."

      The SAT scores prove nothing. Television can't be held re-
sponsible. Literacy crises are historical responses to democ-
ratization and natural language change. Is there a college literacy crisis? The informed answer must be no. We might have come
to the same conclusion if we had looked carefully at the <u>Newsweek</u>
cover photo: Johnny <u>was</u> writing.

Cunningham 10

WORKS CITED

Angoff, William H. "Why the SAT Scores Are Going Down." English Journal 64.3 (March 1975): 10-11.

Baum, Joan. "The Politics of Back-to-Basics." Change 8 (Nov. 1976): 32-36.

Daniels, Harvey. "Is There a Decline in Literacy?" English Journal 65.5 (Sept. 1976): 17+.

Elgin, Suzette Haden. "Why Newsweek Can't Tell Us Why Johnny Can't Write." English Journal 65.7 (Nov. 1976): 29-35.

Fadiman, Clifton, and James Howard. Empty Pages: A Search for Writing Competence in School and Society. Belmont, CA: Fearon Pitman, 1979.

Fischer, John. "Why Nobody Can't Write Good." Harper's 228 (Feb. 1964): 16-26.

Goodman, Kenneth. Celebrate Literacy. Chicago: International Reading Association, 1982.

Hartwell, Patrick. "Grammar, Grammars, and the Teaching of Grammar." College English Feb. 1985: 105-27.

Hillerich, Robert L. "Toward an Assessable Definition of Literacy." English Journal 65.2 (Feb. 1976): 50-55.

Judy, Stephen N. The ABC's of Literacy: A Guide for Parents and Educators. Oxford: Oxford UP, 1980.

Judy, Stephen N. "Who Resurrected Bonehead English?" Editorial. English Journal 64.4 (April 1975).

Katz, Molly. "A Blueprint for Writing." Change 9 (Nov. 1976): 46-47.

Cunningham 11

Lanham, Richard A. <u>Literacy and the Survival of Humanism</u>. New
    Haven: Yale UP, 1983.

''Literacy as a Way of Life.'' Editorial. <u>Change</u> 9 (Nov.
    1976): 8-10.

National Assessment of Educational Progress. <u>Writing Mechan-
    ics, 1969-1974.</u> Washington: GPO, 1975.

Newman, Edwin. <u>Strictly Speaking</u>. New York: Warner, 1974.

Pei, Mario. ''Blurred Vision: The Disturbing Impact of Elec-
    tronic Media.'' <u>Change</u> 9 (Nov. 1976): 42-47.

Stewart, Donald C. ''A Cautionary Tale: The Unteachable Sub-
    ject.'' <u>Change</u> 9 (Nov. 1976): 48-51+.

''Why Johnny Can't Write.'' <u>Newsweek</u> 8 Dec. 1975: 58-63.

THINGS TO DO

1. You've written a term paper citing the following sources. Make three end-of-paper bibliographies, one in each of the following citation systems: MLA citation, APA citation, and numbered citations.

    a. A book called *Down the Spout,* by Ellen Strand, published by Windward Press of Cleveland, Ohio, in 1983.

    b. A book called *Studies in the Grotesque,* by Thomas Nixon and Andrew Gore, published by Androgyne Press of Boothbay, Minnesota, in 1971.

    c. A book called *Literacy Revisited,* edited by Margaret Dumont, published by Rearguard Press of New York City, New York, in 1986.

    d. An article called "Are We Helping the Russians Without Knowing It?," written by Ellen Strand, in *The Voice of the Nation* magazine, Volume #3, Issue #12, dated December 1982. The article begins on page 75 and ends on page 86.

    e. An article called "Negative Camber: Three Approaches," by Morris Wills, in a book called *Suspensions and Their Maintenance,* edited by Stirling Ross and published by Graves and Digger Publishing Company of Houston, Texas, in 1964. The article begins on page 12 and ends on page 212.

    f. A pamphlet from the federal government, with no identified author and no date, called *Wind Shear and Its Effect on House Trailers,* printed by the Government Printing Office in Washington, D.C. It bears the number 3769 and "Department of Transportation" on the title page.

    g. An anonymous article called "Byte Dogs Man," in the *Chicago Tribune* newspaper on November 12, 1975, on page 4 of Section C.

2. Imagine that the following sentences each cite one of the sources in exercise 1, sentence *a* citing source *a,* sentence *b* citing source *b,* and so on. Add parenthetical citations to each sentence in each of our three citation formats. For example, the first sentence with a citation in MLA format might look like this:

> Strand showed that American plumbing has a working life of only five years (12).

Invent page numbers as you need them.

a. Strand showed that American plumbing has a working life of only five years.
b. Gore and Nixon argued in 1971 that "the grotesque is merely the realistic turned on its head."
c. "Literacy is a fiction."
d. Since 1945, our foreign policy has unwittingly played directly into the hands of the Soviets.
e. In 1962, the average negative camber of a Formula One race car was 7 percent.
f. The federal government has concluded that *no* commercial trailer can be expected to withstand winds above 60 mph.
g. Actually, a man once was pursued by a computer—on November 11, 1975, in Flint, Michigan.

APPENDIX A

ESSAY TESTS

There are two kinds of essay exams in college: those that test your expertise in a field like astronomy or sociology and those that test how well you write, like the placement tests designed to identify your literacy level. I'll call the first sort subject tests and the second writing tests. The latter have been proliferating in these days of a "literacy crisis," so that a person who goes through my university and becomes a public school teacher now must pass no fewer than *five*! I'll talk about the universals of essay test-taking first, then I'll talk about the special demands of subject tests and writing tests.

The Universals

Ten tricks will help you do better on every written test you ever take.

1. Warm up beforehand by writing something. We all perform better after we get in the rhythm. A smart test-taker writes a letter to a friend while waiting for the test to begin.

2. Get excited. If you can turn yourself on to what you're saying, get energized by your own performance the way an actor gets energized just by being on the stage in front of an audience, half the battle of writing will be won. As always, the easiest way to excite yourself is to say something that matters to you and to write directly *to* someone with the intent to *stir* him. I grant that many essay test topics make this difficult. Do your best, and remember, a car salesperson isn't excited by the *car*; she's excited by the *selling*.

3. Get down to cases. You may feel you don't have the time, but that's like thinking you're in such a hurry to leave town you don't have time to gas up. No idea is worth a hoot without a "for instance," so, however short the essay, you must have one. If your test answer is two sentences long, make the first a thesis and the second an example.

The rest of the universals all have to do with time saving. In essay tests, time is short, so . . .

4. Take a moment to prewrite. The urge is to go right to paragraph one, but two or three minutes spent mapping will usually pay for themselves by giving you a sense of direction early. Too many essays have discovered their real directions on page 3, too late.

5. Get on with it. Make sure that your first sentence jumps into the heart of things. Skip all essay etiquette, like leisurely introductions. Never repeat yourself.

6. Write in your own language. It takes time to translate your thoughts into someone else's language, time you don't have.

7. Write only one draft. You *won't* have time to rewrite. If you write a few lines and then disown them, just cross them out and keep on writing. Almost any instructor will accept such messiness.

8. Be aware of the time. An unfinished good essay is worse than a finished okay essay.

9. Proofread for garbled meaning. You hate to waste the time, but hasty writing is often garbled in ways that will crack your instructor up or baffle him (omitted *not*s are a favorite). Just skim to see if you wrote the words you intended. It takes less time than you think—perhaps twenty seconds to proofread a thirty-minute quiz.

10. Proofread your mechanics looking only at your pet egregious problems and only if mechanics matter to the instructor. You don't have the time to do a thorough editorial polishing, and few instructors expect you to; but if you know you have one or two mechanical weaknesses serious enough to lower the grade, edit for them alone. If spelling's not a problem for you, ignore it; if it is, proofread for it. If you know you write comma splices, proofread only for them. To do this you need a prioritized list of your writing weaknesses, but a writer needs that always.

Subject Tests

Subject tests are classic examples of audience-driven writing. You're writing to someone who's reading you in a very special way, and her wants are both unusual and specific. Here's what you must do to satisfy her:

Do what the instructor wants. If she's asking a "dump" question to see how much you know, a thesis is irrelevant and possibly a handicap. If she's checking to see how well you've done the reading, the wisest essay in the world that fails to cite the reading loses.

An instructor's purposes in giving a test are rarely self-evident; the only way to find out what they are is to *ask*. Before taking a test, you might want to know

Is there a "right answer"? Or are you being judged just on the quality of your argument?

Does style or mechanics (like spelling) count?

Does the instructor want to see you use the jargon of the course?

Is this in part a check to see if you've done the reading?

Follow directions slavishly. In test-taking this is especially tricky because test questions tend to be lots of little, specific tasks, and as you write your way into the essay, it takes on a life of its own and you forget exactly what you set out to do. The solution is to itemize and number the instructions at the outset and reread them halfway through the essay. How many assigned tasks are there in this exam question?

> Compare and contrast Legitt and Holmes on the role of parental role models in schizophrenia. With whom do you agree? Why? Give three reasons.

I count six: Say how Legitt and Holmes are alike (1); say how they're different (2); agree with one or the other (3); give three reasons why (4, 5, and 6).

Structure to help the instructor read and grade you quickly. Structure rigidly, conservatively, and blatantly. Outlining is strongly recommended. Have a thesis and state it boldly, up front. Let the instructor see when you're performing one of the assigned tasks and when you're performing another. Consider numbering your tasks on the page.

Writing Tests

Purpose

Writing tests have a different purpose than subject tests, and so you approach them differently. The purpose is *to write well,* and that means to do everything we've said leads to good writing: Talk to the reader, be alive and personal, say something you care about, have a real purpose, write to perform, and so on. Doing these things may be more important that staying on the question, thinking well, structuring rigidly, or knowing anything. And, though you'll be expected to be reasonably idiomatic, grammatical, and mechanically sound, almost all test-takers worry about such things far too much and worry not enough about the big things like being human and having some passion. The writing test is the ultimate proof of this book's premise that people write badly because they write for the wrong reasons. People taking such tests feel enormous pressure to "write well," so they try very hard, try to do exactly what they think English teachers want, and end up writing dead, unnatural fakery like this:

> Friendship is a need to which there can be no denying. (Instead of *Everybody knows you need friendship.*)

It is that which brings about a similarity of Anson's view. (Instead of *That's why he agrees with Anson*.)

The harder they try, the worse they write. The people who do best on such tests are those who say, "To heck with the grade; I'm going to have fun!" Write something you'd love to read and you'll do fine.

Structure

On writing tests I think you should avoid the canned, rigidly outlined structure that works so well for subject tests. It'll get you through, and if all you care about is getting through, use it; but it makes it difficult to do really well because it smothers creativity and life. Literacy tests often ask you to compare and discuss two quotations on a single topic, and the canned structure for a response to such a prompt looks like this:

1. Identify and restate the two quotations.
2. State your agreement or disagreement with the first.
3. State your agreement or disagreement with the second.
4. State your personal position on the topic.
5. Summarize.

That's safe but dead; if you have something of your own to say, you should be able to find a livelier, more personal design. Essays that responded to two quotations on individualism in America usually began with a formulaic intro: "Smith and Thompson both raise important issues about individualism." My favorite essay began, "The boys of Delta Sigma had a party last night (and the night before, and the night before)." Wonderful openers like that one don't fit in canned structures.

Push your essay into personal narrative form. Some prompts order you to use a particular structure, in which case of course you must obey, but if you're left free, use the structure that lets you write best. Everyone tells stories about himself better and faster than he writes reasoning processes. Almost any topic can be turned to personal narrative: If the topic is individualism and loneliness, write about a time when you were alone, or a time when you couldn't get any privacy. If the topic is guilt, write about a time you dealt with guilt or saw someone deal with it. Many writing tests help you by asking you to write on personal topics: "Tell about a time when you learned something about yourself." If the topic doesn't do it for you, do it for yourself.

Have a thesis. Don't ask that it be a brilliant insight; you don't need so much. You're not being asked to think a thought no one has thought before; you're being asked to show you can communicate with a reader. A plain thought warmly and humanly expressed will be more than enough.

Methods

Writing tests, by the nature of their clientele, can only give two kinds of prompts. Since the prompt must be something anyone, from any culture, of any age and any upbringing, can respond to, it will either be an invitation to write about personal experience or a huge, umbrella topic like friendship or education. If you get the first, you're home free; if you get the second, use the following guidelines.

Concretize and particularize. The temptation not to is almost overwhelming in the face of an umbrella topic—umbrella topics invite umbrella responses—but you must force yourself. Your grader will love you if you do. I remember reading a dozen umbrella responses on friendship, then reading the sentence "A friend is a person you can tell your real feelings to and not get *punched*" and wanting to run out and kiss the writer for that word.

The best way to concretize is to *begin* concretely: If the topic is loneliness, begin with a place where you like to go when you're alone, a person you know who thrives on solitude or craves a crowd; if the topic is friendship, begin with a particular friend, a particular act of friendship.

Avoid the clichéd response. On any topic there is a response of least imagination and lowest energy, the one that will be used by all the writers who can't find anything better to say:

On individualism: It's important to have some private time and space, but it's important to be able to function as a social being too.

On guilt: Guilt is a good thing because it keeps people on the straight and narrow, but it can get out of hand and become self-destructive.

On friendship: Everybody needs a friend, and a friend is someone you can depend on in the clutch.

If you settle for the clichéd response, you'll bore your reader and make it hard to get better than a grudging C. Use our anticliché exercise (p. 394) to swim against the current:

Individualism is an American curse and an illusion, responsible for most of our culture's ills.

Guilt isn't the voice of conscience telling you you did wrong; guilt is the voice of the Establishment (parents, teachers, bosses) telling you you acted like a person instead of a clone.

The only thing of real value a friend can give is permission to be yourself.

Go beyond agreeing or disagreeing. If you're asked to respond to a provocative statement, a popular version of the clichéd response is simply to agree or disagree. That's a dead end because after you vote yea or nay, the essay's over. Instead, find something personal and provocative to say on the topic; then see how your thesis reflects on the quotation. Good thinking produces more good thinking, not just a yes or no vote. Remind yourself of the Stew Theory from Chapter 17 if you don't see why.

$\mathcal{A}$PPENDIX B

COLLABORATIVE WRITING

The first time an instructor asks you to write an essay as a member of a group, you'll probably say, "Oh dear god, no, please!" My students dread it and often try to drop the course the instant they hear they'll have to do it. I had the same reaction the first time I had to write with partners.

That's natural. Writing and getting along with other human beings are about the two trickiest things you'll ever have to do; now you're being asked to do them at the same time. But take comfort in this student's very typical experience:

The first paper in the term I did by myself. I felt comfortable, and it was all very easy. I knew what I was doing.

The second paper was a whole different story. This time I had a partner, and I had to rearrange my work schedule, compromise, argue. It was a lot more work. We ended up wasting a lot of time, and when it was over I hated the paper.

The third paper was a great learning experience. My partner added a lot of insight. She thought of things I could never have thought up on my own. I wasn't too sure of what I was doing myself, so I needed a partner who was more knowledgeable to help me.

The fourth essay was the most enjoyable of all. I knew my partner ahead of time, and even though we were working we still laughed and had a good time.

The last essay I wrote by myself. It felt strange. I had no one to bounce my ideas off of, and I was very unsure about the worth of what I was doing.

So it can be done.

Why Collaborate?

When I announce that assignments in my classes will be collaborative, students line up to tell me why it's a bad idea. It takes lots more time than solo writing. It's more work, more stress, more worry. People fight. It leads to compromises and middle-of-the-road writing that makes no one happy. Some people do all the work, and the loafers coast. You're suddenly dependent on relative strangers, and if they don't come through you're dragged down with them. The final product seems to belong to no one. It makes grading unfair, because the instructor can't tell who deserves the credit.

All of which is perfectly true. So why do it? Collaborative writing has different goals than solo writing, and as long as you hold on to the principles that have driven your solo schoolwork, collaboration will be as frustrating as trying to drive nails with a screwdriver.

Teachers assign collaborative writing for two reasons. First, almost all of the writing done in the professional world is collaborative, and school is wasting its time if it trains you to do one sort of writing and the rest of your life asks you to do another. *Of course* you'd rather write by yourself; the working world just won't let you.

Professional writers collaborate for one simple reason: Bosses make them do it. And bosses make them do it for one simple reason: Collaborative writing is *better* than solo writing. Most of us refuse to believe it, but groups do more creative work and find better solutions to problems than individuals do. It's just as true in school: My students' collaborative essays are one quantum leap better than their solo work—*even when the writers don't like the results themselves.*

Second, collaboration is a tremendous learning device. If you get together with three classmates and discuss the assignment, agree on strategies for fulfilling it, argue with each other about ways to go, come to consensus, and write two drafts, peer editing each draft as a group, you'll learn more, about the assignment *and* about writing, than you possibly can by writing alone in your room.

Whether or not you call that learning depends on what definition of learning you have in your head. A student will say to me, "Why are we doing this collaborative stuff? I get together with my partner and we never see the assignment the same way. So we just fight. I tell him how I see it, and he says I'm wrong, and he misunderstands me completely so I have to explain myself five different ways, and he tells me how he sees it and it sounds all wrong to me, and we both refuse to give in, so we go around and around for hours, until finally time is running out and we have to write something, so we figure out something we can both live with and hand it in. And he doesn't like my style and I don't like his, so I write it and he takes it and rewrites it into something that doesn't sound at all like me and that I'd never write. And it would be much easier if I could go off and write down what I want to say, without interference."

But to a teacher, all that arguing and compromising and defending of one's position and doing it some way you'd never choose to do it yourself *is learning*—a precious kind of learning so rare in school most of us have learned to call it by derogatory names, like "fighting."

Once you've accepted the idea that collaboration's values are different from what you're used to, but worthy nonetheless, you must next *subjugate the ego*. Most people who want to be writers do so for egocentric reasons, and writing partners are strangers meddling in their most private space. Most writing in school is also egocentric: Students write for their own profit, so they can get clear on what they think. Professional writing, however, is never done for the writer's benefit but for the reader's, and collaborative writing is practice in having that focus. The object of collaborative writing is not to share your personal vision with the world; it's to *get the job done*—to tell the reader how to make veal piccata, give the boss the best advice on how to build the bridge, or plan the subdivision so environmental needs and people's needs are both met. When students complain that their partners forced them to say something other than what they wanted to say, I think to myself, "If your personal vision couldn't sell itself to two *friends*, what kind of appeal can it have for a bunch of *strangers?*"

Part of giving up your egocentric view of writing is giving up your need for a fair division of labor and a personal grade. Yes, it's impossible to make sure everyone in the group pulls his weight; yes, there will be slackers and some people will do more than their share of the work (probably you); yes, the final product will get one grade shared by all members of the group; yes, it's all "unfair." *But that's how life is*, and you might as well get good at living with it now. If you focus on making collaboration fair, you'll be eaten alive by jealousy and be missing the point anyway. The world of work isn't interested in assessing how fairly the work was divided up or assigning grades to individual performances; it cares only about how good the finished product is. Collaboration is a good time to stop writing for grades and personal pats on the head, and start writing *to produce good work*, the way shoemakers work to make good shoes and theatre people work to make good plays. In the end, the rewards of doing good work are profoundly more satisfying than the rewards of grades, anyway.

Techniques

Now that we have the right attitude, we're ready to talk about nuts-and-bolts methods for making the collaboration go well. The eleven rules are in roughly the order in which you might use them.

1. Pick your collaborators carefully.
2. Give the project a lot of time, schedule carefully, and don't procrastinate.

3. Be responsible.
4. Be flexible, but don't be too nice.
5. Write everything down.
6. Don't seek consensus too early.
7. Avoid the tyranny of the mediocre.
8. Alternate between group sessions and solo work.
9. Divide the labor.
10. Explore alternatives to conventional presentation.
11. Don't write drafts with everyone's hands on the keyboard.

Pick your collaborators carefully. With some kinds of collaboration, you choose your collaborators; with other kinds, you don't. In the academic world, collaborators usually pick each other; in the business world, your boss simply assigns you to the team. Your instructor may use either model. If you're assigned partners, make do. But if you can choose, my students unanimously say that *picking the right partner* is the most important step in a successful collaboration.

Although everyone realizes that, almost everyone botches the job. One student said, "Despite the great amount of time I spent plotting who I was going to work with, I ended up choosing the person who was geographically convenient." Another said, "I chose my first partner for her pretty blue eyes. I got a great roommate, but I didn't produce a great essay." If you don't pick the person sitting nearest to you or the sexiest, you pick the nicest because he doesn't scare you, or the most timid because you figure you can boss him around. These are all bad moves.

You're looking for someone with certain characteristics: intelligence, flexibility, an ability to listen and communicate, maturity, and a serious commitment to the course and the work. How can you find such a jewel among a classroom of relative strangers? From the first day of the course, assign yourself the task of smoking out the best potential partners. Listen to the class conversation with that in mind. Read other people's assignments to see how they write and how they think. The people who care, who are engaged, who seem open to others will make themselves known.

Don't seek someone with whom you are too compatible. Okay, you don't want someone you loathe or someone who can only work when you have to sleep, but you don't want someone who thinks just like you either, because then you have nothing to teach each other. Too much agreement is a curse. Find someone who can do things you can't do and vice versa, so you can stretch each other.

You would think that the class stars would be snapped up like burgers at a two-for-one sale, but they aren't. Often my best students are treated like pariahs, because *intelligence is frightening.* Don't deal with the fear by picking someone so dim you feel unthreatened and unchallenged by him. Collaborate with the smartest person you can lasso. You'll learn more, do better work, impress yourself, and get over an ugly anti-intellectual prejudice.

Give the project a lot of time, schedule carefully, and don't procrastinate. Collaboration takes a lot of time—at least three times as long as writing alone. And you can't work whenever you want to, because much of the work can only be done when everyone can get together. If you run out of time or leave things to the last minute, someone will end up doing it alone, badly. So begin early; compare schedules to find available meeting times; schedule *all* meeting times at once, and commit to specific hours; plan more meeting time than you think you'll need; and stick to the schedule.

Be responsible. People's grades are riding on your ability to do what you say you'll do and show up when you say you'll show up. One student said, "To rely on someone else is hard. I would lie awake the night before the paper was due and hope to God my partner would remember to bring it to class." I've had students cry in my office as they realized that their self-destructive behavior just earned their classmates F's. Accept the responsibility, keep it in mind, live up to it.

Be flexible, but don't be too nice. Flexibility is what my students say they like best in a partner. It means an ability to listen to others, to accommodate, to share, to compromise, to change and grow. It means you don't come to the first group session with your mind made up and a determination to get your way.

On the other hand, you mustn't be too nice either. The value of collaboration lies in the diversity, and if you strive above all things to keep conflict to a minimum, you're just pouring water on the bonfire of creativity. Don't make capitulation a virtue. Value your own insights and contributions, state them boldly, defend them vigorously—then back off and help the group come to a decision.

Write everything down. The curse of brainstorming is that everyone wants to talk and no one wants to record. Appoint a secretary, use a tape recorder and appoint a transcriber, take turns keeping notes—somehow make a record of all group conversations.

Don't seek consensus too early. Forcing early decisions breeds absolutism and rigidity. Eventually the group must decide to go one way, but if you try to pick that way too soon you just close doors and cut off the rich diversity and productive messiness that is the glory of group work. Diversity of opinion is not a blemish to be hidden or an obstacle to be overcome. A student who knew this said about one of her collaborations, "It didn't work out; my partner and I thought pretty much the same way, and we just agreed on everything."

I learned about the error of seeking early consensus the first time I was on a jury. When we retired to deliberate on our verdict, I suggested that we begin the discussion by voting, guilty or innocent. I figured if we all happened to feel the same way we wouldn't have to discuss it.

Several wiser people said, "Don't—let's just kick stuff around for a while first." And it was only later that I realized that if we had voted first, two terrible things would have happened: All the diverse views in the room would have been reduced to a sterile two, guilty or innocent, and people would have gotten committed to their vote, dug in, and gotten defensive. So have a long, formless brainstorming period before asking for answers, decisions, or votes.

Avoid the tyranny of the mediocre. Beginning collaborators dreading collaboration see it taking one of three possible forms: endless conflict; capitulation, in which one tyrant gets his way and everyone else gives in; or risk-free consensus, where everyone agrees to put in the final paper only those things that everyone agrees with. Since the first two are night-mares, people often opt for the third. But *all three models are deadly*— even the third, though it may appear "nicer" than the other two, because it produces bland, safe, white-bread thinking and writing. What everyone can agree to is rarely worth saying.

You must find a fourth path. There, everyone's voice is respected. The agreed-upon goal is to make the richest, most stimulating prod-uct—not to make the safest product or to keep all members of the group happy. Consensus is to be sought, but not forced—if consensus isn't achieved, the final product must reflect that, not hide it. The job of each member is to help the other members take their visions as far as they will go. Nobody wants to win. And *nobody has a veto.*

Should you have a group leader? Probably. Democracies are nice ideas, but they're practically impossible to maintain and ponderously inefficient. If you don't openly appoint a leader, one will probably emerge.

Don't pick a leader who thinks he knows the answer or who is the smartest; pick the member most skillful at helping people get along, the best listener. On most committees, the chair doesn't vote, to remind everyone of this point.

Alternate between group sessions and solo work. You're trying to find a structure that nurtures individual contributions, yet also has a sense of group purpose and cooperation. That's tricky, and most people lose the balance and either become tyrants, sycophants, or rebel outcasts. To avoid that, spend part of your time meeting as a group and part of your time working individually. Talk for an hour; then have each member go off and write up thoughts and reactions to the conversation; then come back together and share and react to each member's writing.

There are two times when it's most important for members to work alone. The first is before the first group meeting. Without getting locked in or making decisions, each member must jot down thoughts, sugges-tions, and possibilities and bring them to the meeting. If you don't, you'll be an empty vessel to be filled by the thoughts of your partners, and the power of collaboration is wasted. Make it a hard rule: *No one comes to the first meeting empty-handed.* The second time is after the brainstorming and before the first group draft is attempted. Each member must write her own version of that first draft, and bring the draft to a group session where all versions are read by the other members and critiqued. Typically, each member reads all the drafts by other members and writes reactions in the margins, especially noting good things worth keeping. This approach prevents members from becoming passive yes-men, and it prevents good things in the early drafts from being overlooked and lost in later group revisions.

Divide the labor. The kiss of death for collaborative work is the idea that everyone should have to do everything. Collaboration works because some people are good at one thing and others are good at another. Use that advantage. Let people do what they do well.

Some class projects divide into separate tasks easily: One person does library research, one interviews the university president, one does the drafting, one does the data analysis, one handles the video camera, and the one with the best hair serves as the talking head in front of the camera. Most professional collaborations are strict divisions of labor: One person has the knowledge and the other can write, or one person knows about the literature of the eighteenth century and the other knows about the sociology of the period. But even if the project is just to formulate an opinion, you can divide the labor according to people's gifts. Some people are good drafters, some good brainstormers, some good line editors, some good proofreaders, some good devil's advocates. Some people are idea people, some rule-followers, some grammarians, some logicians. Some people are playful, some are drudges. Some write good dialogue, some write good thesis statements, some are good at abstracting.

Some people call such divisions of labor cheating. When students tell me they couldn't work together because their writing styles were so different and I say, "Why didn't you just have one of you be in charge of the drafting?," they say they didn't know that was fair. Your instructor may agree with them, so ask her if you're in doubt. But most instructors who assign collaborative work accept the division of labor as part of what you're trying to learn to do.

But if you divide up the work, how do you learn? If Chuck is off doing library research and Carla is doing the line editing while your job is to analyze the data, how do you learn to do library research and line editing? You don't . . . *unless you watch.* Have Chuck report to the group about what he did at the library and what the results were. Watch Carla line edit, and have her tell the group what she's doing. Collaboration is everyone's chance to watch masters of the various stages of writing do their thing. The best learning is always done by observing mentors. It's not less educational than writing alone, it's more, because when you write alone you never see researching or line editing done better than you can do it yourself.

There is one exception to the division of labor: Everyone proofreads, because you can never get enough proofreading and different eyes catch different things.

Explore alternatives to conventional presentation. Group projects and conversations often don't fit conveniently into standard essay format, with its thesis in paragraph one and its four reasons following, its single point of view, and its academic style. Good. Now's the time to break out of that dead habit and try something new. Use the new group approach to inspire new essay forms. If consensus was never reached, perhaps you can find a format that uses the disagreement to your advantage. Maybe a dialogue, or a Siskel-and-Ebert kind of debate would work. If there are wildly diverse writing styles in the group, perhaps you can find a format that allows each to have a voice in the essay. Consider interviews, screenplays, fairy tales, parodies, rap lyrics.

Don't write drafts with everyone's hands on the keyboard. Everyone agrees that the easiest part of collaboration is the early brainstorming and the hardest is the actual drafting. How do two or three or four people do the actual composing of the essay?

There is no right answer. Different approaches work for different people. I've known teams who alternated paragraphs—one person would write one, then another would sit down at the keyboard. I've known teams who discussed each new sentence and came to agreement before one person typed it in. If such approaches work for you, use them, but for most people they produce bickering, writer's block, stilted prose, and lots of wasted time. Most people are happiest with an approach like this: Have the group agree on what the draft should do; appoint the best stylist on the team to do the drafting, and leave her alone to do it; peer edit the draft in the group; have the drafter rewrite; then have everybody edit, line edit, and proofread as a group.

A Typical Collaborative Work Schedule

Here's a hypothetical by-the-numbers collaborative experience. Unless your assignment is a big deal and you have a lot of time, you probably won't need such an elaborate structure, but it's nice to know it's there if you need the discipline.

1. Long before the assignment is made, you cruise the class for partners, getting the best students to commit to working with you on the next project.

2. Immediately after the assignment is made, you gather with your collaborators to compare schedules and schedule *all* meeting times. You schedule at least three: one for brainstorming, one for planning the first

draft, and one for peer editing and revising the first draft. The first meeting is in two days. Everyone swears to jot down first thoughts between now and then—nobody comes to the meeting empty-handed.

3. In the next two days, you kick things around in your brain and write them down as they come to you, without getting committed to anything.

4. At the first meeting, you brainstorm. All the rules of brainstorming in Chapter 3 are in force: No one is wrong, etc. All members share the notes they brought—no one is allowed to listen passively. Someone takes notes or tapes the session for transcribing later. The group picks a leader, or one emerges. The group delegates tasks if the project permits. You decide if another brainstorming session is needed. If not, you agree that each member will bring his version of the first draft to the next meeting. You arrange to Xerox the meeting notes and get copies to all members, to aid them in their drafting.

5. At the next meeting, everyone reads everyone else's draft silently, making comments in the margins and noting good things worth keeping. Discussion follows. Someone takes notes. A sense of the collaborative draft emerges. Someone is appointed the task of drafting it, and is given all the drafts and the meeting notes to guide him.

6. The third meeting is held wherever the draft writer's word processor is. Each member silently reads a cleanly typed double-spaced copy of the new draft. A peer editing session follows. The author of the draft revises in the word processor while others coach. Time is set aside for mechanical line editing and checking against the course format, and changes are done in the word processor. Everyone proofreads a copy of the manuscript, and corrections are typed in. Some thoughtful person produces a new ribbon for the printer, and a final handsome copy is run. Someone spots a typo everyone missed, so you reprint that page. It's time to go home, and the assignment isn't even due until the day after tomorrow!

AUTHOR/TITLE INDEX

The following index lists all the student and professional writings that appear in *The Writer's Way*. The first index lists each work by author's name, then cites all pages in *The Writer's Way* that refer to the work. The second index is organized by mode and indicates each work by title.

Essays by Author

Essays by Mode and Title

Personal Essays

Informative Essays

Argumentative Essays

Research Paper

$\mathcal{J}$UBJECT INDEX